Celebration Bar Review

Multistate Workbook 2

©1995-2011 Celebration Bar Review, LLC
  ALL RIGHTS RESERVED
No part of this publication may be reproduced, stored in a retrieval system, or transmitted in any form or by any means, electronic, mechanical, photocopying, recording or otherwise without the prior written permission of the publishers.

PRINTED IN THE USA
NO RESALE PERMITTED

Certain publicly disclosed questions and answers from the July, 1991 MBE and the July 1998 have been included herein with the permission of NCBE, the copyright owner. These questions and answers are the only actual MBE questions and answers included in Celebration Bar Review's Multistate Workbook. Permission to use the NCBE's questions does not constitute an endorsement by NCBE or otherwise signify that NCBE has reviewed or approved any aspect of these materials or the company or individuals who distribute these materials.

All questions, instructions and letter answers copyright ©1995-2011 by the National Conference of Bar Examiners. All rights reserved. All other material © 1995 - 2011 Celebration Bar Review

Table of Contents

MULTISTATE TECHNIQUES — 6
- INTRODUCTION — 6
- WHAT THE MULTISTATE EXAMINERS ARE TRYING TO ACCOMPLISH — 6
- MARKER QUESTIONS — 6
- SKILLS TESTED BY THE EXAMINERS — 7
- LIMITATIONS ON THE EXAMINERS — 7
- ANATOMY OF A MULTISTATE QUESTION — 8
- TECHNIQUES FOR PICKING THE CORRECT OPTION — 9

MULTISTATE NUTSHELLS OF LAW — 25

CONSTITUTIONAL LAW — 25
- SEPARATION OF POWERS — 27
- THE RELATION OF THE NATION AND STATES — 29
- INDIVIDUAL RIGHTS — 31

CONTRACTS AND SALES — 37
- FORMATION OF CONTRACTS — 37
- CONSIDERATION — 39
- THIRD-PARTY BENEFICIARY CONTRACTS — 41
- ASSIGNMENT AND DELEGATION — 42
- STATUTE OF FRAUDS — 42

PAROL EVIDENCE RULE	43
CONDITIONS	44
REMEDIES	45

CRIMINAL LAW AND PROCEDURE — 48

HOMICIDE CRIMES	48
OTHER CRIMES	51
INCHOATE CRIMES	53
GENERAL PRINCIPLES	54
CONSTITUTIONAL PROTECTIONS	56

EVIDENCE — 61

PRESENTATION OF EVIDENCE	61
PRIVILEGES AND EXCLUSIONS	64
RELEVANCY AND ITS COUNTERWEIGHTS	67
WRITINGS AS EVIDENCE	68
HEARSAY	68

PROPERTY — 73

THE ESTATE SYSTEM	73
RIGHTS IN LAND	76
VENDOR AND PURCHASER	78
TITLE	80

TORTS — 84

INTENTIONAL TORTS	84
NUISANCE	85

STRICT LIABILITY	86
NEGLIGENCE	87
DEFAMATION	92
PRIVACY	93
DECEIT	94
JULY, 1991 MULTISTATE BAR EXAM	**97**
JULY, 1998 MULTISTATE BAR EXAM	**203**

MULTISTATE TECHNIQUES

INTRODUCTION

A working knowledge of the objectives of the Multistate Bar Examination, the skills it attempts to test, how it is drafted, the relationship of the Component parts of a Multistate question, and the limitations imposed on its authors can provide a student with a substantial advantage in understanding and passing the exam. These materials are designed to look at the Multistate Bar Examination from the examiners' point of view to help you enhance your Multistate score independent of your knowledge of the law. Obviously, there is no real substitute for knowing the law and how it works in a factual context, but these tips may help you in circumstances where you don't know the answer.

WHAT THE MULTISTATE EXAMINERS ARE TRYING TO ACCOMPLISH

The fundamental objective of the Multistate Examiners is to provide a tool to measure fairly and efficiently which law school graduates have the qualifications to be admitted to the bar and which do not.

The 200-question multiple-choice examination that is used to accomplish this objective must be of a consistent level of difficulty and the level at which the pass/fail decision is made must be achievable by a substantial majority of candidates. These limitations on the examiners lead to the first important insight into preparation for the exam, the kind of questions that really make a difference on whether you pass or fail. An adversarial relationship, which is one of the hallmarks of the legal profession exists between you and the bar examiners when you take the bar exam so that you can enter their profession. The more you know about your adversary and the rules they play by, the easier it is for you to beat them.

MARKER QUESTIONS

For years, performance of students on individual questions during their study has been compared with success or failure on the bar examination. Through an analysis of these statistics, we can identify those questions that are best able to predict performance on the exam. In general, perhaps surprisingly, the hardest questions aren't particularly good predictors, because most of the students who passed them passed the examination. On the other hand, many of the easier questions are very good predictors.

In particular, we identified several questions where students answering them incorrectly failed the bar exam at a rate significantly higher than the usual failure rate of the overall bar exam population.

For example, one of the easiest questions given by the Multistate Examiners in the released February 1978 Exam reads as follows:

Ted frequently visited Janet, his next-door neighbor. Janet was separated from her husband, Howard. Howard resided with his mother but jointly owned the house in which Janet resided. Late one night, Ted and Janet were sitting on the bed in Janet's bedroom drinking when Howard burst through the door and told Ted, "Get out!" When Ted refused, Howard challenged him to go outside and "fight it out." Ted again refused. Howard then pulled a knife from his pocket and lunged at Ted. Ted grabbed a lamp, struck Howard on the head, and killed him. Ted is charged with murder. On a charge of murder, Ted should be found

- (A) not guilty, because Ted had as much right as Howard to be in the house.
- (B) not guilty, because Howard attacked Ted with a deadly weapon.
- (C) guilty, because Ted's presence in Janet's bedroom prompted Howard's attack.
- (D) guilty, because Ted's failure to obey Howard's order to leave the house made him a trespasser.

Of the students who participated in our Analysis, 98% correctly chose (B) as the correct answer. But of the 2% who answered this question incorrectly, 38% failed to pass the bar exam compared to a 20% failure rate overall.

SKILLS TESTED BY THE EXAMINERS

The Examiners test the following skills in the multiple-choice question format.

1. The ability to read a set of facts carefully.
2. The ability to identify the legal issue in a set of facts.
3. Knowledge of the law governing the legal issues found.
4. The ability to apply the correct principle of substantive law to come to the correct conclusion for the right reason.
5. The ability to distinguish between closely related principles of law which are frequently confused.
6. The ability to make reasonable judgments on an ambiguous set of facts.
7. The ability to understand the way in which limiting words make plausible-sounding choices wrong.
8. The ability to guess the right answer by intelligently eliminating incorrect choices.

LIMITATIONS ON THE EXAMINERS

The Examiners are constrained in the way they construct the Multistate Bar Examination. All of the questions have to be related to the subject matter set forth in the outline in their Bulletin for Applicants. While that outline is broad and ambiguous, many years of experience with the Examination has delineated the scope of the material asked, so that you can feel confident that you do not have to go beyond the substantive texts and questions to find the important substantive law and the testable issues which are likely to appear on the Multistate Bar Examination.

The Examiners have specified their sources of authority for the correct answers. In most subjects, it is the generally accepted view of the law in the United States. Decisions of the United States Supreme Court control in Constitutional Law and Criminal Procedure, as does the Uniform Commercial Code in Sales and the Federal Rules in Evidence. In most areas, we have seen enough officially released questions so that we know what the Examiners consider to be the controlling law, and have incorporated that law into our materials. The Examiners are not in a position to change those rules absent a change in the governing law. Recent changes in the law, except U.S. Supreme Court decisions that are more than one year old, will not form the basis for correct answers to questions.

The time between the drafting of a Multistate Bar Examination question and its appearance on the examination is at least one year. After a question is initially drafted, it must be reviewed for substance by a committee responsible for that subject, and then must be reviewed by the technical exam writers working for ACT. It finally appears on an exam which is initially held for back-up in case there is a breach of security for the scheduled exam. The back-up exam is then administered as the scheduled exam during the next administration, six months later. Therefore, the draftsperson of a question which you are taking was not aware of roughly the last two years of decisions by the United States Supreme Court at the time the question was drafted.

The Examiners have an obligation to ask fair questions. While a very careful reading of a fact pattern or item is required in order to reach the right answer, they do not in general rely on "trick" questions. Again, it is the basic, straightforward questions that determine whether you pass, not the occasional oddball or trick question. Reading too much into a question and looking for a trick lurking behind every fact will lead you to the wrong answer more often than it will lead you to the correct answer. Therefore, you should always take questions at face value.

The greatest limitation on the Examiners is that every question must have one demonstrably correct answer and three demonstrably wrong answers. When we look at the details of the construction of the questions, we will see how this limitation sometimes will give you a clue to the correct choice.

The Examiners have the obligation to administer the exam in a secure fashion. They, therefore, must prepare different versions of the exam to be given to persons sitting in close proximity to one another. There is no set order in which you will receive the 100 questions given each session. One group of candidates may get all of the long questions first and think the morning session is very difficult and another group may get easy questions at first and come to the opposite conclusion. You should not discuss the exam at lunch time and become upset because other people have a different impression of the exam than you.

ANATOMY OF A MULTISTATE QUESTION

This officially released question, illustrates the structure of a Multistate question.

ROOT OR FACT PATTERN:

Pemberton and three passengers, Able, Baker, and Charley, were injured when their car was struck by a truck owned by Mammoth Corporation and driven by Edwards. Helper, also a Mammoth employee, was riding in the truck. The issues in *Pemberton v. Mammoth* include the negligence of Edwards in driving too fast and failing to wear glasses, and of Pemberton in failing to yield the right of way.

Pemberton's counsel proffers evidence showing that shortly after the accident, Mammoth put a speed governor on the truck involved in the accident.

STEM OR CALL OF QUESTION The judge should rule the proffered evidence

OPTIONS

DISTRACTER	(A)	admissible as an admission of a party.
DISTRACTER	(B)	admissible as *res gestae*.
KEY	(C)	inadmissible for public policy reasons.
DISTRACTER	(D)	inadmissible, because it would lead to the drawing of an inference on an inference.

You should read the call first because it tells you what task you will be performing when choosing the correct answer, and will help focus your attention when you read the facts. Most of the time, it will be phrased in the positive asking the "best argument" or "most likely result." However, when the call of the question is in the negative, asking for the "weakest argument" or asking which of the options is "not" in a specified category, you must examine each option with the mindset that it if it is wrong, it is the correct answer.

Next, you should read the root or fact pattern, formulating the legal issue involved in those facts and recalling the principles of law or testable points which will resolve the legal issues.

Finally, you should look at each of the options and use the techniques described below to assist you in picking the correct option.

TECHNIQUES FOR PICKING THE CORRECT OPTION

THE PROCESS OF ELIMINATION

Your task in answering a Multistate question is not to find the ideal answer to the question asked, but rather to pick the best of the four options available. Many times when all the options are unattractive, your process is one of elimination. Some options can be positively eliminated because they state an incorrect proposition of law or because they do not appropriately relate to the facts. If you can positively eliminate three choices and the remaining choice is not totally unacceptable, then you should pick it and move on to the next question.

The following question illustrates this point.

Hamilton owns a two-acre ocean-front estate known as "Doubleacre." His three neighbors - Alpha, Beta and Charlie - each own a lot without access to the ocean. Hamilton met Alpha and told him that he was interested in selling his estate for around $700,000 and that he would either sell for all cash or for part cash and part purchase money mortgage. Alpha indicated that he was interested in purchasing the property. A few days later, Alpha phoned Hamilton and informed him that he had secured the financing necessary to purchase the property. Hamilton subsequently met Beta and Charlie at the town dock and indicated to them that he was interested in selling his property and that the price would be around $700,000.

Three weeks later, Hamilton sent three identical letters to Alpha, Beta and Charlie, and did not inform any of them that the letter was being sent to all of them. The letter read as follows:

"As I have previously indicated to you, I am planning to sell Doubleacre for $700,000. I will sell either for $700,000 cash or for $200,000 cash and a promissory note for $500,000 for a term of ten years with interest at 10%. The sale is conditional upon my lawyer, Legalsmith, approving any deed which I give and any note and mortgage which I receive."

(s) Hamilton

Beta immediately drafted a letter that he delivered by messenger to Hamilton which read as follows:

"I accept your offer to purchase Doubleacre for $700,000 cash. I will close at your convenience."
(s) Beta

One day after the Beta letter was received by Hamilton, Alpha delivered a letter to Hamilton as follows:

"I reaffirm my previous offer to purchase Doubleacre for $700,000 cash. I will close at your convenience."
(s) Alpha

Shortly thereafter, Hamilton sold Doubleacre to Stranger for $700,000 cash. If Alpha sues Hamilton for breach of contract, which of the following would be Hamilton's strongest defense?

    (A)   The acceptance sent by Beta was prior in time to that of Alpha and terminated Alpha's power to accept.

    (B)   A binding contract between Hamilton and Alpha could not occur until the occurrence of the condition specified in the offer, namely, that Hamilton's lawyer approve the deed.

    (C)   The letter from Hamilton to Alpha did not state explicitly or by reasonable implication that Alpha could enter into a contractual relationship by manifesting an acceptance.

    (D)   The fact that identical letters were sent to potential buyers indicates that Hamilton did not intend that the letter be an offer.

This is a difficult question because Hamilton will probably lose and your task is to eliminate those defenses that are clearly wrong, and then pick the remaining choice which is not clearly incorrect.

(A) is clearly incorrect, since this is not a real estate brokerage contract which could be terminated without notice to the offeree.

(B) is clearly incorrect. The approval by Hamilton's lawyer would not take place until near the closing, and is at most a condition subsequent which might relieve Hamilton of performance if the buyer insisted on a deed which was unacceptable to Hamilton's lawyer. It would not prevent the formation of a contract in which the approval of the deed was a term of the contract.

(D) would be a strong argument if each of the offerees knew about the multiple addressees, because it would then be unreasonable for an addressee to expect that he had the power to form a contract. However, the facts indicate the addressees did not know that the letter was sent to more than one person and (D) must therefore be wrong.

That leaves you with an unimpressive (C). However, it is possible to read Hamilton's letter as not manifesting an intention to create the power in the addressee to form a contract by accepting, but rather as an invitation for offers only. Accordingly, Hamilton could argue that neither his conversation with Alpha nor his letter to Alpha should be interpreted to give Alpha the power to conclude a contract. It is therefore the correct answer. While it is likely that Hamilton would lose on that argument, the other three choices are wrong and this one is at least plausible.

ELIMINATING SOME CHOICES AND THEN GUESSING

Certain questions on the Multistate Bar Examination are hard because of the difficulty involved in distinguishing between two of the four choices when finally picking the best answer. A common lament from students leaving the bar exam is "I could not decide between the last two choices." The positive side of that problem is that you have eliminated two of the four choices. The arithmetic of the Multistate Bar Examination makes it very likely that you will pass if you have gone about eliminating choices intelligently. If you are sure of the answer to only half of the 200 questions on the exam and can confidently eliminate two of the four choices on the remaining hundred, then you can randomly guess between the two remaining choices, and the odds are that you will get 50 of them right. Those 50, coupled with the 100 questions of which you were sure of the answer, will produce a raw score of 150 on the Multistate Bar Examination, allowing you to pass with room to spare.

An example of that partial elimination process is shown in this Evidence question:

Davis is being tried for the common-law rape of Peg by force. Davis alleges consent.
Quigley, a defense witness, testifies that he had overheard Peg invite Davis to become intimate with her. The prosecution possesses a certified copy of Quigley's three-year old conviction for arson, a crime punishable by five year's imprisonment. Without asking Quigley about the conviction on cross-examination, the prosecution offers the copy of the conviction into evidence on rebuttal. The trial judge should rule the copy of the conviction

(A) inadmissible because the prosecution failed to call the attention of the witness to the conviction on cross-examination.
(B) inadmissible because evidence of convictions to impeach the character of witnesses cannot be shown by extrinsic evidence
(C) admissible only if the trial judge finds that the probative value of admitting the evidence outweighs its prejudicial effect on the accused.
(D) admissible unless its probative value is substantially outweighed by the danger of unfair prejudice.

A student with a rudimentary knowledge of evidence should be able to quickly eliminate (A) and (B), because (A) states the rule with respect to prior inconsistent statements, not convictions, and (B) deals with limitations on extrinsic evidence not applicable to impeachment by convictions. Moreover, given the complex and precise nature of choices (C) and (D), compared to the rather simplistic issues in choices (A) and (B), you should have a sixth sense that the right choice lies between (C) and (D). Choosing between them is difficult because it tests your knowledge of a relatively recent amendment to the Federal Rules of Evidence which relaxed the standard which must be proven by the prosecution when the character of a witness, rather than the character of the criminal defendant, is involved. However, an absolutely random guess between (C) and (D) gives you even odds of answering the question correctly.

THE DOUBLE TRUE/FALSE QUESTION

Because the form of the multiple-choice question used on the Multistate Bar Examination has four options, the double true/false question appears in many forms. In that type of question, the four options are

(A)　proposition A is true.
(B)　proposition B is true.
(C)　both propositions are true.
(D)　neither proposition is true.

In some cases, the propositions are set out with roman numerals in the body of the question itself. In others, combinations of the substance of the propositions appear in the options themselves.

This type of question appeals to the Examiners because the student must judge the truth of each proposition based upon the facts set forth in the root of the question, and little time has to be spent on either the call of the question or the draftsmanship of the options.

In preparing for the exam, it is not necessary to practice on questions that combine the issues to be tested in the precise combination which they are tested on the examination. The important thing to learn is the substantive law governing the issues so that you can correctly judge if a proposition is true or false. Combining two true/false questions in a single multiple-choice question is easy if you can handle each true/false issue separately.

There are no sure rules for guessing on this type of question. Each proposition must be examined independently to determine if it is true or false. The choice of the correct option follows mechanically once that determination is made.

However, where the two propositions are closely related, the Examiner is most often trying to highlight a difference between them, and therefore very often the correct choice is one of the two choices which deals with the two propositions differently.

This is illustrated by this Property Question:

The following conveyances were made of Blackacre by O who holds title in fee simple:

1. I. "To A so long as the premises are used for church purposes, and if they are not so used, then to X."
2. II. "To B, but if the premises should not be used for church purposes, then to X.

O retains an interest in Blackacre

(A) after conveyance I.
(B) after conveyance II.
(C) after both conveyances.
(D) after neither conveyance.

Since propositions I and II look very similar, the shrewd guess is that the examiner is trying to illustrate the difference between them and that O retains an interest after one but not the other. In fact, that is the case. Even if you do not know anything about property law and have to guess between (A) and (B), you have doubled your chances of getting the correct answer.

The statistics on this question illustrate a point made earlier. This question is extremely difficult. Less than one student in four, the result that would occur in random guessing, answered it correctly. Yet, the better students obtained the correct answer twice as often as the poor students. However, it didn't make any difference in the long run whether you got this question right or wrong because those getting it right passed the bar exam at only a slightly higher rate than those answering it incorrectly. This question, which involves the intricacies of determinable fees and the Rule Against Perpetuities is not the kind of question you spend a good deal of time on unless your objective is to obtain a very high score on the Multistate Bar Examination.

MULTIPLE TRUE/FALSE ISSUES

In addition to the double true/false question, the Examiners will sometimes state three propositions in the root of the question, and test some characteristic of those propositions in the call of the question. The choices will list various combinations of propositions. The difference between this type of question and the double true/false question is that only four of the eight possible combinations can be listed in the options. It is therefore possible to reach the correct result if you are not sure of the truth or falsity of all the propositions but are sure of one.

This is illustrated by the following question from the February 1978 Multistate Bar Exam:

Reggie offered Harriet $200 for a 30-day option to buy Harriet's land, Grandvale, for $10,000. As Harriet knew, Reggie, if granted the option, intended to resell Grandvale at a profit. Harriet declined, believing that she could find a desirable purchaser herself. Reggie thereupon said to Harriet, "Make me a written 30-day offer, revocable at your pleasure, to sell me Grandvale at a sale price of $10,000, and tomorrow I will pay you $200 for so doing." Harriet agreed and gave Reggie the following document:

For 30 days I offer my land known as Grandvale to Reggie for $10,000, this offer to be revocable at my pleasure at any time before acceptance.
[signed] Harriet

In a lawsuit by Harriet against Reggie to recover $200, which of the following arguments would plausibly support Reggie's position?

I. Any promise implied by Harriet in making her offer was illusory because of the revocability provision.
II. Since Harriet's offer, if any, was in writing and involved realty, it could not be revoked by telephone.
III. Enforced payment of $200 by Reggie to Harriet would defeat Reggie's reasonable expectation if Harriet's offer was legally open for only one day.

    (A) I and II only
    (B) I and III only
    (C) II and III only
    (D) I, II, and III

This question presents an interesting examsmanship issue. When you are required to determine which of three propositions are true or false, you can sometimes focus on one proposition which you clearly know is false and eliminate all choices where it appears in the answer. Proposition II is such a choice. An offer can be revoked by any means which communicates the revocation to the offeror. It need not be in writing even if the offer must be in writing. If proposition II is false, then (A), (C), and (D), all of which include Proposition II, have to be wrong. Therefore, (B) must be correct because it is the only one that does not contain II. You do not have to determine whether I or III is correct. Both must be correct simply because they appear together in (B), the only one which does not contain II.

THE CORRECTLY STATED BUT INAPPLICABLE PRINCIPLE OF LAW

The task of the Examiners is to make wrong choices look good. One of the best ways to accomplish this is to write a choice which impeccably states a rule of law that is not applicable because of facts in the root of the question.

This is illustrated by the following officially released question:

Trease owned Hilltop in fee simple. By his will, he devised as follows: "Hilltop to such of my grandchildren who shall reach the age of 21; and by this provision I intend to include all grandchildren whenever born." At the time of his death, Trease had three children and two grandchildren.

Courts hold such a devise valid under the common-law Rule Against Perpetuities.
What is the best explanation of that determination?

    (A) All of Trease's children would be measuring lives

(B) The rule of convenience closes the class of beneficiaries when any grandchild reaches the age of 21.

(C) There is a presumption that Trease intended to include only those grandchildren born prior to his death.

(D) There is a subsidiary rule of construction that dispositive instruments are to be interpreted so as to uphold interests, rather than to invalidate them under the Rule Against Perpetuities.

Choice (B) correctly states the rule of convenience as it applies to class gifts. However, the rule of convenience is only a rule of construction, which means that it is not applicable if the grantor has expressed a contrary intent. In this case, the will stated that Trease intended to include all grandchildren whenever born. Therefore, the rule of convenience does not apply, because the body of the question contains facts which make it inapplicable. Be wary of a perfectly stated rule of law. The Examiners usually state a rule that way only when it is not applicable.

ELIMINATION OF CHOICES BY OBSERVING THE INCONSISTENCY BETWEEN THEM AND THE FACT PATTERN

Another method the Examiners use to write appealing but wrong answers is to write a choice which sounds very plausible but is flatly contradicted by the fact pattern. In the process of reaching the correct answer, you must eliminate any choice which states a position inconsistent with the facts of the question.

This is illustrated by the following officially released question:

Trease owned Hilltop in fee simple. By his will, he devised as follows: "Hilltop to such of my grandchildren who shall reach the age of 21; and by this provision I intend to include all grandchildren, whenever born." At the time of his death Trease had three children and two grandchildren.

Which of the following additions to or changes in the facts stated in the previous paragraph would produce a violation of the common-law Rule Against Perpetuities?

(A) A posthumous child was born to Trease.
(B) Trease's will expressed the intention to include all after-born grandchildren in the gift.
(C) The instrument was an inter vivos conveyance rather than a will.
(D) Trease had no grandchildren living at the time of his death.

Choice (B) can be eliminated even if you know nothing about the Rule Against Perpetuities. The focus of the question asks what additions or changes in the preceding paragraph will cause a violation of the Rule. This choice does not represent an addition or change. Trease's will, which is set forth in the root of the question, already expresses the intent to include afterborn grandchildren. Therefore, it must be eliminated, whether or not it would cause a violation of the Rule Against Perpetuities, because it is not an "addition" or "change." It is important when answering these questions to read carefully and compare the choices to the body of the question.

THE THREE-ONE RULE

The author of a question must provide one answer that is correct and three that are not correct. Most questions in which there is a dichotomy of result, such as guilty/not guilty or admissible/inadmissible, will show two choices on each side of the general conclusion. If the question is skewed so that three choices are on one side of the general conclusion and one is on the other, the drafting of the question becomes more difficult if the correct choice is one of the three because the reasoning behind each choice must be distinct from the other choices. On the other hand, if the correct choice is the only one reaching a particular conclusion, there is no requirement to draft a reason why that choice is correct and there is no requirement that the reasoning among the three choices on the other side be clear and distinct. Therefore, the best guess in such a question is the sole choice reaching a conclusion rather than one of the other three choices.

An example of this type of question follows from Criminal Law:

A statute in State X provides: "Arson shall be punishable by a sentence of not more than ten years in state prison." X, during the daytime, went to a house in his neighborhood that was vacant because the previous owners had moved out and the new owners had not yet moved in. He put a lighted torch to the side of the house, and shortly thereafter extinguished the torch. The fire only slightly burned some of the shingles on the house. X is charged with arson. He is

- (A) guilty.
- (B) not guilty, because there was not sufficient burning.
- (C) not guilty, because the house was unoccupied at the time.
- (D) not guilty, because the activity took place during the daytime.

The "guilty" correct answer needs no explanation, and there is no requirement to distinguish between the three "not guilties" because they are all wrong.

THE DISTANCE BETWEEN CHOICES

By far the most common choice pattern is the "two-two" pattern - e.g., two choices which say that P will prevail, and two which say that D will prevail. The best way to approach this kind of question is to rely on your knowledge of the law or on your instinctive feeling as to which general conclusion is correct, then try to distinguish between the explanation following each of the general conclusions and pick the one that best justifies the conclusion. However, if the justifications following the conclusion on the side you chose seem indistinguishable, then look at the explanations for the choices on the other side. If they are readily distinguishable, and one appears reasonable and the other incorrect, then reconsider your initial choice of a general conclusion. Remember that the Examiner is required to provide a clearly distinguishable reason why one explanation of a general conclusion is right and the other is wrong. That obligation does not exist if the general conclusion itself is wrong. If choices (A) and (B) on one side both sound extremely reasonable, and are consistent with the fact pattern and on the other side answer (C) seems clearly wrong, or is inconsistent with the fact pattern, and answer (D) sounds reasonable, then from a purely technical viewpoint, the best guess is answer (D).

This is illustrated by the following Property Question:

In 1976, Barbara was the owner of Blueacre and Gertrude was the owner of the adjoining property, Greenacre. An unpaved driveway running from the main road across a portion of Greenacre gave Gertrude access to her residence. However, Gertrude decided that it would be more convenient for her to use the paved driveway on Blueacre and, in January of 1976, Gertrude began to use this paved driveway without making any effort to obtain Barbara's consent.

Barbara died in 1977 survived by Bonnie, age 12, her sole heir. Prior to her death, Barbara had also used the paved driveway as access to Blueacre but did not discover that Gertrude was also using it.

In 1978, Bonnie's guardian discovered Gertrude's use and orally protested to Gertrude. Gertrude ignored the protest and continued to use the driveway.

In February 1991, Gertrude conveyed Greenacre to Donna, informing Donna that Gertrude had been using the paved driveway on Blueacre. Donna continued to use the driveway until the end of the year, but made no use of it during 1992 or 1993. In January of 1994, Donna decided to begin using the paved driveway again, but when she attempted to do so, he discovered that Evelyn (who had purchased Blueacre from Bonnie in 1990) had erected a fence which blocked access to Greenacre from the paved driveway.

A statute in the jurisdiction provides that: "All actions to recover possession of real property must be brought within fifteen years of the time that the cause of action accrues."

Donna is now claiming that she has acquired an easement in Blackacre, and wishes to compel Evelyn to remove the fence.

Which of- the following is the most accurate statement with regard to the events following Gertrude's conveyance of Greenacre to Donna in February, 1991 ?

(A) The use of the driveway by Donna after her acquisition of Greenacre in 1991 will be "tacked" onto the use by Gertrude to compute the statutory prescriptive period.

(B) Donna's failure to use the driveway during 1992 and 1993 will interrupt the running of the prescriptive period, which is required to be continuous.

(C) The conveyance of Greenacre to Donna also gave her an easement in Blueacre entitling her to the use of the driveway.

(D) Donna's failure to use the driveway during 1992 and 1993 would operate as an abandonment of any rights that she may have theretofore acquired.

The difficulty with this question is that you have to go through 15 years of transactions to determine if Gertrude achieved an easement by prescription before February 1991. Choices (A) and (B) are based on the premise that no easement was obtained, whereas (C) and (D) state conclusions based upon a valid easement by prescription. While a judgment that no easement exists might be reasonable, you can tell that this is not the result envisioned by the Examiners because (A) and (B) are virtually indistinguishable if you come to the conclusion that there was no easement by prescription in 1991. If the easement had not ripened, additional prescriptive time would be tacked on, the conclusion stated by (A). However, the result suggested by (B), that non-use would interrupt the continuous nature of the possession, is also a valid conclusion if there were no easement. Therefore, (A) and (B) must both be wrong and the correct answer must be on the side where the choices are distinguishable. Choice (C) is the right answer because it gives Donna all the rights of an easement-holder, while (D) incorrectly states that she can lose those rights by a short period of non-use.

THE OPPOSITES RULE

Many times the Examiners may desire to test your knowledge of the applicability of a principle of law to a question. Then, often, two of the four choices will be phrased in terms of the applicability of that principle. The other two choices will deal with extraneous issues. When this pattern emerges, the correct answer is usually in one of the two opposites, provided the principle of law they deal with is relevant to a determination of the issue. The choice between those opposites must be made from your knowledge of the substantive law.

An example of this type of question can be found in this officially released question:

Seller and Buyer execute an agreement for the sale of real property on September 1. The jurisdiction in which the property is located recognizes the principle of equitable conversion, and has no statute pertinent to this problem.
Seller dies before closing, and his will leaves personal property to Perry and his real property to Rose. There being no breach of the agreement by either party, which of the following is correct?

    (A)   Death, an eventuality which the parties could have provided for, terminates the agreement if they did not provide otherwise.
    (B)   Rose is entitled to the proceeds of the sale when it closes, because the doctrine of equitable conversion does not apply to these circumstances.
    (C)   Perry is entitled to the proceeds of the sale when it closes.
    (D)   Title was rendered unmarketable by Seller's death.

The fact that the issue is the effect of the doctrine of equitable conversion on the fight to the proceeds can be gleaned from the nature of the choices. (B) and (C) reach the opposite conclusion on this issue, and this narrows your choices to two. The correct answer, (C), is one of those choices.

USE OF THE CONJUNCTIONS, "BECAUSE" "IF" "ONLY IF" AND "UNLESS"'

The conjunctions "because," "if," "only if," and "unless" are commonly used in the options in Multistate questions. This section will explain, regarding each of these conjunctions, the logical thought process that each requires.

For purposes of explaining their use, we will use a simplified set of facts and legal principles dealing with the enforceability of a contract for the sale of land as affected by the Statute of Frauds.

The common part of the fact pattern in each example is that Seller, the owner of Blackacre, offered to sell Blackacre to Buyer for $10,000 on a specific date and Buyer accepted the offer. In some of the examples, there may be facts showing that the offer was in writing or that the offer was oral or the fact pattern may be totally silent on this issue.

The legal issue is the Statute of Frauds, which will prevent the enforceability of the contract unless one of following two conditions are met: (1) there is a memorandum sufficient to satisfy the Statute of Frauds signed by the party to be charged, or (2) part performance takes the agreement out of the Statute of Frauds.

USE OF THE CONJUNCTION "BECAUSE"

The conjunction "because" connects a conclusion with a reason for that conclusion, For an option in a Multistate question using "because" to be the correct answer, the conclusion must be correct and the reason must logically follow based upon the facts and the applicable substantive law.

For example,

(Fact Pattern 1)
Seller, the owner of Blackacre, offered in a writing, signed by him, to sell Blackacre to Buyer for $10,000 on a specific date and Buyer accepted the offer. Seller later refused to perform.
In a suit by Buyer against Seller....

In Fact Pattern 1, an option which said, "Buyer will win because the agreement was in writing" would be correct. It reaches the correct conclusion and states a valid reason both in fact and in law for that conclusion.

Note that the only requirement of the reason following the word "because" is that it logically follow the conclusion and that it be supported by the facts and the substantive law.

However, it need not be the **only** reason that supports the conclusion. For example, in Fact Pattern 1, a choice which said "Buyer will win **because** he accepted Seller's offer" would also be correct since it satisfies the two requirements of the conjunction "because": the general conclusion is correct and the reason logically follows and is supported by the facts and the law.

If either of the two requirements is **not** met, the choice is wrong. For example,

(Fact Pattern 2)

Seller, the owner of Blackacre, offered orally to sell Blackacre to Buyer for $10,000 on a specific date and Buyer accepted the offer. Seller later refused to perform.

In a suit by Buyer against Seller....
The option, "Buyer will win **because** he accepted Seller's offer" would not be correct since the conclusion is incorrect. Buyer would lose because of the absence of a writing. The fact that the reason which follows "because" logically follows and is supported by the facts is irrelevant because the conclusion is wrong.
Likewise, the option is incorrect if the reasoning does not logically follow from the facts. An option following Fact Pattern I which said, "Buyer will win **because** the doctrine of part performance takes the agreement out of the Statute

of Frauds" would be incorrect, even though the conclusion is correct and the principle of law is correctly stated. The reasoning is not supported by the facts and therefore does not follow logically therefrom.

The failure of logical reasoning can apply to legal principles as well as the facts. An option Following Fact Pattern 1 which said, "Buyer will win **because** Seller's offer is admissible under the parol evidence rule" is incorrect, even though it relates to the facts of the question, because the reasoning concerning the parol evidence rule is not a legal basis for Buyer's winning.

The "because" conjunction is heavily used because it requires the applicants to determine the correct conclusion based upon their knowledge of the substantive law and also requires applicants to determine if there is a logical nexus between the conclusion and the reason stated based upon their analysis of the facts in the root of the question and their knowledge of the substantive law.

USE OF THE CONJUNCTION "IF"

The conjunction "if" requires a much narrower focus than "because." The focus of inquiry to make an item correct when it contains an "if" narrows to whether or not the entire statement is true, assuming that the proposition which follows the "if" is true. There is no requirement that facts in the root of the question support the proposition following "if," or if there are facts in the root which might support the proposition, that such a construction be reasonable.

For example,

(Fact Pattern 3)
Seller, the owner of Blackacre, offered to sell Blackacre to Buyer for $10,000 on a specific date and Buyer accepted the offer. Seller later refused to perform.
In a suit by Buyer against Seller....

The option, "Buyer will prevail if Seller's offer was in a writing signed by him" is correct because the contract is enforceable when there is a writing signed by the party to be charged and we must accept the proposition followed by "if" as true. It does not matter that the fact pattern did not mention that the offer was in writing.

There is no requirement of exclusivity when the conjunction "if" is used. "If" is not the equivalent of "only if," discussed below. For example, Buyer would also prevail (even without a writing) if the doctrine of part performance took the contract out of the Statute of Frauds. Nevertheless, the option dealing with a writing is correct.

However, the conjunction "if" does not automatically foreclose inquiry into the legal principles raised by the fact pattern. If, although we must assume the proposition followed by "if" is true, the conclusion is incorrect, then the option is not correct.

This principle can be illustrated by Fact Pattern 2.

(Fact Pattern 2)

Seller, the owner of Blackacre, offered orally to sell Blackacre to Buyer for $10,000 on a specific date and Buyer accepted the offer. Seller later refused to perform.
In a suit by Buyer against Seller....

The option "Buyer will prevail if he accepted Seller's offer in a writing signed by him" is incorrect, even though we must accept the fact that Buyer's acceptance was in writing. The portion of the fact pattern that says that Seller's offer was oral is still an operative fact, because it has not been contradicted by the proposition following the "if." Even if we must take as true that Buyer's acceptance was in writing, Buyer will not prevail because there has been no writing signed by the party to be charged (Seller) and the contract is therefore unenforceable by Buyer against Seller because of the Statute of Frauds.

USE OF THE CONJUNCTION "ONLY IF"

When an option uses the conjunction "only if," we must again accept as true the words following that conjunction and apply the principles discussed above with respect to the correctness of the entire proposition, assuming that it is true. The critical difference, where "only if" is used, is that the proposition cannot be true **except when the condition is true. Exclusivity is required.** The difference can be illustrated by Fact Pattern 3.

(Fact Pattern 3)

Seller, the owner of Blackacre offered to sell Blackacre to Buyer for $10,000 on a specific date and Buyer accepted the offer. Seller later refused to perform.
In a suit by Buyer against Seller....

We previously found that the option, "Buyer will prevail **if** Seller's offer was in a writing signed by him" is correct because the contract is enforceable when there is a writing signed by the party to be charged and we must accept the proposition followed by "if' as true.

If that option were, "Buyer will prevail **only if** Seller's offer was in a writing signed by him," it would be **incorrect.** Even though this is one instance when Buyer will prevail, it is not the **only** instance. If Buyer moved onto the land in reliance on an oral purchase and sale agreement and made substantial improvements on it, the doctrine of part performance would take the contract out of the Statute of Frauds and would allow Buyer to recover on the oral agreement.
Of course, there are circumstances when the option can be correct when it is circumscribed by the "only if" conjunction. Fact Pattern 2 can be used to illustrate this.

(Fact Pattern 2)

Seller, the owner of Blackacre, offered orally to sell Blackacre to Buyer for
$10,000 on a specific date and Buyer accepted the offer. Seller later refused to perform.

In a suit by Buyer against Seller....

If the option were, "Buyer will prevail **only if** the doctrine of part performance takes the contract out of the Statute of Frauds," then it would be correct. The fact pattern clearly indicates that the contract involves the sale of land and that there is no writing that will satisfy the Statute of Frauds. Under these circumstances the **only** way in which Buyer can prevail is if the condition is met, namely that the doctrine of part performance will make the oral contract enforceable. The difference between this example and the previous one where "only if" made the option incorrect, is that, in Fact Pattern 2, we are clearly told that the offer is oral and that the Statute of Frauds has not been satisfied. The only other way that Buyer can win is through the doctrine of part performance.

Therefore, when faced with the conjunction "only if" in an option, make sure that the conclusion cannot be true unless the condition is met.

USE OF THE CONJUNCTION "UNLESS"

The conjunction "unless" performs the same logical function as the conjunction "only if," except that it precedes a negative exclusive condition instead of a positive one. It is essentially the mirror image of an "only if" choice. Thus, the best approach to an option using an "unless" conjunction is to reverse the result and substitute the words "only if" for "unless."

Some of the previous examples will illustrate this point.

(Fact Pattern 3)

Seller, the owner of Blackacre offered to sell Blackacre to Buyer for $10,000 on a specific date and Buyer accepted the offer. Seller later refused to perform.
In a suit by Buyer against Seller....

If the option were "Seller will prevail **unless** his offer was in a writing signed by him," it would be incorrect for the same reason that its functional equivalent, "Buyer will prevail only if Seller's offer was in a writing signed by him" would be incorrect. Buyer will not prevail only if Seller's offer was not in writing. If the circumstances which would give rise to the doctrine of part performance were present, then Buyer would prevail, even if Seller's offer was oral, because the requirements of a writing imposed by the Statute of Frauds will not be applicable. If Buyer moved onto the land in reliance on an oral purchase and sale agreement and made substantial improvements on it, the doctrine of part performance would take the contract out of the Statute of Frauds and would allow Buyer to recover on the oral agreement.

The same reversal process works for the previous illustration where an option containing "only if" was correct.

(Fact Pattern 2)

Seller, the owner of Blackacre, offered orally to sell Blackacre to Buyer for
$10,000 on a specific date and Buyer accepted the offer. Seller later refused to perform.

In a suit by Buyer against Seller....

If the option were, "Seller will prevail **unless** the doctrine of part performance takes the contract out of the Statute of Frauds," then it would be correct for precisely the same reason that the option "Buyer will prevail **only if** the doctrine of part performance takes the contract out of the Statute of Frauds" is correct. The fact pattern clearly indicates that the contract involves the sale of land and that there is no writing that will satisfy the Statute of Frauds. Under these circumstances the only way in which Seller can lose is if the condition is met, namely that the doctrine of part performance makes the oral contract enforceable. The difference between this example and the previous one, where "unless" made the option incorrect, is that in Fact Pattern 2, we are clearly told that the offer is oral and that the Statute of Frauds has not been satisfied. The only other way that Seller can lose is through the doctrine of part performance.
It is much easier to think in the positive than the negative. Therefore, every time you see an "unless" in an option, reverse the result and substitute the words "only if" for unless. "

USE OF THE ADVERBS AND ADJECTIVES "ALL," "ANY," "NEVER," "ALWAYS," AND "EVERY"

In addition to the limitations imposed by the conjunctions discussed above, options can be narrowed by the use of limiting adverbs and adjectives which require that a proposition be true all of the time or none of the time. These are substantial conditions which are designed to make close choices wrong.

This is illustrated by this Evidence Question:

Which of the following statements regarding judicial notice is most accurate?

(A) A court may take judicial notice only when requested by one of the parties.
(B) Once the court takes judicial notice, the jury is required to accept as conclusive any fact judicially noticed in all proceedings.
(C) If a court, on its own authority, takes judicial notice of a fact, a party is not entitled to a hearing as the propriety of the action.
(D) Judicial notice may be taken for the first time during the appellate stages of litigation.

Choice (B) is a very popular wrong answer to this question. While the statement about the conclusive nature of the facts judicially noticed is true in civil cases, it is false in criminal cases. A jury is not required to find in accordance with judicially noticed facts in a criminal case. Therefore, it is incorrect because the choice says that such facts are true concerning **any** fact in **all** proceedings.
The same analysis must be applied to any choice involving an "all," "always, "any," or "every." Irrespective of the facts of the question, the proposition stated must be true no matter what the circumstances. Likewise, the legal principle

stated in a choice including a "never" must be false no matter what the circumstances; if there are any circumstances in which the legal proposition stated is true, the choice is wrong.

TIMING

The time given you to complete a Multistate Bar Examination is ordinarily adequate, if you have practiced enough on questions to improve your speed and efficiency to the required level. The examination is broken into two 100-question segments. You are allowed three hours for each set of 100 questions - one minute and forty-eight seconds per question. However, all questions do not require the same amount of time. You should first check the clock 15 minutes after the examination starts. By then, you should have nine questions completed. You should check at 15-minute intervals thereafter. As long as you have completed 18 questions in the first half hour, 90 in the first two and one-half hours, and 100 after two hours and forty-five minutes, your pace is right.

If you find a particularly hard question or one you do not know the answer to, make a shrewd guess within this time frame and make a note to yourself to come back if time allows. DO NOT LEAVE IT BLANK.

If you find that your natural, careful pace is faster than this, work at your faster pace, but use your extra time fruitfully on the harder questions or in thoroughly rechecking your work at the end.

If you find that you absolutely cannot finish all the questions in the allotted time, then you should skip those questions with a long fact pattern and only one question. If you follow this advice, make sure that you keep your proper place on your answer sheet by skipping the row on the answer sheet corresponding to the question you skipped. Come back to those questions at the end and do as many as you can. Then, before turning your paper in, guess at the rest. In this way, you can reduce the number of random guesses to a minimum. **Make sure that you answer every question,** even if you have not even read the question, since wrong answers do not count against you.

As you decide each correct answer, circle it in your examination book and mark the appropriate block on your answer sheet. At the pace of nine questions per 15 minutes, you should have about seven minutes left at the end. Spend that time proofreading your answer sheet, which is the only paper that will be graded. Check against the answers you circled in the book to be certain that you marked the appropriate block on your answer sheet. Make sure that there are no blanks on your answer sheet and no questions for which you have marked two answers. If you have erased, make sure that your erasure is thorough; otherwise, the computer may reject your answer because it thinks you have marked two answers. DO NOT use this time to change the answer you have already picked unless you have a very good reason to change. If you have time left after your proofreading is done, go back to the difficult questions and re-think the answers you have chosen. But even after careful thought, you should hesitate to change an answer. Do not leave any section of the examination early. Use all the time allotted to you wisely.

MULTISTATE NUTSHELLS OF LAW

The following rules of law have controlled the answers to questions on the Multistate Bar Exam. They should be committed to memory and their application understood before you take the Multistate Bar Exam.

CONSTITUTIONAL LAW

NATURE OF JUDICIAL REVIEW

The Federal and State Court Systems

Congress can require state courts to hear causes of action based upon federal statutes.

State governments or agencies are not citizens of a state for the purpose of federal diversity jurisdiction.

A private citizen cannot sue a state in a federal court.

A private citizen can challenge the constitutionality of a state statute in a federal court by suing a state officer to enjoin the enforcement of the statute on the ground that it is unconstitutional.

Political subdivisions of a state can be sued by citizens in federal court because they do not enjoy the protection afforded a state under the Eleventh Amendment.

Supreme Court Jurisdiction and Review

If a case has been decided by a state court on an independent state ground, there is no jurisdiction for Supreme Court review, even if the state court decides a federal issue in the case which is not essential to the decision. If, on the other hand, the state court decides a state issue on the basis of federal decisions on the same point, then the state ground is not independent and there is a basis for Supreme Court review.

A state has the right to sue another state in the United States Supreme Court on behalf of its citizens on claims affecting a multiplicity of citizens (the *parens patriae* doctrine).

There is no direct right of appeal to the Supreme Court from a federal district court decision holding an act of Congress unconstitutional.

There is no right to appeal a state court advisory opinion to the United States Supreme Court even if it involves federal constitutional issues because there is no case or controversy, as required by the United States Constitution for federal court jurisdiction.

CONGRESSIONAL CONTROL OVER JURISDICTION; ARTICLE I COURTS

Congress has control of the jurisdiction of the federal courts and can establish or abolish lower federal courts.

Congress cannot alter the jurisdiction of the Supreme Court in such a way as to interfere with the Court's essential function of preserving constitutional order.

Congress cannot interfere with inherent judicial functions in courts it has created.

Congress can set up courts pursuant to its powers under Article I of the Constitution. Judges of such courts are not constitutionally entitled to life tenure.

Due process requires that there must ultimately be a right of appeal to an Article III court from the decision of an Article I court or an administrative body.

STANDING; CASE OR CONTROVERSY

A person has standing by virtue of being a taxpayer only to challenge legislation authorizing expenditures on the basis that those expenditures contravene specific constitutional limitations on the spending power.

A mere philosophical, ethical or intellectual interest in the outcome of a case is not sufficient to qualify for standing.

Standing exists in a party that has a close relationship to the party actually injured if the injured party is unlikely to successfully assert its rights.

MOOTNESS AND RIPENESS

A case will not be dismissed for mootness if the issue is capable of repetition and will consistently evade review.

A case will be dismissed as not ripe if events which will raise material issues in the case have not yet occurred.

ABSTENTION

A federal court has discretion to abstain from deciding an issue of state law if a decision by a state court on the state issue might obviate the need for a decision on a federal constitutional issue.

A federal court will abstain from a case asking for an injunction against the enforcement of a state criminal statute if a prosecution under that statute has commenced.

JUSTICIABILITY; POLITICAL QUESTIONS

Under the political question doctrine, the United States Supreme Court will not review an issue on the merits if it determines that the Constitution places final authority to resolve the issue in another branch of government.

Burden of Proof in Constitutional Litigation

If constitutional litigation involves the strict scrutiny tier of equal protection, the denial of substantive due process rights which are highly protected, or the deprivation of the right of free speech or of freedom of religion, the state must show a compelling state need and that no less burdensome method would achieve that objective.

If constitutional litigation involves sexual discrimination, the state must show that the classification has an important governmental objective and is substantially related to achieving those objectives.

If constitutional litigation involves matters other than those described above, the plaintiff must prove that the legislation lacked a rational basis.

The state never has the burden when only lack of rational basis must be shown, and the plaintiff never has the burden when highly protected rights are involved.

SEPARATION OF POWERS

CONGRESSIONAL COMMERCE POWER

The Supremacy Clause itself is not a source of congressional power.

Congress may exercise the commerce power to regulate purely local commerce as long as it affects interstate commerce.

Congress may exercise the commerce power to regulate the conduct of private individuals with respect to racial discrimination (even though such private action could not be regulated by legislation under the Fourteenth Amendment) so long as the individual's conduct affects interstate commerce.

Congress may delegate rulemaking power to an administrative agency, but cannot reserve to itself the right to change such rules by anything short of legislation adopted by the full constitutional process.

CONGRESSIONAL TAXING AND SPENDING POWER

Through Congress's power to condition expenditures on compliance with its standards, Congress can persuade the states and individuals to adopt measures which it could not directly require through legislation.

While Congress can tax and spend for the general welfare, the General Welfare Clause is not a source of congressional regulatory power.

Congress can achieve a regulatory effect through a taxing statute as long as the statute has a revenue-raising purpose.

CONGRESSIONAL PROPERTY POWER AND POWER OVER TERRITORIES

The property power, not the commerce power, is the best source of congressional authority to regulate or dispose of property owned by the United States.

Congress holds all of the regulatory power of territories which would be possessed by the state legislature if the territory were a state.

Judges appointed to serve in the territories are not Article III judges entitled to lifetime tenure.

CONGRESSIONAL DEFENSE AND GENERAL LEGISLATIVE POWERS

Congress has the power to investigate and subpoena witnesses for the purpose of obtaining information with respect to potential legislation which it might pass.

An individual can successfully defend against a contempt of Congress charge for failing to answer a question from a congressional committee only if the witness can show that the subject matter of the questioning was beyond the power of Congress to pass potential legislation or beyond the scope of the power delegated by Congress to that committee.

CONGRESSIONAL POWER TO ENFORCE 13TH, 14TH, AND 15TH AMENDMENTS

Congress has power under the 13th Amendment to affect individual conduct but only to eradicate slavery or the effects of slavery. Pursuant to that authority, it has the power to regulate the manner in which Blacks are treated.

Congress has power under the 14th Amendment only to reach state action (or action accomplished under the color of state law) which abrogates the rights guaranteed by that Amendment.

Congress has power under the 15th Amendment to directly regulate voting procedures in the states for the purpose of eradicating procedures which affect the rights of minorities to vote or to have their vote counted.

POWERS OF THE PRESIDENT

The President is obligated to carry out legislation mandating that the President act in a specific manner.

The pardon power only extends to federal crimes.

Executive privilege is absolute with respect to defense and foreign policy matters. Confidential communications between the President and advisors in all other areas are presumptively privileged; disclosure can be required only when a specific communication is subpoenaed and a substantial governmental interest outweighs the President's interest in nondisclosure.

INTERBRANCH CHECKS ON POWER

Only the President has the right to appoint officers of the United States, and an attempted appointment by Congress or by members thereof is unconstitutional.

The Supreme Court has the right under the Constitution to decide which branch of government is vested with final authority to decide a particular matter.

While the Senate has the right to advise and consent on presidential appointments, it does not have the right to advise and consent when the President removes officers of the Executive branch.

THE RELATION OF THE NATION AND STATES

INTERGOVERNMENTAL IMMUNITIES

Absent congressional intention to the contrary, states can tax buildings leased by the federal government and contractors doing business with the federal government, as long as such tax is not discriminatory.

The federal government has the right to tax and regulate the instrumentalities and employees of state government.

AUTHORITY RESERVED TO THE STATES

A state has the right to regulate interstate commerce as long as it does not contravene an express federal policy, does not discriminate against interstate commerce, and does not unduly burden interstate commerce.

In determining the validity of a state action which burdens interstate commerce, the court will consider whether the state used the least restrictive means to achieve a legitimate state objective.

A state regulatory statute which discriminates in favor of local commerce and against out-of-state commerce is unconstitutional because of the negative implications of the Commerce Clause.

The negative implications of the Commerce Clause prevent a state from requiring that a resource of the state be sold to in-state customers only.

The negative implications of the Commerce Clause prevent a state from excluding trash from a sister state if its landfills accept in-state trash.

A state acting in a proprietary rather than a regulatory capacity may discriminate in favor of local business and against interstate commerce.

Congress has the right to expressly authorize a state to burden commerce or discriminate in favor of local commerce, even if the Supreme Court has held such burden or discrimination unconstitutional under the negative implications of the Commerce Clause.

The police power is a source of state power, not a source of congressional power.

NATIONAL POWER TO OVERRIDE STATE AUTHORITY

The Supremacy Clause is the source of constitutional power for a court to hold state statutes and decisions unconstitutional because they conflict with the Constitution, laws, or treaties of the United States or acts done in furtherance of them.

If Congress has provided a comprehensive scheme of regulation in an area, Congress may be said to have occupied the field and any state regulation (even if complementary to the federal legislation) will be preempted, unless Congress's intent was to allow state regulation. Congress has the ability to permit states to operate in areas where it has legislated.

States may not enact any legislation which affects foreign policy, because foreign policy is the exclusive province of the federal government.

State legislation or decisions which are contrary to a federal policy expressed in an executive agreement are invalid.

A state or municipal law in conflict with a federal regulation dealing with standards applicable to federal offices is invalid because of the Supremacy Clause.

INDIVIDUAL RIGHTS

STATE ACTION

The activity of a state in regulating or taxing an activity does not render the activity itself "state action" subject to 14th Amendment scrutiny.

The action of any political subdivision of a state constitutes state action.

The activities of an entity in which the state has a partnership interest constitute state action.

SUBSTANTIVE DUE PROCESS

An economic regulation violates the substantive strand of the Due Process Clause if there is no rational basis for it.

Substantive due process prohibits states from limiting fundamental privacy interests, absent a showing of a compelling state need. The right to use contraceptives and the right of an extended family to live together are examples of such interests.

A state activity is no more likely to withstand constitutional challenge because it is part of the state constitution or enacted by referendum.

PROCEDURAL DUE PROCESS

Procedural due process is required only if the action of the decisionmaker constitutes state action.

An individual has a property interest in continued employment if the individual has an employment contract or tenure.

The factors in determining what process is "due" are the type of interest infringed, the likelihood of an erroneous decision, and the burden on the government in providing process.

The minimum necessary to satisfy due process is notice and an opportunity to be heard.

Criminal statutes violate due process if they are so vague that they do not inform a citizen of the conduct deemed criminal. A judicial construction of the statute can cure the vagueness with respect to future violators, but not with respect to any person charged before the decision was rendered.

EQUAL PROTECTION - REGULATION OF VOTING AND LEGISLATIVE REPRESENTATION

The Equal Protection Clause is contained in the Fourteenth Amendment and does not apply to the federal government. However, the principles of equal protection are applied to the federal government through the Due Process Clause of the Fifth Amendment.

The one man/one vote rule applies to municipal legislative bodies.

The state may impose limited residency requirements (e.g., two months) on the right to vote to assure that voters are bona fide residents.

The state may impose reasonable requirements regarding filing fees, residency, and petition signatures to achieve ballot access.

EQUAL PROTECTION - REGULATION OF SOCIAL AND ECONOMIC WELFARE

Economic regulation need only satisfy the rational basis standard.

The right to be free from poverty is not a fundamental right.

EQUAL PROTECTION - REGULATION OF OTHER INTERESTS

The right to work is not a fundamental right and the state can impose age classifications on various governmental jobs.

EQUAL PROTECTION - CLASSIFICATION BY RACE OR ALIENAGE

Neither the state nor the federal government can discriminate on the basis of race except to further a compelling state need.

A regulation or decision which classifies on the basis of race in order to remedy specific past racial discrimination is valid.

A classification based upon a racially neutral principle such as residence, which also indirectly discriminates by race, is not unconstitutional unless there is an intention to discriminate by race.

The federal government has broad discretion to discriminate on the basis of alienage in the furtherance of foreign policy. A state cannot discriminate on the basis of alienage except in elective governmental positions and non-elective governmental jobs which formulate or execute public policy.

EQUAL PROTECTION - CLASSIFICATION BY GENDER OR ILLEGITIMACY

Discrimination on the basis of gender is valid only if it serves an important governmental purpose and is substantially related to achieving that purpose.

The state cannot deny worker's compensation benefits, wrongful death benefits, or intestacy benefits based upon illegitimacy where the parent-child relationship has been adjudicated or acknowledged, but can make distinctions where proof of the relationship is difficult.

PRIVILEGES AND IMMUNITIES

The Privileges and Immunities Clause of the Fourteenth Amendment applies only to the privileges of national citizenship and is rarely if ever a valid reason for holding a statute unconstitutional.

The Privileges and Immunities Clause of Article IV of the Constitution is an alternative analysis where the state discriminates on a matter of fundamental interest in favor of its own citizens and against out-of-staters.

OBLIGATIONS OF CONTRACT; BILLS OF ATTAINDER

State legislation which impairs the obligations of a contract is invalid unless there is a valid police power reason for the legislation or unless it only alters the remedies for breach of contract and other feasible remedies are available.

Legislation, either federal or state, which withholds appropriations for a specific job as long as a named individual holds that job is a bill of attainder and unconstitutional.

FIRST AMENDMENT - FREEDOM OF RELIGION

A state has the right to regulate action based upon religious belief if there is a compelling state need.

When religious belief is the basis for resisting government rules (e.g., conscientious objector status) the courts have a right to examine the sincerity of the belief, but not the belief itself.

Courts cannot decide ecclesiastical questions to settle disputes concerning church management or property.

FIRST AMENDMENT - SEPARATION OF CHURCH AND STATE

State aid to religions is constitutional only if the activity reflects a secular purpose, it has a primary effect which neither advances nor inhibits religion, and there is no excessive entanglement between church and state.

State activity which aids all religions equally can still violate the Establishment Clause.

State laws requiring that religious theory be taught in public schools violate the Establishment Clause.

FIRST AMENDMENT - REGULATION OF CONTENT OF SPEECH

Action which is a substitute for words can be protected symbolic speech. However, even if action is intended as symbolic speech, it can be regulated to protect a legitimate government interest divorced from the content of the symbolic speech itself (e.g., burning draft cards).

All speech is protected speech for purposes of content regulation except fighting words, defamatory speech, obscene speech, and to some degree commercial speech.

Neither the state nor the federal government can regulate the content of protected speech unless it can show a compelling state need.

A compelling state need is present and the state can proscribe the content of protected speech which is directed toward inciting immediate lawless action and is likely to incite that action.

Commercial speech can be subject to reasonable governmental regulation for the protection of consumers and other legitimate government interests, but outright prohibition of commercial speech is unconstitutional.

Requiring an individual to display a message prescribed by the state is the equivalent of regulating the content of speech.

The state has an affirmative obligation to protect a speaker before an audience, but the speaker can be required to stop speaking if there is a genuine likelihood of immediate violence which the state cannot prevent.

FIRST AMENDMENT - REGULATION OF TIME, PLACE AND MANNER OF SPEECH

The state cannot completely prohibit the exercise of free speech rights in a public forum such as streets or parks, but can regulate such speech pursuant to narrowly drawn statutes conferring limited discretion on officials to ban speech at particular times and places and in particular ways, as long as the prohibition of speech does not turn on its content.

The state has the right to forbid speech near semi-public forums such as schools, libraries and courthouses to prevent interference with governmental functions.

The state has the right to prohibit the exercise of free speech rights in places closed to the public such as jails, military bases and private government offices.

Unless the regulation of speech on private property becomes state action (as in the operation of a company town), the owner of private property can regulate and prohibit the exercise of speech on that property.

FIRST AMENDMENT - OBSCENITY

Speech is obscene and subject to complete prohibition if it appeals to the prurient interest of an average person applying contemporary community standards, depicts or describes sexual activity in a patently offensive way, and taken as a whole, lacks serious literary, artistic, political or scientific value.

Child pornography is totally unprotected speech.

Communications portraying nudity or sexual activity can be regulated concerning the time, place and manner of their exhibition even if the communication is not pornographic and the regulation is content-based.

FIRST AMENDMENT - PROCEDURAL PROBLEMS

If a court has issued an injunction banning the exercise of free speech rights, the constitutional issues raised by the issuance of the injunction cannot be litigated in a contempt prosecution for violation of the injunction.

A statute which is overly broad (i.e., prohibits protected speech as well as properly regulated speech) or vague (i.e., a person of ordinary intelligence cannot distinguish permitted from prohibited activities) is unconstitutional on its face and can be successfully challenged even by those who could be regulated if the statute were clear and narrowly drawn.

An individual is entitled to notice and a hearing before an injunction is granted limiting the time, place and manner of his expression, unless there is a genuine emergency justifying an ex parte application.

FIRST AMENDMENT - FREEDOM OF ASSOCIATION; LICENSE OR BENEFITS BASED UPON FIRST AMENDMENT RIGHTS

A public employee's freedom of speech with respect to matters of public concern cannot be infringed unless the employer's interest in operating the public service outweighs the employee's interest in expressing the employee's political views.

A public employee who has joined a subversive organization cannot be dismissed from public employment unless the employer can prove that the employee would have been dismissed even if the employee had not exercised the right of freedom of association by joining the organization.

CONTRACTS AND SALES

FORMATION OF CONTRACTS

OFFERS

A communication is an offer for a bilateral contract if it sets forth a proposed exchange of promises in such a manner that the person to whom it is directed reasonably believes that he can enter into a binding contract by accepting those terms.

The person selling goods at auction is not bound by the highest bid unless he advertises the auction as "without reserve," in which case placing the goods at auction is making an offer to the highest bidder.

ACCEPTANCE

At common law, an offer can only be accepted by the offeree agreeing, before the offer is revoked, to all of its terms in the time and manner specified by the offeror (or in a reasonable time and in a reasonable manner, if the offeror did not specify the manner of acceptance).

Unless the offeror specifically states that his offer may be accepted by silence or the course of dealings between the parties indicates that the offer will be accepted if the offeree does nothing, silence will not operate as an acceptance.

Under the UCC, a valid contract is formed if the offeree accepts the offer, even if he proposes different or additional terms. Between merchants, the different or additional terms become part of the contract if they do not materially alter the offer and the offeror does not object.

Under the UCC, a seller can accept an offer either by a promise to sell the goods requested by the buyer or by shipping conforming goods in accordance with the offer.

REVOCATION OF OFFERS

At common law, an offer is generally revocable even if the offer says it will remain open for a specified time. At common law, an offer is irrevocable for the time specified only if an option contract is formed, i.e., if the offeree has given consideration to the offeror in exchange for the offeror's agreement to keep the offer open.

Under the UCC, a "firm offer" cannot be revoked before the expiration date. Such a "firm offer" can only be made by a merchant, must state in writing that the offer is irrevocable until a date certain, and cannot remain irrevocable for more than three months.

An offer for a unilateral contract is irrevocable by the offeror if the offeree has, with the knowledge of the offeror, started substantial performance.

An offer is revoked if the notice of revocation is communicated to the offeree in any manner before the offer is accepted. The notice of revocation can be any communication which fairly indicates to the offeree that the offeror has withdrawn the offer.

In a real estate brokerage transaction where the owner makes an offer for a unilateral contract which the broker accepts by producing a buyer ready, willing and able to buy at the listing price, the offer is automatically revoked by the seller's acceptance of an offer to purchase the property from a buyer not produced by the broker.

An offer for a contract which would fall within the statute of frauds can be revoked orally.

If the offeror dies before the offer is accepted, it is revoked. However, if the offer is accepted, then death does not terminate the obligations of the contract.

REJECTION

If the offeree rejects an offer or makes a counter-offer, the original offer is terminated and cannot thereafter be accepted, even if the time for expiration of the offer has not yet occurred.

If the offeror has made an offer which he permits to be accepted in part, acceptance of part can be considered a rejection of the remainder.

An inquiry in response to an offer ("Would you consider a lesser price?") is not a rejection.

MISTAKE, FRAUD, AND DURESS

A contract can be avoided on the grounds of unilateral mistake if the mistake was so obvious that the offeree should have known of the mistake at the time he accepted the offer.

If each of the parties innocently has a different understanding of the meaning of the words of the agreement, then there is no contract.

A party has the right to rescind a contract if it was entered into in reliance on an untrue material fact.

INDEFINITENESS AND ABSENCE OF TERMS

If the price term is missing in a UCC transaction, there is a contract at a reasonable price.

CAPACITY TO CONTRACT

A minor can disaffirm a contract, even one that has been completed, within a reasonable time of reaching the age of majority.

IMPLIED-IN-FACT CONTRACTS; QUASI CONTRACTS

If a person accepts services from someone in the business of providing those services, there is an implied-in-fact contract to pay for the reasonable value of those services.

If necessary services are rendered to a person at a time when he lacks the mental capacity to request such services, (e.g., he is unconscious at the time medical services are rendered), there is an implied-in-law contract to pay for them.

A quasi contract exists when there is no enforceable contractual relationship between the parties, but one party has conferred a benefit on the other not intended to be gratuitous. The party conferring the benefit is entitled to collect the fair value of the services rendered.

A party does not have the right to sue in *quantum meruit* for a benefit conferred if there is an enforceable right to sue under a contract.

PRE-CONTRACTUAL LIABILITY BASED UPON DETRIMENTAL RELIANCE

If a subcontractor submits an offer to perform a subcontract to a contractor knowing that the contractor will rely on that offer when making a bid to the contracting authority, then under the doctrine of promissory estoppel, the subcontractor may not revoke his offer until the contractor has had an opportunity to accept, if the contractor is the successful bidder.

CONSIDERATION

BARGAIN AND EXCHANGE

The concept of bargain is the essence of consideration. If a party asks for something that he wants, even though it does not directly benefit him, and promises something in return, there is valid bargained-for consideration.

An illusory promise, one which gives the party the unilateral right to do anything they want, is not valid consideration.

A gift contingent on a minor condition which is not bargained for by the donor, such as "I will give you a birthday present if you come down and pick it up," does not amount to a contract supported by consideration.

ADEQUACY OF CONSIDERATION

The value of what a party promises or requests is irrelevant for purposes of determining if there is valid consideration.

If a party to a contract performs the promise he makes, he is entitled to enforce the contract according to its terms, even if he is getting far more than he has given.

MORAL OBLIGATIONS; DETRIMENTAL RELIANCE

One party's promise to make a gift is enforceable under the doctrine of promissory estoppel if (1) the donor-promisor knows that the promise will induce substantial reliance on the part of the promisee, and (2) failure to enforce the promise will cause substantial hardship.

A service which has already been gratuitously rendered is not valid consideration for a later promise to pay for that service.

A promise in writing to pay a debt which is barred by the statute of limitations is enforceable according to its terms without new consideration.

MODIFICATION OF CONTRACTS; PREEXISTING DUTY RULE

In a **non**-UCC contract, consideration is required to support a modification. In a UCC contract, consideration is **not** required to support a modification.

If each side to an existing contract modifies its rights and obligations in exchange for modification of the rights of the party(ies) on the other side, there is consideration.

If the parties agree to rescind an executory (i.e., uncompleted) contract, consideration is found in the mutual agreements to give up rights under the contract.

The agreement to perform an act which a person is already legally obligated to perform is not valid consideration.

COMPROMISE AND SETTLEMENT OF CLAIMS

Forbearance (a promise not to assert a legal right) is valid consideration if the person seeking to enforce the contract reasonably believes that he has a valid legal claim.

OUTPUT AND REQUIREMENTS CONTRACTS

Output or requirements contracts are generally valid.

They are enforceable for the actual amount of the output or requirements as long as those amounts are not unreasonably disproportionate to the expectations of the parties at the time the contract was formed.

Output and requirements contracts are specifically enforceable if the nonbreaching party will have difficulty in obtaining substitute performance.

THIRD-PARTY BENEFICIARY CONTRACTS

INTENDED BENEFICIARIES

Intended beneficiaries are those persons who have a right to sue on a third-party beneficiary contract because the original contracting parties either explicitly or implicitly intended to benefit them.

If the third-party beneficiary contract is designed to satisfy an obligation of the promisee to the third party, the third-party beneficiary does not give up his rights against the promisee until such time as the promisor renders performance to the third-party beneficiary.

INCIDENTAL BENEFICIARIES

An incidental beneficiary, a person that the original contracting parties did not intend to benefit, has no right to enforce a third-party beneficiary contract.

MODIFICATION OF THE THIRD-PARTY BENEFICIARY'S RIGHTS

The promisor and promisee of a third-party beneficiary contract can modify their contract to the detriment of the intended beneficiary only until the beneficiary either assents to the contract at a party's request, sues on the contract, or changes her position in reliance on it.

ENFORCEMENT BY THIRD PARTY

The third party need not provide consideration to be able to sue on a third-party beneficiary contract.

The promisor of a third-party beneficiary contract has a valid defense in a suit by the intended beneficiary if the promisee fails to perform his obligations to the promisor.

ASSIGNMENT AND DELEGATION

ASSIGNMENT OF RIGHTS

The benefits of a UCC contract are assignable even if the contract prohibits assignment.

The benefits of a contract can be assigned without the assignee becoming bound to perform the obligations of the contract.

An assignee takes rights under the contract subject to any defenses which the contracting party has against the assignor.

If a party to a contract is notified of the assignment of rights under that contract, the contracting party cannot raise against the assignee rights against the assignor which accrue after notice of the assignment.

DELEGATION OF DUTIES

A contract is not delegable if the party wishing to delegate possesses unique characteristics such that the performance rendered by a delegatee would vary materially from that bargained for.

A contract is also not delegable if the contract specifically prohibits it.

The party delegating duties (the delegator) remains liable on the contract as a surety for the performance of the delegatee, the party now principally liable on the contract.

STATUTE OF FRAUDS

CONTRACT CANNOT BE PERFORMED WITHIN ONE YEAR

In determining if a contract can be performed within one year, measure from the time of the making of the contract to the time prescribed for the end of performance, not just the time when performance will take place.

A personal services contract for more than a year is within the statute of frauds despite the fact that the contract would be prematurely terminated if the personal service supplier died within the year.

A contract for life is not within the statute of frauds because death could occur within a year, which would be the natural termination of the contract.

SURETYSHIP

An oral promise to pay the debt of another is usually unenforceable because of the statute of frauds. However, if a person agrees to pay the debt of another for the primary purpose of furthering his own goals, rather than those of the debtor, the statute of frauds will not prevent enforcement of the promise.

SALE OF GOODS

Contracts for the sale of goods for $500 or more must satisfy the statute of frauds, unless they are specially manufactured goods and not suitable for sale to others in the ordinary course of business. . (Note that the most recent revision of UCC §2-201 increases this triggering amount to $5,000, but as of 2006 no U.S. state has adopted revised Section 201.)

The statute of frauds is satisfied to the extent that there is part performance.

The statute of frauds with respect to the sale of goods does not apply where the goods have been received and accepted.

The statute of frauds with respect to the sale of goods is satisfied in a contract between merchants where one merchant sends a written, signed memorandum of the transaction sufficient to bind him to the contract and the receiving merchant does not object within ten days.

In a UCC contract, a memorandum satisfies the statute of frauds if it indicates there is a contract, it contains a description of the goods and the quantity, and is signed. It need not contain the price.

A modification of a UCC contract, if it involves a sale of goods for more than $500, requires compliance with the statute of frauds.

LAND CONTRACTS

In a contract for the sale of land, the memorandum required to satisfy the statute of frauds must contain the price.

A real estate brokerage contract is not within the statute of frauds.

PAROL EVIDENCE RULE

PAROL EVIDENCE RULE

Parol evidence is admissible to show that there is a condition precedent to a contract's coming into existence.

Parol evidence is admissible to explain an ambiguity.

Parol evidence is admissible to show that the parties used words in a nontraditional manner or spoke in code.

Parol evidence is admissible to prove a mistake in reducing the terms of an oral agreement to writing.

In a UCC contract, a provision which requires subsequent modifications be in writing is valid. In a **non**-UCC contract, a provision requiring that subsequent modifications be in writing is **in**valid.

Except in a UCC contract requiring subsequent amendments to be in writing, evidence of an oral modification subsequent to the making of a written contract is admissible.

INTERPRETATION OF CONTRACTS

Achieving the intent of the parties is the overriding principle of contract interpretation.

The past course of dealing of the parties is important evidence in interpreting a contract.

CONDITIONS

EXPRESS CONDITIONS

A party seeking to sue on a contract must either show compliance with an express condition, or that the other party was in bad faith with respect to the condition, thereby excusing its performance.

If a contract contains a condition that performance must be satisfactory to the purchaser, that satisfaction will be judged by an objective standard, unless the contract involves personal taste, in which case the performance must be subjectively satisfactory to the purchaser (limited only by the purchaser's obligation to exercise good faith).

CONSTRUCTIVE CONDITIONS OF EXCHANGE

Unless otherwise specified, each party must perform its obligations under the contract to be able to demand performance from the other side. Such mutual conditions precedent are constructive conditions of exchange.

DIVISIBLE CONTRACTS; INSTALLMENT CONTRACTS

If a contract is divisible, then performance of one divisible portion permits the plaintiff to demand performance from the defendant for that divisible portion, even if the plaintiff is in breach with respect to another divisible portion.

The fact that a construction contract requires periodic payments does not make it a divisible contract.

Under the UCC, if a contract is determined to be an installment contract, the buyer can reject a nonconforming shipment only if it substantially impairs the value of the installment and cannot be cured.

Under a UCC installment contract, a breach with respect to one installment is a breach of the total contract only if the nonconformity substantially impairs the value of the entire contract.

IMMATERIAL BREACH AND SUBSTANTIAL PERFORMANCE

Under the common law, the plaintiff can sue for breach of contract if she has substantially performed the contract, even if there is an immaterial (nonwilful) breach.

Under the UCC, except for an installment contract, the seller must tender the correct number of conforming goods at the time specified in the contract or the buyer can reject the goods without liability. However, the seller has a limited right to "cure" after a nonconforming tender.

CONSTRUCTIVE CONDITION OF COOPERATION

A condition of cooperation is implied into every contract. A party who wrongfully hinders the other party's performance breaches the contract.

OBLIGATIONS OF GOOD FAITH AND FAIR DEALING

Each party to a contract has an implied duty to cooperate with the other party in achieving the objects of the contract. Failure of the plaintiff to discharge that implied duty is a defense in a suit on the contract.

SUSPENSION OR EXCUSE OF CONDITIONS BY WAIVER, ELECTION

Waiver occurs when a party affirmatively represents that it will not act on a known right. If the other party relies on the waiver to its detriment, the waiver becomes irrevocable.

REMEDIES

ANTICIPATORY REPUDIATION; DEMAND FOR ASSURANCES

Under the UCC, when a party has reasonable grounds for insecurity, he may demand adequate assurances from the other party and suspend his performance until he receives them.

If a party repudiates a contract before the time for performance, the other party may treat the repudiation as a total breach, seek performance elsewhere, and sue for breach.

If the nonrepudiating party has not canceled the contract or materially changed position, the repudiating party may retract the repudiation, providing he gives adequate assurances. The nonrepudiating party then has no right to sue for breach.

RISK OF LOSS; RIGHTS OF BONA FIDE PURCHASERS

The seller shifts the risk of loss to the buyer when he completes his delivery obligation for conforming goods. If the contract is FOB seller's place of business, the delivery obligation is completed by placing conforming goods on a common carrier with arrangements that they be shipped to the buyer. If the contract is FOB buyer's place of business, the delivery obligation is completed when the goods are delivered to buyer's place of business; the seller retains the risk of loss during transit.

If the seller ships nonconforming goods on a shipment or a destination contract, she retains the risk of loss until the goods are accepted.

If the buyer rightfully revokes acceptance of the goods, the risk of loss is on the seller to the extent that the goods are not covered by buyer's insurance.

If the buyer breaches or repudiates the contract before the risk of loss passes to him, the risk of loss is on the buyer for a commercially reasonable time to the extent that the loss is not covered by seller's insurance.

SELLER'S REMEDIES IN THE EVENT OF BUYER'S BREACH

The seller may sell the goods in a commercially reasonable manner and collect the difference between the contract price and the sales price, plus incidental damages.

If the difference between the sales price and the contract price does not reasonably reflect the seller's damage because he has an unlimited supply of the goods, then the measure of damage is the seller's profit, the difference between his production cost for the goods and the contract price.

The seller may sue for the contract price if the goods cannot be sold in the seller's ordinary course of business.

BUYER'S REMEDIES IN THE EVENT OF SELLER'S BREACH

The buyer may seek specific performance and replevin the goods where they are unique (and in other special circumstances).

The buyer may seek damages - the difference between the market price and the contract price.

The buyer may cover, that is, purchase the goods elsewhere and collect the difference between the cover price and the contract price.

MEASURE OF DAMAGES

The usual contract measure of damages is the amount which will put the nonbreaching party in the position it would have been in had the contract been performed - the amount of unreimbursed money expended on the contract plus the profit which it would have made on the contract.

If expectancy damages are too speculative, the nonbreaching party may seek reliance damages - the amount expended by him to perform the contract.

CONSEQUENTIAL DAMAGES; LIQUIDATED DAMAGES; SPECIFIC PERFORMANCE

Consequential damages are limited to those damages which were reasonably foreseeable.

Liquidated damages are only collectible if the liquidated amount is reasonable either in respect to the amount of damages which the parties anticipated at the time of making the contract, or in respect to the actual damages incurred.

Both the buyer and the seller are entitled to sue for specific performance of enforceable land contracts.

RESTITUTION DAMAGES

If a party is prevented from suing on the contract because the contract is unenforceable or because he has breached the contract, he is entitled to collect restitution damages in *quantum meruit*, measured by the fair value of the benefit conferred on the other party.

IMPOSSIBILITY AND FRUSTRATION

At common law, the excuse of impossibility applies when the subject matter of the contract is destroyed or a party to a personal service contract dies.

Under the UCC doctrine of impracticability, performance is excused when (1) goods identified to the contract are destroyed, (2) performance becomes illegal, or (3) performance is prevented by a nonforeseeable event the nonoccurrence of which was a basic assumption of the contract.

CRIMINAL LAW AND PROCEDURE

HOMICIDE CRIMES

MURDER - INTENTIONAL KILLINGS

A mercy killing is murder because it is an intentional killing, even if the victim asks the person to kill him.

A person who sets up a mechanical device which kills a person is guilty of the crime which would have been committed if the person had personally set off the device intentionally.

If a person takes steps to make substantially certain that an event will occur, he has intended the act even if he subjectively does not desire that the result occur.

MURDER - INTENT TO DO GREAT BODILY HARM

If a person commits an act which would not ordinarily inflict fatal injury, but would likely cause great bodily harm, and the victim dies, that person is guilty of murder, even if the victim died because of a peculiar medical condition.

An intent to do great bodily harm can be inferred from the use of a weapon to inflict bodily injury.

FELONY MURDER

A defendant is not guilty of felony murder unless he is guilty of the commission or attempted commission of the underlying felony.

A defendant is not guilty of felony murder if the commission of the felony has not yet begun or is completed at the time the death occurs.

A co-conspirator of the felon who actually commits the killing is not guilty of felony murder if the killing was beyond the scope of the conspiracy.

The felonies of manslaughter or assault and battery cannot be the underlying felony for felony murder.

If a third party kills a cofelon in the course of a felony, the surviving felon is not guilty of felony murder because the killing is justifiable homicide.

ABANDONED OR MALIGNANT HEART MURDER

Firing bullets in a confined space or through a wall, or playing russian roulette, is abandoned heart murder if a death results.

Deliberately and unjustifiably driving a car onto a crowded sidewalk would constitute abandoned heart murder if a death results.

DEGREES OF MURDER

A homicide accompanied by malice in the form of a deliberate intentional killing is first-degree murder.

A death in the course of the serious common law felonies of Mayhem, Rape, Sodomy, Burglary, Arson, Kidnapping, Escape and Robbery is first-degree murder ("felony murder").

A murder accompanied by malice in the form of intent to do great bodily harm is usually second-degree murder.

A murder accompanied by malice in the form of a depraved heart is second-degree murder.

VOLUNTARY MANSLAUGHTER

To reduce a murder crime to voluntary manslaughter, there must be adequate provocation to inflame a reasonable person into the heat of passion and the defendant must have actually been in such a state. A violent battery, spousal adultery, mutual affray and an illegal arrest are adequate provocation. The killing must also take place in a time frame where the passions of a reasonable person would not have cooled and the passion of the defendant must not in fact have cooled.

A murder crime can be reduced to manslaughter if the defendant had a defense (e.g., a right to defend himself or another), but used that defense imperfectly (e.g., by employing excessive force).

If the defendant would only have been guilty of voluntary manslaughter if she had killed A, she is only guilty of voluntary manslaughter if she shoots at A, misses him and kills V.

INVOLUNTARY MANSLAUGHTER

A death occurring in the course of willful, wanton conduct is involuntary manslaughter.

A death occurring in the course of a misdemeanor malum in se is involuntary manslaughter.

A person under a duty to aid another person because of a contractual or family relationship is guilty of involuntary manslaughter if a death occurs because of unreasonable failure to give that aid. However, a person under no duty can unreasonably refuse to give aid without any criminal liability.

SELF-DEFENSE AND DEFENSE OF OTHERS

An aggressor does not have the right of self-defense, unless he attacked with nondeadly force and is met with deadly force, or unless he completely ends his aggression and makes that known to the person attacked.

A person committing a felony does not have the right of self-defense.

An individual has the right to use deadly force to apprehend a felon committing a dangerous felony or to prevent a dangerous felony from being committed. Only nondeadly force can be used if the crime is a misdemeanor.

Force is classified as deadly or nondeadly by its likelihood to cause death, not whether death in fact occurred.

A belief that the person defended has the right of self-defense is a defense in a criminal prosecution, even if the person defended does not in fact have the right of self-defense (e.g., because he was the aggressor). (To avoid liability in tort, though, the person defended must have **actually** had a right to self-defense.)

A person does not have the right to use self-defense to avoid being arrested by a police officer.

If an individual has a perfect right of self-defense but, in the exercise of that right, kills the wrong person, the homicide is still excused.

OTHER DEFENSES TO HOMICIDE CRIMES

Defense of property is not sufficient to justify the use of deadly force.

A killing commanded by the law, such as an execution or killing on the battlefield in time of war is not murder because it is a justifiable homicide.

Duress relates to coercion by a human force, whereas necessity relates to coercion by nonhuman elements. Duress and necessity cannot be defenses to a homicide crime, but can be defenses to an underlying felony, which would then be a defense to felony murder.

OTHER CRIMES

LARCENY

The specific intent necessary for larceny is not present if the defendant intends to return the property at the time he committed the trespassory taking.

If the defendant intended to return the property, the fact that it was not returned because it was unintentionally destroyed does not transform the intent into an intent to steal. However, an intent to destroy is equivalent to an intent to steal.

If possession is obtained by fraud, the crime is larceny by trick, not embezzlement.

The trespassory act necessary for larceny can be committed by an innocent agent of the defendant.

A person with title to property can be guilty of larceny if he wrongfully takes that property from a person rightfully in possession.

A lower-level employee in possession of the goods of an employer, or a bailee who breaks the bulk of the goods bailed, does not have a sufficient possessory interest to have the taking of those goods constitute embezzlement.

EMBEZZLEMENT

Embezzlement only occurs when a person rightfully gains possession of another's property and then converts it to his own use.

OBTAINING PROPERTY BY FALSE PRETENSES

To be guilty of obtaining property by false pretenses, the victim must give up title to property in reliance on a false representation of material fact by the defendant.

The defendant's honest belief that the representation is true prevents the defendant from having the specific intent necessary for the crime of obtaining property by false pretenses, even if the belief is unreasonable.

RECEIVING STOLEN GOODS

A belief that the goods were not stolen is a defense to the crime of receiving stolen goods.

If the goods are not in fact stolen goods, the defendant cannot be convicted of receiving stolen goods even if he believes that the goods are stolen.

ROBBERY

Larceny is an essential element of (and merges into the more serious crime of) robbery when all of the elements of robbery are found.

The battery which constitutes the force employed in a robbery merges into the more serious crime of robbery.

The use of force or intimidation to retain possession of property already stolen is not robbery.

The threat to use force in the future is the threat necessary for extortion, not robbery.

Burglary

In order to be guilty of burglary, the defendant must have the specific intent to commit a felony on the premises at the moment of the entering.

Burglary is committed if the defendant breaks and enters a part of a dwelling house, even if he does not break and enter when he first enters the dwelling.

The breaking and entering need not occur simultaneously.

The breaking and entering necessary for burglary are present if entry is obtained by fraud.

A person cannot be guilty of burglary for breaking and entering into his own home.

Defendant is guilty of burglary even if not successful in completing the intended felony.

ASSAULT AND BATTERY

The defendant never has the obligation to retreat if he is using nondeadly force as a defense to an assault or battery.

RAPE

Consent to intercourse is not a defense if the victim's assent to the act performed is procured through fraud which obscures the fact that intercourse is taking place.

An underage female who engages in intercourse cannot be held guilty of conspiracy to commit statutory rape or as an accessory to statutory rape.

KIDNAPPING AND ARSON

Demand for a ransom is not an element of simple kidnapping.

A person cannot be guilty of the common law crime of arson for burning his own house.

A minimal burning of part of the dwelling house is all that is required for arson, but the burning of the contents alone is not sufficient.

INCHOATE CRIMES

ATTEMPTS

To be guilty of the crime of attempt, the defendant must intend to commit the crime which she is attempting.

If the act which the defendant intended to accomplish is not a crime, the defendant is not guilty of an attempt even if he thinks he has committed a crime.

If the defendant is successful in his attempt and commits the substantive crime, there is no separate crime of attempt; the attempt and the crime merge.

CONSPIRACY

A co-conspirator is guilty of the substantive crimes committed by any other co-conspirator during the course of the conspiracy and within the scope of the conspiracy.

If a co-conspirator withdraws from the conspiracy and informs his co-conspirators of the withdrawal, he is not guilty of the substantive crimes committed by the conspirators after the withdrawal, but is guilty of the conspiracy crime.

An overt act is not necessary to complete the conspiracy crime at common law, but is required today for federal conspiracy crimes and is required in some states.

The impossibility of accomplishing the object of the conspiracy is not a defense to conspiracy, but there is no conspiracy if the parties mistakenly believe that the lawful object of the conspiracy is a crime.

A person is not a conspirator unless he combines with another human being to commit an unlawful act or a lawful act by unlawful means. Persons who do not have the requisite intent to qualify as a conspirator do not count as that other person.

A person is not a conspirator if he does not intend to combine to commit a crime. For example, a person is not a conspirator if he intends to combine only to do something which he believes is legal.

A person is not guilty of conspiracy if he combines with another person who is essential to the commission of the substantive crime (e.g., adultery).

Conspiracy does not merge into the substantive offense.

SOLICITATION

If the party solicited agrees to commit the crime, there is a conspiracy and the crime of solicitation is merged into it.

PARTIES TO CRIMES

To be guilty as an accomplice, the person must know that the principal is committing a crime and must intend to help the principal.

If the act being committed by the principal is not in fact a crime, the accessory is not guilty despite his intent to help with an illegal act.

Presence at the scene of the crime plus encouragement of the principal to commit the crime is sufficient for accomplice liability.

GENERAL PRINCIPLES

GENERAL INTENT CRIMES

To be guilty of a general intent crime, the intent to accomplish the act must coincide with the doing of the act.

If a person desires a result and that result occurs, even through an unexpected means, the person has intended the act for purposes of the criminal law.

SPECIFIC INTENT CRIMES

To be guilty of a specific intent crime, the defendant must have the required specific intent at the time he is accomplishing the specific act.

STRICT LIABILITY

The doing of the actus reus is all that is required for the defendant to be guilty of a strict liability crime.

Specifically forbidding an agent to perform an illegal act is not a defense for a principal if performing that act constitutes a strict liability offense.

To be guilty of an **attempt** to commit a strict liability offense, the defendant must have the specific intent to commit the offense.

MISTAKE OF FACT

A reasonable mistake of fact is a defense to a general intent crime.

A reasonable or unreasonable mistake of fact which prevents the specific intent from being formed is a valid defense to a specific intent crime.

MISTAKE OF LAW

A mistake of law is not a defense to a general intent crime, but a mistake of law which prevents the specific intent from being formed is a defense to a specific intent crime.

INSANITY

A mental illness which causes delusions will not create the defense of insanity under the *M'Naghten* test if the individual knows what he is doing and knows that it is a crime. The irresistible impulse test is not part of the *M'Naghten* test of insanity.

INTOXICATION

In a specific intent crime, intoxication is a defense if the intoxication prevents the defendant from forming the required specific intent.

Intoxication can prevent the formation of the malice necessary to constitute first-degree murder and reduce the crime to second-degree murder, but not to manslaughter.

CAUSATION

If a person mortally wounds a victim, but death occurs from a totally independent cause, that person is not guilty of murder.

Improper medical treatment resulting in death is within the scope of the risk when an individual causes bodily harm. Therefore, lack of causation is not a defense to a homicide crime if there was the required intent or misconduct.

JUSTIFICATION

A police officer is justified in using deadly force to apprehend a person who it reasonably appears is either committing or escaping from a dangerous felony. The use of deadly force to arrest a person for a nondangerous felony or any misdemeanor is not justified.

A person assisting a police officer is justified in using the same force that a police officer would be justified in using.

CONSTITUTIONAL PROTECTIONS

ARREST

Except in the case of hot pursuit, a warrant is required to arrest an individual in his home.

A police officer has the right to arrest without a warrant outside of the home if he has probable cause to believe that the arrestee committed a misdemeanor in the presence of the officer or committed a felony.

DEFINITION OF A SEARCH

A search involves government intrusion into space or activities where an individual has a reasonable expectation of privacy.

An individual has a reasonable expectation of privacy in his person, his home (including the curtilage), in his desk and file cabinets in a private office at work, and in containers for personal effects.

An individual only has standing to object to searches which violate his own reasonable expectation of privacy.

The Fourth Amendment rules apply only to searches by government authorities or those acting under their express direction. It does not apply to searches by private individuals.

An individual does not have a reasonable expectation of privacy in his financial records in the hands of a third party.

If property is in plain view from a place where a law enforcement officer has a lawful right to be, there is no search.

SEARCH INCIDENT TO A VALID ARREST

If the arrest is invalid, or the search is made before there is a valid ground to arrest, then the evidence obtained by the search is inadmissible.

A search incident to an arrest must be essentially contemporaneous with the arrest and only of the area within the arrestee's immediate control.

CONSENT SEARCHES

The consent given by an individual to search his own property must be voluntary, but the suspect need not be warned that he need not give consent.

A third party can give valid consent to search areas over which he has joint access.

A hotel manager cannot validly consent to the search of rooms in the hotel which are rented to guests.

AUTOMOBILE SEARCHES

The random stopping of automobiles without any probable cause constitutes an invalid search. However, stops of all vehicles at a fixed checkpoint are permissible.

Once an automobile is stopped with probable cause, the entire automobile (including the trunk and containers in the automobile) may be searched. The search need not take place immediately.

The police may stop a car and search containers within the car if they have probable cause as to the containers.

OTHER WARRANTLESS SEARCHES

A search at a border (or the functional equivalent thereof) does not require probable cause or a warrant.

A regulatory search does not require probable cause.

A "stop and frisk" is permitted only if there is a suspicion of criminality and may extend only to a "pat down" search. If the "pat down" uncovers an object which may be a weapon, an intrusive search may be made for weapons.

SEARCHES PURSUANT TO A SEARCH WARRANT

A search warrant can only be issued by a neutral and detached magistrate on the basis of probable cause.

Probable cause can be based on the totality of the circumstances and does not require evidence on both the basis for the search and the reliability of the informant.

The warrant must state with particularity the place to be searched and the objects of the search.

If a magistrate grants a search warrant, and the police execute it believing in good faith that it is valid, the property seized pursuant to the search is admissible.

COERCED CONFESSIONS

If a confession is coerced, even by a private individual, then it is inadmissible for any purpose. However, if improperly admitted, such admission is subject to the harmless error rule.

MIRANDA

Miranda only applies when the suspect is interrogated while he is in custody.

Interrogation can take the form of behavior by the police likely to induce the defendant to make a statement.

If the defendant exercises his *Miranda* rights by demanding a lawyer, no further questioning can take place until a lawyer is present and the defendant agrees to interrogation after consultation with his lawyer.

If a defendant agrees to submit to interrogation, he can be questioned about more subjects than the crime which is the primary object of the police interrogation.

If evidence is inadmissible substantively because of a *Miranda* violation, it is nevertheless admissible to impeach.

LINEUPS AND OTHER FORMS OF IDENTIFICATION

There is a right to counsel at a lineup only after the criminal process has commenced.

If the likelihood of a proper identification is so remote or the lineup is so prejudicial that it offends due process standards, then both testimony about the lineup identification and a subsequent in-court identification are inadmissible.

RIGHT TO COUNSEL

A defendant has the right to counsel in all felonies and all misdemeanors for which he is actually incarcerated.

An individual has the right to act as his own counsel and, if he does, he cannot later complain that he was denied his right to counsel.

A defendant has the right to counsel for one appeal.

The defendant has been deprived of effective assistance of counsel if his attorney has a conflict of interest because he is also representing a co-defendant.

PUBLIC TRIAL; FAIR CONDUCT BY THE PROSECUTOR

Even if both the prosecutor and defendant want a private trial, the public has a right to a public trial. A trial must be public unless there is either a substantial likelihood of prejudice to the defendant or a need to limit access to ensure an orderly proceeding.

A prosecutor has the obligation to disclose to the defendant all exculpatory material known to or in the possession of the prosecutor's office.

JURY TRIAL; SPEEDY TRIAL

The right to speedy trial does not commence to run until the defendant is charged with the crime.

The defendant is not denied the right to a speedy trial solely by the passage of time. There must also be prejudice to the defendant.

The defendant is entitled to be tried by a jury if the period of incarceration can exceed six months.

The defendant is entitled to be tried by a jury chosen from a venire in which there is no systematic racial exclusion. Neither the defendant nor the prosecutor may systematically exclude individuals of one race from the jury by peremptory challenges.

The jury need consist of only six persons. However, if the jury consists of only six persons, the verdict must be unanimous. If the jury consists of twelve persons, a nine-person verdict is constitutional.

CONFRONTATION; SEVERANCE; STANDARD OF PROOF

The confrontation clause is satisfied if the defendant had the right to cross-examine the witness at a pretrial hearing and there is a valid excuse for the witness's absence from the trial.

If the statement of one defendant is admissible against the confessor, but also implicates a co-defendant and is inadmissible against the co-defendant, the court must either excise the offending portions of the statement or grant a severance.

The prosecution must prove all elements of the offense beyond a reasonable doubt. However, the state can place upon the defendant the obligation to plead affirmative defenses and prove them by a preponderance of the evidence.

FAIR TRIAL - POST-TRIAL STAGE

The appellate court may constitutionally order a new trial if the verdict is against the weight of the evidence.

A defendant's criminal record is admissible after the verdict, for purposes of deciding the appropriate sentence.

DOUBLE JEOPARDY

Jeopardy attaches in a criminal jury trial when the jury is sworn, and in a jury-waived trial, when the first witness begins to testify.

Double jeopardy does not apply when the judge declares a mistrial to benefit the defendant or the appellate court orders a new trial as the result of the defendant's appeal.

The prosecution can only appeal a judgment if a victory for the prosecution will not result in a retrial.

COLLATERAL ESTOPPEL

If issues are litigated in one criminal case between the prosecution and the defendant, they cannot be relitigated in a separate criminal case between the same parties.

EVIDENCE

PRESENTATION OF EVIDENCE

PERSONAL KNOWLEDGE

Every witness (except an expert witness and a witness testifying to admissible hearsay) must testify from first-hand knowledge.

LEADING AND ARGUMENTATIVE QUESTIONS

Leading questions are not permitted on direct examination until a witness's memory is exhausted, but are permissible on cross-examination.

An argumentative question (e.g., one that starts "Don't you know that . . .") is inadmissible even on cross-examination.

REFRESHING RECOLLECTION

Present memory refreshed occurs when the witness's memory is revived (e.g., by reference to a document). The witness then testifies to what he remembers. The rules regarding hearsay and admissibility of writings are inapplicable.

On the other hand, past recollection recorded occurs when a witness has made a written record on a matter while his memory was fresh, and his memory of that matter is exhausted and cannot be revived. The document itself, which comes within a hearsay exception, is read to the jury and must satisfy the requirements for admissibility of a writing.

If a witness brings written documents with him while testifying, opposing counsel can examine them as a matter of right in the course of cross-examination.

OBJECTIONS AND OFFERS OF PROOF

Hearsay evidence which would be inadmissible at trial is admissible before a judge hearing evidence on a preliminary question of fact.

An offer of proof is required only when an objection to a question is sustained. The party must state for the record what the answer to the question would be, if known.

To preserve an issue for appeal, counsel must object to the admissibility of evidence at the time it is offered.

LAY OPINIONS AND EXPERT WITNESSES

A layperson can testify in the form of opinion with respect to matters on which laypersons are competent to form opinions, if the opinion is based upon personal knowledge and is helpful to an understanding of the testimony.

A lay witness cannot testify on matters on which only experts are qualified to give opinions, even if the layperson's opinion is based upon first-hand knowledge.

An expert witness need not testify from personal knowledge, but instead may draw inferences from facts presented to him and may rely on the opinions of other experts if to do so is customary in the field of expertise.

An expert witness can be cross-examined about specific instances in his background which bear on his qualification as an expert.

Except for the mental state of a criminal defendant, an expert witness can give an opinion on the ultimate issue in a case.

QUALIFICATIONS AND COMPETENCE OF WITNESSES

The Federal Rules of Evidence require that a federal court apply the state's rule on matters of competency of witnesses and privilege if state law provides the basis for decision in the federal court (as it would in diversity cases).

JUDICIAL NOTICE

A jury in a criminal case is not bound to take as true matters which have been judicially noticed.

CROSS-EXAMINATION

If the opposing party is deprived of his opportunity to cross-examine a witness, the remedy is to strike the direct examination.

If part of a document is admitted in evidence by one party, the opposing party has the right to introduce any other part of the same document which ought in fairness be considered with the part already in evidence, even if such evidence would otherwise be inadmissible.

An out-of-court declarant whose statement is admissible hearsay may be impeached in the same manner as an in-court witness.

PRIOR INCONSISTENT STATEMENTS

A prior inconsistent statement is admissible only to impeach unless it comes within an exception to the hearsay rule or it was given under oath, in which case it is admissible to prove the matter asserted.

Extrinsic evidence of a prior inconsistent statement is inadmissible to impeach credibility unless the attention of the witness is called to the statement.

BIAS

Unless the witness admits the fact relating to bias on cross-examination, extrinsic evidence can be introduced to prove bias.

If offered to prove bias, usually inadmissible evidence (such as insurance coverage and other criminal convictions) is admissible.

IMPEACHMENT - CONVICTIONS

Prior convictions of a person can only be introduced to impeach credibility after that person has testified.

Evidence of convictions for juvenile crimes and for misdemeanors not involving dishonesty or false statement are always inadmissible to impeach credibility.

The party proffering a witness can anticipate impeachment of the witness through the use of prior convictions by introducing the convictions against the witness on direct examination.

The court must admit **any** conviction involving dishonesty or false statement against **any** witness, as long as the conviction is recent (i.e., less than 10 years old).

The court may admit a recent conviction of the **criminal defendant** for a crime punishable by death or at least one year imprisonment only if the impeaching party first shows that the probative value of the conviction outweighs its prejudicial effect. The court must admit a recent conviction of a **witness (other than the accused)** for a nonfraud crime punishable by death or at least one year imprisonment unless the objecting party shows that the prejudicial effect of the impeachment **substantially** outweighs the probative value of the evidence.

A conviction more than 10 years old can only be admitted against **any** witness only if the impeaching party first shows that the probative value of the conviction substantially outweighs its prejudicial effect.

IMPEACHMENT - PRIOR BAD ACTS

Evidence of bad acts which show fraudulent conduct can be inquired into on cross-examination to impeach credibility, but extrinsic evidence of such conduct cannot be introduced.

IMPEACHMENT - REPUTATION FOR VERACITY

Character can be attacked either by opinion evidence or by reputation evidence.

The character of a witness for truthfulness cannot be introduced until that character trait has been attacked.

IMPEACHMENT BY CONTRADICTION

Extrinsic evidence cannot be used to contradict a witness on a collateral matter.

REHABILITATION AND REDIRECT EXAMINATION

Testimony on redirect examination must relate to those matters asked on cross-examination.

A witness's credibility can be rehabilitated only with respect to the manner in which it has been attacked. For example, evidence of good character can only be presented if the witness's character has been attacked.

PRESUMPTIONS

If the party seeking the benefit of a presumption introduces evidence from which the jury can find the basic fact giving rise to the presumption, the party against whom the presumption operates must introduce evidence contradicting the presumed fact or face a directed verdict against him on that fact.

PRIVILEGES AND EXCLUSIONS

HUSBAND-WIFE COMMUNICATIONS

There are two separate marital privileges, with distinct rules. Under the first, a witness-spouse can refuse to testify in a criminal prosecution of the defendant-spouse, but the defendant-spouse cannot keep the witness-spouse off the stand. With respect to this rule, the parties must be married at the time of trial.

The second applies to confidential communications between individuals who are at the time of the communication married to each other. The privilege with respect to such communications survives divorce. The presence of third parties capable of understanding the conversation destroys the confidentiality necessary for this spousal privilege.

ATTORNEY-CLIENT PRIVILEGE

The privilege only applies to confidential communications between a client and an attorney for the purpose of obtaining legal advice.

The privilege applies even if the attorney is not in fact hired by the client.

The privilege applies even if the individual consulted is not an attorney, if the client reasonably believed that he was.

The presence of third parties reasonably necessary for either the attorney or the client to perform their duties does **not** destroy the confidentiality necessary for the privilege.

If two clients consult one lawyer, communications in the presence of both clients and the lawyer are privileged in any suit with a third party, but are not privileged in a suit between the clients.

The privilege is inapplicable if the purpose of the communication was to commit future fraud or future criminal conduct.

The privilege is inapplicable if the client or a disciplinary body calls the attorney's conduct into question and the attorney must reveal the confidential communication to defend herself.

Turning over preexisting documents to an attorney does not make them privileged, but a letter to an attorney seeking legal advice is privileged.

PHYSICIAN-PATIENT PRIVILEGE

The physician-patient privilege is a statutory privilege by which the patient can prevent the disclosure of confidential communications made to a physician, and the disclosure of observations made by him. The confidential nature of the communications or observations is not destroyed by the presence of third persons necessary to the performance of the physician's duties. The privilege is waived if the patient introduces evidence on his physical condition, or sues the physician.

SELF-INCRIMINATING STATEMENTS

The privilege against self-incrimination is a testimonial privilege and does not empower a defendant to refuse to turn over nontestimonial items such as bodily, handwriting, or voice samples.

The privilege against self-incrimination (except for cases where the *Miranda* rule concerning confessions is applicable) operates prospectively, and does not give a defendant the power to suppress a statement already made.

A defendant who testifies on a preliminary matter in a criminal case does **not** waive his right to refuse to testify in the case itself, and cannot be cross-examined in the preliminary hearing on matters beyond the scope of the preliminary hearing.

Admissions of ownership for purposes of asserting standing in a hearing on a motion to suppress evidence are not admissible in the criminal trial.

The government, by granting use and derivative use immunity, can compel testimony despite the privilege against self-incrimination.

SUBSEQUENT SAFETY MEASURES

Evidence of subsequent remedial measures is not admissible to prove negligence or culpable conduct, but is admissible to prove ownership or control.

OFFERS OF SETTLEMENT; PAYMENT OF MEDICAL EXPENSES

An offer to compromise a disputed claim **and all statements made in such a context** are not admissible to prove liability.

However, an offer in compromise is admissible if it is accepted and the party is suing in contract to enforce it.

An offer in compromise cannot qualify as such until the other party has made a claim so that a dispute exists.

An offer to pay or the payment of medical expenses is likewise not admissible to show liability. However, a statement made in connection with an offer to pay medical expenses **is** admissible.

An offer to plea bargain and statements made in connection therewith are not admissible at a subsequent trial.

If the criminal process has not begun, a statement made in an attempt to avoid criminal liability (for example, an offer to pay for goods which were stolen) is admissible at a subsequent trial.

OTHER PRIVILEGES

Other privileges, recognized in some jurisdictions, include a priest-penitent privilege, a social worker-client privilege, and privileges not to disclose one's vote, a newsperson's sources and government secrets.

RELEVANCY AND ITS COUNTERWEIGHTS

PROBATIVE VALUE

Evidence of a rape victim's sexual conduct is admissible only if it involves other sexual conduct with the alleged perpetrator or the alleged victim's sexual conduct with a person other than the defendant at the time of the alleged rape **and** the judge determines that the probative value of the evidence outweighs its prejudicial effect.

USE OF CHARACTER TO PROVE ACTIONS

Evidence of a character trait to show propensity to act in accordance with that trait is **always** inadmissible in a civil case.

The defense in a criminal case can prove, by either opinion or reputation evidence, character traits of the criminal defendant which are inconsistent with the alleged criminal activity. After the defendant introduces such evidence, the prosecution can rebut with similar character evidence.

The prosecution cannot initiate the proof of character in a criminal case, except to prove the peaceful nature of the victim in a homicide case where the defendant has raised the defense of self-defense.

EVIDENCE OF OTHER CRIMES

Evidence of other crimes is admissible only to prove identity, motive, notice, opportunity, plan or similar relevant facts in a criminal case. Conviction of the other crime need **not** be proven.

HABIT, CUSTOM AND ROUTINE PRACTICE

Evidence of regularized conduct which can be characterized as a habit is admissible to prove conduct in accordance with that habit.

SIMILAR HAPPENINGS AND TRANSACTIONS

Evidence of similar events or circumstances is not admissible to prove the relevant event unless the probative value is compelling.

EXPERIMENTAL AND SCIENTIFIC EVIDENCE

Evidence of a scientific test which fairly represents a relevant event is admissible even if the opposing party had no notice of the test and did not participate in it.

DEMONSTRATIVE EVIDENCE

The judge has wide discretion in deciding whether and in what form to allow demonstrative evidence. The judge may exclude demonstrative evidence as unduly inflammatory, even if it is relevant.

WRITINGS AS EVIDENCE

AUTHENTICATION; PROOF OF SIGNATURES

Objects which do not have any identifying characteristics must be authenticated by proving a chain of custody from the point at which the object became relevant to the time of trial.

A photograph is admissible upon testimony that it fairly and accurately depicts a relevant event. The photographer is not required to so testify; any witness may testify.

A telephone voice of an individual is authenticated by testimony either that the witness recognized the voice, or that the witness called the number listed to that individual and the call was answered by a person identifying himself as that individual. A telephone voice of an individual is **not** authenticated if the witness does not recognize the voice and the person **calls the witness** and identifies himself.

A lay witness cannot testify to the genuineness of a signature solely on the basis of comparing the signature in question to an admittedly genuine signature, but a handwriting expert can.

Familiarity with a signature by a witness, even at a distant time, is all that is required to authenticate the signature.

BEST EVIDENCE RULE

Secondary evidence used to prove a collateral matter is admissible despite the best evidence rule.

The best evidence rule does not require the production of a written record of an event if the witness can testify about that event from first-hand knowledge.

HEARSAY

DEFINITION OF HEARSAY

An out-of-court statement is not hearsay if you do not have to believe the statement is true for it to be relevant in the lawsuit.

Nonverbal conduct is hearsay **only** if the person intended to make an assertive statement by the conduct.

EVIDENCE USED CIRCUMSTANTIALLY AS NONHEARSAY

Out-of-court statements which are only used circumstantially - not to prove the truth of the matter asserted - are not hearsay. Examples of this include statements admitted to show: (1) the knowledge or state of mind of either the declarant or the recipient of the statement, when such is relevant to a case, (2) the declarant's lack of credibility, or (3) the meaning to the parties of the words involved in a statement.

NONHEARSAY - PRIOR INCONSISTENT STATEMENT GIVEN UNDER OATH

If a witness testifies on the stand, a prior inconsistent statement by the witness given under oath subject to the penalty of perjury is admissible substantively to contradict the witness.

If the prior inconsistent statement was not made under oath subject to the penalty of perjury, it is only admissible to impeach. If the witness is not on the stand, a prior statement can be admissible under the former testimony exception to the hearsay rule, if the necessary requirements are met (the declarant is unavailable, etc.).

NONHEARSAY - PRIOR CONSISTENT STATEMENT

An out-of-court statement consistent with testimony on the witness stand is admissible substantively for the purpose of showing that the testimony given on the witness stand is not a recent contrivance when the opposing party has impeached credibility by use of a prior inconsistent statement.

An out-of-court statement consistent with testimony on the witness stand is admissible substantively to rebut an inference of bias if the consistent statement was made prior to the time that the reason for the bias occurred.

NONHEARSAY - PRIOR OUT-OF-COURT IDENTIFICATION BY WITNESS AT TRIAL

A prior identification by a witness is admissible if the witness is on the stand and testifying subject to cross-examination.

NONHEARSAY - ADMISSIONS BY PARTY

An out-of-court statement of a party is admissible, even though it was in his interest at the time he made it, and even though he had no personal knowledge of the facts contained in it.

In addition to the statement of a party, his actions which are inconsistent with the position he is taking in a case are admissible against him.

NONHEARSAY - ADOPTIVE ADMISSIONS

Likewise, statements made by others which a party has adopted through his actions are admissions. This most commonly occurs when a party remains silent when a statement is made in his presence which he would deny if it were false. Such statements are not admissible when a defendant is entitled to his *Miranda* rights. A party may adopt a statement without knowing its precise nature if he indicates that its author is a reliable person.

NONHEARSAY - VICARIOUS ADMISSIONS

Statements made by an authorized agent, a partner, or a predecessor in title are admissible.

NONHEARSAY - STATEMENT BY EMPLOYEE

The statement of an employee while still employed concerning matters within the scope of his employment is an admission against his employer, even if the employee was not specifically authorized to speak for the employer.

NONHEARSAY - STATEMENT MADE BY A CONSPIRATOR

Admissions made by one co-conspirator are only admissible against another co-conspirator if made during the course of the conspiracy. A conspiracy ends with the arrest of the co-conspirators.

INADMISSIBLE HEARSAY

Evidence which is hearsay and does not come within any hearsay exception is inadmissible.

HEARSAY EXCEPTION - PRIOR TESTIMONY

Statements made in contemplation of impending death, declarations against interest, former testimony, and statements of personal and family history require unavailability. Other hearsay exceptions do not.

A witness who is available but refuses to answer questions or claims the privilege against self-incrimination is "unavailable" for purposes of the Rule 804 hearsay exceptions.

If prior testimony is offered in a case where the parties are not identical to the case in which the witness testified, the prior testimony is admissible only if the opposing attorney in the first trial had an opportunity and the same motive for cross-examination as the party against whom the statement is offered in the second trial.

HEARSAY EXCEPTION - DECLARATION AGAINST INTEREST

When the out-of-court declarant is unavailable, a statement made by him which was contrary to the declarant's pecuniary or proprietary interest and which would likely subject him to criminal or tort liability, or which would likely render invalid a claim which he might possess, is admissible as an exception to the hearsay rule, provided that it was against his or her interest at the time that it was made. If the statement is offered to exonerate a criminal defendant by showing that the out-of-court declarant committed the crime, the evidence must be corroborated.

HEARSAY EXCEPTION - STATEMENT MADE WITH KNOWLEDGE OF IMPENDING DEATH

A statement of impending death is admissible only in civil cases and criminal homicide prosecutions. The death of the declarant is not required (only unavailability).

HEARSAY EXCEPTION - PRESENT SENSE IMPRESSIONS AND EXCITED UTTERANCES

A present sense impression must be more contemporaneous with the prompting event than an excited utterance, but does not require an **exciting** event.

A witness may testify to a present sense impression stated by the declarant without having been in a position to observe the facts related by the declarant.

HEARSAY EXCEPTION - STATEMENTS OF MENTAL OR PHYSICAL CONDITION

The present mental state exception can be used to prove actions in accordance with that mental state.

Statements of **present** physical condition are admissible if made to anyone. Statements of **past** physical condition are admissible only if made to a doctor or the like for purposes of medical diagnosis.

HEARSAY EXCEPTION - PAST RECOLLECTION RECORDED

The declarant must be on the witness stand for either a past recollection recorded or a nonhearsay statement of prior identification to be admissible.

HEARSAY EXCEPTION - BUSINESS RECORDS

The business record exception is not applicable to a business record made in preparation for a lawsuit.

HEARSAY EXCEPTION - TEXTBOOKS

Where the learned treatise exception applies, the passage in the learned treatise is admitted substantively. However, the treatise itself cannot be admitted as an exhibit.

The learned treatise exception is available only after the opposing expert testifies and the proponent establishes the authority of the treatise. The opposing expert need not admit to the authority of the treatise, but some expert must establish its qualifications.

OTHER EXCEPTIONS

Family records and reputation concerning family history are admissible to prove family relationships. If the declarant is unavailable, his own statement concerning his personal history is admissible.

Documents more than 20 years old in proper custody come within the ancient documents exception to the hearsay rule.

PROPERTY

THE ESTATE SYSTEM

FEE SIMPLE DETERMINABLE AND FEE SIMPLE SUBJECT TO CONDITION SUBSEQUENT

The interest created in the grantor after a **fee simple determinable** ("to X so long as the premises are used for church purposes") is a **possibility of reverter**.

The interest created in the grantor after a **fee simple subject to a condition subsequent** ("to X but if alcoholic beverages are served on the premises, then the grantor has a right to reenter") is a **right of entry for condition broken**.

A fee simple determinable or fee simple subject to a condition subsequent are the only devices which will allow a seller who retains no land to control the use of the property.

The interest created in a third person after a fee simple determinable or a fee simple subject to a condition subsequent is an **executory interest** which is subject to the Rule Against Perpetuities. Unless that interest must vest or fail within the period of the Rule (lives in being plus 21 years) it is void.

FUTURE INTERESTS

If an interest is created in a third party in the same instrument as the prior possessory interest and can take in possession upon the termination of the prior interest it is a remainder.

A remainder is contingent if there is a condition precedent to its becoming possessory or the holders are unascertained.

A remainder is vested if it can take whenever and however the previous estate terminates. The persons taking are ascertained and there is no condition precedent to their taking.

If the named vested remainderman dies before the life tenant, his devisees take his interest if he leaves a will. His heirs take if he dies intestate.

If there is a class gift (a gift to children or grandchildren) afterborn members of the class can join the class until the class closes. If the grantor does not indicate otherwise, the class closes at the time any member of the class is capable of taking possession of the gift.

If there is a remainder to the children of a living person and one or more children are in existence, then during the prior estate the interest in the children is "subject to open," or "subject to partial divestment."

A future interest can be alienated prior to its becoming possessory.

The interest in the "heirs" of a living person is contingent, because heirs cannot be determined until the person's death.

LIFE ESTATES

Any remainderman (including a contingent remainderman) can enjoin a life tenant from committing waste.

The holder of an interest after a qualified fee simple determinable or fee simple subject to a condition subsequent cannot enjoin the holder of the fee simple for waste.

If there is a mortgage on property at the time it is conveyed to a life tenant and a remainderman, the life tenant is responsible for interest and current real estate taxes, and the remainderman is responsible for paying the principal.

THE RULE AGAINST PERPETUITIES

A child conceived but not born at the time of the commencement of the Rule will be considered a life in being.

The Rule Against Perpetuities does not apply to interests in the grantor (reversions, possibilities of reverter, or rights of entry for condition broken) or vested remainders.

The time for determining lives in being when the conveyance is by will is at the death of the testator.

The time for determining lives in being when the conveyance is by inter vivos deed is at the time of the conveyance.

The time for determining lives in being when the conveyance is by irrevocable inter vivos trust is at the time of the conveyance. If the trust is revocable, it is at the time that the power to revoke terminates (either on the death of the testator or earlier if the power to revoke is relinquished).

The Rule Against Perpetuities invalidates rights of first refusal which might not be exercised within the period of the Rule.

Under the common-law Rule Against Perpetuities, any person is irrebuttably presumed capable of having children until death.

If the Rule Against Perpetuities invalidates the interest of one member of a class, the disposition to the entire class is invalid.

If an interest is invalid because of the Rule Against Perpetuities, the disposition is construed with the invalid gift deleted.

If there is no ultimate disposition in a will because of an invalid disposition, then the testator's heirs take.

If there is an incomplete disposition by conveyance because of an invalidity, then the grantor or his heirs have a reversion.

RESTRAINTS ON ALIENATION

A right of first refusal which only requires the seller to sell at market value is not an invalid restraint on alienation.

A prohibition of a grantee's right to alienate property or a provision forfeiting an interest if the grantee attempts to alienate is invalid.

The owner of property can by contract restrict his own right to alienate property.

COTENANCIES BETWEEN HUSBAND AND WIFE

The conveyance of one spouse's interest in a tenancy by the entirety to a third party is invalid and creates no property interest in the third party.

A conveyance to two persons who are not married to each other as tenants by the entirety creates a joint tenancy.

CONVERSION OF JOINT TENANCIES INTO TENANCIES IN COMMON

The granting of a mortgage by one joint tenant does not transform the tenancy into a tenancy in common in a state adopting the lien theory of mortgages, but it does in a title theory state.

If two joint tenants die simultaneously, the estate of each takes one half.

A conveyance by all joint tenants of an undivided portion of their interest to a third party does <u>not</u> destroy the joint tenancy between them in the portion they retain.

CHARACTERISTICS OF COTENANCIES

A cotenant who makes improvements to property cannot charge his cotenants for contribution for the cost of the improvements.

A cotenant who occupies the property owes no rent to his fellow cotenants.

Persons owning property as joint tenants or tenants in common have an inalienable right to partition. Tenants by the entirety have no right to partition.

RIGHTS AND LIABILITIES OF ADJOINING LANDOWNERS

An abutting landowner has an absolute duty of lateral support to his neighbor's land in its natural state, and a duty to avoid negligence regardless.

RIGHTS IN LAND

EXPRESS EASEMENTS

An easement is overburdened if it is used to benefit land other than the dominant estate.

Non-use alone is insufficient to terminate an easement.

An easement by grant must be in writing and signed by the grantor to be valid.

An easement by grant must be recorded in order to bind bona fide purchasers of the benefited land.

An appurtenant easement is automatically transferred with the dominant estate.

A person cannot alienate his interest in an appurtenant easement separate from the alienation of the dominant estate.

The holder of an easement has the right to make repairs to property such as pipes and roads which are associated with the easement.

A person cannot have an easement on land which he owns in fee simple.

If the holder of the dominant estate acquires title to the servient estate, the easement is destroyed by merger and is not reinstated by a later conveyance of the servient estate.

If the owner of an interest in land induces another person to substantially rely on the fact that the owner will not assert his property right, the owner will be prevented from later asserting that right by reason of estoppel.

EASEMENTS BY IMPLICATION AND NECESSITY

An easement by necessity or implication can only be created at the time of the division of a commonly owned parcel.

An easement created by necessity ends when the necessity ends, but the end of the reason for creating an express easement does not terminate an express easement.

An easement for light and air does **not** arise by necessity or implication.

EASEMENTS BY PRESCRIPTION

An easement by prescription need not be recorded to be effective against purchasers.

The scope of an easement by prescription depends upon the scope of the use during the prescriptive period.

Once an easement by prescription ripens with the passage of the appropriate time, continuous use of the easement is not necessary to maintain it.

If use is with the permission of the owner, then no prescriptive rights accrue. If nothing is said, then the use is adverse.

The adverse use of the property need not be exclusive to obtain an easement by prescription.

PROFITS

A person who holds an exclusive profit a prendre has the right to apportion it.

A profit a prendre can be unlimited in time and is created in the same manner as an express easement.

FIXTURES

A tenant has the right to remove personal property which he attached to the real estate, even though the property might otherwise be characterized as a fixture (real estate).

A person having an estate of uncertain duration (e.g., a life estate) who plants crops on that land can enter the land and remove the crops at the end of the growing season.

COVENANTS

The person who imposes a covenant which runs with the land cannot enforce that covenant against a subsequent purchaser unless he is still the owner of some land which was owned by him at the time he imposed the covenant.

For a deed covenant to be enforceable against a subsequent owner of the property restricted, the original parties must have intended that it apply to subsequent owners, the subsequent owners must have actual or record notice of the restriction, and the subject matter of the restriction must touch and concern the land.

The recording by a grantee of a deed containing a covenant running with the land is a satisfactory substitute for a memorandum signed by the grantee, and the defense that the covenant is unenforceable because of the Statute of Frauds is invalid.

COMMON SCHEMES

If the grantor consistently imposes similar covenants on a group of lots in a subdivision, he has created a common scheme and the owner of any lots burdened by the restrictions can sue the owner of any other lot to enforce the restrictions.

If the grantor imposes similar covenants on a group of lots in a subdivision, he has created a common scheme and can be required to impose similar restrictions on all remaining lots in the subdivision, even if he has not promised in writing that he will do so.

CHOICE OF PROPERTY DEVICES

The most useful property device to control the use of land, which does not seriously affect the marketability of title, is usually an easement. However, if the marketability of title is not an issue, a qualified estate is the most certain form of control.

VENDOR AND PURCHASER

STATUTE OF FRAUDS

A written brokerage listing agreement is not a memorandum sufficient to satisfy the Statute of Frauds.

Payment of the purchase price by the buyer is not sufficient part performance to take an oral agreement out of the Statute of Frauds.

A written memorandum is necessary to change co-ownership from one form to another.

EQUITABLE CONVERSION

In a jurisdiction which recognizes equitable conversion, the risk of loss is on the buyer from the time that a binding purchase and sale agreement is executed.

If a purchase and sale agreement is executed in a jurisdiction which recognizes equitable conversion, the buyer's interest is immediately an interest in realty and the seller's interest is immediately an interest in the proceeds (i.e., personalty).

TIME OF CLOSING

If time is of the essence, then the seller and the buyer must each be prepared to close on the date specified in the agreement or each are in default.

MARKETABLE TITLE

Restrictions imposed by zoning ordinances do not render title unmarketable.

The fact that a buyer would be exposed to nonfrivolous litigation is sufficient to render title unmarketable.

An adverse possessor whose title has not been confirmed in a judicial proceeding does not have marketable title.

SURVIVAL OF COVENANTS IN THE PURCHASE AND SALE AGREEMENT

If a purchase and sale agreement is consummated by the delivery of a deed, covenants contained in the purchase and sale agreement are no longer enforceable unless the agreement specifically states that they survive the closing.

MORTGAGES

A person who purchases at a mortgage foreclosure takes free of any encumbrances placed on the land subsequent to the mortgage which is being foreclosed.

If the mortgagor sells property without paying off the mortgage and the buyer agrees to assume and pay the mortgage, the buyer is primarily liable and the mortgagor is only secondarily liable on the mortgage note.

If the mortgagor sells property without paying off the mortgage and the buyer takes subject to the mortgage (i.e., without agreeing to pay the debt), the buyer is not liable for any deficiency judgment on the mortgage note, but can lose the property through foreclosure if he does not pay the mortgage.

If a deed (rather than a mortgage) is given to secure the payment of a debt, the deed is an equitable mortgage. Parol evidence can be used to prove that the deed was intended to be a mortgage.

If there is an equitable mortgage, the grantor/mortgagor can require a reconveyance of the property upon payment of the debt unless the grantee/mortgagee has conveyed the property to a bona fide purchaser.

A mortgage foreclosure is not effective against a junior encumbrance unless notice is given to the holder of the encumbrance.

A purchase money mortgage (a mortgage from the grantee to the grantor to secure part of the purchase price) which is recorded immediately after the deed, takes precedence over any other liens on the property.

MORTGAGES AND OTHER SECURITY DEVICES

A deed which is absolute on its face, but was intended only to convey a security interest, can be reformed by a court into an equitable mortgage, as long as a bona fide purchaser does not now hold title.

Other security devices, such as installment sales contracts, will be treated as a mortgage by a court. The usual procedures required for foreclosure and redemption will be applied.

TITLE

ADVERSE POSSESSION

Open, notorious and exclusive possession by one cotenant for the statutory period will not establish adverse possession unless the other cotenant was ousted at the beginning of that period.

Joint possession with the rightful owner interrupts the adverse possessor's exclusive possession. Adverse possession must start all over again after the rightful owner leaves.

If adverse possession commences against a competent adult, the subsequent ownership by a minor or a person with a disability does not interrupt the statutory period.

It is possible to obtain title by adverse possession to airspace by projections from a structure which overhang another's property.

Transfer of ownership by the true owner does not interrupt the running of the period of adverse possession.

Transfer of rights from one adverse possessor to a subsequent adverse possessor does not interrupt the running of the period of adverse possession.

DELIVERY AND VALIDITY OF A DEED

A forged deed is a nullity conveying no title.

The time of the transfer of title dates back to the time when the deed was delivered into a commercial escrow if the transaction is consummated.

If the owner of property delivers a valid deed to a grantee, title is transferred to the grantee even though the deed is not recorded.

The subsequent redelivery of the original deed from the grantee to the grantor does not retransfer title to the grantor. A new deed signed by the grantee is required for that retransfer.

A grantee who receives a warranty deed does not have to be a bona fide purchaser to sue his grantor for a breach of a warranty.

If the grantee of a validly delivered deed objects to owning the property, title has not been transferred because the grantee has not accepted the deed.

DESCRIPTION OF PROPERTY

Any description of property which describes the property deeded with reasonable certainty is sufficient to make the deed effective. A reference to a survey or plan is sufficient, even if the survey or plan is not recorded. In cases of ambiguity, parol evidence is admissible to clarify the parties' intent. A deed which does not sufficiently describe the property, even after consideration of parol evidence, is invalid.

Where there is a conflict, a description of the property by monuments prevails over a description of the property by distances.

COVENANTS OF TITLE

A quitclaim deed contains no covenants. A warranty deed usually contains both present and future covenants. Future covenants run with the land, while present covenants do not. Thus, the grantee may sue only the immediate grantor for breach of a present covenant (such as the covenant against encumbrances). Present covenants are also breached, if at all, at the time of conveyance.

The covenant of quiet enjoyment (a future covenant) is breached only when the grantee is ousted from possession of (even part of) the land.

ESTOPPEL BY DEED

If a person grants an interest in land which he does not own by a warranty deed to a grantee, the grantee automatically becomes the owner of that interest as soon as the grantor acquires it, because of estoppel by deed.

RECORDING SYSTEM

Recording is not required for an effective transfer of interests between the parties to the transaction.

If the owner of property delivers a deed to a grantee and he records immediately, and the owner then delivers a deed of the same property to a subsequent grantee, the subsequent grantee loses because he has (constructive) notice of the prior deed.

If the owner of property deeds first to one grantee and then to a second grantee, the issue of which grantee prevails does not turn on whether the first grantee is a bona fide purchaser. That inquiry is relevant only with respect to the second grantee.

A deed which is recorded out of order in the chain of title is not constructive notice to a subsequent bona fide purchaser.

TYPES OF RECORDING SYSTEMS

In a notice jurisdiction, the subsequent grantee cuts off the interest of the prior grantee who fails to record if the subsequent grantee is a bona fide purchaser.

In a race-notice jurisdiction, the subsequent grantee cuts off the interest of the prior grantee who fails to record if the subsequent grantee is a bona fide purchaser and records prior to the first grantee.

CHARACTERISTICS OF A BONA FIDE PURCHASER

A person who takes a conveyance in satisfaction of a prior debt is a purchaser.

A person need not actually search title in the registry to be a bona fide purchaser.

Even though a donee is not a purchaser, the donee can sell to a bona fide purchaser who will prevail over a prior grantee.

Persons who take title in a chain where there is a forged deed or where the record owner has lost title by adverse possession are not protected by the recording system.

If the subsequent grantee has actual knowledge of the deed to the prior grantee, he cannot prevail even if the prior grantee's deed is not properly recorded.

LANDLORD-TENANT RELATIONSHIP

A tenant is liable to pay rent during the term even if he has assigned his interest in the leasehold.

A tenant who is denied the beneficial use of the property by the landlord and who moves out is not liable to pay the rent on the theory that he was constructively evicted.

TYPES OF TENANCIES

A periodic tenancy is terminated by notice (from either the landlord or the tenant) before the beginning of a rental period terminating the tenancy at the end of that period.

A term for years is terminated at the end of the term without notice by either party.

ASSIGNMENT AND SUBLETTING OF TENANCIES

An assignee is obligated to pay rent during the time that he possesses the leasehold property, but is not obligated to pay rent if he further assigns his leasehold interest.

Only if the landlord, tenant, and assignee enter into a novation, is the tenant no longer liable for the rent.

When a tenant validly assigns a lease, the assignee and the landlord (or the landlord's successors) are bound by all of the covenants in the lease, such as a covenant to pay taxes or a covenant giving the tenant a right to purchase the property.

A covenant against assignment does not prevent a tenant from subletting the property and vice versa.

TORTS

INTENTIONAL TORTS

ASSAULT

Intent to cause apprehension of contact is (all that is) required. Contact or intent to actually contact is no required.

Words alone are not enough unless accompanied by an ability and intent to act.

There is a privilege to use any assault or reasonable battery in self defense, defense of others, and to eject trespassers. These privileges exist as long as the actor reasonably believed the circumstances called for the conduct, even if there was a mistake.

BATTERY

The plaintiff must show (1) an intentional and (2) unconsented (3) harmful or offensive (4) touching. No actual harm is required, though.

There is a privilege to use any assault or reasonable battery in self defense, defense of others, and to eject trespassers. These privileges exist as long as the actor reasonably believed the circumstances called for the conduct, even if there was a mistake.

FALSE IMPRISONMENT

The plaintiff need not resist confinement to have an action for false imprisonment.

The imprisonment must be (1) intentional and (2) without consent to be actionable.

A shopkeeper has a privilege to reasonably detain someone reasonably suspected of shoplifting.

The plaintiff must have been aware of the confinement.

Any reasonable exist or alternate route confinement defeats the cause of action.

Only a wrongful arrest constitutes false imprisonment. The fact that the plaintiff did not actually commit the crime does not automatically give rise to a cause of action.

TRESPASS TO LAND

Force need not be used to gain entry, but consent (even implied consent) will defeat the cause of action.

There is a privilege to trespass in emergency situations and to protect one's own property, but the trespasser must pay for any damage done by the trespass.

TRESPASS TO CHATTELS AND CONVERSION

Both trespass to chattels and conversion require an intentional interference with the personal property of another. However, like trespass to land, the defendant need not know that the trespass was wrongful for it to be actionable. The defendant need only intend to commit the act which constitutes the trespass.

Only a **substantial** interference with personal property can be the basis for an action of conversion. If the defendant has substantially damaged or lost the personal property or if the defendant refuses to return it after demand has been made, the plaintiff can bring an action for conversion to recover the value of the personal property at the time that the defendant first asserted dominion over it. Any lesser interference with personal property is only the basis for a trespass to chattels action to recover damages for the harm done to the chattel and the plaintiff's lost use of the chattel.

INTENTIONAL INFLICTION OF EMOTIONAL DISTRESS

The defendant's conduct must be extreme and outrageous such that it would be substantially certain to cause severe emotional distress in a person of normal sensitivities. However, the defendant can also be held liable if he knows of the victim's peculiar sensitivities.

Bystanders can recover for emotional distress resulting from an intentional tort to family member only if the defendant knew the bystander was a witness.

NUISANCE

A nuisance exists when the defendant's use of neighboring land unreasonably interferes with the use and enjoyment of the plaintiff's land.

A defendant can be held liable for nuisance even if the offending use is not negligent.

PRIVATE NUISANCE

If there is an actual physical invasion of the plaintiff's land, the cause of action is for trespass, rather than nuisance.

Which use commenced first is a factor to be considered in deciding whether a particular use is a nuisance, but it is not dispositive. (That is, one can "move to the nuisance" and still enjoin it or recover damages in some cases.)

The fact that a particular use is permitted by the applicable zoning regulations does not establish that it is not a nuisance, although it is some proof that the use is reasonable.

Some courts will deny any judgment for plaintiff if the defendant's use of the land is socially useful. Other courts will award damages, but will refuse to enjoin such a use.

PUBLIC NUISANCE

A nuisance is a private nuisance if it interferes with only one neighbor's use and enjoyment of his land. That neighbor has a cause of action for private nuisance.

A nuisance is a public nuisance if it interferes with the use and enjoyment of several neighboring parcels. In general, only the relevant political subdivision (city, county, etc.) has the right to sue for a public nuisance. However, a private plaintiff can sue for public nuisance if the harm to that plaintiff from the nuisance is different in kind from the harm to the public (or if a statute gives the neighbor a private cause of action).

STRICT LIABILITY

PRODUCTS LIABILITY - STRICT LIABILITY OF MANUFACTURERS

A supplier (i.e., a seller or manufacturer) of a product is strictly liable if (1) the product was defective when it left the party's hands and (2) that defect causes the plaintiff harm.

Foreseeable users and even bystanders may recover under a strict liability theory.

Assumption of the risk is a defense in strict products liability actions, but not contributory negligence.

Exercise of utmost care by the defendant in manufacturing or handling the product will not defeat plaintiff's strict liability claim.

Misuse by the plaintiff is not a defense, unless that misuse was unforeseeable.

Alteration of the product after it left the defendant's hands can defeat the plaintiff's strict liability action.

An assembler is liable for the defective parts included in its finished product.

Unavoidably unsafe drugs (including blood) are the basis of strict liability only if the supplier does not notify the physician of the potential dangers.

PRODUCTS LIABILITY - STRICT LIABILITY OF SUBCONTRACTORS AND VENDORS

The manufacturer of a defective component is liable for the defective parts included in the finished product.

ABNORMALLY DANGEROUS ACTIVITIES

There is strict liability for any harm which results from a use of land which (1) is not common to the area, and (2) presents a serious risk of harm even if undertaken with due care. In such a case, the plaintiff need not show that the defendant's conduct of the abnormally dangerous activity was negligent to recover.

ANIMALS

Owners of wild animals are strictly liable for the harm cause by them; owners of domesticated animals are only liable for their own negligence regarding the animals.

NEGLIGENCE

RISK AND DUTY

Generally, one has a duty to act reasonably, but one usually does not have a duty to rescue someone from a danger that he or she did not create. Only the creator of the peril or a close family member (usually a parent) has any duty to rescue someone in danger.

Once one undertakes to rescue, though, one has a duty to act with reasonable care. This is called the Good Samaritan doctrine.

One who has acted negligently is liable not only to direct victims of his negligence, but anyone who undertakes to rescue persons in peril from the defendant's negligence. A defendant who endangers only himself is also liable for his negligence to anyone who tries to rescue him from his own misconduct.

GENERAL STANDARD OF CONDUCT

The usual standard of care is that of a reasonable adult in the circumstances.

Evidence of custom is admissible to establish due care in a particular circumstance or field, but is not binding on the jury.

A manufacturer is not liable (in negligence) if the manufacturer used reasonable care in inspecting component parts assembled into a finished product.

STATUTORY STANDARD OF CONDUCT

Violation of a regulatory statute or ordinance is "negligence per se" (absolute proof of negligence) or some proof of negligence - depending upon the jurisdiction's rule - if the statute or ordinance was promulgated to avoid the harm that resulted. There must also be a causal connection between the violation and the harm.

The fact that the defendant has complied with statutes and ordinances is usually not proof that there was no negligence.

Licensing statutes are irrelevant to the proof of negligence.

The fact that the defendant is guilty of negligence per se does not mean that the plaintiff's own negligence will not defeat or diminish his recovery.

Under "guest statutes," the driver of a car is only liable to a passenger in his car for gross negligence.

STANDARD OF CONDUCT OF CLASSES OF PERSONS

Children under the age of seven are presumed incapable of negligence as a matter of law. (However, children can be held guilty of intentional torts.)

A minor may usually be held to a lower standard of care, but if the minor is engaged in an adult activity (e.g., driving), an adult standard of care will be applied.

Parents can be held liable for the torts of their child only if the parents are guilty of negligence in raising or supervising the child, or the child is acting as an agent of the parents.

METHOD OF PROVING FAULT

Proof of subsequent repairs is not admissible to prove negligence (but may be used to prove other matters, such as control).

Violations of regulatory statutes can be used to prove negligence. (See above.)

Prior misconduct cannot be used to prove negligence unless the misconduct rises to the level of habit.

Negligence need not be proven by direct evidence, but can be proved by inference or circumstantial evidence. (See below.)

However, negligence must be established by a preponderance of the evidence. It must be shown that there is a probability (not merely a possibility) that the defendant was negligent and such negligence caused the plaintiff's harm.

Expert testimony will be required only where the jury cannot determine based on their everyday knowledge and experience whether the defendant was negligent or whether the defendant's negligence was the cause of the plaintiff's harm.

Prior accidents (or lack of prior accidents) is admissible to prove that a situation or condition was negligent (or not negligent) only if the situation or condition was the same in the prior incidents. Regardless, the lack of prior accidents may be admissible solely to prove that the defendant had no notice of the dangerous condition.

RES IPSA LOQUITUR

The plaintiff can prevail without direct proof of the defendant's negligence if he can prove (or the circumstances alone indicate) that he would not have been harmed if the defendant had not been negligent. The plaintiff need only show that it is more likely than not that the defendant was negligent (and that there is a causal connection to the plaintiff's harm).

Res ipsa loquitur is irrelevant if there is direct evidence that the defendant was negligent.

The defendant can defeat a res ipsa loquitur case against him by showing that it is just as likely that someone else's negligence caused the plaintiff's harm.

CAUSATION

The test of factual causation is "but for," i.e., the plaintiff's harm would not have occurred if not for the defendant's negligence.

The chain of causation is broken by a **superseding** intervening cause. However, the defendant is liable for any harm which would have occurred if not for the superseding cause.

A foreseeable intervening cause is not superseding. An unlawful or negligent act may be foreseeable.

Once a plaintiff has recuperated from an injury by the defendant, the defendant is not liable for subsequent injuries just because they would not have happened if not for the plaintiff's weakened condition from the first injury.

Even if there is factual causation, there must be proximate cause (i.e., the plaintiff's harm must not be too remote). A cause cannot be the "proximate" cause unless it is also the factual cause.

Where two or more independent defendants are responsible for the plaintiff's harm, each is generally ultimately liable only for the part of plaintiff's harm for which he is responsible. However, the plaintiff can recover all of his damages from the defendants if their combined negligence causes more harm than their actions alone would have caused (or even if, alone, their actions would not have caused **any** harm).

CONTRIBUTION AMONG JOINT TORTFEASORS

Contribution is available between joint tortfeasors no matter what the relative degrees of fault. Contribution allows a defendant who was held liable to recover a pro rata share of his liability from his joint tortfeasors.

A negligent defendant is only entitled to contribution (not complete indemnification) from a joint tortfeasor.

INDEMNITY OF ONE TORTFEASOR TO ANOTHER

A right of indemnification exists when a non-negligent defendant has been held vicariously liable (i.e., for the negligence of another, e.g., a servant). The non-negligent defendant has the right to recover all of the amount for which he was held liable from the negligent party.

NEGLIGENCE LIABILITY OF OWNERS AND OCCUPIERS OF LAND

At common law, a business invitee was owed a duty of reasonable care. A licensee (social guest) was only owed a duty to warn of dangers known to the owner or occupant but not obvious to the licensee. A trespasser was only owed a duty to avoid gross negligence or wanton, willful misconduct.

The doctrine of "attractive nuisance" only applies if the landowner or occupant has reason to know both that children might come onto the land and that the nuisance might be dangerous to them. Then, the landowner owes a duty of reasonable care to the infant trespasser(s). It is not necessary that the children be attracted onto the land **by** the nuisance.

NEGLIGENT INFLICTION OF MENTAL DISTRESS

A plaintiff can recover for negligent infliction of mental distress only if (a) he experiences some actual physical harm from the defendant's negligence, (b) he is within the zone of danger, or (c) he witnesses harm to a family member.

The plaintiff can only recover if the defendant's conduct was sufficient to cause emotional distress in a person of normal sensitivities. Once this objective test is met, the plaintiff can recover for any emotional harm, even if it is unusual.

VICARIOUS LIABILITY

Employers are liable for the torts of their servants committed within the scope of their employment. An intentional tort is within the scope of employment if it was committed to further the master's business.

A plaintiff who is injured by a servant may sue the servant and/or the employer.

JOINT ENTERPRISE LIABILITY

When two parties enter into a joint enterprise, they are liable for each other's torts within the scope of the joint enterprise activity.

LIABILITY FOR INDEPENDENT CONTRACTORS AND NONDELEGABLE DUTIES

Generally, the employer of an independent contractor is not liable for the torts of the independent contractor. An employee is an independent contractor - as opposed to a servant (see above) - if the employer does not control the employee's performance.

However, an employer is liable for ultrahazardous activity (e.g., blasting) undertaken by an independent contractor. There is said to be a nondelegable duty to see that such activity is performed properly.

An employer of an independent contractor can also be held liable for his negligence in hiring an unfit contractor.

ASSUMPTION OF RISK

A plaintiff's cause of action is defeated by assumption of the risk only if he had actual, subjective knowledge of the risk and voluntarily assumed it.

CONTRIBUTORY NEGLIGENCE AND LAST CLEAR CHANCE

Under a contributory (as opposed to comparative) negligence rule, any negligence on the part of the plaintiff would bar his recovery against the defendant. However, in some jurisdictions, a negligent plaintiff could still recover if the defendant had the last clear chance to avoid the accident.

The contributory negligence of another party will not be attributed to the plaintiff, even if the parties are related. However, under most wrongful death statutes, the contributory negligence of either the decedent or the beneficiaries will bar recovery.

COMPARATIVE NEGLIGENCE

Under a comparative negligence statute, the negligence of the plaintiff will not defeat the plaintiff's cause of action, but her recovery will be reduced by her share of the negligence.

Under a "pure" comparative negligence statute, the plaintiff will recover no matter how negligent she was. Under a "hybrid" comparative negligence statute, she will recover only if her negligence was equal to or less than the combined negligence of the other parties.

Comparative negligence does not change the rule of joint and several liability between joint tortfeasors. A plaintiff can recover all of his damages (minus his share of the negligence) from one defendant; that defendant will then have to seek contribution from the joint tortfeasor (based on the joint tortfeasor's share of the negligence).

ELEMENTS OF TORT DAMAGE

Expert testimony is usually required to prove future medical expenses.

A defendant is liable for all of the damages proximately caused by his negligence, even if the defendant's particular damages were unforeseeable.

PRODUCTS LIABILITY - CLAIMS IN NEGLIGENCE

Contributory negligence is a defense in a products liability action based on negligence.

Exercise of due care by the defendant in manufacturing or handling the product **will** defeat plaintiff's products liability claim in negligence.

DEFAMATION

Material is defamatory if it would lower the person's esteem in the eyes of a reputable segment of the community.

LIBEL

Some jurisdictions treat libel per se and libel per quod differently. Libel per se is that which is libelous on its face. Libel per quod is that which is libelous only when taken in conjunction with facts known by those to whom the libel is published. These jurisdictions allow recovery for libel per quod only if there are "special" (i.e., actual monetary) damages.

There must be a publication - meaning that the defendant must intend or allow that at least one person (other than the defamer and defamed) receive and understand the statement (even if they didn't believe it).

A public official or figure must prove "malice" - that the defendant acted with knowledge of falsity or reckless disregard for the truth - in order to recover for defamation (or invasion of privacy).

Any other plaintiff must at least prove negligence to recover for defamation.

SLANDER

The common law rule is that a plaintiff suing for slander must show special damages unless the slander constitutes slander per se (charging the plaintiff with a crime, a loathsome disease, sexual misconduct or business incompetence).

DEFENSES

Truth is an absolute defense in a defamation action (and a "false light" privacy action).

PRIVILEGES

There is no defamation if the statement was privileged. Relevant statements made in court hearings are absolutely privileged. (A perjury action not a defamation action, is the proper action for lies stated in court.) All other privileged statements (those made by an employer to another employer about an employee, statements in administrative hearings) are only protected by a qualified privilege. Such qualified privileges can be overcome if the statement was made with knowledge that it was false or with reckless disregard for its truth.

CONSTITUTIONAL PROBLEMS

A public official or figure must prove "actual malice" to recover for defamation. "Actual malice" requires that the plaintiff prove that the defendant either knew that the information was false, or acted with reckless disregard for its truth or falsity.

Even private persons must show at least negligence to recover against a media defendant.

PRIVACY

Publication is not required for the tort of intentional intrusion upon seclusion.

Truth is not a defense to the torts of invasion of privacy (except "false light" publicity).

Newsworthiness is a defense to the torts of invasion of privacy.

Publishing information in the public record cannot generally be the basis for a privacy tort.

A defendant can be held liable for giving unreasonable publicity to the plaintiff's private life if the material published would be highly offensive to a reasonable person and is not of legitimate public concern (i.e., newsworthy).

A defendant can be held liable for false light publicity even if the material published is complimentary (as long as it is untrue).

DECEIT

In order to be deceit, there must usually be an affirmative misrepresentation. Silence is a misrepresentation only when the defendant had some legal (e.g., fiduciary) duty to disclose.

A statement of opinion is not an actionable misrepresentation.

July, 1991 MULTISTATE BAR EXAM

(MBE II)

DO NOT TURN THIS PAGE UNTIL YOU ARE INSTRUCTED TO DO SO
OR ARE READY TO BEGIN THE TEST.

The questions and letter answers contained herein have been publicly disclosed from the July, 1991 MBE and are reprinted herein with the permission of NCBE, the copyright owner. Permission to use the NCBE's questions does not constitute an endorsement by NCBE or otherwise signify that NCBE has reviewed or approved any aspect of these materials or the company or individuals who distribute these materials.

All questions, instructions and letter answers copyright ©1996-2009 by the National Conference of Bar Examiners. All rights reserved. All other material © 1996 - 2009 Celebration Bar Review

Celebration Bar Review   **MBE II**

AM Book

Time-3 hours

Directions: Each of the questions or incomplete statements below is followed by four suggested answers or completions. You are to choose the best of the stated alternatives. Answer all questions according to the generally accepted view, except where otherwise noted.

For the purposes of this test, you are to assume that Articles 1 and 2 of the Uniform Commercial Code have been adopted. You are also to assume relevant application of Article 9 of the UCC concerning fixtures. The Federal Rules of Evidence are deemed to control. The terms "Constitution," "constitutional," and "unconstitutional" refer to the federal Constitution unless indicated to the contrary. You are also to assume that there is no applicable community property law, no guest statute, and no No-Fault Insurance Act unless otherwise specified. In negligence cases, if fault on the claimant's part is or may be relevant, the statement of facts for the particular question will identify the contributory or comparative negligence rule that is to be applied.

1. By warranty deed, Marta conveyed Blackacre to Beth and Christine "as joint tenants with right of survivorship." Beth and Christine are not related. Beth conveyed all her interest to Eugenio by warranty deed and subsequently died intestate. Thereafter, Christine conveyed to Darin by warranty deed.

   There is no applicable statute, and the jurisdiction recognizes the common-law joint tenancy.

   Title to Blackacre is in
   (A) Darin.
   (B) Marta.
   (C) Darin and Eugenio.
   (D) Darin and the heirs of Beth.

2. Peavey was walking peacefully along a public street when he encountered Dorwin, who he had never seen before. Without provocation or warning, Dorwin picked up a rock and struck Peavey with it. It was later established that Dorwin was mentally ill and suffered recurrent hallucinations.

   If Peavey asserts a claim against Dorwin based on battery, which of the following, if supported by evidence, will be Dorwin's best defense?
   (A) Dorwin did not understand that his act was wrongful.
   (B) Dorwin did not desire to cause harm to Peavey.
   (C) Dorwin did not know that he was striking a person.
   (D) Dorwin thought Peavey was about to attack him.

3. Penstock owned a large tract of land on the shore of a lake. Drury lived on a stream that ran along one boundary of Penstock's land and into the lake. At some time in the past, a channel had been cut across Penstock's land from the stream to the lake at a point some distance from the mouth of the stream. From where Drury lived, the channel served as a convenient shortcut to the lake. Erroneously believing that the channel was a public waterway, Drury made frequent trips through the channel in his motorboat. His use of the channel caused no harm to the land through which it passed.

   If Penstock asserts a claim for damages against Drury based on trespass, which of the following would be a correct disposition of the case?
   (A) Judgment for Penstock for nominal damages, because Drury intentionally used the channel.
   (B) Judgment for Drury, if he did not use the channel after learning of Penstock's ownership claim.
   (C) Judgment for Drury, because he caused no harm to Penstock's land.
   (D) Judgment for Drury, because when he used the channel he believed it was a public waterway.

Questions 4-5 are based on the following fact situation.

Structo contracted with Bailey to construct for $500,000 a warehouse and an access driveway at highway level. Shortly after commencing work on the driveway, which required for the specified level some excavation and removal of surface material, Structo unexpectedly encountered a large mass of solid rock.

4. For this question only, assume the following facts. Structo informed Bailey (accurately) that because of the rock the driveway as specified would cost at least $20,000 more than figured, and demanded for that reason a total contract price of $520,000. Since Bailey was expecting warehousing customers immediately after the agreed completion date, he signed a writing promising to pay the additional $20,000. Following timely completion of the warehouse and driveway, which conformed to the contract in all respects, Bailey refused to pay Structo more than $500,000.

   What is the maximum amount to which Structo is entitled?

   (A) $500,000, because there was no consideration for Bailey's promise to pay the additional $20,000.
   (B) $500,000, because Bailey's promise to pay the additional $20,000 was exacted under duress.
   (C) $520,000, because the modification was fair and was made in the light of circumstances

not anticipated by the parties when the original contract was made.

(D) $520,000, provided that the reasonable value of Structo's total performance was that much or more.

5. For this question only, assume the following facts. Upon encountering the rock formation, Structo, instead of incurring additional costs to remove it, built the access driveway over the rock with a steep grade down to the highway. Bailey, who was out of town for several days, was unaware of this nonconformity until the driveway had been finished. As built, it is too steep to be used safely by trucks or cars, particularly in the wet or icy weather frequently occurring in the area. It would cost $30,000 to tear out and rebuild the driveway at highway level. As built, the warehouse, including the driveway, has a fair market value of $550,000. Bailey has paid $470,000 to Structo, but refuses to pay more because of the nonconforming driveway, which Structo has refused to tear out and rebuild.

If Structo sues Bailey for monetary relief, what is the maximum amount Structo is entitled to recover?

(A) $30,000, because the fair market value of the warehouse and driveway "as is" exceeds the contract price by $50,000 (more than the cost of correcting the driveway).
(B) $30,000, because Structo substantially performed and the cost of correcting the driveway would involve economic waste.
(C) $30,000, minus whatever amount Structo saved by not building the driveway at the specified level.
(D) Nothing, because Bailey is entitled to damages for the cost of correcting the driveway.

6. Larson was charged with the murder of a man who had been strangled and whose body was found in some woods near his home. Larson suffers from a neurological problem that makes it impossible for him to remember an occurrence for longer than 48 hours.

After Larson was charged, the police visited him and asked if they might search his home. Larson consented. The police found a diary written by Larson. An entry dated the same day as the victim's disappearance read, "Indescribable excitement. Why did no one ever tell me that killing gave such pleasure to the master?"

Larson was charged with murder. His attorney has moved to exclude the diary from evidence on the ground that its admission would violate Larson's privilege against self-incrimination. Counsel has also argued that Larson could not give informed consent to the search because more than 48 hours had passed since the making of the entry and hence he could not remember the existence of the incriminating entry at the time he gave his consent. There is no evidence that the police officers who secured Larson's consent to the search were aware of his memory impairment.
With regard to the diary, the court should

(A) admit it, because Larson's consent was not obtained by intentional police misconduct and Larson was not compelled to make the diary entry.
(B) admit it, pursuant to the good-faith exception to the exclusionary rule.
(C) exclude it, because Larson was not competent to consent to a search.
(D) exclude it, because use of the diary as evidence would violate Larson's privilege against self-incrimination.

7. In contract litigation between Pixley and Dill, a fact of consequence to the determination of the action is whether Pixley provided Dill with a required notice at Dill's branch office "in the state capital." Pixley introduced evidence that he gave notice at Dill's office in the city of Capitan. Although Capitan is the state's capital, Pixley failed to offer proof of that fact.

Which of the following statements is most clearly correct with respect to possible judicial notice of the fact that Capitan is the state's capital?

(A) The court may take judicial notice even though Pixley does not request it.
(B) The court may take judicial notice only if Pixley provides the court with an authenticated copy of the statute that designates Capitan as the capital.
(C) If the court takes judicial notice, the burden of persuasion on the issue of whether Capitan is the capital shifts to Dill.
(D) If the court takes judicial notice, it should instruct the jury that it may, but is not required to, accept as conclusive the fact that Capitan is the capital.

8. A statute of the state of East Dakota requires each insurance company that offers burglary insurance policies in the state to charge a uniform rate for such insurance to all of its customers residing within the same county in that state. So long as it complies with this requirement, a company is free to charge whatever rate the market will bear for its burglary insurance policies.

An insurance company located in the state of East Dakota files suit in federal district court against appropriate East Dakota state officials to challenge this statute on constitutional grounds. The insurance company wishes to charge customers residing within the same county in East Dakota rates for burglary insurance policies that will vary because they would be based on the specific nature of the customer's business, on its precise location, and on its past claims record.

In this suit, the court should
(A) hold the statute unconstitutional, because the statute deprives the insurance company of its liberty or property without due process of law.
(B) hold the statute unconstitutional, because the statute imposes an undue burden on interstate commerce.
(C) hold the statute constitutional, because the statute is a reasonable exercise of the state's police power.

(D) abstain from ruling on the merits of this case until the state courts have had an opportunity to pass on the constitutionality of this state statute.

9. Dawson was charged with felony murder because of his involvement in a bank robbery. The evidence at trial disclosed that Smith invited Dawson to go for a ride in his new car, and after a while asked Dawson to drive. As Smith and Dawson drove around town, Smith explained to Dawson that he planned to rob the bank and that he needed Dawson to drive the getaway car. Dawson agreed to drive to the bank and to wait outside while Smith went in to rob it. As they approached the bank, Dawson began to regret his agreement to help with the robbery. Once there, Smith got out of the car. As Smith went out of sight inside the bank, Dawson drove away and went home. Inside the bank, Smith killed a bank guard who tried to prevent him from leaving with the money. Smith ran outside and, finding that his car and Dawson were gone, ran down an alley. He was apprehended a few blocks away. Dawson later turned himself in after hearing on the radio that Smith had killed the guard.

The jurisdiction has a death penalty that applies to felony murder.
Consistent with the law and the Constitution, the jury may convict Dawson of

(A) felony murder and impose the death penalty.
(B) felony murder but not impose the death penalty.
(C) bank robbery only.
(D) no crime.

10. In an automobile negligence action by Popkin against Dwyer, Juilliard testified for Popkin. Dwyer later called Watts, who testified that Juilliard's reputation for truthfulness was bad.

On cross-examination of Watts, Popkin's counsel asks, "Isn't it a fact that when you bought your new car last year, you made a false affidavit to escape paying the sales tax?"

This question is

(A) proper, because it will indicate Watt's standard of judgment as to reputation for truthfulness.
(B) proper, because it bears on Watt's credibility.
(C) improper, because character cannot be proved by specific instances of conduct.
(D) improper, because one cannot impeach an impeaching witness.

11. David built in his backyard a garage that encroached two feet across the property line onto property owned by his neighbor, Prudence. Thereafter, David sold his property to Drake. Prudence was unaware, prior to David's sale to Drake, of the encroachment of the garage onto her property. When she thereafter learned of the encroachment, she sued David for damages for trespass.

In this action, will Prudence prevail?

(A) No, unless David was aware of the encroachment when the garage was built.
(B) No, because David no longer owns or possesses the garage.
(C) Yes, because David knew where the garage was located, whether or not he knew where the property line was.
(D) Yes, unless Drake was aware of the encroachment when he purchased the property.

12. Poole sued Darrel for unlawfully using Poole's idea for an animal robot as a character in Darrell's science fiction movie. Darrel admitted that he had received a model of an animal robot from Poole, but he denied that it had any substantial similarity to the movie character. After the model had been returned to Poole, Poole destroyed it.

In order for Poole to testify to the appearance of the model, Poole

(A) must show that he did not destroy the model in bad faith.
(B) must give advance notice of his intent to introduce the oral testimony.
(C) must introduce a photograph of the model if one exists.
(D) need do none of the above, because the "best evidence rule" applies only to writings, recordings, and photographs.

13. Lanny, the owner of Whiteacre in fee simple, leased Whiteacre to Teri for a term of ten years by properly executed written instrument. The lease was promptly and properly recorded. It contained an option for Teri to purchase Whiteacre by tendering $250,000 as purchase price any time "during the term of this lease." One year later, Teri, by a properly executed written instrument, purported to assign the option to Oscar, expressly retaining all of the remaining term of the lease. The instrument of assignment was promptly and properly recorded.

Two years later, Lanny contracted to sell Whiteacre to Jones and to convey a marketable title "subject to the rights of Teri under her lease." Jones refused to close because of the outstanding option assigned to Oscar.

Lanny brought an appropriate action against Jones for specific performance.

If judgment is rendered in favor of Lanny, it will be because the relevant jurisdiction has adopted a rule on a key issue as to which various state courts have split.

Which of the following identifies the determinative rule or doctrine upon which the split occurs, and states the position favorable to Lanny?

(A) In a contract to buy, any form of "subject to a lease" clause that fail: to mention expressly an existing option means that the seller is agreeing to sell free and clear of any option originally included in the lease.
(B) Marketable title can be conveyed so long as any outstanding option not mentioned in the purchase

contract has not yet been exercised.

(C) Options to purchase by lessees are subject to the Rule Against Perpetuities.

(D) Options to purchase contained in a lease cannot be assigned separately from the lease.

14. Daniel and a group of his friends are fanatical basketball fans who regularly meet at each others' homes to watch basketball games on television. Some of the group are fans of team A, and others are fans of team B. When the group has watched televised games between these two teams, fights sometimes have broken out among the group. Despite this fact, Daniel invited the group to his home to watch a championship game between teams A and B.

During the game, Daniel's guests became rowdy and antagonistic. Fearing that they would begin to fight, and that a fight would damage his possessions, Daniel asked his guests to leave. They refused to go and soon began to fight. Daniel called the police, and Officer was sent to Daniel's home. Officer sustained a broken nose in his efforts to stop the fighting.

Officer brought an action against Daniel alleging that Daniel was negligent in inviting the group to his house to watch this championship game. Daniel has moved to dismiss the complaint.

The best argument in support of this motion would be that

(A) a rescuer injured while attempting to avert a danger cannot recover damages from the endangered person.

(B) a police officer is not entitled to a recovery based upon the negligent conduct that created the need for the officer's professional intervention.

(C) as a matter of law, Daniel's conduct was not the proximate cause of Officer's injury.

(D) Daniel did not owe Officer a duty to use reasonable care, because Officer was a mere licensee on Daniel's property.

15. In a prosecution of Drew for forgery, the defense objects to the testimony of West, a government expert, on the ground of inadequate qualifications. The government seeks to introduce a letter from the expert's former criminology professor, stating that West is generally acknowledged in his field as well qualified.

On the issue of the expert's qualifications, the letter may be considered by

(A) the jury, without regard to the hearsay rule.

(B) the judge, without regard to the hearsay rule.

(C) neither the judge nor the jury, because it is hearsay not within any exception.

(D) both the judge and the jury, because the letter is not offered for a hearsay purpose.

Questions 16-17 are based on the following fact situation.

Responding to County Is written advertisement for bids, Tyres was the successful bidder for the sale of tires to County for County's vehicles. Tyres and County entered into a signed, written agreement that specified, "It is agreed that Tyres will deliver all tires required by this agreement to County, in accordance with the attached bid form and specifications, for a one-year period beginning September 1, 1990" Attached to the agreement was a copy of the bid form and specifications. In the written advertisement to which Tyres had responded, but not in the bid form, County had stated, "Multiple awards may be issued if they are in the best interests of County." No definite quantity of tires to be bought by County from Tyres was specified in any of these documents.

In January 1991, Tyres learned that County was buying some of its tires from one of Tyres's competitors. Contending that the Tyres-County agreement was a requirements contract, Tyres sued County for the damages caused by County's buying some of its tires from the competitor.

16. If County defends by offering proof of the advertisement concerning the possibility of

multiple rewards, should the court admit the evidence?

(A) Yes, because the provision in the written agreement, "all tires required by this agreements" is ambiguous.
(B) Yes, because the advertisement was in writing.
(C) No, because of the parol evidence rule.
(D) No, because it would make the contract illusory.

17. If the court concludes that the Tyres-County contract is an agreement by County to buy its tire requirements from Tyres, Tyres probably will

(A) recover under the contracts clause of the United States Constitution.
(B) recover under the provisions of the Uniform Commercial Code.
(C) not recover, because the agreement lacks mutuality of obligation.
(D) not recover, because the agreement is indefinite as to quantity.

18. Supermarket is in a section of town where there are sometimes street fights and where pedestrians are occasionally the victims of pickpockets and muggers. In recognition of the unusual number of robberies in the area, the supermarket posted signs in the store and in its parking lot that read:

Warning: There are pickpockets and muggers at work in this part of the city. Supermarket is not responsible for the acts of criminals.

One evening, Lorner drove to Supermarket to see about a special on turkeys that Supermarket was advertising. She decided that the turkeys were too large and left the store without purchasing anything. In the parking lot, she was attacked by an unknown man who raped her and then ran away.

If Lorner sues Supermarket, the result should be for the

(A) plaintiff, if Supermarket failed to take reasonable steps to protect customers against criminal attack in its parking lot.
(B) plaintiff, because Supermarket is liable for harm to business invitees on its premises.
(C) defendant, if the warning signs were plainly visible to Lorner.
(D) defendant, because the rapist was the proximate cause of Lorner's injuries.

19. Jones wanted to kill Adams because he believed Adams was having an affair with Jones's wife. Early one morning, armed with a pistol, he crouched behind some bushes on a park hillside overlooking a path upon which Adams frequently jogged. On this morning, however, Jones saw Adams jogging on another path about a half mile away. Nonetheless, Jones fired five shots at Adams. None of the five shots came anywhere close to Adams as he was well out of the range of the pistol Jones was using.

Jones is

(A) guilty of attempted murder, if he was not aware of the limited range of his pistol.
(B) guilty of attempted murder, if a reasonable person would not have been aware of the limited range of his pistol.
(C) not guilty of attempted murder, or any lesser included offense, because, under the circumstances, it was impossible for him to have killed Adams.
(D) not guilty of attempted murder, but guilty of assault.

20. Widgets are manufactured wholly from raw materials mined and processed in the state of Green. The only two manufacturers of widgets in the United States are also located in that state. However, their widgets are purchased by retailers located in every state. The legislature of the state of Green is considering the adoption of a statute that would impose a tax solely on the manufacture of widgets. The tax is to be calculated at 3% of their wholesale value.

Which of the following arguments would be LEAST helpful to the state in defending the constitutionality of this proposed state tax on widgets?

(A) At the time widgets are manufactured and taxed they have not yet entered the channels of interstate commerce.
(B) The economic impact of this tax will be passed on to both in-state and out-of-state purchasers of widgets and, therefore, it is wholly nondiscriminatory in its effect.
(C) Because of the powers reserved to them by the Tenth Amendment, states have plenary authority to construct their tax system in any manner they choose.
(D) A tax on the manufacture of widgets may be imposed only by the state in which the manufacturing occurs and, therefore, it is not likely to create the danger of a multiple tax burden on interstate commerce.

21. Blackacre is a large tract of land owned by a religious order known as The Seekers. On Blackacre, The Seekers erected a large residential building where its members reside. Blackacre is surrounded by rural residential properties and its only access to a public way is afforded by an easement over a strip of land 30 feet wide. The easement was granted to The Seekers by deed from Sally, the owner of one of the adjacent residential properties. The Seekers built a driveway on the strip, and the easement was used for 20 years without incident or objection.

Last year, as permitted by the applicable zoning ordinance, The Seekers constructed a 200-bed nursing home and a parking lot on Blackacre, using all of Blackacre that was available for such development. The nursing home was very successful, and on Sundays visitors to the nursing home overflowed the parking facilities on Blackacre and parked all along the driveway from early in the morning through the evening hours. After two Sundays of the resulting congestion and inconvenience, Sally erected a barrier across the driveway on Sundays preventing any use of the driveway by anyone seeking access to Blackacre. The Seekers objected.

Sally brought an appropriate action to terminate the easement.

The most likely result in this action is that the court will hold for

(A) Sally, because The Seekers excessively expanded the use of the dominant tenement.
(B) Sally, because the parking on the driveway exceeded the scope of the easement.
(C) The Seekers, because expanded use of the easement does not terminate the easement.
(D) The Seekers, because Sally's use of self-help denies her the right to equitable relief.

22. Ralph and Sam were engaged in a heated discussion over the relative merits of their favorite professional football teams when Ralph said, "You have to be one of the dumbest persons around." Sam slapped Ralph. Ralph drew a knife and stabbed Sam in the stomach. Other persons then stepped in and stopped any further fighting. Despite the pleas of the other persons, Sam refused to go to a hospital or to seek medical treatment About two hours later, he died as the result of a loss of blood. Ralph was charged with the murder of Sam. At trial, medical evidence established that if Sam had been taken to a hospital, he would have survived.

At the end of the case, Ralph moves for a judgment of acquittal or, in the alternative, for an instruction on the elements of voluntary manslaughter.

The court should

(A) grant the motion for acquittal.
(B) deny the motion for acquittal, but instruct on manslaughter because there is evidence of adequate provocation.
(C) deny both motions, because Ralph failed to retreat.

(D) deny both motions, because malice may be proved by the intentional use of a deadly weapon on a vital part of the body.

23. Three months ago, Bert agreed in writing to buy Sam's single-family residence, Liveacre, for $110,000. Bert paid Sam a $5,000 deposit to be applied to the purchase price. The contract stated that Sam had the right at his option to retain the deposit as liquidated damages in the event of Bert's default. The closing was to have taken place last week. Six weeks ago, Bert was notified by his employer that he was to be transferred to another job 1,000 miles away. Bert immediately notified Sam that he could not close, and therefore he demanded the return of his $5,000. Sam refused, waited until after the contract closing date, listed with a broker, and then conveyed Liveacre for $108,000 to Conner, a purchaser found by the real estate broker. Conner paid the full purchase price and immediately recorded his deed. Conner knew of the prior contract with Bert. In an appropriate action, Bert seeks to recover the $5,000 deposit from Sam.

The most probable result will be that Sam

(A) must return the $5,000 to Bert, because Sam can no longer carry out his contract with Bert.
(B) must return the $5,000 to Bert, because Bert was legally justified in not completing the contract.
(C) must return $3,000 to Bert, because Sam's damages were only $2,000.
(D) may keep the $5,000 deposit, because Bert breached the contract.

24. Rollem, an automobile retailer, had an adult daughter, Betsy, who needed a car in her employment but had only $3,000 with which to buy one. Rollem wrote to her, "Give me your $3,000 and I'll give you the car on our lot that we have been using as a demonstrator." Betsy thanked her father and paid him the $3,000. As both Rollem and Betsy knew, the demonstrator was reasonably worth $10,000. After Betsy had paid the $3,000, but before the car had been delivered to her, one of Rollem's sales staff sold and delivered the same car to a customer for $10,000. Neither the salesperson nor the customer was aware of the transaction between Rollem and Betsy.

Does Betsy, after rejecting a tendered return of the $3,000 by Rollem, have an action against him for breach of contract?

(A) Yes, because Rollem's promise was supported by bargained-for consideration.
(B) Yes, because Rollem's promise was supported by the moral obligation a father owes his child as to the necessities of modern life.
(C) No, because the payment of $3,000 was inadequate consideration to support Rollem's promise.
(D) No, because the salesperson's delivery of the car to the customer made it impossible for Rollem to perform.

25. Peter, who was 20 years old, purchased a new, high-powered sports car that was marketed with an intended and recognized appeal to youthful drivers. The car was designed with the capability to attain speeds in excess of 100 miles per hour. It was equipped with tires designed and tested only for a maximum safe speed of 85 miles per hour. The owner's manual that came with the car stated that "continuous driving over 90 miles per hour requires high-speed - capability tires," but the manual did not describe the speed capability of the tires sold with the car.

Peter took his new car out for a spin on a straight, smooth country road where the posted speed limit was 55 miles per hour. Intending to test the car's power, he drove for a considerable distance at over 100 miles per hour. While he was doing so, the tread separated from the left rear tire, causing the car to leave the road and hit a tree. Peter sustained severe injuries.

Peter has brought a strict product liability action in tort against the manufacturer of the car. You should assume that pure comparative fault principles apply to this case.

Will Peter prevail?

(A) No, because Peter's driving at an excessive speed constituted a misuse of the car.
(B) No, because the car was not defective.
(C) Yes, if the statement in the manual concerning the tires did not adequately warn of the danger of high-speed driving on the tires mounted on the car.
(D) Yes, unless Peter's driving at a speed in excess of the posted speed limit was negligence *per se* that, by the law of the jurisdiction, was not excusable.

26. In a federal court diversity action by Plant against Decord on an insurance claim, a question arose whether the court should apply a presumption that, where both husband and wife were killed in a common accident, the husband died last.

Whether this presumption should be applied is to be determined according to

(A) traditional common law.
(B) federal statutory law.
(C) the law of the state whose substantive law is applied.
(D) the federal common law.

27. Plagued by neighborhood youths who had been stealing lawn furniture from his back yard, Armando remained awake nightly watching for them. One evening Armando heard noises in his backyard. He yelled out, warning intruders to leave. Receiving no answer, he fired a shotgun filled with nonlethal buckshot into bushes along his back fence where he believed the intruders might be hiding. A six-year-old child was hiding in the bushes and was struck in the eye by some of the pellets, causing loss of sight.

If Armando is charged with second degree assault, which is defined in the jurisdiction as "maliciously causing serious physical injury to another," he is

(A) not guilty, because the child was trespassing and he was using what he believed was nondeadly force.
(B) not guilty, because he did not intend to kill or to cause serious physical injury.
(C) guilty, because he recklessly caused serious physical injury.
(D) guilty, because there is no privilege to use force against a person who is too young to be criminally responsible.

28. Twenty percent of the residents of Green City are members of minority racial groups. These residents are evenly distributed among the many different residential areas of the city. The five city council members of Green City are elected from five single-member electoral districts that are nearly equally populated. No candidate has ever been elected to the city council who was a member of a minority racial group.

A group of citizens who are members of minority racial groups file suit in federal district court seeking a declaratory judgment that the single-member districts in Green City are unconstitutional. They claim that the single-member distracting system in that city diminishes the ability of voters who are members of minority racial groups to affect the outcome of city elections. They seek an order from the court forcing the city to adopt an at-large election system in which the five candidates with the greatest vote totals would be elected to the city council. No state or federal statutes are applicable to the resolution of this suit.

Which of the following constitutional provisions provides the most obvious basis for plaintiffs' claim in this suit?

(A) The Thirteenth Amendment.
(B) The due process clause of the Fourteenth Amendment.
(C) The privileges and immunities clause of the Fourteenth Amendment.
(D) The Fifteenth Amendment.

29. Loomis, the owner and operator of a small business, encourages "wellness" on the part

of his employees and supports various physical-fitness programs to that end. Learning that one of his employees, Graceful, was a dedicated jogger, Loomis promised to pay her a special award of $100 if she could and would run one mile in less than six minutes on the following Saturday. Graceful thanked him, and did in fact run a mile in less than six minutes on the day specified. Shortly thereafter, however, Loomis discovered that for more than a year Graceful had been running at least one mile in less than six minutes every day as a part of her personal fitness program. He refused to pay the $100.

In an action by Graceful against Loomis for breach of contract, which of the following best summarizes the probable decision of the court?

(A) Loomis wins, because it is a compelling inference that Loomis's promise did not induce Graceful to run the specified mile.
(B) Loomis wins, because Graceful's running of the specified mile was beneficial, not detrimental, to her in any event.
(C) Graceful wins, because running a mile in less than six minutes is a significantly demanding enterprise.
(D) Graceful wins, because she ran the specified mile as requested, and her motives for doing so are irrelevant.

30. Able was the owner of Blackacre, an undeveloped city lot. Able and Baker executed a written document in which Able agreed to sell Blackacre to Baker and Baker agreed to buy Blackacre from Able for $100,000; the document did not provide for an earnest money down payment. Able recorded the document, as authorized by statute.

Able orally gave Baker permission to park his car on Blackacre without charge prior to the closing. Thereafter, Baker frequently parked his car on Blackacre.

Another property came on the market that Baker wanted more than Blackacre. Baker decided to try to escape any obligation to Able.

Baker had been told that contracts for the purchase and sale of real property require consideration and concluded that because he had made no earnest money down payment, he could refuse to close and not be liable. Baker notified Able of his intention not to close and, in fact, did refuse to close on the date set for the closing. Able brought an appropriate action to compel specific performance by Baker.

If Able wins, it will be because

(A) Baker's use of Blackacre for parking constitutes part performance.
(B) general contract rules regarding consideration apply to real estate contracts.
(C) the doctrine of equitable conversion applies.
(D) the document was recorded.

Questions 31-32 are based on the following fact situation.

Under the terms of a written contract, Karp agreed to construct for Manor a garage for $10,000. Nothing was said in the parties' negotiations or in the contract about progress payments during the course of the work.

31. For this question only, assume the following facts. After completing 25% of the garage strictly according to Manor's specifications, Karp demanded payment of $2,000 as a "reasonable progress payment." Manor refused, and Karp abandoned the job.

If each party sues the other for breach of contract, which of the following will the court decide?

(A) Both parties are in breach, and each is entitled to damages, if any, from the other.
(B) Only Karp is in breach, and liable for Manor's damages, if any.
(C) Only Manor is in breach and liable for Karp's damages, if any.

(D) Both parties took reasonable positions, and neither is in breach.

32. For this question only, assume the following facts. After completing 25% of the garage strictly according to Manor's specifications, Karp assigned his rights under the contract to Banquo as security for an $8,000 loan. Banquo immediately notified Manor of the assignment. Karp thereafter, without legal excuse, abandoned the job before it was half-complete. Karp subsequently defaulted on the loan from Banquo. Karp has no assets. It will cost Manor at least $8,000 to get the garage finished by another builder.

If Banquo sues Manor for $8,000, which of the following will the court decide?

(A) Banquo wins, because the Karp-Manor contract was in existence and Karp was not in breach when Banquo gave Manor notice of the assignment.
(B) Banquo wins, because Banquo as a secured creditor over Karp is entitled to priority over Manor's unsecured claim against Karp.
(C) Manor wins, because his right to recoupment on account of Karp's breach is available against Banquo as Karp's assignee.
(D) Manor wins, because his claim against Karp arose prior to Karp's default on his loan from Banquo.

33. The Sports Championship Revenue Enhancement Act is a federal statute that was enacted as part of a comprehensive program to eliminate the federal budget deficit. That act imposed, for a period of five years, a 50% excise tax on the price of tickets to championship sporting events. Such events included the World Series, the Super Bowl, major college bowl games, and similar championship sports events.

This federal tax is probably

(A) constitutional, because the compelling national interest in reducing the federal budget deficit justifies this tax as a temporary emergency measure.
(B) constitutional, because an act of Congress that appears to be a revenue raising measure on its face is not rendered invalid because it may have adverse economic consequences for the activity taxed.
(C) unconstitutional, because a 50% tax is likely to reduce attendance at championship sporting events and, therefore, is not rationally related to the legitimate interest of Congress in eliminating the budget deficit.
(D) unconstitutional, because Congress violates the equal protection component of the Fifth Amendment by singling out championship sporting events for this tax while failing to tax other major sporting, artistic, or entertainment events to which tickets are sold.

34. On June 1, Topline Wholesale, Inc., received a purchase-order form from Wonder-Good, Inc., a retailer and new customer, in which the latter ordered 1,000 anti-recoil widgets for delivery no later than August 30 at a delivered total price of $10,000, as quoted in Topline's current catalog. Both parties are merchants with respect to widgets of all types. On June 2, Topline mailed to Wonder-Good its own form, across the top of which Topline's president had written, "We are pleased to accept your order." This form contained the same terms as Wonder-Good's form except for an additional printed clause in Topline's form that provided for a maximum liability of $100 for any breach of contract by Topline.

As of June 5, when Wonder-Good received Topline's acceptance form, which of the following is an accurate statement concerning the legal relationship between Topline and Wonder-Good?

(A) There is no contract, because the liability-limitation clause in Topline's form is a material alteration of Wonder-Good's offer.
(B) There is no contract, because Wonder-Good did not consent to

the liability-limitation clause in Topline's form.
(C) There is an enforceable contract whose terms include the liability-limitation clause in Topline's form, because liquidation of damages is expressly authorized by the Uniform Commercial Code.
(D) There is an enforceable contract whose terms do not include the liability-limitation clause in Topline's form.

35. Electco operates a factory that requires the use of very high voltage electricity. Paul owns property adjacent to the Electco plant where he has attempted to carry on a business that requires the use of sensitive electronic equipment. The effectiveness of Paul's electronic equipment is impaired by electrical interference arising from the high voltage currents used in Electco's plant. Paul has complained to Electco several times, with no result. There is no way that Electco, by taking reasonable precautions, can avoid the interference with Paul's operation that arises from the high voltage currents necessary to Electco's operation.

In Paul's action against Electco to recover damages for the economic loss caused to him by the electrical interference, will Paul prevail?

(A) Yes, because Electco's activity is abnormally dangerous.
(B) Yes, for loss suffered by Paul after Electco was made aware of the harm its activity was causing to Paul.
(C) No, unless Electco caused a substantial and unreasonable interference with Paul's business.
(D) No, because Paul's harm was purely economic and did not arise from physical harm to his person or property.

36. Les leased a barn to his neighbor, Tom, for a term of three years. Tom took possession of the barn and used it for his farming purposes. The lease made Les responsible for structural repairs to the barn, unless they were made necessary by actions of Tom.

One year later, Les conveyed the barn and its associated land to Lottie "subject to the lease to Tom." Tom paid the next month's rent to Lottie. The next day a portion of an exterior wall of the barn collapsed because of rot in the interior structure of the wall. The wall had appeared to be sound, but a competent engineer, on inspection, would have discovered its condition. Neither Lottie nor Tom had the barn inspected by an engineer. Tom was injured as a result of the collapse of the wall.

Les had known that the wall was dangerously weakened by rot and needed immediate repairs, but had not told Tom or Lottie. There is no applicable statute.

Tom brought an appropriate action against Les to recover damages for the injuries he sustained. Lottie was not a party.

Which of the following is the most appropriate comment concerning the outcome of this action?

(A) Tom should lose, because Lottie assumed all of Les's obligations by reason of Tom's attornment to her.
(B) Tom should recover, because there is privity between lessor and lessee and it cannot be broken unilaterally.
(C) Tom should recover, because Les knew of the danger but did not warn Tom.
(D) Tom should lose, because he failed to inspect the barn.

37. Dahle is charged with possession of heroin. Prosecution witness Walker, an experienced dog trainer, testified that he was in the airport with a dog trained to detect heroin. As Dahle approached, the dog immediately became alert and pawed and barked frantically at Dahle's briefcase. Dahle managed to run outside and throw his briefcase into the river, from which it could not be recovered. After Walker's experience is established, he is asked to testify as an expert that the dog's reaction told him that Dahle's briefcase contained heroin.

Walker's testimony is

(A) admissible, as evidence of Dahle's guilt.
(B) admissible, because an expert may rely on hearsay.
(C) inadmissible, because it is based on hearsay not within any exception.
(D) inadmissible, because of the unreliability of the reactions of an animal.

38. Doe negligently caused a fire in his house, and the house burned to the ground. As a result, the sun streamed into Peter's yard next door, which previously had been shaded by Doe's house. The sunshine destroyed some delicate and valuable trees in Peter's yard that could grow only in the shade. Peter has brought a negligence action against Doe for the loss of Peter's trees. Doe has moved to dismiss the complaint.

    The best argument in support of this motion would be that

    (A) Doe's negligence was not the active cause of the loss of Peter's trees.
    (B) Doe's duty to avoid the risks created by a fire did not encompass the risk that sunshine would damage Peter's trees.
    (C) the loss of the trees was not a natural and probable consequence of Doe's negligence.
    (D) Peter suffered a purely economic loss, which is not compensable in a negligence action.

39. Phillips bought a new rifle and wanted to try it out by doing some target shooting. He went out into the country to an area where he had previously hunted. Much to his surprise, he noticed that the area beyond a clearing contained several newly constructed houses that had not been there before. Between the houses there was a small playground where several children were playing. Nevertheless, Phillips nailed a paper target to a tree and went to a point where the tree was between himself and the playground. He then fired several shots at the target. One of the shots missed the target and the tree and hit and killed one of the children in the playground.

    Phillips was convicted of murder. He appealed, contending that the evidence was not sufficient to support a conviction of murder.

    The appellate court should

    (A) affirm the conviction, as the evidence is sufficient to support a conviction of murder.
    (B) reverse the conviction and remand for a new trial, because the evidence is not sufficient for murder but will support a conviction of voluntary manslaughter.
    (C) reverse the conviction and remand for a new trial, because the evidence is not sufficient for murder but will support a conviction of involuntary manslaughter.
    (D) reverse the conviction and order the case dismissed, because the evidence is sufficient only for a finding of negligence and negligence alone cannot support a criminal conviction.

Questions 40-41 are based on the following fact situation.

Dominique obtained a bid of $10,000 to tear down her old building and another bid of $90,000 to replace it with a new structure in which she planned to operate a sporting goods store. Having only limited cash available, Dominique asked Hardcash for a $100,000 loan. After reviewing the plans for the project, Hardcash in a signed writing promised to lend Dominique $100,000 secured by a mortgage on the property and repayable over ten years in equal monthly installments at 10% annual interest. Dominique promptly accepted the demolition bid and the old building was removed, but Hardcash thereafter refused to make the loan. Despite diligent efforts, Dominique was unable to obtain a loan from any other source.

40. Does Dominique have a cause of action against Hardcash?

(A) Yes, because by having the building demolished, she accepted Hardcash's offer to make the loan.
(B) Yes, because her reliance on Hardcash's promise was substantial, reasonable, and foreseeable.
(C) No, because there was no bargained-for exchange of consideration for Hardcash's promise to make the loan.
(D) No, because Dominique's inability to obtain a loan from any other source demonstrated that the project lacked the financial soundness that was a constructive condition to Hardcash's performance.

41. For this question only, assume that Dominique has a cause of action against Hardcash.

    If she sues him for monetary relief, what is the probable measure of her recovery?
    (A) Expectancy damages, measured by the difference between the value of the new building and the old building, less the amount of the proposed loan ($100,000).
    (B) Expectancy damages, measured by the estimated profits from operating the proposed sporting goods store for ten years, less the cost of repaying a $100,000 loan at 10% interest over ten years.
    (C) Reliance damages, measured by the $10,000 expense of removing the old building, adjusted by the decrease or increase in the market value of Dominique's land immediately thereafter.
    (D) Nominal damages only, because both expectancy and reliance damages are speculative, and there is no legal or equitable basis for awarding restitution.

42. Dan, an eight-year-old, rode his bicycle down his driveway into a busy highway and Driver had to stop her car suddenly to avoid colliding with the bike. Because of the sudden stop, Driver's two-year-old son, Peter, who was sitting on the seat without any restraint, was thrown into the dashboard and injured. Had Peter been properly restrained in a baby car seat, as required by a state safety statute of which his mother was a 'ware, he would not have been injured.

    In an action brought on Peter's behalf against Dan's parents to recover for Peter's injuries, Peter will

    (A) not prevail, because parents are not vicariously liable for the negligent acts of their children.
    (B) not prevail, because Peter's injury was attributable to his mother's knowing violation of a safety statute.
    (C) prevail, if Dan's parents knew that he sometimes drove into the highway, and they took no steps to prevent it.
    (D) prevail, if Dan's riding into the highway was negligent and the proximate cause of Peter's injuries.

43. While Hill was in her kitchen, she heard the screech of automobile tires. She ran to the window and saw a tricycle flying through the air. The tricycle had been hit by a car driven by Weber, who had been speeding. She also saw a child's body in the grass adjacent to the street. As a result of her shock from this experience, Hill suffered a heart attack.

    In a claim by Hill against Weber, the issue on which Hill's right to recover will depend is whether

    (A) a person can recover damages based on the defendant's breach of a duty owed to another.
    (B) it is foreseeable that a person may suffer physical harm caused solely by an injury inflicted on another.
    (C) a person can recover damages caused by shock unaccompanied by bodily impact.
    (D) a person can recover damages for harm resulting from shock caused solely by another's peril or injury.

44. Suffering from painful and terminal cancer, Willa persuaded Harold, her husband, to kill her to end her misery. As they reminisced about their life together and reaffirmed their

love for each other, Harold tried to discourage Willa from giving up. Willa insisted, however, and finally Harold held a gun to her head and killed her.

The most serious degree of criminal homicide of which Harold can be legally convicted is

(A) no degree of criminal homicide.
(B) involuntary manslaughter.
(C) voluntary manslaughter.
(D) murder.

45. Peterson sued Dylan for libel. After Peterson testified that Dylan wrote to Peterson's employer that Peterson was a thief, Dylan offers evidence that Peterson once stole money from a former employer.

The evidence of Peterson's prior theft is

(A) admissible, as substantive evidence to prove that Peterson is a thief.
(B) admissible, but only to impeach Peterson's credibility.
(C) inadmissible, because character may not be shown by specific instances of conduct.
(D) inadmissible, because such evidence is more unfairly prejudicial than probative.

46. The Federal Computer Abuse Act establishes the Federal Computer Abuse Commission, authorizes the Commission to issue licenses for the possession of computers on terms that are consistent with the purposes of the act, and makes the unlicensed possession of a computer a crime. The provisions of the Federal Computer Abuse Act are inseverable.

User applied to the Federal Computer Abuse Commission for a license to possess a computer. The Commission held, and User participated in, a trial type proceeding on User's license application. In that proceeding it was demonstrated that User repeatedly and intentionally used computers to introduce secret destructive computer programs (computer viruses) into electronic data banks without the consent of their owners. As a result, the Commission denied User's application for a license. The license denial was based on a Commission rule authorized by the Computer Abuse Act that prohibited the issuance of computer licenses to persons who had engaged in such conduct. Nevertheless, User retained and continued to use his computer. He was subsequently convicted of the crime of unlicensed possession of a computer. On appeal, he challenges the constitutionality of the licensing provision of the Federal Computer Abuse Act.

In this case, the reviewing court would probably hold that act to be

(A) constitutional, because the Constitution generally authorizes Congress to enact all laws that are necessary and proper to advance the general welfare, and Congress could reasonably believe that possession of computers by people like User constitutes a threat to the general welfare.
(B) constitutional, because Congress may use the authority vested in it by the commerce clause to regulate the possession of computers and the provisions of this act do not violate any prohibitory provision of the Constitution.
(C) unconstitutional, because Congress may not impose a criminal penalty on action that is improper only because it is inconsistent with an agency rule.
(D) unconstitutional, because the mere possession of a computer is a wholly local matter that is beyond the regulatory authority of Congress.

47. Defendant left her car parked on the side of a hill. Two minutes later, the car rolled down the hill and struck and injured Plaintiff.

In Plaintiff's negligence action against Defendant, Plaintiff introduced into evidence the facts stated above, which are undisputed. Defendant testified that, when she parked her car, she turned the front wheels into the curb and put on her emergency brakes, which were in good working order. She also introduced evidence that, in the weeks before this incident, juveniles had been seen tampering with cars in the neighborhood. The jury returned a verdict in favor of Defendant, and Plaintiff moved for a judgment notwithstanding the verdict.

Plaintiff's motion should be

(A) granted, because it is more likely than not that Defendant's negligent conduct was the legal cause of Plaintiff's injuries.
(B) granted, because the evidence does not support the verdict.
(C) denied, because, given Defendant's evidence, the jury was not required to draw an inference of negligence from the circumstances of the accident.
(D) denied, if Defendant was in no better position than Plaintiff to explain the accident.

48. Able conveyed Blackacre to Baker by a warranty deed. Baker recorded the deed four days later. After the conveyance but prior to Baker's recording of the deed, Smollett properly filed a judgment against Able.

The two pertinent statutes in the jurisdiction provide the following: 1) any judgment properly filed shall, for ten years from filing, be a lien on the real property then owned or subsequently acquired by any person against whom the judgment is rendered, and 2) no conveyance or mortgage of real property shall be good against subsequent purchasers for value and without notice unless the same be recorded according to law.

The recording act has no provision for a grace period.

Smollett joined both Able and Baker in an appropriate action to foreclose the judgment lien against Blackacre.

If Smollett is unsuccessful, it will be because

(A) Able s warranty of title to Baker defeats Smollett's claim.
(B) Smollett is not a purchaser for value.
(C) any deed is superior to a judgment lien.
(D) four days is not an unreasonable delay in recording a deed.

49. The United States Department of Energy regularly transports nuclear materials through Centerville on the way to a nuclear weapons processing plant it operates in a nearby state. The city of Centerville recently adopted an ordinance prohibiting the transportation of any nuclear materials in or through the city. The ordinance declares that its purpose is to protect the health and safety of the residents of that city.

May the Department of Energy continue to transport these nuclear materials through the city of Centerville?

(A) No, because the ordinance is rationally related to the public health and safety of Centerville residents.
(B) No, because the Tenth Amendment reserves to the states certain enumerated sovereign powers.
(C) Yes, because the Department of Energy is a federal agency engaged in a lawful federal function and, therefore, its activities may not be regulated by a local government without the consent of Congress.
(D) Yes, because the ordinance enacted by Centerville is invalid because it denies persons transporting such materials the equal protection of the laws.

50. Dart is charged with the statutory offense of "knowingly violating a regulation of the State Alcoholic Beverage Control Board" and specifically that he knowingly violated regulation number 345-90 issued by the State Alcoholic Beverage Control Board. That regulation prohibits the sale of alcoholic beverages to any person under the age of 18 and also prohibits the sale of any alcoholic beverage to a person over the age

of 17 and under the age of 22 without the presentation of such person's driver's license or other identification showing the age of the purchaser to be 18 or older.

The evidence showed that Dart was a bartender in a tavern and sold a bottle of beer to a person who was 17 years old and that Dart did not ask for or see the purchaser's driver's license or any other identification.

Which of the following, if found by the jury, would be of the most help to Dart?

(A) The purchaser had a driver's license that falsely showed his age to be 21.
(B) Dart had never been told he was supposed to check identification of persons over 17 and under 22 before selling them alcohol.
(C) Dart did not know that the regulations classified beer as an alcoholic beverage.
(D) Dart mistakenly believed the purchaser to be 24 years old.

Questions 51-52 are based on the following fact situation.

In a writing signed by both parties on December 1, Kranc agreed to buy from Schaff a gasoline engine for $1,000, delivery to be made on the following February 1. Through a secretarial error, the writing called for delivery on March 1, but neither party noticed the error until February 1. Before signing the agreement, Kranc and Schaff orally agreed that the contract of sale would be effective only if Kranc should notify Schaff in writing not later than January 2 that Kranc had arranged to resell the engine to a third person. Otherwise, they agreed orally, "There is no deal." On December 15, Kranc entered into a contract with Trimota to resell the engine to Trimota at a profit.

51. For this question only, assume the following facts. Kranc did not give Schaff notice of the resale until January 25, and Schaff received it by mail on January 26. Meantime, the value of the engine had unexpectedly increased about 75% since December 1, and Schaff renounced the agreement.

If Kranc sues Schaff on February 2 for breach of contract, which of the following is Schaff's best defense?

(A) The secretarial error in the written delivery-term was a mutual mistake concerning a basic fact, and the agreement is voidable by either party.
(B) Kranc's not giving written notice by January 2 of his resale was a failure of a condition precedent to the existence of a contract.
(C) In view of the unexpected 75% increase in value of the engine after December 1, Schaff's performance is excused by the doctrine of commercial frustration.
(D) The agreement, if any, is unenforceable because a material term was not included in the writing.

52. For this question only, assume the following facts. On December 16, Kranc notified Schaff by telephone of Kranc's resale agreement with Trimota, and explained that a written notice was unfeasible because Kranc's secretary was ill. Schaff replied, "That's okay. I'll get the engine to you on February 1, as we agreed." Having learned, however, that the engine had increased in value about 75% since December 1, Schaff renounced the agreement on February 1.

If Kranc sues Schaff on February 2 for breach of contract, which of the following concepts best supports Kranc's claim?

(A) Substantial performance.
(B) Nonoccurrence of a condition subsequent.
(C) Waiver of condition.
(D) Novation of buyers.

53. David owned a shotgun that he used for hunting. David knew that his old friend, Mark, had become involved with a violent gang that recently had a shootout with a rival gang. David, who was going to a farm to hunt quail, placed his loaded shotgun on the back seat of his car. On his way to the farm, David picked up Mark to give him a ride to a friend's house. After dropping off Mark at the friend's house, David proceeded

to the farm, where he discovered that his shotgun was missing from his car. Mark had taken the shotgun and, later in the day, Mark used it to shoot Paul, a member of the rival gang. Paul was severely injured.

Paul recovered a judgment for his damages against David, as well as Mark, on the ground that David was negligent in allowing Mark to obtain possession of the gun, and was therefore liable jointly and severally with Mark for Paul's damages. The jurisdiction has a statute that allows contribution based upon proportionate fault and adheres to the traditional common-law rules on indemnity.

If David fully satisfies the judgment, David then will have a right to recover from Mark

(A) indemnity for the full amount of the judgment, because Mark was an intentional tortfeasor.
(B) contribution only, based on comparative fault, because David himself was negligent.
(C) one-half of the amount of the judgment.
(D) nothing, because David's negligence was a substantial proximate cause of the shooting.

54. The legislature of the state of Chetopah enacted a statute requiring that all law enforcement officers in that state be citizens of the United States. Alien, lawfully admitted to permanent residency five years before the enactment of this statute, sought employment as a forensic pathologist in the Chetopah coroner's office. He was denied such a job solely because he was not a citizen.

Alien thereupon brought suit in federal district court against appropriate Chetopah officials seeking to invalidate this citizenship requirement on federal constitutional grounds.

The strongest ground upon which to attack this citizenship requirement is that it

(A) constitutes an ex post facto law as to previously admitted aliens.
(B) deprives an alien of a fundamental right to employment without the due process of law guaranteed by the Fourteenth Amendment.
(C) denies an alien a right to employment in violation of the privileges and immunities clause of the Fourteenth Amendment.
(D) denies an alien the equal protection of the laws guaranteed by the Fourteenth Amendment.

55. Olwen owned 80 acres of land, fronting on a town road. Two years ago, Olwen sold to Buck the back 40 acres. The 40 acres sold to Buck did not adjoin any public road. Olwen's deed to Buck expressly granted a right-of-way over a specified strip of Olwen's retained 40 acres, so Buck could reach the town road. The deed was promptly and properly recorded.

Last year, Buck conveyed the back 40 acres to Sam. They had discussed the right-of-way over Olwen's land to the road, but Buck's deed to Sam made no mention of it. Sam began to use the right-of-way as Buck had, but Olwen sued to enjoin such use by Sam.

The court should decide for

(A) Sam, because he has an easement by implication.
(B) Sam, because the easement appurtenant passed to him as a result of Buck's deed to him.
(C) Olwen, because Buck's easement in gross was not transferable.
(D) Olwen, because Buck's deed failed expressly to transfer the right-of-way to Sam.

56. Dickinson was charged with possession of cocaine. At Dickinson's trial, the prosecution established that, when approached by police on a suburban residential street corner, Dickinson dropped a plastic bag and ran, and that when the police returned to the corner a few minutes later after catching Dickinson, they found a plastic bag containing white powder. Dickinson objects to introduction of this bag (the contents of which would later be

established to be cocaine), citing lack of adequate identification.

The objection should be

(A) overruled, because there is sufficient evidence to find that the bag was the one Dickinson dropped.
(B) overruled, because the objection should have been made on the basis of incomplete chain of custody.
(C) sustained, because Dickinson did not have possession of the bag at the time he was arrested.
(D) sustained, unless the judge makes a finding by a preponderance of the evidence that the bag was the one dropped by Dickinson.

57. Chemco manufactured a liquid chemical product known as XRX. Some XRX leaked from a storage tank on Chemco's property, seeped into the groundwater, flowed to Farmer's adjacent property, and Polluted Farmer's well. Several of Farmer's cows drank the Polluted well water and died. If Farmer brings an action against Chemco to recover the value of the cows that died, Farmer will

(A) prevail, because a manufacturer is strictly liable for harm caused by its products.
(B) prevail, because the XRX escaped from Chemco's premises.
(C) not prevail, unless Farmer can establish that the storage tank was defective.
(D) not prevail, unless Chemco failed to exercise reasonable care in storing the XRX.

58. A threatening telephone call that purports to be from Defendant to Witness is most likely to be admitted against Defendant if

(A) the caller identified himself as Defendant.
(B) Witness had previously given damaging testimony against Defendant in another lawsuit.
(C) Witness had given his unlisted number only to Defendant and a few other persons.
(D) Witness believes that Defendant is capable of making such threats.

59. The open-air amphitheater in the city park of Rightville has been utilized for concerts and other entertainment programs. Until this year, each of the groups performing in that city facility was allowed to make its own arrangements for sound equipment and sound technicians.

After recurring complaints from occupants of residential buildings adjacent to the city park about intrusive noise from some performances held in the amphitheater, the Rightville City Council passed an ordinance establishing city control over all sound amplification at all programs held there. The ordinance provided that Rightville's Department of Parks would be the sole provider in the amphitheater of sound amplification equipment and of the technicians to operate the equipment "to ensure a proper balance between the quality of the sound at such performances and respect for the privacy of nearby residential neighbors."

Which of the following standards should a court use to determine the constitutionality on its face of this content neutral ordinance?

(A) The ordinance is narrowly tailored to serve a substantial government interest, and does not unreasonably limit alternative avenues of expression.
(B) The ordinance is rationally related to a legitimate government interest, and does not unreasonably limit alternative avenues of expression.
(C) The ordinance is rationally related to a legitimate government interest and restricts the expressive rights involved no more than is reasonable under the circumstances.
(D) The ordinance is substantially related to a legitimate governmental interest and restricts the expressive rights involved no

more than is reasonable in light of the surrounding circumstances.

60. Smith and Penn were charged with murder. Each gave a confession to the police that implicated both of them. Smith later retracted her confession, claiming that it was coerced.

Smith and Penn were tried together. The prosecutor offered both confessions into evidence. Smith and Penn objected. After a hearing, the trial judge found that both confessions were voluntary and admitted both into evidence. Smith testified at trial. She denied any involvement in the crime and claimed that her confession was false and the result of coercion. Both defendants were convicted.

On appeal, Smith contends her conviction should be reversed because of the admission into evidence of Penn's confession.

Smith's contention is

(A) correct, unless Penn testified at trial.
(B) correct, whether or not Penn testified at trial.
(C) incorrect, because Smith testified in her own behalf.
(D) incorrect, because Smith's own confession was properly admitted into evidence.

61. The state of Orrington wanted to prevent its only major league baseball team, the privately owned and operated Orrington Opossums, from moving to the rival state of Atrium. After a heated political debate in the legislature, Orrington enacted legislation providing for a one-time grant of $10 million in state funds to the Opossums to cover part of the projected income losses the team would suffer during the next five years if it remained in that state. The legislation required that the team remain in the state for at least ten years if it accepted the grant.

After accepting the grant, the owners of the Opossums decided to build a new $150 million stadium in Orrington. As plans for the construction of the new stadium proceeded, it became evident that all of the contractors and subcontractors would be white males, and that they had been chosen by the owners of the Opossums without any public bids because these contractors and subcontractors had successfully built the only other new baseball stadium in the region. Several contractors who were females or members of minority racial groups filed suit against the owners of the Opossums in federal district court to compel public solicitation of bids for the construction of its new stadium on an equal opportunity basis, and to enjoin construction of the stadium until compliance was ensured. Their only claim was that the contracting practices of the owners of the Opossums denied them the equal protection of the laws in violation of the Fourteenth Amendment.

In this suit, the court will probably rule that

(A) the nexus between the actions of the owners of the Opossums and the one-time grant of monies to them by the state is sufficiently substantial to subject their actions to the limitations of the Fourteenth Amendment.
(B) the intense public preoccupation with the activities of major league baseball teams coupled with the fact that baseball is considered to be our national pastime is sufficient to justify application of the Fourteenth Amendment to the activities of major league teams.
(C) in the absence of additional evidence of state involvement in the operations or decisions of the owners of the Opossums, a one-time grant of state monies to them is insufficient to warrant treating their actions as subject to the limitations of the Fourteenth Amendment.
(D) the issues presented by this case are nonjusticiable political questions because there is a lack of judicially manageable standards to resolve them and they are likely to be deeply involved in partisan politics.

Questions 62-63 are based on the following 63. fact situation.

Walker, who knew nothing about horses, inherited Aberlone, a thoroughbred colt whose disagreeable behavior made him a pest around the barn. Walker sold the colt for $1,500 to Sherwood, an experienced racehorse-trainer who knew of Walker's ignorance about horses. At the time of sale, Walker said to Sherwood, "I hate to say it, but this horse is bad-tempered and nothing special."

62. For this question only, assume that soon after the sale, Aberlone won three races and earned $400,000 for Sherwood.

Which of the following additional facts, if established by Walker, would best support his chance of obtaining rescission of the sale to Sherwood?

(A) Walker did not know until after the sale that Sherwood was an experienced racehorse-trainer.
(B) At a pre-sale exercise session of which Sherwood knew that Walker was not aware, Sherwood clocked Aberlone in record-setting time, far surpassing any previous performance.
(C) Aberlone was the only thoroughbred that Walker owned, and Walker did not know how to evaluate young and untested racehorses.
(D) At the time of the sale, Walker was angry and upset over an incident in which Aberlone had reared and thrown a rider.

63. Which one of the following scenarios would best support an action by Sherwood, rather than Walker, to rescind the sale?

(A) In his first race after the sale, Aberlone galloped to a huge lead but dropped dead 100 yards from the finish line because of a rare congenital heart defect that was undiscoverable except by autopsy.
(B) Aberlone won $5 million for Sherwood over a three-year racing career but upon being retired was found to be incurably sterile and useless as a breeder.
(C) After Aberlone had won three races for Sherwood, it was discovered that by clerical error, unknown to either party, Aberlone's official birth registration listed an undistinguished racehorse as the sire rather than the famous racehorse that in fact was the sire.
(D) A week after the sale, Aberlone went berserk and inflicted injuries upon Sherwood that required his hospitalization for six months and a full year for his recovery.

64. Sixty years ago by a properly executed and recorded deed, Albert conveyed Greenacre, a tract of land: "To Louis for life, then to Louis's widow for her life, then to Louis's child or children in equal shares." At that time, Louis, who was Albert's grandson, was six years old.

Shortly thereafter, Albert died testate. Louis was his only heir at law. Albert's will left his entire estate to First Church.

Twenty-five years ago, when he was 41, Louis married Maria who was then 20 years old; they had one child, Norman. Maria and Norman were killed in an automobile accident three years ago when Norman was 21. Norman died testate, leaving his entire estate to the American Red Cross. His father, Louis, was Norman's sole heir at law.

Two years ago, Louis married Zelda. They had no children. This year, Louis died testate, survived by his widow, Zelda, to whom he left his entire estate.

The common-law Rule Against Perpetuities is unchanged by statute in the jurisdiction.

In an appropriate action to determine the ownership of Greenacre, the court should find that title is vested in

(A) First Church, because the widow of Louis was unborn at the time of conveyance and, hence, the

remainder violated the Rule Against Perpetuities.
(B) Zelda, because her life estate and her inheritance from Louis (who was Albert's sole heir at law and who was Norman's sole heir at law) merged the entire title in her.
(C) the American Red Cross, because Norman had a vested remainder interest (as the only child of Louis) that it inherited, the life estate to Louis's widow being of no force and effect.
(D) Zelda for life under the terms of Albert's deed, with the remainder to the American Red Cross as the successor in interest to Norman, Louis's only child.

65. In an automobile collision case brought by Poe against Davies, Poe introduced evidence that Ellis made an excited utterance that Davies ran the red light.

Davies called Witt to testify that later Ellis, a bystander, now deceased, told Witt that Davies went through a yellow light.

Witt's testimony should be

(A) excluded, because it is hearsay not within any exception.
(B) excluded, because Ellis is not available to explain or deny the inconsistency.
(C) admitted only for the purpose of impeaching Ellis.
(D) admitted as impeachment and as substantive evidence of the color of the light.

66. Plaintiff, a jockey, was seriously injured in a race when another jockey, Daring, cut too sharply in front of her without adequate clearance. The two horses collided, causing Plaintiff to fall to the ground, sustaining injury. The State Racetrack Commission ruled that, by cutting in too sharply, Daring committed a foul in violation of racetrack rules requiring adequate clearance for crossing lanes. Plaintiff has brought an action against Daring for damages in which one count is based on battery.

Will Plaintiff prevail on the battery claim?

(A) Yes, if Daring was reckless in cutting across in front of Plaintiff's horse.
(B) Yes, because the State Racetrack Commission determined that Daring committed a foul in violation of rules applicable to racing.
(C) No, unless Daring intended to cause impermissible contact between the two horses or apprehension of such contact by Plaintiff.
(D) No, because Plaintiff assumed the risk of accidental injury inherent in riding as a jockey in a horse race.

67. Able entered into a written contract with Baker to sell Greenacre. The contract was dated June 19 and called for a closing date on the following August 19. There was no other provision in the contract concerning the closing date. The contract contained the following clause: "subject to the purchaser, Baker, obtaining a satisfactory mortgage at the current rate." On the date provided for closing, Baker advised Able that he was unable to close because his mortgage application was still being processed by a bank. Able desired to declare the contract at an end and consulted his attorney in regard to his legal position.

Which of the following are relevant in advising Able of his legal position?

I. Is time of the essence?
II. Parol evidence rule.
III. Statute of Frauds.
IV. Specific performance.

(A) I and III only.
(B) II and IV only.
(C) II, III, and IV only.
(D) I, II, III, and IV.

68. Lester was engaged to marry Sylvia. One evening, Lester became enraged at the comments of Sylvia's eight-year-old daughter, Cynthia, who was complaining, in her usual fashion, that she did not want her mother to marry Lester. Lester, who had had too much to drink, began beating her.

Cynthia suffered some bruises and a broken arm. Sylvia took Cynthia to the hospital. The police were notified by the hospital staff. Lester was indicted for felony child abuse.

Lester pleaded with Sylvia to forgive him and to run away with him. She agreed. They moved out of state and took Cynthia with them. Without the testimony of the child, the prosecution was forced to dismiss the case.

Some time later, Sylvia returned for a visit with her family and was arrested and indicted as an accessory-after-the-fact to child abuse.

At her trial, the court should

(A) dismiss the charge, because Lester had not been convicted.
(B) dismiss the charge, because the evidence shows that any aid she rendered occurred after the crime was completed.
(C) submit the case to the jury, on an instruction to convict only if Sylvia knew Lester had been indicted.
(D) submit the case to the jury, on an instruction to convict only if her purpose in moving was to prevent Lester's conviction.

69. In response to massive layoffs of employees of automobile assembly plants located in the state of Ames, the legislature of that state enacted a statute which prohibits the parking of automobiles manufactured outside of the United States in any parking lot or parking structure that is owned or operated by the state or any of its instrumentalities. This statute does not apply to parking on public streets.

Which of the following is the strongest argument with which to challenge the constitutionality of this statute?

(A) The statute imposes an undue burden on foreign commerce.
(B) The statute denies the owners of foreign-made automobiles the equal protection of the laws.
(C) The statute deprives the owners of foreign-made automobiles of liberty or property without due process of law.
(D) The statute is inconsistent with the privileges and immunities clause of the Fourteenth Amendment.

70. Pate sued Dr. Doke for psychiatric malpractice and called Dr. Will as an expert witness. During Will's direct testimony, Will identified a text as a reliable authority in the field. He seeks to read to the jury passages from this book on which he had relied in forming his opinion on the proper standard of care.

The passage is

(A) admissible, as a basis for his opinion and as substantive evidence of the proper standard of care.
(B) admissible, as a basis for his opinion but not as substantive evidence of the proper standard of care.
(C) inadmissible, because a witness's credibility cannot be supported unless attacked.
(D) inadmissible, because the passage should be received as an exhibit and not read to the jury by the witness.

71. The Daily Sun, a newspaper, printed an article that stated:

Kitchen, the popular restaurant on the town square, has closed its doors. Kitchen employees have told the Daily Sun that the closing resulted from the owner's belief that Kitchen's general manager has embezzled thousands of dollars from the restaurant over the last several years. A decision on reopening the restaurant will be made after the completion of an audit of Kitchen's books.

Plaintiff, who is Kitchen's general manager, brought a libel action against the Daily Sun based on the publication of this article. The parties stipulated that Plaintiff never embezzled any funds from Kitchen. They also stipulated that Plaintiff is well known among many people in the community because of his job with Kitchen.

The case went to trial before a jury.

The defendant's motion for a directed verdict in its favor, made at the close of the evidence, should be granted if the

(A) record contains no evidence that Plaintiff suffered special harm as a result of the publication.
(B) record contains no evidence that the defendant was negligent as to the truth or falsity of the charge of embezzlement.
(C) evidence is not clear and convincing that the defendant published the article with "actual malice."
(D) record contains uncontradicted evidence that the article accurately reported what the employees told the Daily Sun.

72. Surgeon performed a sterilization operation on Patient. After the surgery, Surgeon performed a test that showed that Patient's fallopian tubes were not severed, as was necessary for sterilization. Surgeon did not reveal the failure of the operation to Patient, who three years later became pregnant and delivered a baby afflicted with a severe birth defect that will require substantial medical care throughout its life. The birth defect resulted from a genetic defect unknown to, and undiscoverable by, Surgeon. Patient brought an action on her own behalf against Surgeon, seeking to recover the cost of her medical care for the delivery of the baby, and the baby's extraordinary future medical expenses for which Patient will be responsible.

Which of the following questions is relevant to the lawsuit and currently most difficult to answer?

(A) Did Surgeon owe a duty of care to the baby in respect to medical services rendered to Patient three years before the baby was conceived?
(B) Can a person recover damages for a life burdened by a severe birth defect based on a physician's wrongful failure to prevent that person's birth from occurring?
(C) Did Surgeon owe a duty to Patient to inform her that the sterilization operation had failed?
(D) Is Patient entitled to recover damages for the baby's extraordinary future medical expenses?

73. Robert walked into a store that had a check-cashing service and tried to cash a $550 check which was payable to him. The attendant on duty refused to cash the check because Robert did not have two forms of identification, which the store's policies required. Robert, who had no money except for the check and who needed cash to pay for food and a place to sleep, became agitated. He put his hand into his pocket and growled, "Give me the money or I'll start shooting." The attendant, who knew Robert as a neighborhood character, did not believe that he was violent or had a gun. However, because the attendant felt sorry for Robert, he handed over the cash. Robert left the check on the counter and departed. The attendant picked up the check and found that Robert had failed to endorse it.

If Robert is guilty of any crime, he is most likely guilty of

(A) robbery.
(B) attempted robbery.
(C) theft by false pretenses.
(D) larceny by trick.

Questions 74-75 are based on the following fact situation.

Kabb, the owner of a fleet of taxis, contracted with Petrol, a dealer in petroleum products, for the purchase and sale of Kabb's total requirements of gasoline and oil for one year. As part of that agreement, Petrol also agreed with Kabb that for one year Petrol would place all his advertising with Ada Artiste, Kabb's wife, who owned her own small advertising agency. When Artiste was informed of the Kabb-Petrol contract, she declined to accept an advertising account from the Deturgid Soap Company because she could not handle both the Petrol and Deturgid accounts during the same year.

74. For this question only, assume the following facts. During the first month of the contract, Kabb purchased substantial amounts of his gasoline from a supplier other than Petrol, and Petrol thereupon notified Artiste that he would no longer place his advertising with her agency.

   In an action against Petrol for breach of contract, Artiste probably will

   (A) succeed, because she is a third-party beneficiary of the Kabb-Petrol contract.
   (B) succeed, because Kabb was acting as Artiste's agent when he contracted with Petrol.
   (C) not succeed, because the failure of constructive condition precedent excused Petrol's duty to place his advertising with Artiste.
   (D) not succeed, because Artiste did not provide any consideration to support Petrol's promise to place his advertising with her.

75. For this question only, make the following assumptions. Artiste was an intended beneficiary under the Kabb-Petrol contract. Kabb performed his contract with Petrol for six months, and during that time Petrol placed his advertising with Artiste. At the end of the six months, Kabb and Artiste were divorced, and Kabb then told Petrol that he had no further obligation to place his advertising with Artiste. Petrol thereupon notified Artiste that he would no longer place his advertising with her.

   In an action against Petrol for breach of contract, Artiste probably will

   (A) succeed, because, on the facts of this case, Petrol and Kabb could not, without Artiste's consent, modify their contract so as to discharge Petrol's duties to Artiste.
   (B) succeed, because Kabb acted in bad faith in releasing Petrol from his duty with respect to Artiste.
   (C) not succeed, because, absent a provision in the contract to the contrary, the promisor and promisee of a third-party beneficiary contract retain by law the right to modify or terminate the contract.
   (D) not succeed, because the agency relationship, if any, between Kabb and Artiste terminated upon their divorce.

76. Drew, the owner of a truck leasing company, asked Pat, one of Drew's employees, to deliver $1,000 to the dealership's main office. The following week, as a result of a dispute over whether the money had been delivered, Drew instructed Pat to come to the office to submit to a lie detector test.

   When Pat reported to Drew's office for the test, it was not administered. Instead, without hearing Pat's story, Drew shouted at him, "You're a thief!" and fired him. Drew's shout was overheard by several other employees who were in another office, which was separated from Drew's office by a thin partition. The next day, Pat accepted another job at a higher salary. Several weeks later, upon discovering that the money had not been stolen, Drew offered to rehire Pat.

   In a suit for slander by Pat against Drew, Pat will

   (A) prevail, because Pat was fraudulently induced to go to the office for a lie detector test, which was not, in fact, given.
   (B) prevail, if Drew should have foreseen that the statement would be overheard by other employees.
   (C) not prevail, if Drew made the charge in good faith, believing it to be true.
   (D) not prevail, because the statement was made to Pat alone and intended for his ears only.

77. Adam owns his home, Blackacre, which was mortgaged to Bank by a duly recorded purchase money mortgage. Last year, Adam replaced all of Blackacre's old windows with new windows.

Each new window consists of a window frame with three inserts: regular windows, storm windows, and screens. The windows are designed so that each insert can be easily inserted or removed from the window frame without tools to adjust to seasonal change and to facilitate the cleaning of the inserts.

The new windows were expensive. Adam purchased them on credit, signed a financing statement, and granted a security interest in the windows to Vend, the supplier of the windows. Vend promptly and properly filed and recorded the financing statement before the windows were installed. Adam stored the old windows in the basement of Blackacre.

This year, Adam has suffered severe financial reverses and has defaulted on his mortgage obligation to Bank and on his obligation to Vend.

Bank brought an appropriate action to enjoin Vend from its proposed repossession of the window inserts.

In the action, the court should rule for

(A) Bank, because its mortgage was recorded first.
(B) Bank, because windows and screens, no matter their characteristics, are an integral part of a house.
(C) Vend, because the inserts are removable.
(D) Vend, because the availability of the old windows enables Bank to return Blackacre to its original condition.

78. In a suit by Palmer against Denby, Palmer sought to subpoena an audiotape on which Denby had narrated his version of the dispute for his attorney. Counsel for Denby moves to quash the subpoena on the ground of privilege.

The audiotape is most likely to be subject to subpoena if

(A) Denby played the audiotape for his father to get his reactions.

(B) the lawsuit involved alleged criminal behavior by Denby.
(C) Denby has been deposed and there is good reason to believe that the audiotape may contain inconsistent statements.
(D) Denby is deceased and thus unavailable to give testimony in person.

79. The National Ecological Balance Act prohibits the destruction or removal of any wild animals located on lands owned by the United States without express permission from the Federal Bureau of Land Management. Violators are subject to fines of up to $1,000 per offense.

After substantial property damage was inflicted on residents of the state of Arkota by hungry coyotes, the state legislature passed the Coyote Bounty Bill, which offers $25 for each coyote killed or captured within the state. The Kota National Forest, owned by the federal government, is located entirely within the state of Arkota. Many coyotes live in the Kota National Forest.

Without seeking permission from the Bureau of Land Management, Hunter shot several coyotes in the Kota National Forest and collected the bounty from the state of Arkota. As a result, he was subsequently tried in federal district court, convicted, and fined $1,000 for violating the National Ecological Balance Act. Hunter appealed his conviction to the United States Court of Appeals.

On appeal, the Court of Appeals should hold the National Ecological Balance Act, as applied to Hunter, to be

(A) constitutional, because the property clause of Article IV, Section 3, of the Constitution authorizes such federal statutory controls and sanctions.
(B) constitutional, because Article I, Section 8, of the Constitution authorizes Congress to enact all laws necessary and proper to advance the general welfare.
(C) unconstitutional, because Congress may not use its

(D) unconstitutional, because Congress violates the full faith and credit clause of Article IV when it punishes conduct that has been authorized by state action.

80. A kidnapping statute in State A makes it a crime for a person, including a parent, to "take a child from the custody of his custodial parent, knowing he has no privilege to do so."

After a bitter court battle Ann and Dave were divorced and Ann was given custody of their daughter, Maria. Dave later moved to State B where he brought an action to obtain custody of Maria. A local judge awarded him custody. His attorney incorrectly advised him that, under this award, he was entitled to take Maria away from Ann. Dave drove to State A, picked Maria up at her preschool, and took her back to State B with him.

He was indicted for kidnapping in State A, extradited from State B, and tried. At trial, he testified that he had relied on his attorney's advice in taking Maria, and that at the time he believed his conduct was not illegal.

If the jury believes his testimony, Dave should be

(A) acquitted, because he acted on the advice of an attorney.
(B) acquitted, because he lacked a necessary mental element of the crime.
(C) convicted, because reliance on an attorney's advice is not a defense.
(D) convicted, provided a reasonable person would have known that the attorney's advice was erroneous.

81. Owen, the owner of Greenacre, a tract of land, mortgaged Greenacre to ABC Bank to secure his preexisting obligation to ABC Bank. The mortgage was promptly and properly recorded. Owen and Newton then entered into a valid written contract for the purchase and sale of Greenacre, which provided for the transfer of "a marketable title, free of encumbrances." The contract did not expressly refer to the mortgage.

Shortly after entering into the contract, Newton found another property that much better suited her needs and decided to try to avoid her contract with Owen. When Newton discovered the existence of the mortgage, she asserted that the title was encumbered and that she would not close. Owen responded by offering to provide for payment and discharge of the mortgage at the closing from the proceeds of the closing. Newton refused to go forward, and Owen brought an appropriate action against her for specific performance.

If the court holds for Owen in this action, it will most likely be because

(A) the mortgage is not entitled to priority because it was granted for preexisting obligations.
(B) the doctrine of equitable conversion supports the result.
(C) Owen's arrangements for the payment of the mortgage fully satisfied Owen's obligation to deliver marketable title.
(D) the existence of the mortgage was not Newton's real reason for refusing to close.

82. Pawn sued Dalton for injuries received when she fell down a stairway in Dalton's apartment building. Pawn, a guest in the building, alleged that she caught the heel of her shoe in a tear in the stair carpet. Pawn calls Witt, a tenant, to testify that Young, another tenant, had said to him a week before Pawn's fall: "When I paid my rent this morning, I told the manager he had better fix that torn carpet."

Young's statement, reported by Witt, is

(A) admissible, to prove that the carpet was defective.
(B) admissible, to prove that Dalton had notice of the defect.

(C) admissible, to prove both that the carpet was defective and that Dalton had notice of the defect.
(D) inadmissible, because it is hearsay not within any exception.

83. A law of the state of Wonatol imposed a generally applicable sales tax payable by the vendor. That law exempted from its provisions the sale of "all magazines, periodicals, newspapers, and books." In order to raise additional revenue, the state legislature eliminated that broad exemption and substituted a narrower exemption. The new, narrower exemption excluded from the state sales tax only the sale of those "magazines, periodicals, newspapers, and books that are published or distributed by a recognized religious faith and that consist wholly of writings sacred to such a religious faith."

Magazine is a monthly publication devoted to history and politics. Magazine paid under protest the sales tax due on its sales according to the amended sales tax law. Magazine then filed suit against the state in an appropriate state court for a refund of the sales taxes paid. It contended that the state's elimination of the earlier, broader exemption and adoption of the new, narrower exemption restricted to sacred writings of recognized religious faiths violates the First and Fourteenth Amendments to the Constitution.

In this case, the court will probably rule that

(A) Magazine lacks standing to sue for a refund of sales taxes imposed by a generally applicable state law because Article III of the Constitution precludes taxpayers from bringing such suits.
(B) the Eleventh Amendment bars the state court from exercising jurisdiction over this suit in the absence of a law of Wonatol expressly waiving the state's immunity.
(C) the new, narrower exemption from the state sales tax law violates the establishment clause of the First and Fourteenth Amendments by granting preferential state support to recognized religious faiths for the communication of their religious beliefs.
(D) the new, narrower exemption from the state sales tax law violates the freedom of the press guaranteed by the First and Fourteenth Amendments because it imposes a prior restraint on nonreligious publications that are required to pay the tax.

84. For five years, Rancher had kept his horse in a ten-acre field enclosed by a six-foot woven wire fence with six inches of barbed wire on top. The gate to the field was latched and could not be opened by an animal. Rancher had never had any trouble with people coming onto his property and bothering the horse, and the horse had never escaped from the field. One day, however, when Rancher went to the field, he found that the gate was open and the horse was gone. Shortly before Rancher's discovery, Driver was driving with due care on a nearby highway when suddenly Rancher's horse darted in front of his car. When Driver attempted to avoid hitting the horse, he lost control of the car, which then crashed into a tree. Driver was injured.

Driver sued Rancher to recover damages for his injuries and Rancher moved for summary judgment.

If the facts stated above are undisputed, the judge should

(A) deny the motion, because, pursuant to the doctrine of *res ipsa loquitur*, a jury could infer that Rancher was negligent.
(B) deny the motion, because an animal dangerous to highway users escaped from Rancher's property and caused the collision.
(C) grant the motion, because there is no evidence that Rancher was negligent.
(D) grant the motion, because Rancher did not knowingly permit the horse to run at large.

85. Defendant was prosecuted for bankruptcy fraud. Defendant's wife, now deceased, had

testified adversely to Defendant during earlier bankruptcy proceedings that involved similar issues. Although the wife had been cross-examined, no serious effort was made to challenge her credibility despite the availability of significant impeachment information. At the fraud trial, the prosecutor offers into, evidence the testimony given by Defendant's wife at the bankruptcy proceeding.

This evidence should be

(A) admitted, under the hearsay exception for former testimony.
(B) admitted, because it is a statement by a person identified with a party.
(C) excluded, because it is hearsay not within any exception.
(D) excluded, because Defendant has the right to prevent use of his spouse's testimony against him in a criminal case.

Questions 86-87 are based on the following fact situation.

Mermaid owns an exceptionally seaworthy boat that she charters for sport fishing at a $500 daily rate. The fee includes the use of the boat with Mermaid as the captain, and one other crew member, as well as fishing tackle and bait. On May 1, Phinney agreed with Mermaid that Phinney would have the full-day use of the boat on May 15 for himself and his family for $500. Phinney paid an advance deposit of $200 and signed an agreement that the deposit could be retained by Mermaid as liquidated damages in the event Phinney canceled or failed to appear.

86. For this question only, assume the following facts. At the time of contracting, Mermaid told Phinney to be at the dock at 5 a.m. on May 15. Phinney and his family, however, did not show up on May 15 until noon. Meantime, Mermaid agreed at 10 a.m. to take Tess and her family out fishing for the rest of the day. Tess had happened to come by and inquire about the possibility of such an outing. In view of the late hour, Mermaid charged Tess $400 and stayed out two hours beyond the customary return time. Phinney's failure to appear until noon was due to the fact that he had been trying to charter another boat across the bay at a lower rate and had gotten lost after he was unsuccessful in getting such a charter.

Which of the following is an accurate statement concerning the rights of the parties?

(A) Mermaid can retain the $200 paid by Phinney, because it would be difficult for Mermaid to establish her actual damages and the sum appears to have been a reasonable forecast in light of anticipated loss of profit from the charter.
(B) Mermaid is entitled to retain only $50 (10% of the contract price) and must return $150 to Phinney.
(C) Mermaid must return $100 to Phinney in order to avoid her own unjust enrichment at Phinney's expense.
(D) Mermaid must return $100 to Phinney, because the liquidated-damage clause under the circumstances would operate as a penalty.

87. For this question only, assume the following facts. On May 15 at 1 a.m., the Coast Guard had issued offshore "heavy weather" warnings and prohibited all small vessels the size of Mermaid's from leaving the harbor. This prohibition remained in effect throughout the day. Phinney did not appear at all on May 15, because he had heard the weather warnings on his radio.

Which of the following is an accurate statement?

(A) The contract is discharged because of impossibility, and Phinney is entitled to return of his deposit.
(B) The contract is discharged because of mutual mistake concerning an essential fact, and Phinney is entitled to return of his deposit.
(C) The contract is not discharged, because its performance was possible in view of the exceptional seaworthiness of Mermaid's boat, and Phinney is not entitled to return of his deposit.
(D) The contract is not discharged, and Phinney is not entitled to return of

his deposit, because the liquidated-damage clause in effect allocated the risk of bad weather to Phinney.

88. Eight years ago, Orben, prior to moving to a distant city, conveyed Blackacre, an isolated farm, to his son, Sam, by a quitclaim deed. Sam paid no consideration. Sam, who was 19 years old, without formal education, and without experience in business, took possession of Blackacre and operated the farm but neglected to record his deed. Subsequently, Orben conveyed Blackacre to Fred by warranty deed. Fred, a substantial land and timber promoter, paid valuable consideration for the deed to him. He was unaware of Sam's possession, his quitclaim deed, or his relationship to Orben. Fred promptly and properly recorded his deed and began removing timber from the land. Immediately upon learning of Fred's actions, Sam recorded his deed and brought an appropriate action to enjoin Fred from removing the timber and to quiet title in Sam. The recording act of the jurisdiction provides:

"No conveyance or mortgage of real property shall be good against subsequent purchasers for value and without notice unless the same be recorded according to law."

In this actions Fred should

(A) prevail, because a warranty deed for valuable consideration takes priority over a quitclaim deed without consideration.
(B) prevail, because Orben's subsequent conveyance to Fred revoked the gift to Sam.
(C) lose, because Sam's possession charged Fred with notice.
(D) lose, because the equities favor Sam.

89. Brown owned Blackacre, a tract of undeveloped land. Blackacre abuts Whiteacre, a tract of land owned by Agency, the state's governmental energy agency. At Whiteacre, Agency has operated a waste-to-electricity recycling facility for 12 years. Blackacre and Whiteacre are in a remote area and Whiteacre is the only developed parcel of real estate within a ten-mile radius. The boundary line between Blackacre and Whiteacre had never been surveyed or marked on the face of the earth.

During the past 12 years, some of the trucks bringing waste to the Agency facility have dumped their loads so that the piles of waste extend from Whiteacre onto a portion of Blackacre. However, prior to the four-week period during each calendar year when the Agency facility is closed for inspection and repairs, the waste piles are reduced to minimal levels so that during each of the four-week closures no waste was, in fact, piled on Blackacre. Neither Brown nor any representative of Agency knew the facts about the relation of the boundary line to the waste piles.

The time for acquiring title by adverse possession in the jurisdiction is ten years.

Last year, Brown died, and his son, Silas, succeeded him as the owner of Blackacre. Silas became aware of the facts, demanded that Agency stop using Blackacre for the piling of waste, and, when Agency refused his demand, brought an appropriate action to enjoin any such use of Blackacre in the future.

If Agency prevails in that action, it will be because

(A) the facts constitute adverse possession and title to the portion of Blackacre concerned has vested in Agency.
(B) Brown's failure to keep himself informed as to Agency's use of Blackacre and his failure to object constituted implied consent to the continuation of that use.
(C) the interest of the public in the conversion of waste to energy overrides any entitlement of Silas to equitable remedies.
(D) the power of eminent domain of the state makes the claim of Silas moot.

90. Defendant was charged with possession of cocaine with intent to distribute. He had

been stopped while driving a car and several pounds of cocaine were found in the trunk. In his opening statement, defendant's counsel asserted that his client had no key to the trunk and no knowledge of its contents. The prosecutor offers the state motor vehicle registration, shown to have been found in the glove compartment of the car, listing Defendant as the owner.

The registration should be

(A) admitted, as a statement against interest.
(B) admitted, as evidence of Defendant's close connection with the car and, therefore, knowledge of its contents.
(C) excluded, unless authenticated by testimony of or certification by a state official charged with custody of vehicle registration records.
(D) excluded, as hearsay not within any exception.

91. Donald was arrested in Marilyn's apartment after her neighbors had reported sounds of a struggle and the police had arrived to find Donald bent over Marilyn's prostrate body. Marilyn was rushed to the hospital where she lapsed into a coma. Despite the explanation that he was trying to revive Marilyn after she suddenly collapsed, Donald was charged with attempted rape and assault after a neighbor informed the police that she had heard Marilyn sobbing, "No, please no, let me alone."

At trial, the forensic evidence was inconclusive. The jury acquitted Donald of attempted rape but convicted him of assault. While he was serving his sentence for assault, Marilyn, who had never recovered from the coma, died. Donald was then indicted and tried on a charge of felony murder. In this common-law jurisdiction, there is no statute that prevents a prosecutor from proceeding in this manner, but Donald argued that a second trial for felony murder after his original trial for attempted rape and assault would violate the double jeopardy clause.

His claim is

(A) correct, because he was acquitted of the attempted rape charge.
(B) correct, because he was convicted of the assault charge.
(C) incorrect, because Marilyn had not died at the-time of the first trial and he was not placed in jeopardy for murder.
(D) incorrect, because he was convicted of the assault charge.

92. Ogle owned Greenacre, a tract of land, in fee simple. Five years ago, he executed and delivered to Lilly an instrument in the proper form of a warranty deed that conveyed Greenacre to Lilly "for and during the term of her natural life." No other estate or interest or person taking an interest was mentioned. Lilly took possession of Greenacre and has remained in possession.

Fifteen months ago, Ogle died, leaving a will that has been duly admitted to probate. The will, inter alia, had the following provision:

"I devise Greenacre to Mina for her natural life and from and after Mina's death to Rex, his heirs and assigns, forever."

Administration of Ogle's estate has been completed. Mina claims the immediate right to possession of Greenacre. Rex also asserts a right to immediate possession.

In an appropriate lawsuit to which Lilly, Mina, and Rex are parties, who should be adjudged to have the right to immediate possession?

(A) Lilly, because no subsequent act of Ogle would affect her life estate.
(B) Mina, because Ogle's will was the final and definitive expression of his intent.
(C) Mina, because Lilly's estate terminated with the death of Ogle.
(D) Rex, because Lilly's estate terminated with Ogle's death and all that Ogle had was the right to transfer his reversion in fee simple.

93. Devlin was charged with murder. Several witnesses testified that the crime was committed by a person of Devlin's general description who walked with a severe limp. Devlin in fact walks with a severe limp. He objected to a prosecution request that the court order him to walk across the courtroom in order to display his limp to the jury to assist it in determining whether Devlin was the person that the witnesses had seen.

    Devlin's objection will most likely be

    (A) sustained, because the order sought by the prosecution would violate Devlin's privilege against self-incrimination.
    (B) sustained, because the order sought by the prosecution would constitute an illegal search and seizure.
    (C) denied, because the order sought by the prosecution is a legitimate part of a proper courtroom identification process.
    (D) denied, because a criminal defendant has no legitimate expectation of privacy.

94. A statute of the state of Kiowa provided state monetary grants to private dance, theater, and opera groups located in that state. The statute required recipients of such grants to use the granted monies for the acquisition, construction, and maintenance of appropriate facilities for the public performance of their performing arts. The last section of the statute conditioned the award of each such grant on the recipient's agreement to refrain from all kinds of political lobbying calculated to secure additional tax support for the performing arts.

    The strongest constitutional basis for an attack upon the validity of the last section of the statute would be based upon the

    (A) commerce clause.
    (B) obligation of contracts clause.
    (C) Fifth Amendment.
    (D) First and Fourteenth Amendments.

95. Penkov suffered a severe loss when his manufacturing plant, located in a shallow ravine, was flooded during a sustained rainfall. The flooding occurred because City had failed to maintain its storm drain, which was located on City land above Penkov's premises, and because Railroad had failed to maintain its storm drain, which was located on Railroad land below Penkov's premises. The flooding would not have occurred if either one of the two storm drains had been maintained properly.

    Penkov sued Railroad to recover compensation for his loss. The evidence in the case established that the failures of the two drains were caused by the respective negligence of City and Railroad. There is no special rule insulating City from liability.

    In his action against Railroad, Penkov should recover

    (A) nothing, because he should have joined City, without whose negligence he would have suffered no loss.
    (B) nothing, unless he introduces evidence that enables the court reasonably to apportion responsibility between City and Railroad.
    (C) one-half his loss, in the absence of evidence that enables the court to allocate responsibility fairly between City and Railroad.
    (D) all of his loss, because but for Railroad's negligence none of the flooding would have occurred.

96. Smith asked Jones if he would loan him $500, promising to repay the amount within two weeks. Jones loaned him the $500. The next day Smith took the money to the race track and lost all of it betting on horse races. He then left town for six months. He has not repaid Jones.

    Smith has committed

    (A) both larceny by trick and obtaining money by false pretenses (although he can only be convicted of one offense).
    (B) larceny by trick only.

(C) obtaining money by false pretenses only.
(D) neither larceny by trick nor obtaining money by false pretenses.

97. Assume that Congress passed and the President signed the following statute:

"The appellate jurisdiction of the United States Supreme Court shall not extend to any case involving the constitutionality of any state statute limiting the circumstances in which a woman may obtain an abortion, or involving the constitutionality of this statute."

The strongest argument against the constitutionality of this statute is that

(A) Congress may not exercise its authority over the appellate jurisdiction of the Supreme Court in a way that seriously interferes with the establishment of a supreme and uniform body of federal constitutional law.
(B) Congress may only regulate the appellate jurisdiction of the Supreme Court over cases initially arising in federal courts.
(C) the appellate jurisdiction of the Supreme Court may only be altered by constitutional amendment.
(D) the statute violates the equal protection clause of the Fourteenth Amendment.

98. The federal statute admitting the state of Blue to the Union granted Blue certain public lands, and established some very ambiguous conditions on the subsequent disposition of these lands by Blue. This federal statute also required the new state to write those exact same conditions into its state constitution. One hundred years later, a statute of Blue dealing with the sale of these public lands was challenged in a state court lawsuit on the ground that it was inconsistent with the conditions contained in the federal statute, and with the provisions of the Blue Constitution that exactly copy the conditions contained in the federal statute. The trial court decision in this case was appealed to the Blue Supreme Court. In its opinion, the Blue Supreme Court dealt at length with the ambiguous language of the federal statute and with cases interpreting identical language in federal statutes admitting other states to the union. The Blue Supreme Court opinion did not discuss the similar provisions of the Blue Constitution, but it did hold that the challenged Blue statute is invalid because it is "Inconsistent with the language of the federal statute and therefore is inconsistent with the identical provisions of our state constitution."

If the losing party in the Blue Supreme Court seeks review of the decision of that court in the United States Supreme Court, the United States Supreme Court should

(A) accept the case for review and determine the validity and interpretation of the federal statute if it is an important and substantial question.
(B) ask the Blue Supreme Court to indicate more clearly whether it relied on the state constitutional provision in rendering its decision.
(C) decline to review the case on the ground that the decision of the Blue Supreme Court rests on an adequate and independent state ground.
(D) decline to review the case because a decision by a state supreme court concerning the proper disposition of state public lands is not reviewable by the United States Supreme Court.

99. Trawf, the manager of a state fair, contracted with Schweinebauch, a renowned hog breeder, to exhibit Schweinebauch's world champion animal, Megahawg, for the three weeks of the annual fair, at the conclusion of which Schweinebauch would receive an honorarium of $300. Two days before the opening of the fair, Megahawg took sick with boarsitis, a communicable disease among swine, and, under the applicable state quarantine law, very probably could not be exhibited for at least a month.

Upon learning this, Trawf can legally pursue which of the following courses of action with respect to his contract with Schweinebauch?

(A) Suspend his own performance, demand assurances from Schweinebauch, and treat a failure by Schweinebauch to give them as an actionable repudiation.
(B) Suspend his own performance and recover damages from Schweinebauch for breach of contract unless Schweinebauch at once supplies an undiseased hog of exhibition quality as a substitute for Megahawg.
(C) Terminate his own performance and treat Megahawg's illness as discharging all remaining duties under the contract.
(D) Terminate the contract, but only if he (Trawf) seeks promptly to obtain for the exhibit a suitable substitute for Megahawg from another hog owner.

100. The manager of a department store noticed that Paula was carrying a scarf with her as she examined various items in the blouse department. The manager recognized the scarf as an expensive one carried by the store. Paula was trying to find a blouse that matched a color in the scarf, and, after a while, found one. The manager then saw Paula put the scarf into her purse, pay for the blouse, and head for the door. The manager, who was eight inches taller than Paula, blocked Paula's way to the door and asked to see the scarf in Paula's purse. Paula produced the scarf, as well as a receipt for it, showing that it had been purchased from the store on the previous day. The manager then told Paula there was no problem, and stepped out of her way.

If Paula brings a claim against the store based on false imprisonment, the store's best defense would be that

(A) by carrying the scarf in public view and then putting it into her purse, Paula assumed the risk of being detained.
(B) the manager had a reasonable belief that Paula was shoplifting and detained her only briefly for a reasonable investigation of the f acts.
(C) Paula should have realized that her conduct would create a reasonable belief that facts existed warranting a privilege to detain.
(D) Paula was not detained, but was merely questioned about the scarf.

STOP

IF YOU FINISH BEFORE TIME IS CALLED, CHECK YOUR WORK ON THIS TEST.

Multistate Bar Examination

PM Book
Time-3 hours

Directions: Each of the questions or incomplete statements below is followed by four suggested answers or completions. You are to choose the best of the stated alternatives. Answer all questions according to the generally accepted view, except where otherwise noted.

For the purposes of this test, you are to assume that Articles 1 and 2 of the Uniform Commercial Code have been adopted. You are also to assume relevant application of Article 9 of the UCC concerning fixtures. The Federal Rules of Evidence are deemed to control. The terms "Constitution," "constitutional," and "unconstitutional" refer to the federal Constitution unless indicated to the contrary. You are also to assume that there is no applicable community property law, no guest statute, and no No-Fault Insurance Act unless otherwise specified. In negligence cases, if fault on the claimant's part is or may be relevant, the statement of facts for the particular question will identify the contributory or comparative negligence rule that is to be applied.

101. A proposed federal statute would prohibit all types of discrimination against black persons on the basis of their race in every business transaction executed anywhere in the United States by any person or entity, governmental or private.

Is this proposed federal statute likely to be constitutional?

(A) Yes, because it could reasonably be viewed as an exercise of Congress's authority to enact laws for the general welfare.
(B) Yes, because it could reasonably be viewed as a means of enforcing the provisions of the Thirteenth Amendment.
(C) No, because it would regulate purely local transactions that are not in interstate commerce.
(D) No, because it would invade the powers reserved to the states by the Tenth Amendment.

102. Sam told Horace, his neighbor, that he was going away for two weeks and asked Horace to keep an eye on his house. Horace agreed. Sam gave Horace a key to use to check on the house.

Horace decided to have a party in Sam's house. He invited a number of friends. One friend, Lewis, went into Sam's bedroom, took some of Sam's rings, and put them in his pocket.

Which of the following is true?

(A) Horace and Lewis are guilty of burglary.
(B) Horace is guilty of burglary and Lewis is guilty of larceny.
(C) Horace is guilty of trespass and Lewis is guilty of larceny.
(D) Lewis is guilty of larceny and Horace is not guilty of any crime.

103. John's father, Jeremiah, died in Hospital. Hospital maintains a morgue with refrigerated drawers a bit larger than a human body. Jeremiah's body was placed in such a drawer awaiting pickup by a mortician. Before the mortician called for the body, a Hospital orderly placed two opaque plastic bags in the drawer with Jeremiah's body. One bag contained Jeremiah's personal effects, and the other contained an amputated leg from some other Hospital patient. It is stipulated that Hospital was negligent to allow the amputated leg to get into Jeremiah's drawer. The mortician delivered the two opaque plastic bags to John, assuming both contained personal effects. John was shocked when he opened the bag containing the amputated leg. John sued Hospital to recover for his emotional distress. At the trial, John testified that the experience had been extremely upsetting that he had had recurring nightmares about it, and that his family and business relationships had been adversely affected for a period of several months. He did not seek medical or psychiatric treatment for his emotional distress.

Who should prevail?

- (A) John, because of the sensitivity people have regarding the care of the bodies of deceased relatives.
- (B) John, because hospitals are strictly liable for mishandling dead bodies.
- (C) Hospital, because John did not require medical or psychiatric treatment.
- (D) Hospital, because John suffered no bodily harm.

104. Able was the owner of Greenacre, a large tract of land. Able entered into a binding written contract with Baker for the sale and purchase of Greenacre for $125,000. The contract required Able to convey marketable record title.

Baker decided to protect his interest and promptly and properly recorded the contract.

Thereafter, but before the date scheduled for the closing, Charlie obtained and properly filed a final judgment against Able in the amount of $1 million in a personal injury suit. A statute in the jurisdiction provides: "Any judgment properly filed shall, for ten years from filing, be a lien on the real property then owned or subsequently acquired by any person against whom the judgment is rendered."

The recording act of the jurisdiction authorizes recording of contracts and also provides: "No conveyance or mortgage of real property shall be good against subsequent purchasers for value and without notice unless the same be recorded according to law."

There are no other relevant statutory provisions.

At the closing, Baker declined to accept the title of Able on the ground that Charlie's judgment lien encumbered the title he would receive and rendered it unmarketable. Able brought an appropriate action against Baker for specific performance of the contract and joined Charlie as a party.

In this action, the judgment should be for

- (A) Able, because in equity a purchaser takes free of judgment liens.
- (B) Able, because the contract had been recorded.
- (C) Baker, because Able cannot benefit from Baker's action in recording the contract.
- (D) Baker, because the statute creating judgment liens takes precedence over the recording act.

105. Post sued Dint for dissolution of their year-long partnership. One issue concerned the amount of money Post had received in cash. It was customary for Dint to give Post money from the cash register as Post needed it for personal expenses. Post testified that, as he received money, he jotted down the amounts in the partnership ledger. Although Dint had access to the ledger, he made no changes in it. The ledger was admitted into evidence. Dint seeks to testify to his memory of much larger amounts he had given Post.

Dint's testimony is

- (A) admissible, because it is based on Dint's firsthand knowledge.
- (B) admissible, because the ledger entries offered by a party opponent opened the door.
- (C) inadmissible, because the ledger is the best evidence of the amounts Post received.
- (D) inadmissible, because Dint's failure to challenge the accuracy of the ledger constituted an adoptive admission.

106. In a signed writing, Nimrod contracted to purchase a 25-foot travel trailer from Trailco for $15,000, cash on delivery no later than June 1. Nimrod arrived at the Trailco sales lot on Sunday, May 31, to pay for and take delivery of the trailer, but refused to do so when he discovered that the spare tire was missing.

Trailco offered to install a spare tire on Monday when its service department would open, but Nimrod replied that he did not want the trailer and would purchase another one elsewhere.

Which of the following is accurate?

(A) Nimrod had a right to reject the trailer, but Trailco was entitled to a reasonable opportunity to cure the defect.
(B) Nimrod had a right to reject the trailer and terminate the contract under the perfect tender rule.
(C) Nimrod was required to accept the trailer, because the defect could be readily cured.
(D) Nimrod was required to accept the trailer, because the defect did not substantially impair its value.

107. Oker owned in fee simple two adjoining lots, Lots 1 and 2. He conveyed in fee simple Lot 1 to Frank. The deed was in usual form of a warranty deed with the following provision inserted in the appropriate place:

"Grantor, for himself, his heirs and assigns, does covenant and agree that any reasonable expense incurred by grantee, his heirs and assigns, as the result of having to repair the retaining wall presently situated on Lot 1 at the common boundary with Lot 2, shall be reimbursed one-half the costs of repairs; and by this provision the parties intend a covenant running with, the land."

Frank conveyed Lot 1 in fee simple to Sara by warranty deed in usual and regular form. The deed omitted any reference to the retaining wall or any covenant. Fifty years after Oker's conveyance to Frank, Sara conveyed Lot 1 in fee simple to Tim by warranty deed in usual form; this deed omitted any reference to the retaining wall or the covenant.

There is no statute that applies to any aspect of the problems presented except a recording act and a statute providing for acquisition of title after ten years of adverse possession.

All conveyances by deeds were for a consideration equal to fair market value.

The deed from Oker to Frank was never recorded. All other deeds were promptly and properly recorded.

Lot 2 is now owned by Henry, who took by intestate succession from Oker, now dead.

Tim expended $3,500 on the retaining wall. Then he obtained all of the original deeds in the chain from Oker to him. Shortly thereafter, Tim discovered the covenant in Oker's deed to Frank. He demanded that Henry pay $1,750, and when Henry refused, Tim instituted an appropriate action to recover that sum from Henry. In such action, Henry asserted all defenses available to him.

If judgment is for Henry, it will be because

(A) Tim is barred by adverse possession.
(B) Frank's deed from Oker was never recorded.
(C) Tim did not know about the covenant until after he had incurred the expenses and, hence, could not have relied on it.
(D) Tim's expenditures were not proved to be reasonable and customary.

108. While Prudence was leaving an elevator, it suddenly dropped several inches, causing her to fall. An investigation of the accident revealed that the elevator dropped because it had been negligently maintained by the Acme Elevator Company. Acme had a contract with the owner of the building to inspect and maintain the elevator. Prudence's fall severely aggravated a preexisting physical disability.

If Prudence sues Acme Elevator Company for damages for her injuries, she should recover

(A) nothing, if Acme could not reasonably have been expected to foresee the extent of the harm that Prudence suffered as a result of the accident.
(B) nothing, if the accident would not have caused significant harm to an ordinarily prudent elevator passenger.

(C) damages for the full amount of her disability, because a tortfeasor must take its victim as it finds her.
(D) damages for the injury caused by the falling elevator, including the aggravation of her preexisting disability.

109. Dix is on trial for killing Vetter. prosecutor calls Winn to testify that after being shot, Vetter said, "Dix did it." Before the testimony is given, Dix's lawyer asks for a hearing on whether Vetter believed his death was imminent when he made the statement.

Before permitting evidence of the dying declaration, the judge should hear evidence on the issue from

(A) both sides, with the jury not present, and decide whether Winn may testify to Vetter's statement.
(B) both sides, with the jury present, and decide whether Winn may testify to Vetter's statement.
(C) both sides, with the jury present, and allow the jury to determine whether Winn may testify to Vetter's statement.
(D) the prosecutor only, with the jury not present, and if the judge believes a jury could reasonably find that Vetter knew he was dying, permit Winn to testify to the statement, with Dix allowed to offer evidence on the issue as a part of the defendant's case.

110. Police received an anonymous tip that Tusitala was growing marijuana in her backyard, which was surrounded by a 15-foot high, solid wooden fence. Officer Boa was unable to view the yard from the street, so he used a police helicopter to fly over Tusitala's house. Boa identified a large patch of marijuana plants growing right next to the house and used this observation to obtain a search warrant.

Tusitala is prosecuted for possession of marijuana and moves to suppress use of the marijuana in evidence.

The court should

(A) grant the motion, because the only purpose of Boals flight was to observe the yard.
(B) grant the motion, because Tusitala had a reasonable expectation of privacy in the curtilage around her house and the police did not have a warrant.
(C) deny the motion, because a warrant is not required for a search of a residential yard.
(D) deny the motion, because Tusitala had no reasonable expectation of privacy from aerial observation.

111. Buyem faxed the following signed message to Zeller, his long-time widget supplier: "Urgently need blue widgets. Ship immediately three gross at your current list price of $600." Upon receipt of the fax, Zeller shipped three gross of red widgets to Buyem, and f axed to Buyem the following message: "Temporarily out of blue. In case red will help, am shipping three gross at the same price. Hope you can use them."

Upon Buyem's timely receipt of both the shipment and Zeller's fax, which of the following best describes the rights and duties of Buyem and Zeller?

(A) Buyem may accept the shipment, in which case he must pay Zeller the list price, or he must reject the shipment and recover from Zeller for total breach of contract.
(B) Buyem may accept the shipment, in which case he must pay Zeller the list price, or he may reject the shipment, in which case he has no further rights against Zeller.
(C) Buyem may accept the shipment, in which case he must pay Zeller the list price, less any damages sustained because of the nonconforming shipment, or he may reject the shipment and recover from Zeller for total breach of contract, subject to Zeller's right to cure.
(D) Buyem may accept the shipment, in which case he must pay Zeller the list price, less any damages sustained because of the nonconforming shipment, or he

may reject the shipment provided that he promptly covers by obtaining conforming widgets from another supplier.

112. Members of a religious group calling itself the Friends of Lucifer believe in Lucifer as their Supreme Being. The members of this group meet once a year on top of Mt. Snow, located in a U.S. National Park, to hold an overnight encampment and a midnight dance around a large campfire. They believe this overnight encampment and all of its rituals are required by Lucifer to be held on the top of Mt. Snow. U.S. National Park Service rules that have been consistently enforced prohibit all overnight camping and all campfires on Mt. Snow because of the very great dangers overnight camping and campfires would pose in that particular location. As a result, the park Superintendent denied a request by the Friends of Lucifer for a permit to conduct these activities on top of Mt. Snow. The park Superintendent, who was known to be violently opposed to cults and other unconventional groups had, in the past, issued permits to conventional religious groups to conduct sunrise services in other areas of that U.S. National Park.
The Friends of Lucifer brought suit in Federal Court against the U.S. National Park Service and the Superintendent of the park to compel issuance of the requested permit.

As a matter of constitutional law, the most appropriate result in this suit would be a decision that denial of the permit was

(A) invalid, because the free exercise clause of the First Amendment prohibits the Park Service from knowingly interfering with religious conduct.
(B) invalid, because these facts demonstrate that the action of the Park Service purposefully and invidiously discriminated against the Friends of Lucifer.
(C) valid, because the establishment clause of the First Amendment prohibits the holding of religious ceremonies on federal land.
(D) valid, because religiously motivated conduct may be subjected to nondiscriminatory time, place, and manner restrictions that advance important public interests.

113. Park sued Davis Co. for injuries suffered in the crash of Park's dune buggy, allegedly caused by a defective auto part manufactured by Davis Co. Davis Co. claims that the part was a fraudulent imitation, not produced by Davis Co.

Which of the following is NOT admissible on the issue of whether the part was manufactured by Davis Co.?

(A) The fact that the defective part bears Davis Co.'s insignia or trademark.
(B) Testimony that the part was purchased from a parts house to which Davis Co. regularly sold parts.
(C) The part itself and a concededly genuine part manufactured by Davis Co. (for the jury's comparison).
(D) A judgment for another plaintiff against Davis Co. in another case involving substantially similar facts.

114. Anna entered into a valid written contract to purchase Blackacre, a large tract of land, from Jones for its fair market value of $50,000. The contract was assignable by Anna. Anna duly notified Jones to convey title to Anna and Charles, Charles being Anna's friend whom Anna had not seen for many years.
When Anna learned that Charles would have to sign certain documents in connection with the closing, she prevailed upon her brother, Donald, to attend the closing and pretend to be Charles. Anna and Donald attended the closing, and Jones executed an instrument in the proper form of a deed, purporting to convey Blackacre to Anna and Charles, as tenants in common. Donald pretended that he was Charles, and he signed Charles's name to all the required documents. Anna provided the entire $50,000 consideration for the transaction. The deed was promptly and properly recorded.

Unknown to Anna or Donald, Charles had died several months before the closing. Charles's will, which was duly probated, devised "All my real estate to my nephew, Nelson" and the residue of his estate to Anna.

Anna and Nelson have been unable to agree as to the status or disposition of Blackacre. Nelson brought an appropriate action against Jones and Anna to quiet legal title to an undivided one-half interest in Blackacre.

The court should hold that legal title to Blackacre is vested

(A) all in Jones.
(B) all in Anna.
(C) one-half in Anna and one-half in Jones.
(D) one-half in Anna and one-half in Nelson.

Questions 115-116 are based on the following fact situation.

Staff, Inc., a flour wholesaler, contracted to deliver to Eclaire, a producer of fine baked goods, her flour requirements for a one-year period. Before delivery of the first scheduled installment, Staff sold its business and "assigned" all of its sale contracts to Miller, Inc., another reputable and long-time flour wholesaler. Staff informed Eclaire of this transaction.

115. For this question only, assume that when Miller tendered the first installment to Eclaire in compliance with the Staff-Eclaire contract, Eclaire refused to accept the goods.

Which of the following arguments, if any, legally support(s) Eclaire's rejection of the goods?

I. Executory requirements contracts are nonassignable.
II. Duties under an executory bilateral contract are assumable only by an express promise to perform on the part of the delegates.
III. Language of "assignment" in the transfer for value of a bilateral sale-of-goods contract effects only a transfer of rights, not a delegation of duties.

(A) I only.
(B) II and III only.
(C) I and II and III.
(D) Neither I nor II nor III.

116. For this question only, assume that Eclaire accepted Miller's delivery of the first installment under the Staff-Eclaire contract, but that Eclaire paid the contract price for that installment to Staff and refused to pay anything to Miller.

In an action by Miller against Eclaire for the contractual amount of the first installment, which of the following, if any, will be an effective defense for Eclaire?

I. Eclaire had not expressly agreed to accept Miller as her flour supplier.
II. Eclaire's payment of the contractual installment to Staff discharged her obligation.
III. Staff remained obligated to Eclaire even though Staff had assigned the contract to Miller.

(A) I only.
(B) II only.
(C) I and III only.
(D) Neither I nor II nor III.

117. On October 22, Officer Jones submitted an application for a warrant to search 217 Elm Street for cocaine. In the application, Officer Jones stated under oath that he believed there was cocaine at that location because of information supplied to him on the morning of October 22 by Susie Schultz. He described Schultz as a cocaine user who had previously supplied accurate information concerning the use of cocaine in the community and summarized what Schultz had told him as follows: the previous night, October 21, Schultz was in Robert Redd's house at 217 Elm Street. Redd gave her cocaine. She also saw three cellophane bags containing cocaine in his bedroom.

The warrant was issued and a search of 217 Elm Street was conducted on October 22. The search turned up a quantity of marijuana but no cocaine. Robert Redd was arrested and charged with possession of marijuana. Redd moved to suppress the use of the marijuana as evidence contending that Susie Schultz was not in 217 Elm Street on October 21 or at any other time.

If, after hearing evidence, the judge concludes that the statement in the application attributed to Susie Schultz is incorrect, the judge should grant the motion to suppress

(A) because the application contains a material statement that is false.
(B) because of the false statement and because no cocaine was found in the house.
(C) only if he also finds that Susie Schultz's statement was a deliberate lie.
(D) only if he also finds that Officer Jones knew the statement was false.

118. The Personnel Handbook of Green City contains all of that city's personnel policies. One section of the handbook states that "where feasible and practicable supervisors are encouraged to follow the procedures specified in this Handbook before discharging a city employee." Those specified procedures include a communication to the employee of the reasons for the contemplated discharge and an opportunity for a pretermination trial-type hearing at which the employee may challenge those reasons. After a year of service, Baker, the secretary to the Green City Council, was discharged without receiving any communication of reasons for her contemplated discharge and without receiving an opportunity for a pretermination trial-type hearing. Baker files suit in federal district court to challenge her discharge solely on constitutional grounds.

Which of the following best describes the initial burden of persuasion in that suit?

(A) The Green City Council must demonstrate that its personnel handbook created no constitutionally protected interest in city employment or in the procedures by which such employment is terminated.
(B) The Green City Council must demonstrate that Baker's termination was for good cause.
(C) Baker must demonstrate that state law creates a constitutionally protected interest in her employment or in the procedures by which her employment is terminated.
(D) Baker must demonstrate that she reasonably believed that she could work for Green City for as long as she wished.

119. Dean was prosecuted in federal court for making threats against the President of the United States. Dean was a voluntary patient in a private psychiatric hospital and told a nurse, shortly before the President came to town, that Dean planned to shoot the President. The nurse reported the threat to FBI agents.

Dean's motion to prevent the nurse's testifying is likely to be

(A) successful, because the statement was made in a medical setting.
(B) successful, because the nurse violated a confidence in reporting the statement.
(C) unsuccessful, because the statement was not within any privilege.
(D) unsuccessful, because Dean had not been committed involuntarily by court order.

120. Able, who owned Blackacre, a residential lot improved with a dwelling, conveyed it for a valuable consideration to Baker. The dwelling had been constructed by a prior owner. Baker had inspected Blackacre prior to the purchase and discovered no defects. After moving in, Baker became aware that sewage seeped into the basement when the toilets were flushed. Able said that this defect had been present for years and that he had taken no steps to hide the facts from Baker. Baker paid for the necessary repairs and brought an appropriate action against Able to recover his cost of repair.

If Baker wins, it will be because

(A) Able failed to disclose a latent defect.
(B) Baker made a proper inspection.
(C) the situation constitutes a health hazard.
(D) Able breached the implied warranty of habitability and fitness for purpose.

121. Gardner's backyard, which is landscaped with expensive flowers and shrubs, is adjacent to a golf course. While Driver was playing golf on the course, a thunderstorm suddenly came up. As Driver was returning to the clubhouse in his golf cart, lightning struck a tree on the course, and the tree began to fall in Driver's direction. In order to avoid being hit by the tree, Driver deliberately steered his cart onto Gardner's property, causing substantial damage to Gardner's expensive plantings.

In an action by Gardner against Driver to recover damages for the harm to his plantings, Gardner will

(A) prevail, because, although occasioned by necessity, Driver's entry onto Gardner's property was for Driver's benefit.
(B) prevail, for nominal images only, because Driver was privileged to enter Gardner's property.
(C) not prevail, because the lightning was an act of God.
(D) not prevail, because Driver's entry onto Gardner's property was occasioned by necessity and therefore privileged.

122. Steve, in desperate need of money, decided to hold up a local convenience store. Determined not to harm anyone, he carried a toy gun that resembled a real gun. In the store, he pointed the toy gun at the clerk and demanded money. A customer who entered the store and saw the robbery in progress pulled his own gun and fired at Steve. The bullet missed Steve but struck and killed the clerk.

Steve was charged with felony murder.

His best argument for being found NOT guilty is that he

(A) did not intend to kill.
(B) did not commit the robbery because he never acquired any money from the clerk.
(C) did not intend to create any risk of harm.
(D) is not responsible for the acts of the customer.

123. Client consulted Lawyer about handling the sale of Client's building, and asked Lawyer what her legal fee would be. Lawyer replied that her usual charge was $100 per hour, and estimated that the legal work on behalf of Client would cost about $5,000 at that rate. Client said, "Okay; let's proceed with it," and Lawyer timely and successfully completed the work. Because of unexpected title problems, Lawyer reasonably spent 75 hours on the matter and shortly thereafter mailed Client a bill for $7,500, with a letter itemizing the work performed and time spent. Client responded by a letter expressing his good-faith belief that Lawyer had agreed to a total fee of no more than $5,000. Client enclosed a check in the amount of $5,000 payable to Lawyer and conspicuously marked, "Payment in full for legal services in connection with the sale of Client's building." Despite reading the "Payment in full ... " language, Lawyer, without any notation of protest or reservation of rights, endorsed and deposited the check to her bank account. The check was duly paid by Client's bank. A few days later, Lawyer unsuccessfully demanded payment from Client of the $2,500 difference between the amount of her bill and the check, and now sues Client for that difference.

What, if anything, can Lawyer recover from Client?

(A) Nothing, because the risk of unexpected title problems in a real-property transaction is properly allocable to the seller's attorney and thus to Lawyer in this case.
(B) Nothing, because the amount of Lawyer's fee was disputed in good

faith by Client, and Lawyer impliedly agreed to an accord and satisfaction.

(C) $2,500, because Client agreed to an hourly rate for as many hours as the work reasonably required, and the sum of $5,000 was merely an estimate.

(D) The reasonable value of Lawyer's services in excess of $5,000, if any, because there was no specific agreement on the total amount of Lawyer's fee.

124. Pauline and Doris own adjacent parcels of land. On each of their parcels was a low-rise office building. The two office buildings were of the same height.

Last year Doris decided to demolish the low-rise office building on her parcel and to erect a new high-rise office building of substantially greater height on the parcel as permitted by the zoning and building ordinances. She secured all the governmental approvals necessary to pursue her project.

As Doris's new building was in the course of construction, Pauline realized that the shadows it would create would place her (Pauline's) building in such deep shade that the rent she could charge for space in her building would be substantially reduced.

Pauline brought an appropriate action against Doris to enjoin the construction in order to eliminate the shadow problem and for damages. Pauline presented uncontroverted evidence that her evaluation as to the impact of the shadow on the fair rental value of her building was correct. There is no statute or ordinance (other than the building and zoning ordinances) that is applicable to the issues before the court.

The court should

(A) grant to Pauline the requested injunction.
(B) award Pauline damages measured by the loss of rental value, but not an injunction.
(C) grant judgment for Doris, because she had secured all the necessary governmental approvals for the new building.
(D) grant judgment for Doris, because Pauline has no legal right to have sunshine continue to reach the windows of her building.

Questions 125-126 are based on the following fact situation.

Dumont, a real estate developer, was trying to purchase land on which he intended to build a large commercial development. Perkins, an elderly widow, had rejected all of Dumont's offers to buy her ancestral home, where she had lived all her life and which was located in the middle of Dumont's planned development. Finally, Dumont offered her $250,000. He told her that it was his last offer and that if she rejected it, state law authorized him to have her property condemned.

Perkins then consulted her nephew, a law student, who researched the question and advised her that Dumont had no power of condemnation under state law. Perkins had been badly frightened by Dumont's threat, and was outraged when she learned that Dumont had lied to her.

125. If Perkins sues Dumont for damages for emotional distress, will she prevail?

(A) Yes, if Dumont's action was extreme and outrageous.
(B) Yes, because Perkins was frightened and outraged.
(C) No, if Perkins did not suffer emotional distress that was severe.
(D) No, if it was not Dumont's purpose to cause emotional distress.

126. If Perkins asserts a claim based on misrepresentation against Dumont, will she prevail?

(A) Yes, if Dumont knew he had no legal power of condemnation.
(B) Yes, if Dumont tried to take unfair advantage of a gross difference between himself and Perkins in commercial knowledge and experience.
(C) No, if Dumont's offer of $250,000 equaled or exceeded the market value of Perkins's property.
(D) No, because Perkins suffered no pecuniary loss.

127. State Y employs the Model Penal Code or American Law Institute test for insanity, and requires the state to prove sanity, when it is in issue, beyond a reasonable doubt. At Askew's trial for murder, he pleaded insanity. The state put on an expert psychiatrist who had examined Askew. He testified that, in his opinion, Askew was sane at the time of the murder. Askew's attorney did not introduce expert testimony on the question of sanity. Rather, he presented lay witnesses who testified that, in their opinion, Askew was insane at the time of the murder. At the end of the trial, each side moves for a directed verdict on the question of sanity.

Which of the following correctly describes the judge's situation?

(A) She may grant a directed verdict for the defense if she believes that the jury could not find the prosecution to have proved sanity beyond a reasonable doubt.
(B) She may grant a directed verdict for the prosecution if she believes that Askew's witnesses on the insanity question are not believable.
(C) She may not grant a directed verdict for the defense, because the state had expert testimony and the defense only lay witnesses.
(D) She may grant a directed verdict for the prosecution if she is convinced by their experts that Askew was sane beyond a reasonable doubt.

128. Trelawney worked at a day-care center run by the Happy Faces Day Care Corporation. At the center, one of the young charges, Smith, often arrived with bruises and welts on his back and legs. A statute in the jurisdiction requires all day-care workers to report to the police cases where there is probable cause to suspect child abuse and provides for immediate removal from the home of any suspected child abuse victims. Trelawney was not aware of this statute. Nevertheless, he did report Smith's condition to his supervisor, who advised him to keep quiet about it so the day-care center would not get into trouble for defaming a parent. About two weeks after Trelawney first noticed Smith's condition, Smith was beaten to death by his father. Trelawney has been charged with murder in the death of Smith. The evidence at trial disclosed, in addition to the above, that the child had been the victim of beatings by the father for some time, and that these earlier beatings had been responsible for the marks that Trelawney had seen. Smith's mother had been aware of the beatings but had not stopped them because she was herself afraid of Smith's father.

Trelawney's best argument that he is NOT guilty of murder is

(A) he was not aware of the duty-to-report statute.
(B) he lacked the mental state necessary to the commission of the crime.
(C) his omission was not the proximate cause of death.
(D) the day-care corporation, rather than Trelawney, was guilty of the omission, which was sanctioned by its supervisory-level agent.

Questions 129-130 are based on the following fact situation.

Perkins and Morton were passengers sitting in adjoining seats on a flight on Delval Airline. There were many empty seats on the aircraft.

During the flight, a flight attendant served Morton nine drinks. As Morton became more and more obviously intoxicated and attempted to engage Perkins in a conversation, Perkins chose to ignore Morton. This angered Morton, who suddenly struck Perkins in the face, giving her a black eye.

129. If Perkins asserts a claim for damages against Delval Airline based on negligence, Perkins will

(A) not recover, because a person is not required by law to come to the assistance of another who is imperiled by a third party.
(B) not recover, if Perkins could easily have moved to another seat.

(C) recover, because a common carrier is strictly liable for injuries suffered by a passenger while aboard the carrier.

(D) recover, if the flight attendants should have perceived Morton's condition and acted to protect Perkins before the blow was struck.

130. If Perkins asserts a claim for damages against Delval Airline based on battery, she will

(A) prevail, because she suffered an intentionally inflicted harmful or offensive contact.
(B) prevail, if the flight attendant acted recklessly in continuing to serve liquor to Morton.
(C) not prevail, because Morton was not acting as an agent or employee of Delval Airline.
(D) not prevail, unless she can establish some permanent injury from the contact.

131. Terrorists in the foreign country of Ruritania kidnapped the United States ambassador to that country. They threatened to kill her unless the President of the United States secured the release of an identified person who was a citizen of Ruritania and was held in a prison of the state of Aurora in the United States pursuant to a valid conviction by that state.

The President responded by entering into an agreement with Ruritania which provided that Ruritania would secure the release of the United States ambassador on a specified date in return for action by the President that would secure the release of the identified person held in the Aurora prison. The President then ordered the governor of Aurora to release the prisoner in question. The governor refused. No federal statutes are applicable.

Which of the following is the strongest constitutional argument for the authority of the President to take action in these circumstances requiring the governor of Aurora to release the Aurora prisoner?

(A) The power of the President to conduct the foreign affairs of the United States includes a plenary authority to take whatever action the President deems wise to protect the safety of our diplomatic agents.
(B) The power of the President to appoint ambassadors authorizes him to take any action that he may think desirable to protect them from injury because, upon appointment, those officials become agents of the President.
(C) The power of the President to negotiate with foreign nations impliedly authorizes the President to make executive agreements with them which prevail over state law.
(D) The duty of the President to execute faithfully the laws authorizes him to resolve finally any conflicts between state and federal interests, making the determination of such matters wholly nonjusticiable.

132. Damson was charged with murder, and Wagner testified for the prosecution. On cross-examination of Wagner, Damson seeks to elicit an admission that Wagner was also charged with the same murder and that the prosecutor told her, "If you testify against Damson, we will drop the charges against you after the conclusion of Damson's trial."

The evidence about the prosecutor's promise is

(A) admissible, as proper impeachment of Wagner.
(B) admissible, as an admission by an agent of a party-opponent.
(C) inadmissible, because the law encourages plea-bargaining.
(D) inadmissible, because the evidence is hearsay not within any exception.

Questions 133-134 are based on the following fact situation.

On November 1, Debbit, an accountant, and Barrister, a lawyer, contracted for the sale by Debbit to Barrister of the law books Debbit had inherited from his father. Barrister agreed to pay the purchase price of $10,000 when Debbit delivered the books on December 1.

On November 10, Barrister received a signed letter from Debbit that stated: "I have decided to dispose of the book stacks containing the law books you have already purchased. If you want the stacks, I will deliver them to you along with the books on December 1 at no additional cost to you. Let me know before November 15 whether you want them. I will not sell them to anyone else before then." On November 14, Barrister faxed and Debbit received the following message: "I accept your offer of the stacks." Debbit was not a merchant with respect to either law books or book stacks.

133. Debbit is contractually obligated to deliver the stacks because

(A) Barrister provided a new bargained-for exchange by agreeing to take the stacks.
(B) Debbit's letter (received by Barrister on November 10) and Barrister's fax-message of November 14 constituted an effective modification of the original sale-of-books contract.
(C) Barrister's tax-message of November 14 operated to rescind unilaterally the original sale-of-books contract.
(D) Debbit's letter (received by Barrister on November 10) waived the bargained-for consideration that would otherwise be required.

134. For this question only assume that on November 12 Debbit told Barrister that he had decided not to part with the stacks.

Will this communication operate as a legally effective revocation of his offer to deliver the stacks?

(A) Yes, because Barrister had a pre-existing obligation to pay $10,000 for the law books.
(B) Yes, because Debbit was not a merchant with respect to book stacks.
(C) No, because Debbit had given a signed assurance that the offer would be held open until November 15.
(D) No, because by delaying his acceptance until November 14, Barrister detrimentally relied on Debbit's promise not to sell the stacks to anyone else in the meantime.

135. Seller owned Blackacre, improved with an aging four-story warehouse. The warehouse was built to the lot lines on all four sides. On the street side, recessed loading docks permitted semi trailers to be backed in. After the tractors were unhooked, the trailers extended into the street and occupied most of one lane of the street. Over the years, as trailers became larger, the blocking of the street became more severe. The municipality advised Seller that the loading docks could not continue to be used because the trailers blocked the street; it gave Seller 90 days to cease and desist.

During the 90 days, Seller sold and conveyed Blackacre by warranty deed for a substantial consideration to Buyer. The problem of the loading docks was not discussed in the negotiations.

Upon expiration of the 90 days, the municipality required Buyer to stop using the loading docks. This action substantially reduced the value of Blackacre.

Buyer brought an appropriate action against Seller seeking cancellation of the deed and return of all monies paid.

Such action should be based upon a claim of

(A) misrepresentation.
(B) breach of the covenant of warranty.
(C) failure of consideration.
(D) mutual mistake.

136. Prescott sued Doxie for fraud. After verdict for Prescott, Doxie talked with juror Wall about the trial.

Doxie's motion for a new trial would be most likely granted if Wall is willing to testify that he voted for Prescott because he

(A) misunderstood the judge's instructions concerning the standard of proof in a fraud case.
(B) was feeling ill and needed to get home quickly.
(C) relied on testimony that the judge had stricken and ordered the jury to disregard.
(D) learned from a court clerk that Doxie had been accused of fraud in several recent lawsuits.

137. Despondent over losing his job, Wilmont drank all night at a bar. While driving home, he noticed a car following him and, in his intoxicated state, concluded he was being followed by robbers. In fact, a police car was following him on suspicion of drunk driving. In his effort to get away, Wilmont sped through a stop sign and struck and killed a pedestrian. He was arrested by the police.

Wilmont is prosecuted for manslaughter.

He should be

(A) acquitted, because he honestly believed he faced an imminent threat of death or severe bodily injury.
(B) acquitted, because his intoxication prevented him from appreciating the risk he created.
(C) convicted, because he acted recklessly and in fact was in no danger.
(D) convicted, because he acted recklessly and his apprehension of danger was not reasonable.

138. Ody, owner of Profitacre, executed an instrument in the proper form of a deed, purporting to convey Profitacre "to Leon for life, then to Ralph in fee simple." Leon, who is Ody's brother and Ralph's father, promptly began to manage Profitacre, which is valuable income producing real estate. Leon collected all rents and paid all expenses, including real estate taxes. Ralph did not object, and this state of affairs continued for five years until 1987. In that year, Leon executed an instrument in the proper form of a deed, purporting to convey Profitacre to Mona. Ralph, no admirer of Mona, asserted his right to ownership of Profitacre. Mona asserted her ownership and said that if Ralph had any rights he was obligated to pay real estate taxes, even though Leon had been kind enough to pay them in the past. Income from Profitacre is ample to cover expenses, including real estate taxes.

In an appropriate action to determine the rights of the parties, the court should decide

(A) Leon's purported deed forfeited his life estate, so Ralph owns Profitacre in fee simple.
(B) Mona owns an estate for her life, entitled to all income, and must pay real estate taxes; Ralph owns the remainder interest.
(C) Mona owns an estate for the life of Leon and is entitled to all income, and must pay real estate taxes; Ralph owns the remainder interest.
(D) Mona owns an estate for the life Leon and is entitled to all income; Ralph owns the remainder interest, and must pay real estate taxes.

139. Homer Ethel were jointly in possession of Greenacre in fee simple as tenants in common. They joined in a mortgage of Greenacre to Fortunoff Bank. Homer erected a fence along what he considered to be the true boundary between Greenacre and the adjoining property, owned by Mitchell. Shortly thereafter, Homer had an argument with Ethel and gave up his possession to Greenacre. The debt secured by the mortgage had not been paid.

Mitchell surveyed his land and found that the fence erected a year earlier by Homer did not follow the true boundary. Part of the fence was within Greenacre. Part of the fence encroached on Mitchell's land. Mitchell and Ethel executed an agreement fixing the boundary line in accordance with the fence constructed by Homer. The agreement, which met all the formalities required in the jurisdiction, was promptly and properly recorded.

A year after the agreement was recorded, Homer temporarily reconciled his differences with Ethel and resumed joint possession of Greenacre. Thereafter, Homer repudiated the boundary line agreement and brought an appropriate action against Mitchell and Ethel to quiet title along the original true boundary.

In such action, Homer will

(A) win, because Fortunoff Bank was not a party to the agreement.
(B) win, because one tenant in common; cannot bind another tenant in common to a boundary line agreement.
(C) lose, because the agreement, as a matter of law, was mutually beneficial to Ethel and Homer.
(D) lose, because Ethel was in sole possession of said premises at the time the agreement was signed.

140. At the trial of an action against Grandmother on behalf of Patrick, the following evidence has been introduced. Grandson and his friend, Patrick, both aged eight, were visiting at Grandmother's house when, while exploring the premises, they discovered a hunting rifle in an unlocked gun cabinet. They removed it from the cabinet and were examining it when the rifle, while in Grandson's hands, somehow discharged. The bullet struck and injured Patrick. The gun cabinet was normally locked. Grandmother had opened it for dusting several days before the boys' visit, and had then forgotten to relock it. She was not aware that it was unlocked when the boys arrived.

If the defendant moves for a directed verdict in her favor at the end of the plaintiff's case, that motion should be

(A) granted, because Grandmother is not legally responsible for the acts of Grandson.
(B) granted, because Grandmother did not recall that the gun cabinet was unlocked.
(C) denied, because a firearm is an inherently dangerous instrumentality.
(D) denied, because a jury could find that Grandmother breached a duty of care she owed to Patrick.

Questions 141-142 are based on the following fact situation.

On November 15, Joiner in a signed writing contracted with Galley for an agreed price to personally remodel Galley's kitchen according to specifications provided by Galley, and to start work on December 1. Joiner agreed to provide all materials for the job in addition to all of the labor required.

141. For this question only, assume that on November 26 Joiner without legal excuse repudiated the contract and that Galley, after a reasonable and prolonged effort, could not find anyone to remodel his kitchen for a price approximating the price agreed to by Joiner.

If one year later Galley brings an action for specific performance against Joiner, which of the following will provide Joiner with the best defense?

(A) An action for equitable relief not brought within a reasonable time is barred by laches.
(B) Specific performance is generally not available as a remedy to enforce a contractual duty to perform personal services.
(C) Specific performance is generally not available as a remedy in the case of an anticipatory repudiation.
(D) Specific performance is not available as a remedy where even nominal damages could have been recovered as a remedy at law.

142. For this question only, assume the following facts. On November 26, Galley without legal excuse repudiated the contract. Notwithstanding Galley's repudiation, however, Joiner subsequently purchased for $5,000 materials that could only be used in remodeling Galley's kitchen, and promptly notified Galley, "I will hold you to our contract." If allowed to perform, Joiner

would have made a profit of $3,000 on the job.

If Galley refuses to retract his repudiation, and Joiner sues him for damages, what is the maximum that Joiner is entitled to recover?

(A) Nothing, because he failed to mitigate his damages.
(B) $3,000, his expectancy damages.
(C) $5,000, on a restitutionary theory.
(D) $5,000, his reliance damages, plus $3,000, his expectancy damages.

Questions 143-144 are based on the following fact situation.

The police suspected that Yancey, a 16-year-old high school student, had committed a series of burglaries. Two officers went to Yancey's high school and asked the principal to call Yancey out of class and to search his backpack. While the officers waited, the principal took Yancey into the hall where she asked to look in his backpack. When Yancey refused, the principal grabbed it from him, injuring Yancey's shoulder in the process. In the backpack, she found jewelry that she turned over to the officers.

The officers believed that the jewelry had been taken in one of the burglaries. They arrested Yancey, took him to the station, and gave him Miranda warnings. Yancey asked to see a lawyer. The police called Yancey's parents to the station. When Yancey's parents arrived, the police asked them to speak with Yancey. They put them in a room and secretly recorded their conversation with a concealed electronic device. Yancey broke down and confessed to his parents that he had committed the burglaries.

Yancey was charged with the burglaries.

143. Yancey moves to suppress the use of the jewelry.

The court should

(A) deny the motion on the ground that the search was incident to a lawful arrest.
(B) deny the motion on the ground that school searches are reasonable if conducted by school personnel on school grounds on the basis of reasonable suspicion.
(C) grant the motion on the ground that the search was conducted with excessive force.
(D) grant the motion on the ground that the search was conducted without probable cause or a warrant.

144. Assume for this question only that the court denied the motion to suppress the jewelry. Yancey moves to suppress the use of the statement Yancey made to his parents.

The best argument for excluding it would be that

(A) Yancey was in custody at the time the statement was recorded.
(B) the police did not comply with Yancey's request for a lawyer.
(C) once Yancey had invoked his right to counsel, it was improper for the police to listen to any of his private conversations.
(D) the meeting between Yancey and his parents was arranged by the police to obtain an incriminating statement.

145. A newly enacted federal statute appropriates $100 million in federal funds to support basic research by universities located in the United States. The statute provides that "the ten best universities in the United States" will each receive $10 million. It also provides that "the ten best universities" shall be "determined by a poll of the presidents of all the universities in the nation, to be conducted by the United States Department of Education." In responding to that poll, each university president is required to apply the well-recognized and generally accepted standards of academic quality that are specified in the statute. The provisions of the statute are inseverable.
Which of the following statements about this statute is correct?

(A) The statute is unconstitutional, because the reliance by Congress on a poll of individuals who are not federal officials to determine the recipients of its appropriated funds is an unconstitutional delegation of legislative power.

(B) The statute is unconstitutional, because the limitation on recipients to the ten best universities is arbitrary and capricious and denies other high quality universities the equal protection of the laws.

(C) The statute is constitutional, because Congress has plenary authority to determine the objects of its spending and the methods used to achieve them, so long as they may reasonably be deemed to serve the general welfare and do not violate any prohibitory language in the Constitution.

(D) The validity of the statute is nonjusticiable, because the use by Congress of its spending power necessarily involves political considerations that must be resolved finally by those branches of the government that are closest to the political process.

146. Which of the following fact patterns most clearly suggests an implied-in-fact contract?

(A) A county tax assessor mistakenly bills Algernon for taxes on Bathsheba's property, which Algernon, in good faith, pays.
(B) Meddick, a physician, treated Ryder without Ryder's knowledge or consent, while Ryder was unconscious as the result of a fall from his horse.
(C) Asphalt, thinking that he was paving Customer's driveway, for which Asphalt had an express contract, mistakenly paved Nabor's driveway while Nabor looked on without saying anything or raising any objection.
(D) At her mother's request, Iris, an accountant, filled out and filed her mother's "E-Z" income-tax form (a simple, short form).

147. Ashton owned Woodsedge, a tract used for commercial purposes, in fee simple and thereafter mortgaged it to First Bank. She signed a promissory note secured by a duly executed and recorded mortgage. There was no "due on sale" clause, that is, no provision that, upon sale, the whole balance then owing would become due and owing. Ashton conveyed Woodsedge to Beam "subject to a mortgage to First Bank, which the grantee assumes and agrees to pay." Beam conveyed Woodsedge to Carter it subject to an existing mortgage to First Bank." A copy of the note and the mortgage that secured it had been exhibited to each grantee.

After Carter made three timely payments, no further payments were made by any party. In fact, the real estate had depreciated to a point where it was worth less than the debt.

There is no applicable statute or regulation.

In an appropriate foreclosure action, First Bank joined Ashton, Beam, and Carter as defendants. At the foreclosure sale, although the fair market value for Woodsedge in its depreciated state was obtained, a deficiency resulted.

First Bank is entitled to collect a deficiency judgment against

(A) Ashton only.
(B) Ashton and Beam only.
(C) Beam and Carter only.
(D) Ashton, Beam, and Carter.

148. Landco purchased a large tract of land intending to construct residential housing on it. Landco hired Poolco to build a large in-ground swimming pool on the tract. The contract provided that Poolco would carry out blasting operations that were necessary to create an excavation large enough for the pool. The blasting caused cracks to form in the walls of Plaintiff Is home in a nearby residential neighborhood.

In Plaintiff's action for damages against Landco, Plaintiff should

(A) prevail, only if Landco retained the right to direct and control Poolco's construction of the pool.
(B) prevail, because the blasting that Poolco was hired to perform damaged Plaintiff's home.

(C) not prevail, if Poolco used reasonable care in conducting the blasting operations.

(D) not prevail, if Landco used reasonable care to hire a competent contractor.

149. The state of Atlantica spends several million dollars a year on an oyster conservation program. As part of that program, the state limits, by statute, oyster fishing in its coastal waters to persons who have state oyster permits. In order to promote conservation, it issues only a limited number of oyster permits each year. The permits are effective for only one year from the date of their issuance and are awarded on the basis of a lottery, in which there is no differentiation between resident and nonresident applicants. However, each nonresident who obtains a permit is charged an annual permit fee that is $5 more than the fee charged residents.

Fisher, Inc., is a large fishing company that operates from a port in another state and is incorporated in that other state. Each of the boats of Fisher, Inc., has a federal shipping license that permits it "to engage in all aspects of the coastal trade, to fish and to carry cargo from place to place along the coast, and to engage in other lawful activities along the coast of the United States." These shipping licenses are authorized by federal statute. Assume no other federal statutes or administrative rules apply.

Although it had previously held an Atlantica oyster permit, Fisher, Inc., did not obtain a permit in that state's lottery this year.

Which of the following is the strongest argument that can be made in support of a continued right of Fisher, Inc., to fish for oysters this year in the coastal waters of Atlantica?

(A) Because the Atlantica law provides higher permit charges for nonresidents, it is an undue burden on interstate commerce.

(B) Because the Atlantica law provides higher permit charges for nonresidents, it denies Fisher, Inc., the privileges and immunities of state citizenship.

(C) Because it holds a federal shipping license, Fisher, Inc., has a right to fish for oysters in Atlantica waters despite the state law.

(D) Because Fisher, Inc., previously held an Atlantica oyster permit and Atlantica knows that company is engaged in a continuing business operation, the refusal to grant Fisher, Inc., a permit this year is a taking of its property without due process of law.

150. The United States Department of the Interior granted Concessionaire the food and drink concession in a federal park located in the state of New Senora. Concessionaire operated his concession out of federally owned facilities in the park. The federal statute authorizing the Interior Department to grant such concessions provided that the grantees would pay only a nominal rental for use of these federal facilities because of the great benefit their concessions would provide to the people of the United States.

The legislature of the state of New Senora enacted a statute imposing an occupancy tax on the occupants of real estate within that state that is not subject to state real estate taxes. The statute was intended to equalize the state tax burden on such occupants with that on people occupying real estate that is subject to state real estate taxes. Pursuant to that statute, the New Senora Department of Revenue attempted to collect the state occupancy tax from Concessionaire because the federal facilities occupied by Concessionaire were not subject to state real estate taxes. Concessionaire sued to invalidate the state occupancy tax as applied to him.

The strongest ground upon which Concessionaire could challenge the occupancy tax is that it violates the

(A) commerce clause by unduly burdening the interstate tourist trade.

(B) privileges and immunities clause of the Fourteenth Amendment by

(C) interfering with the fundamental right to do business on federal property.
(C) equal protection of the laws clause of the Fourteenth Amendment because the tax treats him less favorably than federal concessionaires in other states who do not have to pay such occupancy taxes.
(D) supremacy clause of Article VI and the federal statute authorizing such concessions.

151. Davis has a small trampoline in his backyard which, as he knows, is commonly used by neighbor children as well as his own. The trampoline is in good condition, is not defective in any way, and normally is surrounded by mats to prevent injury if a user should fall off. Prior to leaving with his family for the day, Davis leaned the trampoline up against the side of the house and placed the mats in the garage.

While the Davis family was away, Philip, aged 11, a new boy in the neighborhood, wandered into Davis's yard and saw the trampoline. Philip had not previously been aware of its presence, but, having frequently used a trampoline before, he decided to set it up, and started to jump. He lost his balance on one jump and took a hard fall on the bare ground, suffering a serious injury that would have been prevented by the mats.

An action has been brought against Davis on Philip's behalf to recover damages for the injuries Philip sustained from his fall. In this jurisdiction, the traditional common-law rules pertaining to contributory negligence have been replaced by a pure comparative negligence rule.

In his action against Davis, will Philip prevail?

(A) No, if children likely to be attracted by the trampoline would normally realize the risk of using it without mats.
(B) No, if Philip failed to exercise reasonable care commensurate with his age, intelligence, and experience.
(C) No, because Philip entered Davis's yard and used the trampoline without Davis's permission.
(D) No, because Philip did not know about the trampoline before entering Davis's yard and thus was not "lured" onto the premises.

152. Deben was charged with using a forged prescription from a Dr. Kohl to obtain Percodan from Smith's Drugstore on May 1. At trial, Smith identified Deben as the customer, but Deben testified that he had not been in the store.

In rebuttal, the prosecutor calls Wallman and Witler to testify that on May 1 a man they identified as Deben had presented prescriptions for Percodan from a Dr. Kohl at, respectively, Wallman's Drugs and Witler's Drugstore.

Wallman's and Witler's testimony is

(A) admissible, to prove a pertinent trait of Deben's character and Deben's action in conformity therewith.
(B) admissible, to identify the man who presented the prescription at Smith's Drugstore.
(C) inadmissible, because it proves specific acts rather than reputation or opinion.
(D) inadmissible, because other crimes may not be used to show propensity.

153. An ordinance of the city of Green requires that its mayor must have been continuously a resident of the city for at least five years at the time he or she takes office. Candidate, who is thinking about running for mayor in an election that will take place next year, will have been a resident of Green for only four and one-half years at the time the mayor elected then takes office. Before he decides whether to run for the position of mayor, Candidate wants to know whether he could lawfully assume that position if he were elected. As a result, Candidate files suit in the local federal district court for a declaratory judgment that the Green five-year-residence requirement is unconstitutional and that he is entitled to a

place on his political party's primary election ballot for mayor. He names the chairman of his political party as the sole defendant but does not join any election official. The chairman responds by joining Candidate in requesting the court to declare the Green residence requirement invalid.

In this case, the court should

(A) refuse to determine the merits of this suit, because there is no case or controversy.
(B) refuse to issue such a declaratory judgment, because an issue of this kind involving only a local election does not present a substantial federal constitutional question.
(C) issue the declaratory judgment, because a residency requirement of this type is a denial of the equal protection of the laws.
(D) issue the declaratory judgment, because Candidate will have substantially complied with the residency requirement.

154. Oliver, owner of Blackacre, needed money. Blackacre was fairly worth $100,000, so Oliver tried to borrow $60,000 from Len on the security of Blackacre. Len agreed, but only if Oliver would convey Blackacre to Len outright by warranty deed, with Len agreeing orally to reconvey to Oliver once the loan was paid according to its terms. Oliver agreed, conveyed Blackacre to Len by warranty deed, and Len paid Oliver $60,000 cash. Len promptly and properly recorded Oliver's deed.

Now, Oliver has defaulted on repayment with $55,000 still due on the loan. Oliver is still in possession.

Which of the following best states the parties' rights in Blackacre?

(A) Len's oral agreement to reconvey is invalid under the Statute of Frauds, so Len owns Blackacre outright.
(B) Oliver, having defaulted, has no further rights in Blackacre, so Len may obtain summary eviction.
(C) The attempted security arrangement is a creature unknown to the law, hence a nullity; Len has only a personal right to $55,000 from Oliver.
(D) Len may bring whatever foreclosure proceeding is appropriate under the laws of the jurisdiction.

155. Big City High School has had a very high rate of pregnancy among its students : In order to assist students who keep their babies to complete high school, Big City High School has established an infant day-care center for children of its students, and also offers classes in childcare. Because the child-care classes are always overcrowded, the school limits admission to those classes solely to Big City High School students who are the mothers of babies in the infant day-care center.

Joe, a student at Big City High School, has legal custody of his infant son. The school provides care for his son in its infant day-care center, but will not allow Joe to enroll in the child-care classes. He brings suit against the school challenging, on constitutional grounds, his exclusion from the childcare classes.

Which of the following best states the burden of persuasion in this case?

(A) Joe must demonstrate that the admission requirement is not rationally related to a legitimate governmental interest.
(B) Joe must demonstrate that the admission requirement is not as narrowly drawn as possible to achieve a substantial governmental interest.
(C) The school must demonstrate that the admission policy is the least restrictive means by which to achieve a compelling governmental interest.
(D) The school must demonstrate that the admission policy is substantially related to an important governmental interest.

156. Defendant was upset because he was going to have to close his liquor store due to competition from a discount store in a new shopping mail nearby. In desperation, he decided to set fire to his store to collect the insurance. While looking through the basement for flammable material, he lit a match to read the label on a can. The match burned his finger and, in a reflex action, he dropped the match. It fell into a barrel and ignited some paper. Defendant made no effort to put out the fire but instead left the building. The fire spread and the store was destroyed by fire. Defendant was eventually arrested and indicted for arson.

    Defendant is

    (A) guilty, if he could have put out the fire before it spread and did not do so because he wanted the building destroyed.
    (B) guilty, if he was negligent in starting the fire.
    (C) not guilty, because even if he wanted to burn the building there was no concurrence between his *mens rea* and the act of starting the fire.
    (D) not guilty, because his starting the fire was the result of a reflex action and not a voluntary act.

157. In his employment, Grinder operates a grinding wheel. To protect his eyes, he wears glasses, sold under the trade name "Safety Glasses," manufactured by Glassco. The glasses were sold with a warning label stating that they would protect only against small, flying objects. One day, the grinding wheel Grinder was using disintegrated and fragments of the stone wheel were thrown off with great force. One large fragment hit Grinder, knocking his safety glasses up onto his forehead. Another fragment then hit and injured his eye.

    Grinder brought an action against Glassco for the injury to his eye. The jurisdiction adheres to the traditional common-law rule pertaining to contributory negligence.

    In this action, will Grinder prevail?

    (A) Yes, because the safety glasses were defective in that they did not protect him from the disintegrating wheel.
    (B) Yes, because the glasses were sold under the trade name "Safety Glasses."
    (C) No, because the glasses were not designed or sold for protection against the kind of hazard Grinder encountered.
    (D) No, if Grinder will be compensated under the workers' compensation law.

Questions 158-160 are based on the following Fact situation.

Oscar purchased a large bottle of NoFlake dandruff shampoo, manufactured by Shampoo Company. The box containing the bottle stated in part: "CAUTION--Use only 1 capful at most once a day. Greater use may cause severe damage to the scalp." Oscar read the writing on the box, removed the bottle, and threw the box away. Oscar's roommate, Paul, asked to use the No-Flake, and Oscar said, "Be careful not to use too much." Paul thereafter used No-Flake twice a day, applying two or three capfuls each time, notwithstanding the label statement that read: "Use no more than one capful per day. See box instructions." The more he used NoFlake, the more inflamed his scalp became, the more it itched, and the more he used. After three weeks of such use, Paul finally consulted a doctor who diagnosed his problem as a serious and irreversible case of dermatitis caused by excessive exposure to the active ingredients in No-Flake. These ingredients are uniquely effective at controlling dandruff, but there is no way to remove a remote risk to a small percentage of persons who may contract dermatitis as the result of applying for prolonged periods of time amounts of NoFlake substantially in excess of the directions. This jurisdiction adheres to the traditional common-law rules pertaining to contributory negligence and assumption of risk.

158. Based upon the foregoing facts, if Paul sues Shampoo Company to recover damages for his dermatitis, his most promising theory of liability will be that the No-Flake shampoo

    (A) had an unreasonably dangerous manufacturing defect.
    (B) had an unreasonably dangerous design defect.

(C) was inherently dangerous.
(D) was inadequately labeled to warn of its dangers.

159. If Paul asserts a claim for his injuries against Shampoo Company based on strict liability in tort, which of the following would constitute a defense?

   I. Paul misused the No-Flake shampoo.
   II. Paul was contributorily negligent in continuing to use No-Flake shampoo when his scalp began to hurt and itch.
   III. Paul was a remote user and not in privity with Shampoo Company.

   (A) I only.
   (B) I and II only.
   (C) II and III only.
   (D) Neither I, nor II, nor III.

160. If Paul asserts a claim against Oscar for his dermatitis injuries, Oscar's best defense will be that

   (A) Paul was contributorily negligent.
   (B) Paul assumed the risk.
   (C) Oscar had no duty toward Paul, who was a gratuitous donee.
   (D) Oscar had no duty toward Paul, because Shampoo Company created the risk and had a nondelegable duty to foreseeable users.

161. Unprepared for a final examination, Slick asked his girlfriend, Hope, to set off the fire alarms in the university building 15 minutes after the test commenced. Hope did so. Several students were injured in the panic that followed as people were trying to get out of the building. Slick and Hope are prosecuted for battery and for conspiracy to commit battery.
   They are

   (A) guilty of both crimes.
   (B) guilty of battery but not guilty of conspiracy.
   (C) not guilty of battery but guilty of conspiracy.
   (D) not guilty of either crime.

162. A statute of the state of Wasminia prohibits the use of state-owned or state-operated facilities for the performance of abortions that are not "necessary to save the life of the mother." That statute also prohibits state employees from performing any such abortions during the hours they are employed by the state.

Citizen was in her second month of pregnancy. She sought an abortion at the Wasminia State Hospital, a state-owned and state-operated facility. Citizen did not claim that the requested abortion was necessary to save her life. The officials in charge of the hospital refused to perform the requested abortion solely on the basis of the state statute. Citizen immediately filed suit against those officials in an appropriate federal district court. She challenged the constitutionality of the Wasminia statute and requested the court to order the hospital to perform the abortion she sought.

In this case, the court will probably hold that the Wasminia statute is

(A) unconstitutional, because a limit on the availability of abortions performed by state employees or in state-owned or state-operated facilities to situations in which it is necessary to save the life of the mother impermissibly interferes with the fundamental right of Citizen to decide whether to have a child.
(B) unconstitutional, because it impermissibly discriminates against poor persons who cannot afford to pay for abortions in privately owned and operated facilities and against persons who live far away from privately owned and operated abortion clinics.
(C) constitutional, because it does not prohibit a woman from having an abortion or penalize her for doing so, it is rationally related to the legitimate governmental goal of encouraging childbirth, and it does not interfere with the voluntary performance of abortions by

private physicians in private facilities.
(D) constitutional, because the use of state-owned or state-operated facilities and access to the services of state employees are privileges and not rights and, therefore, a state may condition them on any basis it chooses.

163. Oscar, owner of Greenacre, conveyed Greenacre by quitclaim deed as a gift to Ann, who did not then record her deed. Later, Oscar conveyed Greenacre by warranty deed to Belle, who paid valuable consideration, knew nothing of Ann's claim, and promptly and properly recorded. Next, Ann recorded her deed. Then Belle conveyed Greenacre by quitclaim deed to her son Cal as a gift. When the possible conflict with Ann was discovered Cal recorded his deed.

Greenacre at all relevant times has been vacant unoccupied land.

The recording act of the jurisdiction provides: "No unrecorded conveyance or mortgage of real property shall be good against subsequent purchasers for value without notice, who shall first record." No other statute is applicable.

Cal has sued Ann to establish who owns Greenacre.

The court will hold for

(A) Cal, because Ann was a donee.
(B) Cal, because Belle's purchase cut off Ann's rights'
(C) Ann, because she recorded before Cal.
(D) Ann, because Cal was a subsequent donee.

164. While Driver was taking a leisurely spring drive, he momentarily took his eyes off the road to look at some colorful trees in bloom. As a result, his car swerved a few feet off the roadway, directly toward Walker, who was standing on the shoulder of the road waiting for a chance to cross. When Walker saw the car bearing down on him, he jumped backwards, fell, and injured his knee. Walker sued Driver for damages, and Driver moved for summary judgment. The foregoing facts are undisputed.

Driver's motion should be

(A) denied, because the record shows that Walker apprehended an imminent, harmful contact with Driver's car.
(B) denied, because a jury could find that Driver negligently caused Walker to suffer a legally compensable injury.
(C) granted, because the proximate cause of Walker's injury was his own voluntary act.
(D) granted, because it is not unreasonable for a person to be distracted momentarily.

165. In which of the following situations is the defendant most likely to be convicted, even though he did not intend to bring about the harm that the statute defining the offense is designed to prevent?

(A) Defendant was the president of an aspirin manufacturing company. A federal inspector discovered that a large number of aspirin tablets randomly scattered through several bottles in a carton ready for shipment were laced with arsenic. Defendant is charged with attempted introduction of adulterated drugs into interstate commerce.
(B) Defendant struck Victim in the face with a baseball bat, intending to inflict a serious injury. Victim died after being hospitalized for three days. Defendant is charged with murder.
(C) Defendant burglarized a jewelry store, intending to steal some diamonds. As he entered the store, he short-circuited the store's burglar alarm system, thereby preventing a warning of his entry to police. The smoldering wires eventually caused a fire that destroyed the store. Defendant is charged with arson.

(D) Defendant wanted to frighten Victim's friend by placing a plastic rattlesnake in his lunch box. When Victim mistakenly took the lunch box and opened it, believing it to be his own, the plastic rattlesnake popped out. As a result of the fright, Victim suffered a heart attack and died. Defendant is charged with manslaughter.

166. Happy-Time Beverages agreed in writing with Fizzy Cola Company to serve for three years as a distributor in a six-county area of Fizzy Cola, which contains a small amount of caffeine. Happy-Time promised in the contract to "promote in good faith the sale of Fizzy Cola" in that area; but the contract said nothing about restrictions on the products that Happy-Time could distribute.

Six months later, Happy-Time agreed with the Cool Cola Company to distribute its caffeine-free cola beverages in the same six-county area.

If Fizzy Cola Company sues Happy-Time for breach of their distribution contract, which of the following facts, if established, would most strengthen Fizzy's case?

(A) Cool Cola's national advertising campaign disparages the Fizzy Cola product by saying, "You don't need caffeine and neither does your cola."
(B) Since Happy-Time began to distribute Cool Cola, the sales of Fizzy Cola have dropped 3% in the six-county area.
(C) Prior to signing the contract with Fizzy Cola Company, a representative of Happy-Time said that the deal with Fizzy would be "an exclusive."
(D) For many years in the soft-drink industry, it has been uniform practice for distributors to handle only one brand of cola.

167. Dove is on trial for theft. At trial, the prosecutor called John and May Wong. They testified that, as they looked their apartment window, they saw thieves across the street break the window of a jewelry store, take jewelry, and leave in a car. Mrs. Wong telephoned the police and relayed to them the license number of the thieves' car as Mr. Wong looked out the window with binoculars and read it to her. Neither of them has any present memory of the number. The prosecutor offers as evidence a properly authenticated police tape recording of May Wong's telephone call with her voice giving the license number, which is independently shown to belong to Dovel's car.

The tape recording of May Wong's stating the license number is

(A) admissible, under the hearsay exception for present sense impressions.
(B) admissible, as nonhearsay circumstantial evidence.
(C) inadmissible, because it is hearsay not within any exception.
(D) inadmissible, because May Wong never had firsthand knowledge of the license number.

168. Diggers Construction Company was engaged in blasting operations to clear the way for a new road. Diggers had erected adequate barriers and posted adequate warning signs in the vicinity of the blasting. Although Paul read and understood the signs, he entered the area to walk his dog. As a result of the blasting, Paul was hit by a piece of rock and sustained head injuries. The jurisdiction follows the traditional common-law rules governing the defenses of contributory negligence, assumption of risk, and last clear chance.

In an action by Paul against Diggers to recover damages for his injuries, Paul will

(A) not prevail, if Diggers exercised reasonable care to protect the public from harm.
(B) not prevail, because Paul understood the signs and disregarded the warnings.
(C) prevail, because Paul was harmed by Diggers's abnormally dangerous activity.

(D) prevail, unless Paul failed to use reasonable care to protect himself from harm.

169. Pike sued Day City Community Church for damages he suffered when Pike crashed his motorcycle in an attempt to avoid a cow that had escaped from its corral' The cow and corral belonged to a farm that had recently been left by will to the church. At trial, Pike seeks to ask Defendant's witness, Winters, whether she is a member of that church.

The question is

(A) improper, because evidence of a witness's religious beliefs is not admissible to impeach credibility.
(B) improper, because it violates First Amendment and privacy rights.
(C) proper, for the purpose of ascertaining partiality or bias.
(D) proper, for the purpose of showing capacity to appreciate the nature and obligation of an oath.

170. Radon is a harmful gas found in the soil of certain regions of the United States. A statute of the state of Magenta requires occupants of residences with basements susceptible to the intrusion of radon to have their residences tested for the presence of radon and to take specified remedial steps if the test indicates the presence of radon above specified levels. The statute also provides that the testing for radon may be done only by testers licensed by a state agency. According to the statute, a firm may be licensed to test for radon only if it meets specified rigorous standards relating to the accuracy of its testing. These standards may easily be achieved with current technology; but the technology required to meet them is 50% more expensive than the technology required to measure radon accumulations in a slightly less accurate manner.

The United States Environmental Protection Agency (EPA) does not license radon testers. However, a federal statute authorizes the EPA to advise on the accuracy of various methods of radon testing and to provide to the general public a list of testers that use methods it believes to be reasonably accurate.

WeTest, a recently established Magenta firm, uses a testing method that the EPA has stated is reasonably accurate. WeTest is also included by the EPA on the list of testers using methods of testing it believes to be reasonably accurate. WeTest applies for a Magenta radon testing license, but its application is denied because WeTest cannot demonstrate that the method of testing for radon it uses is sufficiently accurate to meet the rigorous Magenta statutory standards. WeTest sues appropriate Magenta officials in federal court claiming that Magenta may not constitutionally exclude WeTest from performing the required radon tests in Magenta.

In this suit, the court will probably rule in favor of

(A) WeTest, because the full faith and credit clause of the Constitution requires Magenta to respect and give effect to the action of the EPA in including WeTest on its list of testers that use reasonably accurate methods.
(B) WeTest, because the supremacy clause of the Constitution requires Magenta to respect and give effect to the action of the EPA in including WeTest on its list of testers that use reasonably accurate methods.
(C) Magenta, because the federal statute and the action of the EPA in including WeTest on its list of testers that use reasonably accurate methods are not inconsistent with the more rigorous Magenta licensing requirement, and that requirement is reasonably related to a legitimate public interest.
(D) Magenta, because radon exposure is limited to basement areas, which, by their very nature, cannot move in interstate commerce.

171. Bitz, an amateur computer whiz, agreed in writing to design for the Presskey Corporation, a distributor of TV game

systems, three new games a year for a five-year period. The writing provided, in a clause separately signed by Bitz, that "No modification shall be binding on Presskey unless made in writing and signed by Presskey's authorized representative."

Because of family problems, Bitz delivered and Presskey accepted only two game-designs a year for the first three years; but the games were a commercial success and Presskey made no objection. Accordingly, Bitz spent substantial sums on new computer equipment that would aid in speeding up future design work. In the first quarter of the fourth year, however, Presskey terminated the contract on the ground that Bitz had breached the annual quantity term.

In Bitz's suit against Presskey for damages, the jury found that the contract had been modified by conduct and the trial court awarded Bitz substantial compensatory damages.

Is this result likely to be reversed on appeal?

(A) Yes, because the contract's no-oral-modification clause was not expressly waived by Presskey.
(B) Yes, because the contract's no-oral-modification clause was a material part of the agreed exchange and could not be avoided without new consideration.
(C) No, because the contract's no-oral-modification clause was unconscionable as against an amateur designer.
(D) No, because Presskey by its conduct waived the annual-quantity term and Bitz materially changed his position in reasonable reliance on that waiver.

172. Test owned Blackacre, a vacant one-acre tract of land in State. Five years ago, he executed a deed conveying Blackacre to "Church for the purpose of erecting a church building thereon." Three years ago, Test died leaving Sonny as his sole heir at law. His duly probated will left Hall my Estate, both real and personal, to my friend Fanny."

Church never constructed a church building on Blackacre and last month Church, for a valid consideration, conveyed Blackacre to Developer.

Developer brought an appropriate action to quiet title against Sonny, Fanny, and Church, and joined the appropriate state official. Such official asserted that a charitable trust was created which has not terminated.

In such action, the court should find that title is now in

(A) Developer.
(B) Sonny.
(C) Fanny.
(D) the state official.

173. Mr. Denby was charged with the sale of narcotics. The federal prosecutor arranged with Mrs. Denby for her to testify against her husband in exchange for leniency in her case. At trial, the prosecution calls Mrs. Denby, who had been granted immunity from prosecution, to testify, among other things, that she saw her husband sell an ounce of heroin.

Which of the following statements is most clearly correct in the federal courts?

(A) Mrs. Denby cannot be called as a witness over her husband's objection.
(B) Mrs. Denby can be called as a witness but cannot testify, over Mr. Denby's objection, that she saw him sell heroin.
(C) Mrs. Denby can refuse, to be a witness against her husband.
(D) Mrs. Denby can be required to be a witness and to testify that she saw her husband sell heroin.

174. Freund, a U.S. west-coast manufacturer, gave Wrench, a hardware retailer who was relocating to the east coast, the following "letter of introduction" to Tuff, an east-coast hardware wholesaler.

This will introduce you to my good friend and former customer, Wrench, who will be seeking to arrange the purchase of hardware inventory from you on credit. If you will let him have the goods, I will make good any loss up to $25,000 in the event of his default.

/Signed/Freund

Wrench presented the letter to Tuff, who then sold and delivered $20,000 worth of hardware to Wrench on credit. Tuff promptly notified Freund of this sale.

Which of the following is NOT an accurate statement concerning the arrangement between Freund and Tuff?

(A) It was important to enforceability of Freund's promise to Tuff that it be embodied in a signed writing.
(B) By extending the credit to Wrench, Tuff effectively accepted Freund's offer for a unilateral contract.
(C) Although Freund received no consideration from Wrench, Freund's promise is enforceable by Tuff.
(D) Freund's promise is enforceable by Tuff whether or not Tuff gave Freund seasonable notice of the extension of credit to Wrench.

175. The legislature of the state of Gray recently enacted a statute forbidding public utilities regulated by the Gray Public Service Commission to increase their rates more than once every two years. Economy Electric Power Company, a public utility regulated by that commission, has just obtained approval of the commission for a general rate increase. Economy Electric has routinely filed for a rate increase every ten to 14 months during the last 20 years. Because of uncertainties about future fuel prices, the power company cannot ascertain with any certainty the date when it will need a further rate increase; but it thinks it may need such an increase sometime within the next 18 months.

Economy Electric files an action in the federal district court in Gray requesting a declaratory judgment that this new statute of Gray forbidding public utility rate increases more often than once every two years is unconstitutional. Assume no federal statute is relevant.

In this case, the court should

(A) hold the statute unconstitutional, because such a moratorium on rate increases deprives utilities of their property without due process of law.
(B) hold the statute constitutional, because the judgment of a legislature on a matter involving economic regulation is entitled to great deference.
(C) dismiss the complaint, because this action is not ripe for decision.
(D) dismiss the complaint, because controversies over state-regulated utility rates are outside of the jurisdiction conferred on federal courts by Article III of the Constitution.

176. Daniel is on trial for evading $100,000 in taxes. The prosecution offers in evidence an anonymous letter to the IRS, identified as being in Daniel's handwriting, saying, "I promised my mother on her deathbed I would try to pay my back taxes. Here is $10,000. I'll make other payments if you promise not to prosecute. Answer yes by personal ad saying, 'OK on tax deal.'

The letter is

(A) admissible, as a statement of present intention or plan.
(B) admissible, as an admission of a party opponent.
(C) inadmissible, because it is an effort to settle a claim.
(D) inadmissible, because the probative value is substantially outweighed by the risk of unfair prejudice.

Questions 177-178 are based on the following fact situation.

Broker needed a certain rare coin to complete a set that he had contracted to assemble and sell to Collecta. On February 1, Broker obtained such a coin from Hoarda in exchange for $1,000 and Broker's signed, written promise to re-deliver to

Hoarda "not later than December 31 this year" a comparable specimen of the same kind of coin without charge to Hoarda. On February 2, Broker consummated sale of the complete set to Collecta.

On October 1, the market price of rare coins suddenly began a rapid, sustained rise; and on October 15 Hoarda wrote Broker for assurance that the latter would timely meet his coin-replacement commitment. Broker replied, "In view of the surprising market, it seems unfair that I should have to replace your coin within the next few weeks."

177. For this question only, assume the following facts. Having received Broker's message on October 17, Hoarda sued Broker on November 15 for the market value of a comparable replacement-coin as promised by Broker in February. The trial began on December 1.

If Broker moves to dismiss Hoarda's complaint, which of the following is Broker's best argument in support of the motion?

(A) Broker did not repudiate the contract on October 17, and may still perform no later than the contract deadline of December 31.

(B) Even if Broker repudiated on October 17, Hoarda's only action would be for specific performance because the coin is a unique chattel.

(C) Under the doctrine of impossibility, which includes unusually burdensome and unforeseen impracticability, Broker is temporarily excused by the market conditions from timely performance of his coin-replacement obligation.

(D) Even if Broker repudiated on October 17, Hoarda has no remedy without first demanding in writing that Broker retract his repudiation.

178. For this question only, assume the following facts. After receiving Broker's message on October 17, Hoarda telephoned Broker, who said, "I absolutely will not replace your coin until the market drops far below its present level." Hoarda then sued Broker on November 15 for the market value of a comparable replacement-coin as promised by Broker in February. The trial began on December 1.

If Broker moves to dismiss Hoarda's complaint, which of the following is Hoarda's best argument in opposing the motion?

(A) Hoarda's implied duty of good faith and fair dealing in enforcement of the contract required to mitigate her losses on the rising market by suing promptly, as she did, after becoming reasonably apprehensive of a prospective breach by Broker.

(B) Although the Joetrine of anticipatory breach is not applicable under the prevailing view if, at the time of repudiation, the repudiates owes the repudiator no remaining duty of performance, the doctrine applies in this case because Hoarda, the repudiates, remains potentially liable under an implied warranty that the coin advanced to Broker was genuine.

(C) When either party to a sale-of-goods contract repudiates with respect to a performance not yet due, the loss of which will substantially impair the value of the contract to the other, the aggrieved party may in good faith resort to any appropriate remedy for breach.

(D) Anticipatory repudiation, as a deliberate disruption without legal excuse of an ongoing contractual relationship between the parties, may be treated by the repudiates at her election as a present tort, actionable at once.

179. Alice owned a commercial property, Eastgate, consisting of a one-story building rented to various retail stores and a very large parking lot. Two years ago, Alice died and left Eastgate to her nephew, Paul, for life, with remainder to her godson, Richard, his heirs and assigns. Paul was 30 years old and Richard was 20 years old when Alice died. The devise of Eastgate was made

subject to any mortgage on Eastgate in effect at the time of Alice's death.

When Alice executed her will, the balance of the mortgage debt on Eastgate was less than $5,000. A year before her death, Alice suffered financial reverses; and in order to meet her debts, she had mortgaged Eastgate to secure a loan of $150,000. The entire principal of the mortgage remained outstanding when she died. As a result, the net annual income from,. Eastgate was reduced not only by real estate taxes and regular maintenance costs, but also by the substantial mortgage interest payments that were due each month.

Paul was very dissatisfied with the limited benefit that he was receiving from the life estate. When, earlier this year, Acme, Inc., proposed to purchase Eastgate, demolish the building, pay off the mortgage, and construct a 30-story office building, Paul was willing to accept Acme's offer. However, Richard adamantly refused the offer, even though Richard, as the remainderman, paid the principal portion of each monthly mortgage amortization payment. Richard was independently wealthy and wanted to convert Eastgate into a public park when he became entitled to possession.

When Acme realized that Richard would not change his mind, Acme modified its proposal to a purchase of the life estate of Paul. Acme was ready to go ahead with its building plans, relying upon a large life insurance policy on Paul's life to protect it against the economic risk of Paul's death. Paul's life expectancy was 45 years.

When Richard learned that Paul had agreed to Acme's modified proposal, Richard brought an appropriate action against them to enjoin their carrying it out.

There is no applicable statute.

The best argument for Richard is that

(A) Acme cannot purchase Paul's life estate, because life estates are not assignable.
(B) the proposed demolition of the building constitutes waste.
(C) Richard's payment of the mortgage principal has subrogated him to Paul's rights as a life tenant and bars Paul's assignment of the life estate without Richard's consent.
(D) continued existence of the one-story building is more in harmony with the ultimate use as a park than the proposed change in use.

180. Doppler is charged with aggravated assault on Vezy, a game warden. Doppler testified that, when he was confronted by Vezy, who was armed and out of uniform, Doppler believed Vezy was a robber and shot in self-defense. The state calls Willy to testify that a year earlier, he had seen Doppler shoot a man without provocation and thereafter falsely claim self-defense.

Wilay's testimony is

(A) admissible, as evidence of Doppler's untruthfulness.
(B) admissible, as evidence that Doppler did not act in self-defense on this occasion.
(C) inadmissible, because it is improper character evidence.
(D) inadmissible, because it is irrelevant to the defense Doppler raised.

181. Eddie worked as the cashier in a restaurant. One night after the restaurant had closed, Eddie discovered that the amount of cash in the cash register did not match the cash register receipt tapes. He took the cash and the tapes, put them in a bag, gave them to Rita, the manager of the restaurant, and reported the discrepancy. Rita immediately accused him of taking money from the register and threatened to fire him if he did not make up the difference. Rita placed the bag in the office safe. Angered by what he considered to be an unjust accusation, Eddie waited until Rita left the room and then reached into the still open safe, took the bag containing the cash, and left.

Eddie is guilty of

(A) larceny.
(B) embezzlement.

(C) either larceny or embezzlement but not both.
(D) neither larceny nor embezzlement.

182. A grand jury returned an indictment charging Daniels with bank robbery, and when he could not make bond he was jailed pending trial. He had received Miranda warnings when arrested and had made no statement at that time. The prosecutor arranged to have Innis, an informant, placed as Daniels's cellmate and instructed Innis to find out about the bank robbery without asking any direct questions about it. Innis, once in the cell, constantly boasted about the crimes that he had committed. Not to be outdone, Daniels finally declared that he had committed the bank robbery with which he was charged.

A Daniels's trial, his attorney moved to exclude any testimony from Innis concerning Daniels's boast.

The motion should be

(A) granted, because Daniels's privilege against self-incrimination was violated.
(B) granted, because Daniels's right to counsel was violated.
(C) denied, because Daniels had received Miranda warnings.
(D) denied, because Daniels was not interrogated by Innis.

183. Pamela sued Driver for damages for the death of Pamela's husband Ronald, resulting from an automobile collision. At trial, Driver calls Ronald's doctor to testify that the day before his death, Ronald, in great pain, said, "It was my own fault; there's nobody to blame but me."

The doctor's testimony should be admitted as

(A) a statement against interest.
(B) a dying declaration.
(C) a statement of Ronald's then existing state of mind.
(D) an excited utterance.

184. Clerk is a clerical worker who has been employed for the past two years in a permanent position in the Wasmania County Public Records Office in the state of Orange. Clerk has been responsible for copying and filing records of real estate transactions in that office. Clerk works in a nonpublic part of the office and has no contact with members of the public. However, state law provides that all real estate records in that office are to be made available for public inspection.

On the day an attempted assassination of the governor of Orange was reported on the radio, Clerk remarked to a coworker, "Our governor is such an evil man, I am sorry they did not get him." Clerk's coworker reported this remark to Clerk's employer, the county recorder. After Clerk admitted making the remark, the county recorder dismissed him stating that "there is no room in this office for a person who hates the governor so much."

Clerk sued for reinstatement and back pay. His only claim is that the dismissal violated his constitutional rights.

In this case, the court should hold that the county recorder's dismissal of Clerk was

(A) unconstitutional, because it constitutes a taking without just compensation of Clerk's property interest in his permanent position with the county.
(B) unconstitutional, because in light of Clerk's particular employment duties his right to express himself on a matter of public concern outweighed any legitimate interest the state might have had in discharging him.
(C) constitutional, because the compelling interest of the state in having loyal and supportive employees outweighs the interest of any state employee in his or her job or in free speech on a matter of public concern.
(D) nonjusticiable, because public employment is a privilege rather than a right and, therefore, Clerk lacked standing to bring this suit.

185. Slalome, a ski-shop operator, in a telephone conversation with Mitt, a glove manufacturer, ordered 12 pairs of vortex-lined ski gloves at Mitt's list price of $600 per dozen "for delivery in 30 days." Mitt orally accepted the offer, and immediately faxed to Slalome this signed memo: "Confirming our agreement today for your purchase of a dozen pairs of vortex-lined ski gloves for $600, the shipment will be delivered in 30 days." Although Slalome received and read Mitt's message within minutes after its dispatch, she changed her mind three weeks later about the purchase and rejected the conforming shipment when it timely arrived.

On learning of the rejection, does Mitt have a cause of action against Slalome for breach of contract?

(A) Yes, because the gloves were identified to the contract and tendered to Slalome.
(B) Yes, because Mitt's faxed memo to Slalome was sufficient to make the agreement enforceable.
(C) No, because the agreed price was $600 and Slalome never signed a writing evidencing a contract with Mitt.
(D) No, because Slalome neither paid for nor accepted any of the goods tendered.

186. A burglar stole Collecta's impressionist painting valued at $400,000. Collecta, who had insured the painting for $300,000 with Artistic Insurance Co., promised to pay $25,000 to Snoop, a full-time investigator for Artistic, if he effected the return of the painting to her in good condition. By company rules, Artistic permits its investigators to accept and retain rewards from policyholders for the recovery of insured property. Snoop, by long and skillful detective work, recovered the picture and returned it undamaged to Collecta.

If Collecta refuses to pay Snoop anything, and he sues her for $25,000, what is the probable result under the prevailing modern rule?

(A) Collecta wins, because Snoop owed Artistic a preexisting duty to recover the picture if possible.
(B) Collecta wins, because Artistic, Snoop's employer, had a preexisting duty to return the recovered painting to Collecta.
(C) Snoop wins, because Collecta will benefit more from return of the $400,000 painting than from receiving the $300,000 policy proceeds.
(D) Snoop wins, because the preexisting duty rule does not apply if the promisee's (Snoop's) duty was owed to a third person.

187. Oren owned Purpleacre, a tract of land, in fee simple. By will duly admitted to probate after his death, Oren devised Purpleacre to "any wife who survives me with remainder to such of my children as are living at her death."

Oren was survived by Well, his wife, and by three children, Cynthia, Cam, and Camelia. Thereafter, Cam died and by will duly admitted to probate devised his entire estate to David. Cynthia and Camelia were Cam's heirs at law.

Later Well died. In appropriate lawsuit to which Cynthia, Camelia, and David are parties, title to Purpleacre is at issue.

In such lawsuit, judgment should be that title to Purpleacre is in

(A) Cynthia, Camelia, and David, because the earliest vesting of remainders is favored and reference to Well's death should be construed as relating to time of taking possession.
(B) Cynthia, Camelia, and David, because the provision requiring survival of children violates the Rule Against Perpetuities since the surviving wife might have been a person unborn at the time of writing of the will.
(C) Cynthia and Camelia, because Cam's remainder must descend by intestacy and is not devisable.

(D) Cynthia and Camelia, because the remainders were contingent upon surviving the life tenant.

188. Allen and Bradley were law school classmates who had competed for the position of editor of the law review. Allen had the higher grade point average, but Bradley was elected editor, largely in recognition of a long and important note that had appeared in the review over her name.

During the following placement interview season, Allen was interviewed by a representative of a nationally prominent law firm. In response to the interviewer's request for information about the authorship of the law review note, Allen said that he had heard that the note attributed to Bradley was largely the work of another student.

The firm told Bradley that it would not interview her because of doubts about the authorship of the note. This greatly distressed Bradley. In fact the note had been prepared by Bradley without assistance from anyone else.

If Bradley asserts a claim against Allen based on defamation, Bradley will

(A) recover, because Allen's statement was false.
(B) recover, if Allen had substantial doubts about the accuracy of the information he gave the interviewer.
(C) not recover, unless Bradley proves pecuniary loss.
(D) not recover,- because the statement was made by Allen only after the interviewer inquired about the authorship of the note.

Questions 189-190 are based on the following fact situation.

Sue Starr, a minor both in fact and appearance, bought on credit and took delivery of a telescope from 30-year-old Paul Prism for an agreed price of $100. Upon reaching her majority soon thereafter, Starr encountered Prism and said, "I am sorry for not having paid you that $100 for the telescope when the money was due, but I found out it was only worth $75. So I now promise to pay you $75." Starr subsequently repudiated this promise and refused to pay Prism anything.

189. In an action for breach of contract by Prism against Starr, Prism's probable recovery is

(A) nothing, because Starr was a minor at the time of the original transaction.
(B) nothing, because there was no consideration for the promise made by Starr after reaching majority.
(C) $75.
(D) $100.

190. For this question only, assume that Starr bought the telescope from Prism after reaching her majority and promised to pay $100 "as soon as I am able."

What effect does this quoted language have on enforceability of the promise.

(A) None.
(B) It makes the promise illusory.
(C) It requires Starr to prove her inability to pay.
(D) It requires Prism to prove Starr's ability to pay.

191. Beach owned a tract of land called Blackacre. An old road ran through Blackacre from the abutting public highway. The road had been used to haul wood from Blackacre. Without Beach's permission and with no initial right, Daniel, the owner of Whiteacre, which adjoined Blackacre, traveled over the old road for a period of 15 years to obtain access to Whiteacre, although Whiteacre abutted another public road. Occasionally, Daniel made repairs to the old road.

The period of time to acquire rights by prescription in the jurisdiction is ten years.

After the expiration of 15 years, Beach conveyed a portion of Blackacre to Carrol. The deed included the following clause: "together with the right to pass and repass at all times and for all purposes over the old road." Carrol built a house fronting on the old road.

The road was severely damaged by a spring flood, and Carrol made substantial repairs to the road. Carrol asked Daniel and Beach to contribute one-third each to the cost of repairing the flood damage. They both refused, and Carrol brought an appropriate action to compel contribution from Beach and Daniel.

In this action, Carrol will

(A) lose as to both defendants.
(B) win as to both defendants.
(C) win as to Beach, but lose as to Daniel.
(D) win as to Daniel, but lose as to Beach.

192. Prine sued Dover for an assault that occurred March 5 in California. To support his defense that he was in Utah on that date, Dover identifies and seeks to introduce a letter he wrote to his sister a week before the assault in which he stated that he would see her in Utah on March 5.

The letter is
(A) admissible, within the state of mind exception to the hearsay rule.
(B) admissible, as a prior consistent statement to support Dover's credibility as a witness.
(C) inadmissible, because it lacks sufficient probative value.
(D) inadmissible, because it is a statement of belief to prove the fact believed.

193. Maple City has an ordinance that prohibits the location of "adult theaters and bookstores" (theaters and bookstores presenting sexually explicit performances or materials) in residential or commercial zones within the city. The ordinance was intended to protect surrounding property from the likely adverse secondary effects of such establishments. "Adult theaters and bookstores" are freely permitted in the areas of the city zoned industrial, where those adverse secondary effects are not as likely. Storekeeper is denied a zoning permit to open an adult theater and bookstore in a building owned by him in an area zoned commercial. As a result, Storekeeper brings suit in an appropriate court challenging the constitutionality of the zoning ordinance. Which of the following statements regarding the constitutionality of this Maple City ordinance is most accurate?

(A) The ordinance is valid, because a city may enforce zoning restrictions on speech-related businesses to ensure that the messages they disseminate are acceptable to the residents of adjacent property.
(B) The ordinance is valid, because a city may enforce this type of time, place, and manner regulation on speech-related businesses, so long as this type of regulation is designed to serve a substantial governmental interest and does not unreasonably limit alternative avenues of communication.
(C) The ordinance is invalid, because a city may not enforce zoning regulations that deprive potential operators of adult theaters and bookstores of their freedom to choose the location of their businesses.
(D) The ordinance is invalid, because a city may not zone property in a manner calculated to protect property from the likely adverse secondary effects of adult theaters and bookstores.

194. Kingsley was prosecuted for selling cocaine to an undercover police agent. At his trial, he testified that he only sold the drugs to the agent, whom Kingsley knew as "Speedy," because Speedy had told him that he (Speedy) would be killed by fellow gang members unless he supplied them with cocaine. The prosecution did not cross-examine Kingsley. As rebuttal evidence, however, the prosecutor introduced records, over Kingsley's objection, showing that Kingsley had two prior convictions for narcotics-related offenses. The court instructed the jury concerning the defense of entrapment and added, also over Kingsley's objection but in accord with state law, that it should acquit on the ground of entrapment only if it found that the defendant had established the elements of the defense by a

preponderance of the evidence. Kingsley was convicted.

On appeal, Kingsley's conviction should be

(A) reversed, because it was an error for the court to admit the evidence of his prior convictions as substantive evidence.
(B) reversed, because it was a violation of due process to impose on the defense a burden of persuasion concerning entrapment.
(C) reversed, for both of the above reasons.
(D) affirmed, because neither of the above reasons constitutes a ground for reversal.

Questions 195-196 are based on the following fact situation.

Pat sustained personal injuries in a three-car collision caused by the concurrent negligence of the three drivers, Pat, Donald, and Drew. In Pat's action for damages against Donald and Drew, the jury apportioned the negligence 30% to Pat, 30% to Donald, and 40% to Drew. Pat's total damages were $100,000.

195. Assume for this question only that a state statute provides for a system of pure comparative negligence, joint and several liability of concurrent tortfeasors, and contribution based upon proportionate fault.

If Pat chooses to execute against Donald alone, she will be entitled to collect at most

(A) $70,000 from Donald, and then Donald will be entitled to collect $40,000 from Drew.
(B) $30,000 from Donald, and then Donald will be entitled to collect $10,000 from Drew.
(C) $30,000 from Donald, and then Donald will be entitled to collect nothing from Drew.
(D) nothing from Donald, because Donald's percentage of fault is not greater than that of Pat.

196. Assume for this question only that the state has retained the common-law rule pertaining to contribution and that the state's comparative negligence statute provides for a system of pure comparative negligence but abolishes joint and several liability.

If Pat chooses to execute against Donald alone, she will be entitled to collect at most

(A) $70,000 from Donald, and then Donald will be entitled to collect $40,000 from Drew.
(B) $30,000 from Donald, and then Donald will be entitled to collect $10,000 from Drew.
(C) $30,000 from Donald, and then Donald will be entitled to collect nothing from Drew.
(D) nothing from Donald, because Donald's percentage of fault is not greater than that of Pat.

197. Tess Traviata owed Dr. Paula Pulmonary, a physician, $25,000 for professional services. Dr. Pulmonary orally assigned this claim to her adult daughter, Bridey, as a wedding gift. Shortly thereafter, on suffering sudden, severe losses in the stock market, Dr. Pulmonary assigned by a signed writing the same claim to her stockbroker, Margin, in partial satisfaction of advances legally made by Margin in Dr. Pulmonary's previous stock-market transactions. Subsequently, Traviata, without knowledge of either assignment, paid Dr. Pulmonary the $25,000 then due, which Dr. Pulmonary promptly lost at a horse track, although she remains solvent.

Assuming that Article 9 of the Uniform Commercial Code does NOT apply to either of the assignments in this situation, which of the following is a correct statement of the parties' rights and liabilities?

(A) As the assignee prior in time, Bridey can recover $25,000 from Traviata, who acted at her peril in paying Dr. Pulmonary.
(B) As the sole assignee for value, Margin can recover $25,000 from Traviata, who acted at her peril in paying Dr. Pulmonary.
(C) Neither Bridey nor Margin can recover from Traviata, but Bridey, though not Margin, can recover $25,000 from Dr. Pulmonary.

(D) Neither Bridey nor Margin can recover from Traviata, but Margin, though not Bridey, can recover $25,000 from Dr. Pulmonary.

198. Patten suffered from a serious, though not immediately life-threatening, impairment of his circulatory system. Patten's cardiologist recommended a cardiac bypass operation and referred Patten to Dr. Cutter. Cutter did not inform Patten of the 2% risk of death associated with this operation. Cutter defended his decision not to mention the risk statistics to Patten because "Patten was a worrier and it would significantly lessen his chances of survival to be worried about the nonsurvival rate."

Cutter successfully performed the bypass operation and Patten made a good recovery. However, when Patten learned of the 2% risk of death associated with the operation, he was furious that Cutter had failed to disclose this information to him.

If Patten asserts a claim against Cutter based on negligence, will Patten prevail?

(A) No, if Cutter used his best personal judgment in shielding Patten from the risk statistic.
(B) No, because the operation was successful and Patten suffered no harm.
(C) Yes, if Patten would have refused the operation had he been informed of the risk.
(D) Yes, because a patient must be told the risk factor associated with a surgical procedure in order to give an informed consent.

199. A statute of the state of Orrington provides that assessments of real property for tax purposes must represent the "actual value" of the property. The Blue County Tax Commission, in making its assessments, has uniformly and consistently determined the "actual value" of real property solely by reference to the price at which the particular property was last sold. In recent years, the market values of real property in Blue County have been rising at the rate of 15% per year.

Owner is required to pay real estate taxes on her home in Blue County that are 200% to 300% higher than those paid by many other owners of similar homes in similar neighborhoods in that county, even though the current market values of their respective homes and Owner's home are nearly identical. The reason the taxes on Owner's home are higher than those imposed on the other similar homes In similar neighborhoods is that she bought her home much more recently than the other owners and therefore, it Is assessed at a much higher "actual value" than their homes. Persistent efforts by Owner to have her assessment - reduced or the assessments of the others raised by the Blue County Tax Commission have failed.

Owner has now filed suit against the Blue County Tax Commission, charging only that the tax assessment on her property is unconstitutional.

The strongest constitutional argument to support Owner's claim is that the comparative overvaluation of Owner's property by the Blue County Tax Commission in making tax assessments over time

(A) deprives Owner of the equal protection of the laws.
(B) deprives Owner of a privilege or immunity of national citizenship.
(C) constitutes a taking of private property for public use without just compensation.
(D) constitutes an ex post facto law.

200. Plaza Hotel sued Plaza House Hotel for infringement of its trade name. To establish a likelihood of name confusion, Plaintiff Plaza Hotel offers a series of memoranda which it had asked its employees to prepare at the end of each day listing instances during the day in which telephone callers, cab drivers, customers, and others had confused the two names.

The memoranda should be

(A) excluded, because they are more unfairly prejudicial and confusing than probative.

(B) excluded, because they are hearsay not within any exception.
(C) admitted, because they are records of regularly conducted business activity.
(D) admitted, because they are past recollection recorded.

STOP
IF YOU FINISH BEFORE TIME IS CALLED, CHECK YOUR WORK ON THIS TEST.

If you use the questions in this publication as a practice exam, you should not rely on your raw score to identify how well you are doing. MBE raw scores are converted to scaled scores through an equating procedure that is designed to ensure that the level of difficulty of the examination remains consistent from administration to administration. The Raw Score Conversion Table following the Answer Key will help you determine where your performance would have placed you had you taken the test in 1991.

Item	Answer	Subject	Item	Answer	Subject
001	C	REAL PROP	054	D	CONST LAW
002	C	TORTS	055	B	REAL PROP
003	A	TORTS	056	A	EVIDENCE
004	C	CONTRACTS	057	B	TORTS
005	D	CONTRACTS	058	C	EVIDENCE
006	A	CRIM LAW	059	A	CONST LAW
007	A	EVIDENCE	060	A	CRIM LAW
008	C	CONST LAW	061	c	CONST LAW
009	B	CRIM LAW	062	B	CONTRACTS
010	B	EVIDENCE	063	A	CONTRACTS
011	C	TORTS	064	D	REAL PROP
012	D	EVIDENCE	065	C	EVIDENCE
013	D	REAL PROP	066	C	TORTS
014	B	TORTS	067	D	REAL PROP
015	B	EVIDENCE	068	D	CRIM LAW
016	A	CONTRACTS	069	A	CONST LAW
017	B	CONTRACTS	070	A	EVIDENCE
018	A	TORTS	071	B	TORTS
019	A	CRIM LAW	072	D	TORTS
020	C	CONST LAW	073	B	CRIM LAW
021	C	REAL PROP	074	C	CONTRACTS
022	A,B,D*	CRIM LAW	075	A	CONTRACTS
023	D	REAL PROP	076	B	TORTS
024	A	CONTRACTS	077	C	REAL PROP
025	C	TORTS	078	A	EVIDENCE
026	C	EVIDENCE	079	A	CONST LAW
027	C	CRIM LAW	080	B	CRIM LAW
028	D	CONST LAW	081	c	REAL PROP
029	D	CONTRACTS	082	D	EVIDENCE
030	B	REAL PROP	083	C	CONST LAW
031	B	CONTRACTS	084	A,C*	TORTS
032	C	CONTRACTS	085	A	EVIDENCE
033	B	CONST LAW	086	A	CONTRACTS
034	D	CONTRACTS	087	A	CONTRACTS
035	C	TORTS	088	C	REAL PROP
036	C	REAL PROP	089	A	REAL PROP
037	A	EVIDENCE	090	B	EVIDENCE
038	B	TORTS	091	A	CRIM LAW
039	A	CRIM LAW	092	A	REAL PROP
040	B	CONTRACTS	093	C	CRIM LAW
041	C	CONTRACTS	094	D	CONST LAW
042	C	TORTS	095	D	TORTS
043	D	TORTS	096	D	CRIM LAW
044	D	CRIM LAW	097	A	CONST LAW
045	A	EVIDENCE	098	A	CONST LAW
046	B	CONST LAW	099	C	CONTRACTS
047	C	TORTS	100	B	TORTS
048	B	REAL PROP	101	B	CONST LAW
049	C	CONST LAW	102	D	CRIM LAW
050	B	CRIM LAW	103	A	TORTS
051	B	CONTRACTS	104	B	REAL PROP
052	C	CONTRACTS	105	A	EVIDENCE
053	A	TORTS	106	A	CONTRACTS

#	Ans	Subject	#	Ans	Subject
107	D	REAL PROP	154	D	REAL PROP
108	D	TORTS	155	D	CONST LAW
109	A	EVIDENCE	156	A	CRIM LAW
110	D	CRIM LAW	157	C	TORTS
111	B	CONTRACTS	158	D	TORTS
112	D	CONST LAW	159	D	TORTS
113	D	EVIDENCE	160	A	TORTS
114	C	REAL PROP	161	B,D*	CRIM LAW
115	D	CONTRACTS	162	C	CONST LAW
116	D	CONTRACTS	163	B	REAL PROP
117	D	CRIM LAW	164	B	TORTS
118	C	CONST LAW	165	B	CRIM LAW
119	C	EVIDENCE	166	D	CONTRACTS
120	A	REAL PROP	167	A	EVIDENCE
121	A	TORTS	168	B	TORTS
122	D	CRIM LAW	169	C	EVIDENCE
123	B	CONTRACTS	170	C	CONST LAW
124	D	REAL PROP	171	D	CONTRACTS
125	C	TORTS	172	A	REAL PROP
126	D	TORTS	173	C	EVIDENCE
127	A	CRIM LAW	174	D	CONTRACTS
128	B	CRIM LAW	175	C	CONST LAW
129	D	TORTS	176	B	EVIDENCE
130	C	TORTS	177	A	CONTRACTS
131	C	CONST LAW	178	C	CONTRACTS
132	A	EVIDENCE	179	B	REAL PROP
133	B	CONTRACTS	180	C	EVIDENCE
134	B	CONTRACTS	181	A	CRIM LAW
135	A	REAL PROP	182	D	CRIM LAW
136	D	EVIDENCE	183	A	EVIDENCE
137	D	CRIM LAW	184	B	CONST LAW
138	C	REAL PROP	185	B	CONTRACTS
139	B	REAL PROP	186	D	CONTRACTS
140	D	TORTS	187	D	REAL PROP
141	B	CONTRACTS	188	B	TORTS
142	B	CONTRACTS	189	C	CONTRACTS
143	D	CRIM LAW	190	D	CONTRACTS
144	D	CRIM LAW	191	A	REAL PROP
145	C	CONST LAW	192	A	EVIDENCE
146	C	CONTRACTS	193	B	CONST LAW
147	B	REAL PROP	194	D	CRIM LAW
148	B	TORTS	195	A	TORTS
149	C	CONST LAW	196	C	TORTS
150	D	CONST LAW	197	D	CONTRACTS
151	A	TORTS	198	B	TORTS
152	B	EVIDENCE	199	A	CONST LAW
153	A	CONST LAW	200	B	EVIDENCE

*Immediately following the administration of an MBE, preliminary scoring is conducted to identify any unanticipated item functioning or unusual response patterns. For example, an item might be flagged if a large number of applicants who did well on the test overall selected an option other than the key on that item. Flagged items are then reviewed by the MBE Drafting Committees to assure there are no ambiguities and that they have been keyed correctly. If a content problem is identified, an item may be double-keyed, triple-keyed, or eliminated from scoring by having all four options keyed correct. In a typical administration of the MBE, more than one option may be scored as correct on one or more of the 200 items.

RAW SCORE CONVERSION TABLE

RAW SCORE	SCALED SCORE	PERCENTILE RANK
161-167	170-175	97.6-99.4
154-160	163-169	92.2-97.1
147-153	157-162	82.6-91.1
140-146	151-156	68.7-80.8
133-139	145-150	53.3-66.6
126-132	139-144	38.0-51.1
119-125	133-138	25.0-35.9
112-118	126-132	15.0-23.5
105-111	120-126	8.3-13.9

The raw score is the total number of correct answers given by an examinee. A statistical procedure is used to convert raw scores to scaled scores to provide comparison of scores across test forms. The scaled score represents a comparable level of achievement for all forms of the MBE and scaled scores on one test form can be used interchangeable with the scaled scores on another test form.

The percentile rank shows an examinee's relative position in a group of examinees in terms of the percentage of examinees scoring below the specified score. On this exam, those examinees who obtained a raw score of 153 scored better than 91 percent of all examinees who took the exam initially. Likewise, a raw score of 119 placed an examinee at the 25th percentile, indicating that the examinee scored higher than only 25 percent of the group. A raw score of 132 converted to a scaled score of 144 and placed an applicant at the 51st percentile.

Multistate Bar Examination Answers

1. This question deals with the termination of a joint tenancy in real property by a conveyance during a joint tenant's lifetime. A joint tenant may convey her interest in jointly owned property by deed before her death, so Beth's conveyance to Eugenio is valid. There is no reversion to the joint tenants' grantor upon this event, nor will the property pass to Beth's heirs. (B) and (D) are incorrect.
    After the conveyance by Beth, Christine and Eugenio held the property as tenants in common. Christine was free to convey her interest to Darin. Darin and Eugenio now hold as tenants in common, so (C) is correct.

2. (A) is incorrect because the law of torts generally requires merely that the defendant have intended to commit the act, not that he have understood it was wrongful.
    (B) is incorrect because the intent required for a battery is merely to bring about an unpermitted touching. No actual harm must have been intended.
    (D) is incorrect because the defense of self-defense requires a reasonable belief that the force used was needed to repel an attack. Dorwin could not reasonably have believed that he was under attack by Peavey.
    (C) is correct because intent to bring about the nonconsensual touching of a person is a required element of a battery.

3. (B) is incorrect because it is irrelevant when, or whether, Drury knew he was committing a trespass.
    (C) is incorrect because harm to the plaintiff's property is not an element of trespass. The tort of trespass involves merely an interference with the plaintiff's possessory interest.
    (D) is incorrect because the intent required for a trespass is merely the intent to enter the property. The defendant need not have known it was the plaintiff's property; a good faith mistake about the ownership of the property will not excuse the defendant.
    (A) is correct because nominal damages may be recovered for interference with the plaintiff's right to possession, even where there was no actual harm to the land and the defendant did not know he was trespassing.

4. (A) is incorrect because a contract may be modified where there is an unforeseen hardship making it difficult for the promisor to complete the work. The additional work required for Structo to overcome the hardship caused by the unanticipated presence of the rock constituted consideration for Bailey's promise to pay an additional $20,000.
    (B) is incorrect. There was no duress because there was no wrongful act by Structo that deprived Bailey of a meaningful choice.
    (D) is incorrect because there was consideration for Bailey's promise to pay $20,000; Structo need not prove the reasonable value of the total performance.
    (C) is correct; it states the standard for modification of an existing contract for unforeseen hardship.

5. (A) is incorrect because Structo's expectancy damages would be the contract price *minus* the market value of his services. There are no benefit of the bargain damages to be recovered by the seller where the value of his goods or services exceeds the contract price.
    (B) is incorrect because fixing the driveway so that it can safely be used would not constitute "economic waste."
    (C) is incorrect because it assumes no breach of contract by Structo. While Structo might have been justified in demanding additional consideration to complete the contract in light of the unforeseen hardship, he was not entitled to perform in a way that did not meet Bailey's requirements.
    (D) is correct because Bailey has paid the contract price minus the cost of correcting the driveway, which is the measure of consequential damages from Structo's breach.

6. The "good faith" exception to the exclusionary rule involves police officers reasonably relying on a facially valid search warrant. There was no warrant to search Larson's home, so (B) is incorrect.
    (C) is incorrect because the nature of Larson's neurological problem would not per se make him incapable of giving consent; mental condition alone does not vitiate consent unless there was also official coercion, of which there is no evidence on these facts.

The diary entry discloses incriminating evidence but is not protected by the privilege against self-incrimination because it was voluntarily prepared. The Fifth Amendment protects against compelled self-incrimination only, so (D) is incorrect.

(A) states the correct result under the applicable standards of both the Fourth and Fifth Amendments.

7. A court *may* take judicial notice of its own volition; the court *must* take judicial notice of facts for which counsel provides the proper means of verification. (B) is incorrect because it does not recognize that the court may take judicial notice even when the proof is not provided by counsel.

The burden of proof does not shift to the other party. In fact, no evidentiary proof is permitted to contradict a judicially noticed fact. Thus, (C) is incorrect.

A judicially noticed fact is conclusive in a civil case, so (D) is incorrect.

(A) is correct.

8. (B) is incorrect. The statute imposes no undue burden on interstate commerce because the same requirements apply to policies offered by all companies, whether local or out-of-state.

Federal courts should abstain from hearing cases that might be decided on adequate and independent state grounds in a way that avoids the federal question. However, the basis for challenge here seems to be the federal constitution, not the state constitution or other state law, so the federal courts need not abstain. The presence of a federal basis for jurisdiction lowers the likelihood of abstention. (D) is incorrect.

(A) is incorrect because questions of substantive due process involve merely whether the statute has a rational basis. The statute presumably has a rational basis, and (C) is correct.

9. Robbery is a serious felony giving rise to the felony-murder rule when someone dies as a result of the commission or attempted commission of the robbery. Dawson may be punished as an accomplice to the felony murder because he was an accessory before the fact to the bank robbery. (C) is incorrect.

Going home did not constitute withdrawal; to avoid liability, Dawson would have had to attempt to thwart the commission of the crime as well as communicate his withdrawal to Smith. Thus, (D) is incorrect.

Although he may be convicted of felony murder, it would violate the Eighth Amendment to impose the death penalty on one who aids and abets a felony in the course of which murder is committed by others but who does not himself kill, attempt to kill, or intend to kill. *Enmund v. Florida*, 458 U.S. 782 (1982).

(B) is correct because Dawson may be convicted of felony murder but may not receive the death penalty.

10. It is permissible to attack the credibility of any witness, so (D) is incorrect.

Watts was called to the stand to testify to Juilliard's reputation for truthfulness; Watts' standard of judgment as to Juilliard's reputation is not at issue, so (A) is incorrect.

Federal Rule 608(b) permits questions on cross-examination about specific instances of the witness's conduct that involve honesty or dishonest, so (C) is incorrect, and (B) is correct.

11. This question deals with a continuing trespass to land. For damages in trespass, the defendant's entry onto the land must have been intentional, but he need not have known he was committing a trespass. Thus, (A) is incorrect.

Where the initial trespass was tortious, not pursuant to a license or privilege, the original trespasser remains liable for damages under a continuing trespass theory even though it has subsequently become impossible or impracticable for him to terminate the intrusion on the plaintiff's land. *Rest.2d, Torts,* § 161, Comment *e*. Prudence may proceed against David even though David no longer owns the garage, so (B) is incorrect.

Where ownership of the thing that was tortiously placed on the land is transferred, the transferee comes under a duty to the possessor to remove the thing upon acquiring knowledge that the thing is wrongfully on the land. *Rest.2d, Torts,* § 161, Comment *f*. Even if Drake has become liable for the trespass, however, David is not relieved of responsibility. Thus, (D) is incorrect.

(C) is correct because David's liability for trespass was established by his knowledge of where the garage was being built, regardless of whether he knew it was encroaching onto Prudence's property, and his liability is not relieved by his sale of the property to Drake, regardless of whether Drake had knowledge of the encroachment.

12. If the piece of evidence involved were a writing, recording, or photograph, the best evidence rule would require the original to be produced unless it were shown to be unavailable for some reason other than the serious fault

of the proponent. Duplicates, including photographs of the original, may be introduced if the original is shown to be unavailable, unless a genuine question is raised as to the authenticity of the original. If the original has been destroyed and no copies exist, oral testimony may be admitted to describe the lost item. However, the requirements of the best evidence rule do not apply to physical evidence, such as the model in question. (D) is correct, and the other answers are incorrect.

13. (D) is correct. The rule on which courts are split is whether options to purchase contained in a lease can be assigned separately from the lease. If they cannot be assigned, then Jones takes the property subject only to Teri's lease.

14. (A) is not Daniel's best argument because "danger invites rescue," meaning that rescue attempts are foreseeable when a person places himself or others in danger.

Policemen and firemen entering under authority of law, but without any element of business dealings with the landholder, are commonly held to stand on the same footing as licensees, *i.e.*, they have a privilege to enter but are not owed a duty of reasonable care as to conditions on the land because they may enter at unforeseeable times and under emergency circumstances under which careful preparation for their visit cannot reasonably be expected. *Rest.2d, Torts,* § 345, Comment *c*. As a licensee, Officer would be owed only a duty to be warned of dangerous conditions on the land known to the possessor of the land. Although (D) states a true principle of law, the sort of danger Officer faced did not arise from the condition of the property, so (D) is incorrect.

Daniel's conduct could be considered the proximate cause of Officer's injury despite the tortious nature of the guests' behavior. When the defendant's conduct creates a situation which is utilized by a third person to inflict intentional harm upon another, but the defendant had no reason to expect that the third person would so act, the defendant is not responsible for the harm thus inflicted unless he has special reasons for anticipating criminal action by the third person. *Rest.2d, Torts,* § 448, Comment *a*. However, if the likelihood that a third person may act in a particular manner is the very hazard which makes the defendant negligent, the third person's act, even if intentionally tortious or criminal, does not prevent the defendant from being liable for harm caused thereby. *Rest.2d, Torts,* §§ 302B, 449. Thus, (C) is incorrect. Even though Daniel's conduct could be considered the proximate cause of Officer's injury, Officer will not be able to recover because he assumes these risks in his job. (B) is correct.

15. The professor's statement is offered to establish West's expert qualifications, not for any substantive purpose in the lawsuit. Thus, it is not hearsay. (C) is incorrect. The qualification of an expert is a preliminary evidentiary issue which should be determined by the judge, not the jury. (B) is correct.

16. A requirements contract involves a promise to purchase all of the buyer's needs for particular goods from a particular seller. The consideration is the promise not to purchase those goods from others; if the promisor may buy only as much as he wants under the contract, his promise may be deemed illusory. County may attempt to show that the contract was illusory for this reason, so (D) is incorrect.

Although the advertisement was in writing, the question of whether or not it can be admitted as an expression of the parties' intent is governed by the parol evidence rule. It is not admissible solely because it is in writing, so (B) is incorrect. The parol evidence rule permits evidence outside the written contract to show the meaning of terms when there is an ambiguity on the face of the written agreement. Here there is an ambiguity as to the meaning of "all tires," so (A) is correct and (C) is incorrect.

17. The Contracts Clause of the U.S. Constitution prohibits the states from passing any law impairing contract obligations. The Supreme Court has applied a stricter scrutiny when the state is attempting to avoid its own contractual obligations than when it is invalidating the obligations of third parties. (A) is incorrect because there was no state law involved in County's breach of its agreement with Tyres, leaving Tyres to a private means of enforcing its contract rights.

The U.C.C. favors enforcement of a requirements contract to the extent of the quantity of goods actually required by the buyer, rather than finding the agreement illusory for indefiniteness of quantity or mutuality of obligation. (B) is correct, and (C) and (D) are incorrect.

18. Where the defendant can be found negligent for failure to take reasonable measures to protect against the act of a third party, the third person's act, even if intentionally tortious or criminal, does not cut off the defendant's liability. *Rest.2d, Torts,* §§ 302B, 449. (D) is incorrect.

A possessor of land who holds it open to the public for entry for business purposes is subject to liability to members of the public, while they are upon the land for such a purpose, for physical harm caused by the accidental, negligent, or intentionally harmful acts of third persons. The landholder has a duty to exercise reasonable care to discover that such acts are being done or likely to be done and give adequate warnings or otherwise protect visitors from such harm. *Rest.2d, Torts,* § 344. The landholder is not an insurer of the visitor's safety, so (B) is incorrect because it is too broad a statement, but if he knows or has reason to know from past experience that there is a likelihood of criminal conduct by third persons, he has a duty to take precautions against it, not only to warn visitors but also to provide a "sufficient number of servants to afford a reasonable protection." *Id.*, Comment *f.* (C) is incorrect, and (A) is correct.

19. An attempt requires a substantial step in the direction of committing a crime, coupled with an intention to commit that crime and the apparent ability to complete it. Factual impossibility to commit the crime is not a defense, so (C) is incorrect. However, an attempt to commit murder requires an intent to kill, which would be negated if Jones knew he could not hit Adams with that gun. The standard is subjective, not what a reasonable person would have known. (A) is correct and (B) is incorrect.

Assault itself is an attempt (to commit a battery). The same question of intent arises, so (D) is incorrect.

20. (A), (B), and (D) represent reasonable arguments in favor of the validity of the tax under a Commerce Clause analysis, and thus none of these is the correct answer.

The Tenth Amendment does not give states plenary authority to construct their tax systems without limitation. State taxes are subject to various federal constitutional limitations, including those imposed under the Commerce Clause. (C) is the correct answer because it is the least helpful argument.

21. Where an easement is created by express grant, courts will allow for a reasonable expansion to preserve the usefulness of the easement to the dominant estate. An easement may not be terminated by expanded use that is reasonably related to the purpose for which the easement was granted. (B) is incorrect, and (C) is correct.

22. The Multistate Bar Examiners accepted (A), (B), and (D) as answers to this question, all but throwing it away.

23. Bert's transfer would not have made it impossible for him to purchase Sam's home, merely more difficult, so his refusal to perform constitutes breach of the contract and (B) is incorrect.

Pursuant to the liquidated damages provision of the contract, Sam may keep the deposit and had no duty to mitigate damages. (C) is incorrect.

Where the contract for sale provides for the deposit to serve as liquidated damages, the seller may keep the deposit if the buyer fails to perform. (D) is correct.

24. Even though the car has been delivered to another customer, this is not a case for Rollem to claim impossibility of performance. The doctrine is usually applied where a unique property that was the subject of the contract was unforeseeably destroyed without fault by the promisor. Here Rollem's own agent caused the breach of contract. Even though a specific car was named in the contract, Rollem could have provided a similar car that would meet Betsy's needs. (D) is incorrect.

Courts rarely find a contract supported by "moral consideration" and these facts present an unlikely case. Betsy is an adult, and her father has no legal or even moral obligation to continue to support her. Furthermore, Betsy has a much sounder argument for an enforceable contract based on bargained-for consideration. (B) is incorrect.

Courts of law generally do not look into the adequacy of consideration. Betsy gave value for the automobile, and it is irrelevant that she paid $3,000 for a car worth $10,000. (C) is incorrect, and (A) is correct.

25. (A) is incorrect because a manufacturer may have a duty to warn of known dangers from foreseeable uses of the product, even an abnormal or unintended use or misuse such as driving at excessive speeds.

(B) is incorrect because the discrepancy between the speed capability of the car and of its tires constitutes a design defect or at least a foreseeable danger against which the manufacturer has a duty to warn the consumer.

Contributory negligence is not a complete bar to recovery in a comparative fault jurisdiction, so (D) is incorrect.

(C) is correct because the failure to warn of a foreseeable danger or defect may be the basis of liability in this case.

26. Although this case is being tried in federal court, it does not arise under the federal Constitution or federal statutes. This type of issue is traditionally resolved by state courts, and does not require nationwide uniformity. The issue is not one to be resolved by either federal statute or federal common law. (B) and (D) are incorrect.

The applicability of the presumption should be decided under the law of the state under which other substantive issues in the case will be determined, including the common law but also any applicable statutes. (C) is a more complete answer than (A).

27. Nondeadly force may be used to prevent unlawful trespass and carrying away of the defendant's personal property. However, the use of force must be reasonable under the circumstances and necessary to prevent the crime. This is not a subjective standard, and (A) is incorrect. Although Armando may thus have exceeded his privilege, or had no privilege due to the age of the child, (D) is incorrect because (C), stating the basis for Armando's liability, is a better answer. The absence of a privilege does not in itself make Armando guilty.

The mental state required by the statute is "malice," which does not require an intent to kill or to cause serious physical injury. (B) is incorrect. Reckless conduct posing a high risk of substantial harm to others may constitute malice. (C) is correct.

28. The 13th Amendment outlaws slavery and gives Congress the power to pass any law necessary and proper to eliminate all badges and incidents of slavery. It applies to actions by individuals and the states, but the 13th Amendment has generally been applied to support the federal Civil Rights Acts barring private acts of discrimination in housing and employment. It has not been invoked in voting rights cases, for which there are other bases for authority. (A) is incorrect.

Most challenges to voting districts are waged under the Equal Protection Clause rather than the Due Process Clause, which requires a showing of a deprivation of life, liberty or property. (B) is incorrect.

The Privileges and Immunities Clause of the 14th Amendment protects rights of national citizenship, not state citizenship. It would not be implicated in a city council election issue. (C) is incorrect.

The 15th Amendment provides that the right to vote shall not be denied or abridged by the United States or by any State on account of race, color, or previous condition of servitude. Various voting rights issues have been addressed under this Amendment. (D) is the correct answer.

29. The basic definition of consideration is legal detriment plus a bargained-for exchange. Legal detriment does not mean that the performance must be detrimental to the actor, but merely something that the actor was under no legal requirement to do. (B) is incorrect. The required action may be minimal; it need not be "significantly demanding." (C) reaches the right result for the wrong reason. Running the mile at the time requested by Loomis was something Graceful was under no obligation to do, and her act thus constituted legal detriment even if it was relatively easy for her to do.

It seems clear from the facts that Graceful's performance and Loomis's payment of the $100 were a bargained-for exchange, so (A) is incorrect.

(D) best summarizes the court's probable decision, although the reference to "motives" is unclear. If she ran to collect on Loomis's promise to pay her $100, she was entitled to the payment even if she did not reveal to Loomis her prior experience in this activity.

30. Part performance is a doctrine that might allow Baker to obtain specific performance from Able if Baker has substantially performed. Baker's performance involves payment of the purchase price; his parking his car on Blackacre does not constitute substantial performance. Even if it did, Baker would have a right to specific performance against Able, not vice versa. (A) is incorrect.

Equitable conversion is a doctrine that treats the purchaser as the owner for certain purposes, such as risk of loss, between the date of the contract and the date of the closing. Equitable conversion requires that the purchaser's obligation to buy be specifically enforceable; it is not a doctrine that independently supports an action for specific performance. (C) is incorrect.

Recordation of an instrument for the sale of real property does not affect the enforceability of the contract for sale. General contract rules determine the enforceability of the contract. (D) is incorrect, and (B) is correct.

31. The basic rule under the doctrine of constructive conditions of exchange in a bilateral contract is that a party who is to perform work must substantially perform before he is entitled to payment. Periodic "progress" payments are not implied. By demanding such payments before finishing the work, Karp has anticipatorily breached the contract. Manor is not in breach for refusing to pay before the work is complete. (B) is correct.

32. An assignee (here, Banquo) obtains whatever rights his assignor (Karp) had under the contract, and the assignee takes subject to any defenses the obligor (Manor) could have raised against the assignor. If the obligor has a right of set-off, it can be raised against the assignee if the alleged set-off arises out of the same transaction as the original contract. It is not a question of priority between secured and unsecured claims or the date of the breach versus the date of the assignment, so (C) is correct and the other responses are incorrect.

33. Congress's power to raise revenues is broad and plenary, subject only to due process and certain requirements of geographical uniformity. Due process challenges to taxes are rarely successful, however, and Congress need not "justify" a tax, so (A), (C), and (D) are incorrect.

Congress may determine which activities should bear the burden of taxation. (B) is the correct answer.

34. This is a contract between merchants, so Article 2 of the Uniform Commercial Code applies. Unlike the common law, the U.C.C. does not treat a proposal for additional terms as a rejection of the offer. UCC § 2-207 would treat Topline's form as an acceptance of Wonder-Good's offer, even though it contained an additional term, and even if deemed a material alteration, because Topline's acceptance was not made conditional on assent to the additional term. (A) and (B) are incorrect.

The additional terms do not automatically become part of the contract, however, if they materially alter it; Wonder-Good would have to assent. While liquidated damages clauses may be negotiated in U.C.C. contracts, they are not necessarily a part of any contract. (C) is incorrect, and (D) is correct.

35. (A) is incorrect. Electco's activity was probably not abnormally dangerous because the value and apprpriateness of the activity to the community in which it is located is a factor that weighs against a finding that it is abnormally dangerous.

(D) is incorrect because economic harm is compensable. However, Paul must show that Electco caused a substantial and unreasonable interference with Paul's business. Electco's knowledge of Paul's harm is not at issue, so (B) is incorrect.

(C) is correct. Paul must prove a substantial and unreasonable interference.

36. If the landlord knows of a dangerous condition on the property and has reason to believe that the condition is not readily discoverable by the tenant in an ordinary inspection, the landlord has a duty to disclose it or be liable for injuries to the tenant. The tenant does not have a duty to hire an engineer to inspect the premises. (D) is incorrect, and (C) is correct.

37. An expert witness is allowed greater latitude than a lay witness to base his opinion testimony on reports of others that are not admissible as evidence, so long as such reports are of a type reasonably upon by experts in the particular field in forming opinions on the subject. (B) is incorrect because it is too broad a statement of the rule, and because the dog's behavior was not hearsay. Hearsay is a verbal or nonverbal assertion of a person. FRE 801. (C) is also incorrect because the dog's behavior was not hearsay.

(D) is incorrect because a properly qualified expert could testify regarding the degree of reliability of animal behavior.

(A) is correct.

38. The traditional rule does not permit recovery in negligence by a plaintiff who suffers purely intangible economic loss, but Peter in fact has suffered tangible property damage in the loss of the trees. Even under the traditional rule, this is compensable, so (D) is incorrect.

(A) is incorrect because Doe was the active cause of the loss (the sunshine being the "passive" cause). (C) is incorrect because the loss of the trees was a natural consequence (there was no supervening cause). Whether it was a "probable" consequence, however, is debatable.

(B) is the best answer because this is an issue of foreseeability and the scope of the risk created by Doe's negligence.

39. Criminal negligence can support a conviction for manslaughter. (D) is incorrect. Phillips' actions went beyond negligence, however, since he knew of the presence of children within range of his rifle. (C) is incorrect. Voluntary manslaughter involves either provocation or imperfect use of a defense. (B) is incorrect.

Phillips could not be convicted of first-degree murder because he lacked premeditation/deliberation, but the evidence is sufficient to support a conviction of second-degree murder on the basis of a willful and wanton disregard of an unreasonable risk to human life. (A) is correct.

40. Having the building demolished was not an acceptance of Hardcash's offer; Hardcash was bargaining for the payment of interest after the loan funds were granted, not the demolition of the building or proof that the project was financially sound. (A) and (D) are incorrect.

Even though the contract is not enforceable on the basis of bargained-for consideration, it may be at least partially enforceable on the basis of promissory estoppel. The doctrine of promissory estoppel applies where substantial reliance on a promise was foreseeable and in fact occurred, as here. (C) is incorrect, and (B) is correct.

41. Since Dominique's cause of action is based on promissory estoppel, she is entitled to reliance damages only to the extent of her loss related to such reliance. (C) is correct. Some damages clearly are provable, so (D) is incorrect. There are no expectancy or benefit-of-the-bargain damages since that is not the basis of Dominique's action, so (A) and (B) are incorrect.

42. (B) is incorrect because Peter's mother's negligence will not be imputed to Peter. A child who suffers physical harm is not barred from recovery by the negligence of his parent. *Rest.2d, Torts,* § 488.

(D) is incorrect because Dan's negligence would not support a cause of action against his parents. The common law does not recognize vicarious liability of parents for torts committed by their children.

(A) is true so far as it goes with respect to the lack of vicarious liability, but that is not the end of the analysis. The parents may be held liable for negligent supervision of the child, *i.e.*, failing to take corrective measures when they had reason to know of the child's propensity for dangerous conduct. (C) is correct.

43. (A) is incorrect because it is too broad a statement of the potential liability of a negligent tortfeasor to third parties. The other three answers all attempt to state a narrower basis for any liability of Weber to Hill. The question does not ask whether Hill will recover, and in fact she probably will not. Hill was inside her kitchen and not in personal danger from the speeding vehicle; moreover, she was apparently not related to the child. The traditional rule allows recovery for purely emotional distress at observing harm to others if the plaintiff was also in the zone of danger (or if the victim was a close relative). *Rest.2d, Torts,* § 436, 436A. (D) is correct because it is the most precise statement of the issue.

44. Under the Model Penal Code and some state statutes, assisting in suicide is at most a manslaughter offense. However, this is not the majority rule. At common law, which is still the majority rule, Harold could be convicted of murder because he deliberately killed Willa, regardless of his motives in doing so. (D) is correct.

45. Truth is a defense to libel, making the proffered evidence relevant and admissible substantively. (A) is correct.

46. (A) makes an incorrect statement of the "necessary and proper" clause. Congress has no general power to legislate for the general welfare, but does have the power to enact laws that are appropriate to the exercise of legislative powers that are specifically delegated to Congress. The "necessary and proper" clause would be a good answer only if the power Congress was attempting to exercise did not appear to be directly authorized by one of the Constitution's direct grants of legislative power. In this case, the Commerce Clause provides a basis for Congressional action.

The Federal Computer Abuse Act itself provides for criminal penalties for unlicensed use, and it was proper for Congress to delegate to a federal agency the authority to define the terms on which such licenses would be issued. (C) is incorrect.

The possession and use of a computer without a license, unlike the possession of a firearm in a school zone in *United States v. Lopez* (1995), is an activity with potential economic implications for interstate commerce and thus is not a "wholly local matter" beyond the regulatory authority of Congress. (D) is incorrect.

(B) is the correct answer. The activity that Congress is attempting to regulate could have a substantial effect on economic activity in interstate commerce.

47. The theory of *res ipsa loquitur* permits an inference that harm suffered by the plaintiff was caused by the defendant's negligence when the event is of a kind which ordinarily does not occur in the absence of negligence, other responsible causes are sufficiently eliminated, and the negligence falls within the scope of the defendant's duty to the plaintiff. The inference can support a verdict, so (B) is incorrect.

The majority rule today does not require the defendant to be in a better position than the plaintiff to explain the occurrence. *Rest.2d, Torts,* § 328D, Comment *b*. Thus, (D) is incorrect. However, potential third party causes must be sufficiently eliminated, so (A) is incorrect and (C) is correct.

48. There is no rule that a deed is always superior to a judgment lien. When a judgment lien is properly recorded against property, subsequent purchasers of the property (even purchasers for value) take subject to the lien if it is not satisfied at the time of the transfer. (C) is incorrect.

Neither is there a rule that forgives "reasonable delay" in recording a deed. Absent a statutory grace period or notice requirements, the "first in time, first in right" rule applies. (D) is incorrect.

Breach of a warranty of title could make Able liable to Baker for damages caused by Smollett's claim; the warranty would not defeat Smollett's claim. (A) is incorrect.

The only possible defense against Smollett is (B). Some jurisdictions might look at the timing and basis for Smollett's claim to determine whether he should be treated as a purchaser for value under the statute. This defense is not likely to be successful since in most jurisdictions an unrecorded deed is void as to docketed judgment creditors, whether the debt was contracted before or after the date of the unrecorded deed.

49. The ordinance may be rationally related to local interests, but that is not the end of the analysis when federal interests are also involved. (A) is incorrect. Persons transporting dangerous materials are not a suspect class, and the ordinance has a rational basis. (D) is incorrect. The Tenth Amendment reserves powers to the states when they do not conflict with federal powers. Here, the Supremacy Clause rules. (B) is incorrect. (C) is the correct answer.

50. The regulation involved creates a strict liability "public welfare offense." Mistake of law, *i.e.*, the actor does not know that the particular act is criminal, does not constitute a defense to a strict liability crime. (C) is incorrect. Even a reasonable mistake of fact is not a defense. One who sells liquor to a minor cannot defend on the ground that he believed the minor was of age. Both (A) and (D) are incorrect.

(B) would be the most helpful to Dart because, even if his employer's culpability does not relieve Dart of liability, Dart may be able to obtain partial or full indemnity from his employer, who should have trained Dart to comply with the law.

51. A contract is voidable for a mutual mistake that goes to a basic assumption on which the contract was made and that has a material effect on the bargain. That is not the case here, however. This is a proper case for reformation of the written contract to reflect the mutual understanding and agreement of the parties, and where reformation is available, neither party can void the contract. (A) is incorrect.

Frustration of purpose is seldom applied to excuse performance. The doctrine is generally applied only when the property subject to the contract is destroyed through an unforeseeable event. Price increases do not rise to this level of frustration, so (C) is incorrect.

A condition precedent to the existence of a contract may be shown by parol evidence. This does not mean that a material term was missing from the written contract, but rather that the parties agreed that no binding effect would be given to the contract terms unless the pre-condition occurred. (D) is incorrect.

(B) is correct. Although Kranc's contract with Trimota might appear to have affirmed his intent to perform the contract, he did not give written notice in the form required before January 2.

52.   Kranc has not substantially performed, since his required performance is the payment of the purchase price. (A) is incorrect.
        Nor has there been a novation. Schaff did not agree to release Kranc from his payment obligation, so (D) is incorrect.
        The written notice was a condition precedent, not a condition subsequent, and it was waived by Schaff's oral agreement. (B) is incorrect, and (C) is correct.

53.   David's negligence was a proximate cause of Paul's injury since David knew or should have known of the likelihood that his conduct would create an opportunity for Mark to harm someone. *Rest.2d, Torts,* § 448. However, Mark's intentional act means that David may seek full indemnification from Mark. The Restatement notes that indemnity may be sought where the two parties are guilty of different types of tortious conduct or are held to different standards of care, e.g., one is negligent and the other is guilty of reckless or intentional misconduct. *Rest.2d, Torts,* § 886B, Comment *k*. One who has been found liable but who was not an active wrongdoer may seek indemnification for the entire amount against the actual wrongdoer, not merely contribution for a portion of the harm, so (A) is incorrect.

54.   An ex post facto law criminalizes conduct that was not criminal when committed. It is not an ex post facto law merely to change Alien's job prospects. (A) is incorrect.
        The Due Process Clause protects property rights that have vested in some way, not merely job prospects. (B) is incorrect.
        The Privileges and Immunities Clause of the 14th Amendment protects rights of "citizens of the United States." It does not apply to non-citizens. (C) is incorrect.
        Aliens who are lawful residents of the United States are "persons" within the protection of the Equal Protection Clause, alienage is a protected status, and the right to earn a living is a fundamental interest, making the Equal Protection Clause Alien's strongest ground to challenge the state law. (D) is the correct answer.

55.   An easement by implication is created at the time commonly owned property is divided. Since the ownership of the two parcels had previously been separated before Sam acquired his land, he does not hold an easement by implication and (A) is incorrect.
        Sam has an easement appurtenant. An easement is appurtenant if the easement owner holds it only by virtue of his status as the owner or possessor of land that is benefited by the easement. Such an easement is useless without concurrent ownership of the land, and the appurtenant easement is automatically transferred with the land benefited, regardless of whether the easement is mentioned in the instrument of conveyance. (D) is incorrect. An easement in gross, by contrast, benefits no particular parcel of land and is generally not transferable. The right to use a strip of land to reach the road obviously benefited the owner of the land, not Buck personally, so (C) is incorrect. (B) is correct.

56.   The foundation required to admit a piece of physical evidence is a showing of reasonable certainty that the item offered into evidence may be identified with the defendant and has not been exchanged, contaminated or tampered with. Chain of custody is a way of providing adequate identification, so (B) is incorrect. The chain of custody requirement is not absolute; it merely must be sufficiently complete to render it reasonably probable that the offered item is the original item at issue. The police need not have taken the bag from Dickinson directly, and (C) is incorrect. The location of the bag in the same place where the police saw Dickinson drop it, and the fact that only a few minutes had passed, in the absence of evidence showing a likelihood of someone tampering with the bag, should be sufficient evidence of the connection to Dickinson. (A) is correct. The standard is reasonable probability, not a preponderance of the evidence, so (D) is incorrect.

57.   A manufacturer's liability extends to those who purchase or use products obtained through the marketplace. The product in question had not reached the market, so (A) is incorrect. Farmer will prevail on a strict liability theory relating to the escape of a dangerous substance from Chemco's premises under the theory of *Rylands v. Fletcher*. It is not necessary for the plaintiff to show negligence, because one who carries on an abnormally dangerous activity is liable for resulting harm even though he has exercised the utmost care to prevent the harm. *Rest.2d, Torts,* § 519. (C) and (D) are incorrect, and (B) is correct.

58. When the relevancy of a voice communication depends on identification of the owner of the voice, the identification must be authenticated. Authentication can be provided by a witness who is familiar with the caller's voice. Identification of a party to a telephone call can also be authenticated by the witness's testimony that he called the party's number and the party identified himself. It is not necessarily authenticated if the owner of the voice called the witness and identified himself, so (A) is incorrect. Other facts may also logically identify the caller, such as if the communication reveals that the speaker had knowledge of facts that only the caller would be likely to know. *Santora, McKay & Ranieri v. Franklin*, 339 S.E.2d 799 (1986). Limited access to the witness's phone number makes the identification substantially more certain, so (C) is correct. Witness's motive is tangential to authentication and can be addressed on cross-examination, so (A) and (D) are incorrect.

59. The Court will uphold time, place or manner restrictions on speech if they are content-neutral, narrowly tailored to serve a substantial government interest, and leave open ample alternative channels of communication. *United States v. Grace*, 461 U.S. 171 (1983).
    (A) is the correct statement of the test. The other statements are incorrect because they refer only to a "legitimate" rather than a "substantial" government interest and do not contain the "narrowly tailored" standard.

60. The use of a non-testifying co-defendant's confession against the accused at trial presumptively violates the accused's Sixth Amendment right of confrontation. It is thus significant whether or not Penn testified at trial to provide a right to confrontation. (A) is the correct answer.

61. The fact that partisan politics are involved does not render an issue a nonjusticiable political question. (D) is incorrect.
    The question turns on a nexus with the state sufficient to constitute state action. The fact that baseball is "the national pastime" clearly does not render everything involving baseball subject to the 14th Amendment.
    A one-time grant of state funds is not a sufficient nexus to evidence state involvement in the operations of the team. Building sports facilities is not traditionally or exclusively a government function within the state action concept. (A) is incorrect, and (C) is correct.

62. This is a case of unilateral mistake. Walker's misconception about the value of his own horse will not, without some affirmative overreaching on Sherwood's part, give Walker a right to rescind the contract. Sherwood was under no duty to inform Walker of the value of Walker's horse, and (C) is incorrect.
    Likewise, Sherwood was under no duty to disclose the extent of his own experience with horses, so long as he made no affirmative misrepresentations in this regard. (A) is incorrect.
    (D) is clearly not an argument for rescission because it involves a fact known to Walker only and could have legitimately affected the value of the horse to Walker on the ground that the horse was "bad tempered."
    (B) is the best answer because Sherwood might have a duty to disclose facts solely within his knowledge affecting a basic assumption of Walker's, *i.e.*, that the horse was "nothing special."

63. In each of these instances, the event leading Sherwood to seek rescission occurred after the sale, so presumably he needs restitution of the price he paid. Generally, rescission and restitution of the price paid or the value of services performed is allowed when a party that has partially performed finds the remainder of his performance excused by impossibility or frustration of purpose. See *Rest.2d, Torts,* § 377. The requirements for excuse on the grounds of frustration of purpose are that an event have occurred "the non-occurrence of which was a basic assumption on which the contract was made." *Rest.2d, Torts,* § 265. The purpose that is frustrated must have been a principal purpose of the party in making the contract, without which the transaction would make little sense, and the frustration must be substantial, not merely causing the party some disappointment or loss. Sherwood may have hoped that Aberlone would make him additional money for stud services, but after earning $5 million over three years (many times what Sherwood paid for the horse), it could not be said that the value of the contract to Sherwood was substantially impaired. The principal purpose of the contract, to provide Sherwood with a competitive racehorse, was fulfilled. (B) is incorrect.
    The clerical error in (C) can probably be corrected and does not go to the underlying assumption that Aberlone was sired by a famous racehorse. The frustration must be so severe that it is not fairly regarded as within the risks that the party assumed under the contract.

(D) is incorrect because, although Sherwood's injuries were severe, Sherwood was warned that the horse was bad-tempered and assumed the risk of this type of problem. Furthermore, Aberlone's attack on Sherwood does not go to his basic qualities as a racehorse.

The death of the horse in his first race would frustrate the purpose of the contract as none of the other problems would. Walker could argue that Sherwood assumed the risk of undiscoverable health problems and might win on this point, but (A) would be Sherwood's strongest scenario for rescission. A party seeking restitution must return or offer to return any property he received in exchange in substantially as good condition as when he received it. However, this requirement does not apply if the property was worthless when received or has been destroyed as a result of its own defects. *Rest.2d, Torts,* § 384. Such would be the case with Aberlone's heart defect in the first scenario, so (A) is correct.

64. Under the common-law Rule Against Perpetuities, the "unborn widow" rule does not void the life interest in Louis's widow because her interest was certain to vest within the period of the Rule (at Louis's death). Maria never became Louis's widow, since she predeceased him. Louis's widow is Zelda and Zelda's life estate is valid. The MBE published (D) as the correct answer, but (B) appears more likely, since Norman's interest under the deed would be voided by the unborn widow problem, and Norman predeceased Louis.

65. When a hearsay statement has been admitted into evidence, the credibility of the declarant may be attacked by his inconsistent statements or conduct. FRE 806. Availability of the declarant is not required. (B) is incorrect, and (C) is correct.

66. Under the majority rule, a willing participant in a normally dangerous professional sport may recover only for intentional attacks, not for negligent or even reckless rule violations because a professional athlete is deemed to understand the usual incidents of competition resulting from the foreseeable carelessness or roughness of other players. (C) is correct. This is a close question because there is a judicial trend toward deeming *some* reckless rule violations outside the scope of a participant's consent, and *Rest.2d, Torts,* § 50, Comment *b* treats *any* violation of a safety rule as outside the scope of a participant's consent. Courts often look at the circumstances with reference to the way each particular sport is played, *i.e.*, the rules and customs that shape the participants' ideas of foreseeable conduct in the course of the game. Whether a sport is normally contact or non-contact may not be determinative. In the game of golf, for example, "a golfer accepts the risk of coming in contact with wayward golf shots on the links," but "a player who hurls a club into the air in a moment of pique and injures another golfer should be held accountable." *Thompson v. McNeill,* 559 N.E.2d 705 (Ohio 1990). In a hockey game, "[b]utt-ending [the practice of taking the end of the stick which does not come into contact with the puck and driving this part of the stick into another player's body] is unexpected and unsportsmanlike conduct for a hockey game" and has been found actionable as a "reckless disregard of safety." *Gauvin v. Clark,* 537 N.E.2d 94 (Mass. 1989). In horse racing, the violation of rules prohibiting "foul riding" or failure to control a horse does not necessarily give rise to liability since such dangers are "inherent in the sport." *Turcotte v. Fell,* 502 N.E.2d 964 (N.Y. 1986). Thus, (B) is incorrect. [The case said the violation does not, without more, constitute recklessness, but said that if a showing of recklessness could be made the court would find liability.]

67. Whether time is of the essence (I) will affect whether or not Baker is in breach. A reasonable delay will not constitute a breach unless time is of the essence, either as stated in the contract or as inferred from the circumstances.

The parol evidence rule (II) could be involved with respect to the question of whether the condition was a condition precedent to the activation of the contract.

Of course, a contract for the sale of land is subject to the Statute of Frauds (III), but it may be supplemented or reformed in appropriate cases so long as the essential terms are stated with reasonable certainty. Baker may attempt to enforce the contract in an action for specific performance (IV) if he can show there is a contract and he is not in breach of the contract. (D) is correct because all of these issues may be involved.

68. At common law, an accessory could be convicted only if the principal had been apprehended, charged and convicted. This is not a requirement, however, where the accessory's acts prevented apprehension or conviction. (A) is incorrect.

An accessory after the fact must have known of the commission of the felony (not of the felon's indictment, so (C) is incorrect) and have given aid to the felon for the purpose of hindering the felon's apprehension, conviction, or punishment. As the name suggests, such aid is typically given after the commission of the felony, and (B) is incorrect. (D) is correct.

69. The owners of foreign-made autos are not a suspect class, so the Equal Protection Clause is not a strong argument. (B) is incorrect.

A prohibition or limitation on parking does not deprive auto owners of their property, so the Due Process Clause is not a likely argument. (C) is incorrect.

The Privileges and Immunities Clause of the 14th Amendment is seldom invoked and is not generally a good answer. It protects incidents of national citizenship, which automobile ownership is not. (D) is incorrect.

Congress holds plenary power to regulate commerce with foreign nations, but there may be room for state regulation where Congress has not acted and there is little need for national uniformity. However, as under the interstate Commerce Clause, a court examining a state's action in the area of foreign commerce should first look at whether the state had a discriminatory purpose or intent, which was clearly the case here. (A) is the strongest argument and thus the correct answer.

70. (A) is correct. FRE 803 permits a learned treatise to be relied upon in direct examination as a basis for the expert's opinion; it is not being used as extraneous evidence to support the witness's credibility.

(D) is incorrect because a published treatise must be admitted by being read to the jury. It is not admissible as an exhibit.

71. Defamatory statements in a printed newspaper article may be actionable as libel, which, unlike slander, does not require proof of special damages. (A) is incorrect.

A showing of malice is required with respect to the publication of defamatory statements about public figures, and the standard of proof in such cases is clear and convincing evidence on the issue of malice, but merely being well known in certain circles is not enough to make a private citizen a public figure unless the plaintiff has "thrust [himself] to the forefront of particular public controversies." *Gertz v. Robert Welch, Inc.*, 418 U.S. 323 (1974). Since that does not appear to be the case with Kitchen's general manager, he should not be required to show malice, so (C) is incorrect.

The defendant's motion for a directed verdict should be granted if the plaintiff has produced no evidence of the defendant's negligence. The defendant need not show "uncontradicted evidence" of accurate reporting, and merely reporting accurately what the employees said would not necessarily discharge the defendant's duty of care with respect to the truth or falsity of the charge of embezzlement. (D) is incorrect, and (B) is correct.

72. It seems clear that Surgeon owed Patient a disclosure about the failure of the operation so that Patient could take corrective action if so desired. Thus, (C), while relevant, is not the most difficult question to answer.

(A) and (B) would argue a duty of care toward the baby to prevent its "wrongful life." Courts do not accept this cause of action, and Patient is not seeking such recovery.

(D) is the best answer, seeking medical damages for "wrongful birth." Some courts allow parents to recover for medical expenses from a child's unintended or damaged birth.

73. Larceny by trick involves obtaining possession of another's property by lying or trickery, and theft by false pretenses involves obtaining title by such means. Here there were no misrepresentations or false pretenses, so (C) and (D) are incorrect.

Robbery is a larceny from the person by violence or intimidation. Here, no violence or intimidation actually occurred because the attendant was not alarmed by Robert's actions. (A) is incorrect.

(B) is correct because Robert intended to commit the crime of robbery and took a substantial step toward it when he threatened to shoot.

74. Kabb was a principal to the contract with Petrol, not merely Artiste's agent, so (B) is incorrect.

Artiste is an intended beneficiary of the Kabb-Petrol contract because Kabb intended to give Artiste the benefit of Petrol's performance. Her rights vested when she changed her position in justifiable reliance on Petrol's promise by declining the Detrugid account. She need not have provided consideration, so (D) is incorrect.

As an intended beneficiary with vested rights under the contract, Artiste may have a cause of action against Petrol, but Petrol can raise any defenses against Artiste that he could raise against Kabb on their contract, including the failure of a condition precedent. Kabb breached the requirements contract by purchasing substantial amounts from another supplier. Petrol can raise this breach by Kabb to excuse his duty to Artiste. (A) is incorrect and (C) is correct.

75. Artiste's rights are not based upon an agency relationship with Kabb, so (D) is incorrect.
Artiste has enforceable legal rights under the contract, not merely an equitable argument of "bad faith," so (D) is incorrect.
The original parties to a third-party beneficiary contract may modify the contract after the beneficiary's rights have vested only with the beneficiary's consent. Artiste's rights vested when she relied upon the Petrol contract to turn down the Deturgid contract, so her consent was required to any modification that would alter or discharge Petrol's performance to her. (A) is correct, and (C) is incorrect.

76. (A) is incorrect because these facts are not relevant to the issues in a suit for slander.
Pat is not a public figure, so negligence, not malice, is the basis of liability and Drew's state of mind is not relevant to his negligence. (C) is incorrect.
Publication of defamatory matter is its communication intentionally or by a negligent act to one other than the person defamed. *Rest.2d, Torts,* § 577(1). Calling Pat a thief in a loud voice when Drew knew or should have known other people in the office could overhear him constituted publication of the defamation, so (B) is the correct answer.

77. The windows are fixtures. Fixtures may be the subject of security interests separate from a mortgage on the real property unless they become an unremovable part of the property such as bricks and cement. The windows are removable, so (B) is incorrect and (C) is correct. A purchase-money security interest in fixtures takes priority over a prior mortgage on the real property if the PMSI is recorded within a statutory period (10 or 20 days) after annexation of the fixture to the property. Vend recorded its PMSI before the windows were installed, so (A) is incorrect.

78. This question involves the scope of, and exceptions to, the attorney-client privilege. The privilege applies to confidential communications between an attorney and his client for the purpose of facilitating the rendition of professional legal services to the client.
Discussions of past crimes are generally within the privilege, so (B) is not the most likely basis for allowing a subpoena.
Prior inconsistent statements may be admissible for certain purposes under the hearsay rules, but this is not an exception to the attorney-client privilege. (C) is incorrect.
Death does not terminate the attorney-client privilege, nor permit disclosure on the ground that the client is unavailable. (D) is incorrect.
The tape is no longer confidential if Denby played it for one who does not fall within the attorney-client relationship. His father is not a person within the privilege because he is not a representative of either Denby or his lawyer. (A) is the correct answer.

79. The Article IV, Section 3 power of Congress over federal property such as wild animals on federal lands is plenary and not subject to state action. *Kleppe v. New Mexico*, 426 U.S. 529 (1976) (state could not round up wild burros on federal land protected by federal law). (C) and (D), which would leave room for state action involving federal property, are incorrect.
On the other hand, the federal power in Article I, Section 8 is overstated in (B), which confuses the power to tax and spend for the general welfare with the power to make laws necessary and proper to execute Congress's enumerated powers. (A) is the correct answer.

80. The kidnapping statute requires knowledge of lack of privilege to take the child and thus creates a specific intent crime. Reliance on erroneous advice from a private attorney does not establish a mistake of law defense, so (A) is incorrect. This is true even if such reliance was reasonable and in good faith. (D) is incorrect.
It might thus seem that (C) is the correct answer, but the knowledge requirement is subjective. If the defendant's lack of knowledge is bona fide, the reason for his ignorance does not matter. (B) is correct.

81. Although a purchase-money mortgage may take priority over a mortgage to secure a preexisting obligation, Owen was selling the property to Newton, not mortgaging it. Newton's purchase of the property would have been subject to the mortgage if the sale had proceeded without satisfaction of the mortgage obligation. (A) is incorrect.

Under the doctrine of equitable conversion the buyer is treated as holding title for some purposes between the date of the contract of sale and the closing, e.g., risk of loss. However, if the seller's title is unmarketable, equitable conversion will not take place In other words, the seller must prove he is entitled to specific performance before claiming that the risk of loss has passed to the buyer or that equitable conversion otherwise applies, so (B) begs the question.

(C) is correct. Marketable title does not contemplate any encumbrances on the property, whether or not specifically named, but a mortgage is not an encumbrance if the seller pays it off before the closing. Owen has offered to do so, and Newton is in breach by refusing to close. It is not necessary to examine Newton's "real reason" for the refusal (D), only her behavior, to find her in breach of the contract.

82. Young's statement is hearsay because it was made by an out-of-court declarant whether it is offered to prove that the carpet was defective or that Dalton knew of the defect. (D) is the correct answer.

83. *Flast v. Cohen* recognized that taxpayers had standing to bring suit to challenge federal taxing and spending where there is a logical nexus between the taxpayer status and the claim sought to be adjudicated. Magazine as a payer of the disputed tax could allege competitive disadvantages, and (A) is incorrect.

The 11th Amendment prohibits suits by citizens of one state against another state in federal court. This case was brought in Wonatol state court, so the 11th Amendment is not implicated, and (B) is incorrect.

(C) is the correct answer. In *Texas Monthly, Inc. v. Bullock*, 489 U.S. 1 (1989), a state statute exempting religious publications from sales taxes was held to violate the Establishment Clause. The reason was that the exemption in effect provided a subsidy for those promoting religious beliefs, not that it was a prior restraint on nonreligious publications that had to pay the tax, and (D) is incorrect.

84. The liability of an owner for harm done by his livestock and other domestic animals is for negligence (*Rest.2d, Torts,* § 518), unless the owner knows of a dangerous propensity of the animal giving rise to strict liability (*Rest.2d, Torts,* § 509), or the animal trespasses off the owner's land (*Rest.2d, Torts,* § 504) . Here the horse had no dangerous propensities and had not been known to escape before. Nor did the horse commit a trespass in this instance, since the harm occurred on the highway and did not involve entry on or harm to Driver's land. The relevant standard is not strict liability in this case, so (B) is incorrect.

Rancher need not be shown to have intentionally let the horse run at large, so (D) is incorrect. The applicable standard is negligence, but the NCBE accepted both (A) and (C) as correct answers to this question.

85. Spousal immunity belongs to the witness spouse, not the defendant spouse, so (D) is incorrect.

FRE 804(b)(1) recognizes a hearsay exception, when the declarant is unavailable for testimony, for testimony given under oath in another proceeding at which the declarant was available for cross-examination, whether or not that opportunity was effectively used at the time. (A) is the correct answer.

86. A liquidated damages clause is enforceable if the amount of damages stipulated is reasonable in relation to either the actual damages suffered or the damages reasonably anticipated at the time the contract was made. Even though Mermaid actually lost only $100 because she was able to find a late rental at a reduced rate, the reasonable anticipation at the time she made the contract with Phinney was that Mermaid might not be able to find a substitute rental prospect. There is no general rule that liquidated damages clauses are penalties unless limited to 10% or 20% of the contract price. (B) and (D) are incorrect. Nor must Mermaid refund any amount in excess of her actual damages. (C) is incorrect.

(A) correctly states the standards for validity of a liquidated damages clause.

87. The contract is discharged due to impossibility. The liquidated damages clause is intended to cover a breach of contract, not discharge due to impossibility, in which circumstances the parties should be returned to the status quo ante. (D) is incorrect. The storm warnings were an supervening event that could not be predicted at the time the contract was made, not a mistake as to a fact that could have been ascertained by one or both parties. (B) is incorrect, and (A) is correct.

88.   There is no rule that a warranty deed takes priority over a quitclaim deed. Whether the deed was conveyed for consideration is relevant only when a subsequent deed is delivered as a gift, in which case it cannot defeat a prior deed. The fact that Orben's subsequent deed to Fred was for consideration does not automatically defeat Sam's prior deed, even though it was a gift. Thus, (A) and (B) are incorrect.
        The public interest in certainty with respect to land titles generally forecloses results based solely on equitable considerations. (D) is incorrect.
        (C) is correct because Sam's possession put Fred on "inquiry notice," meaning that he had a duty to investigate Sam's rights to the property. A purchaser generally has a duty to inspect the property before buying it and cannot claim lack of notice of obvious facts giving rise to questions about ownership interests.

89.   (C) is a broad public policy argument that can be eliminated preliminarily on the ground that such arguments are rarely the correct answer.
        (D) is incorrect because the exercise of eminent domain requires that the state pay just compensation
        The use of Brown's land by Agency constitutes adverse possession because the use has been open and notorious for the statutory period, and the periodic breaks in the use while the facility was closed would not be deemed to interrupt Agency's "continuous" possession. Brown's acquiescence permitted adverse possession to occur, but all the elements of adverse possession are also present, so (B) is incorrect and (A) is correct.

90.   The vehicle registration statement is not hearsay because the document has operative legal effect. Since it is not hearsay, no exception need be found. (A) and (D) are incorrect.
        A certified copy of a public record is self-authenticating without testimony of a state official under FRE 902(4). (C) is incorrect.
        The evidence is relevant to a material issue in the case and is admissible. (B) is correct.

91.   The Double Jeopardy Clause would not prevent Donald from later being tried for murder if the victim of a felony for which he was convicted subsequently died. Although Donald was convicted of assault, he was acquitted of the greater offense of attempted rape. Assault is a misdemeanor at common law, so it could not provide a basis for felony-murder liability, and he was acquitted of the potential felony charge. (A) is correct.

92.   An inter vivos grant is not revoked by a subsequent testamentary provision for the property. On the contrary, a testamentary gift lapses if the property has already been disposed of and is no longer in the decedent's estate. Thus, (B) is incorrect.
        (C) and (D) are incorrect because Lilly's life estate lasts for her life, not Ogle's. The lack of a remainderman would cause a reversion to Ogle's estate only after Lilly's death.
        (A) is correct. Lilly has a life estate that could not subsequently be affected by Ogle.

93.   It is not the law that a criminal defendant has no privacy expectations merely because he is on trial. (D) is incorrect. However, there is no reasonable expectation of privacy in one's physical characteristics, so requiring Devlin to display his limp would not be a Fourth Amendment search. (B) is incorrect.
        The Fifth Amendment privilege against self-incrimination protects only testimonial evidence, not physical evidence or physical characteristics. His limp is not intended to make an assertion. (A) is incorrect.
        (C) is correct. Requiring Devlin to walk across the room would be a legitimate part of the courtroom identification process.

94.   The strongest argument would be that the prohibition on lobbying would be an unconstitutional condition, denying the recipients their First Amendment rights to free speech and association, as applied to the states through the 14th Amendment. The law permits some restrictions in this area. For example, *Regan v. Taxation with Representation of Washington,* 461 U.S. 540 (1983), upheld Internal Revenue Code Section 501(C)(3), which grants special tax exempt status to organizations that are prohibited from using their tax-deductible contributions for lobbying activities. In this question, however, the state of Kiowa's grant would prevent the recipient from all lobbying activities of a specified type, regardless of whether the organization receives additional funding for such activities. (D) is the correct answer.

95. City and Railroad are jointly and severally liable to Penkov because their concurrent negligence brought about Penkov's harm and it is not possible to separate portions of the harm as attributable to each defendant. An inability to apportion the harm does not relieve joint tortfeasors of liability, so (B) is incorrect.

The effect of joint and several liability is that each defendant is liable for the entire amount of the plaintiff's damages, so (C) is incorrect. The plaintiff is not required to join them both in the same action, so (A) is incorrect.

Railroad's negligence was a "but for" cause of Penkov's harm because if Railroad had properly maintained its storm drain, the flooding would not have occurred. (D) is correct. Under joint and several liability, Penkov may recover all of his loss from Railroad, which may then attempt to obtain contribution from City.

96. Obtaining property by false pretenses requires that the defendant know that his representation is false, and thereby intends to defraud the owner. Smith made no false representations of fact to Jones at the time he borrowed the money. A false promise to return the money would not constitute a false representation in most jurisdictions, and it is not apparent that Smith had no intention to return the money at the time he borrowed it. (A) and (C) are incorrect.

Larceny by trick involves obtaining mere possession of another's property by lying or trickery. Smith merely asked to borrow the money, which is more consistent with obtaining possession than title, but again, there is no evidence that Smith lied or made a misrepresentation in that he had no intent to return the money when he borrowed it; few people gamble with the intention to lose money. (B) is incorrect, and (D) is correct.

97. Congress may make "exceptions" to Supreme Court jurisdiction without constitutional amendment, so (C) is incorrect. Congress can limit Supreme Court jurisdiction over cases arising in state courts, so (B) is incorrect.

The strongest argument is that Congress cannot alter federal court jurisdiction in a way that would violate individual rights guaranteed by the Constitution or otherwise interfere with the establishment of a supreme and uniform body of federal constitutional law. (A) is the correct answer.

98. Although involving state lands, the case also involved a federal statute; it could be and in fact was decided under federal law. The United States Supreme Court may review by certiorari state court decisions in cases involving matters of federal law, in order to ensure uniform interpretation of such laws. (D) is incorrect. It is unimportant whether the Blue Supreme Court also relied on the state law, so (B) is incorrect.

The issues involved are the same under the state statute and the federal statute it was patterned after. Thus, the state grounds would not be "independent" of the federal issues that are proper for Supreme Court review, and (C) is incorrect.

(A) is the correct answer.

99. Megahawg appears to be a unique property, the unavailability of which effectively makes the contract impossible or impracticable to perform. Trawf need not demand assurances or accept another hog from Schweinebauch before terminating his own performance. (C) is the correct answer.

100. Paula was detained if the manager was blocking her only reasonable exit without her consent, so (D) is incorrect.

(A) and (C) are difficult to distinguish, and both are incorrect. A merchant has a privilege to detain a person whom the merchant has reasonable grounds to believe is stealing or attempting to steal his property, and Paula's behavior may have contributed to the reasonableness of the manager's belief. However, the reasonableness of such belief is not the only requirement for the merchant's privilege. The detention must be conducted in a reasonable manner and last only for a reasonable period of time. Thus, (B) is the store's best defense.

101. Congress has power under Article I, § 8, cl. 1 to *spend* for the general welfare, not to *legislate* for the general welfare. (A) is incorrect.

An exercise of legislative power under the Commerce Clause may regulate some purely local transactions of a type that also affect interstate commerce. A broad attempt to prohibit discrimination in all business transactions throughout the country could be justified under an expansive interpretation of the Commerce Clause. (C) is incorrect.

(D) is incorrect because the 10th Amendment merely preserves to the states powers not specifically granted to the federal government.

The 13th Amendment specifically grants Congress the power to legislate against the badges and incidents of slavery, including private, individual acts of discrimination. *Jones v. Alfred H. Mayer Co.,* 392 U.S. 409 (1968). (B) is correct.

102. Neither Horace nor Lewis is guilty of burglary because there was no breaking. Horace had a key and permission to enter any time during the two weeks Sam was away, and Horace gave Lewis ingress. (A) and (B) are incorrect.
   Lewis is clearly guilty of larceny in taking the rings. Horace is not guilty of trespass because he had permission to enter the property. (D) is correct.

103. Liability for infliction of emotional distress is based on the outrageousness of the conduct and the severity of the distress, but severe emotional distress is presumed from the mishandling of a dead relative's remains. (Even though the leg was not Jeremiah's, John would not have known that.) Proof of bodily harm or medical or psychiatric treatment is not required. (C) and (D) are incorrect.
   Hospital is not strictly liable; its liability is based on a showing of recklessness or intent. (B) is incorrect, and (A) is correct.

104. The judgment lien statute does not take precedence over the recording act; priority is determined by the time of filing under one statute or the other. (D) is incorrect.
   The conveyance from Able to Baker will not be encumbered by Charlie's judgment lien, not because such liens are not enforced in equity but because Baker recorded the conveyance prior to entry of the judgment lien, making Baker a purchaser for value without notice. (A) is incorrect, and (B) is correct.

105. Even if Dint's failure to challenge the ledger is treated as an adoptive admission, that would not prevent Dint from introducing evidence to contradict the inferences to be drawn from the admission. (D) is incorrect.
   The best evidence rule applies when the document itself has operative legal effect and its contents must be proven. It does not apply to contemporaneously made records of events where the event and not the record is in issue, particularly where the witness has personal knowledge and present memory of the event in question. (C) is incorrect, and (A) is correct.

106. The law of contracts recognizes the doctrine of substantial performance, but in contracts for the sale of goods by a merchant under Article 2 there is a "perfect tender" rule that gives Nimrod the right to reject nonconformance, even if insubstantial. The UCC allows the seller to cure the defect before his time for performance has expired, however. Trailco should have the opportunity to cure the defect on June 1, the latest delivery date under the contract. (A) is correct.

107. The covenant to pay for repairs to the retaining wall meets all of the requirements for a covenant to run with the land. For Tim to enforce the covenant, it is not necessary for Tim to have relied on it when making the expenditures, but it is necessary for him to show that his expenditures were reasonable and customary. (D) is correct.

108. So long as damages to a passenger were foreseeable as a result of Acme's negligence, Acme must "take the plaintiff as it finds her" and foreseeability of the extent of the harm is not required. (A) is incorrect.
   Acme is liable for injuries related to the fall, including the aggravation of Prudence's disability, but is not liable "for the full amount of her disability" to the extent of problems unrelated to the falling elevator. (C) is incorrect, and (D) is correct.

109. Preliminary questions concerning the admissibility of evidence are determined by the judge, out of the hearing of the jury when clearly prejudicial, with both parties present to argue the issues related to admissibility. (A) is correct.

110. There is no reasonable expectation of privacy from aerial observation of one's yard. In *Florida v. Riley*, 488 U.S. 445 (1989), the Supreme Court held that an officer's observation, with his naked eye from a helicopter, of the interior of a greenhouse in a residential backyard did not constitute a "search" because the accused could not reasonably have expected that his greenhouse was protected from public or official observation from a helicopter that was not violating the law or FAA regulations. (D) is correct.

111. This contract is governed by UCC Article 2, which allows the buyer to accept a nonconforming tender or reject it. If he accepts the goods, he must pay the list price and may not seek damages for the nonconformance. If he rejects, he has no further rights against Zeller. (B) is the correct answer.

112. It is not discriminatory for the Park Service to distinguish between traditional sunrise services and an overnight stay involving a campfire in a fire-sensitive area of a national park. (B) is incorrect.
    The Establishment Clause would not be offended by permitting religious groups to hold ceremonies on federal land so long as any group with a similar request is treated similarly. (C) is incorrect.
    The substantial government interest in protecting the park and its visitors would provide adequate justification for placing some restrictions on the time, place and manner of this form of religious expression. (A) is incorrect, and (D) is correct.

113. (A), (B), and (C) all represent relevant and legitimate ways to identify the defective part as one manufactured by Davis Co. (D), on the other hand, is the correct answer because evidence of similar transactions, accidents, or lawsuits is generally not admissible since it is most likely to be found more prejudicial than relevant, except on certain limited issues.

114. The attempted conveyance by Jones to Anna and Charles was ineffective as to Charles, since he was not living at the time and did not sign the required documents. The grantor, Jones, retains the interest that was not effectively conveyed, leaving Jones a co-owner of the property with Anna. (C) is correct.

115. There is no general rule that requirements contracts are nonassignable, and the facts here do not show a material change to the detriment of Eclaire, so (I) is not a good choice.
    Whether Miller had expressly agreed to perform the contract for Staff would affect Staff or Eclaire's right to sue Miller for non-performance but would not give Eclaire a right to reject conforming goods tendered by Miller. (II) is incorrect.
    The modern rule under the *Restatement (Second)* § 328 and Article 2 (§ 2-210(4)) is that language attempting to "assign the contract" presumptively intends not only to assign the rights but also to delegate the duties, so (III) is incorrect.
    Since none of these arguments would support Eclaire's rejection of the goods, (D) is correct.

116. Whether or not Eclaire agreed to accept Miller's performance would affect whether there is a novation releasing Staff from further performance, but not whether Eclaire must pay Miller for his conforming performance. (I) will not be an effective defense.
    Once notice of the assignment is given, payment to the assignor is no defense. Since Eclaire had notice, her payment to Staff did not discharge her obligation to Miller. (II) is incorrect.
    Although it may be true that Staff remains obligated on the contract, that argument is not a defense available to Eclaire in an action by Miller for the first installment.
    (D) is the correct answer.

117. The validity of the search warrant is based on a police officer's personal knowledge or reliance on reasonably trustworthy information from a reliable informant. Since Susie had previously been reliable, Officer Jones was justified in relying on her statements in this case, and the inaccuracy of her statement, whether deliberate or not, does not invalidate the warrant unless Jones knew her statement to be false. (D) is correct.

118. The initial burden in a government employment termination case is for the employee to show that the nature of her employment agreement created a constitutionally protected interest giving rise to certain due process protections. The basis is not her reasonable belief, but objectively verifiable terms of employment as found in state law and employee handbooks. (D) is incorrect. (C) is correct and (A) is incorrect because the initial burden on this issue is not on the government. Green City Council need not demonstrate cause for the termination unless Baker first shows that she had a right to hear and contest such reasons at a pretermination hearing. (B) is incorrect.

119. (A) is too broad a statement of the physician-patient privilege. It does not apply to every statement made in "a medical setting," but only to those made for purposes of diagnosis or treatment.

It is not relevant to the privilege whether Dean was voluntarily or involuntarily committed. (D) is incorrect. It might be relevant whether the hospital personnel were under some legal duty to report further threats by Dean, but this is not specified in the facts.

Dean's statement was not within the psychotherapist-patient privilege because the statement was apparently not made for purposes of diagnosis or treatment but merely because Dean felt compelled to make another threat against the President. Statements made to a nurse may or may not be subject to the privilege, depending on whether the nurse was or was not under the direction of Dean's doctors and more significantly whether the conversation was related to diagnosis or treatment. (C) is the most likely answer.

120. A seller of a used home has no liability based on an implied warranty of habitability, so (C) and (D) are incorrect. However, the seller may be liable for misrepresentation if he knowingly makes any false statements of material facts or conceals conditions that would substantially change the value of the property to the buyer. The modern rule extends such liability not only to active concealment but also to failure to disclose known defects that are not readily discoverable by the buyer, i.e., "latent defects." The bar examiners chose (A) as the correct answer. (B) is a close call because it seems to prove the defect was not discoverable by an ordinary inspection, but the basis of liability is the failure to disclose.

121. The privilege to enter onto someone's land without permission in an emergency is complete (i.e., no damages are compensable) if the actor was attempting to protect the public generally. If the actor who entered onto the land was attempting to protect his own person or property, he is not technically considered a trespasser, but must pay the owner for any damage done to the property. Gardner can collect for the damage to his plantings. (A) is correct.

122. Robbery is an inherently dangerous felony that may give rise to liability for felony murder. It is inherent in the nature of the act that it creates a risk of harm. (C) is not a viable argument. So long as the death was foreseeable, it does not matter that the defendant had no actual intent to kill. (A) is incorrect.

It is irrelevant whether or not the underlying felony was completed, so long as the death occurred during the commission or attempted commission of such felony. (B) is incorrect.

The only issue on which Steve could make an argument for non-liability for the death would be the foreseeability of the customer's actions. It is unlikely that he would be successful, but (D) is the best answer.

123. If a drawer of a check tenders the check "in full satisfaction" of a claim, there is an offer of an accord and satisfaction as to the compromise amount of the check. If the payee endorses the check, she will likely be bound by the accord and satisfaction, even if she attempts a "reservation of rights." UCC § 1-207(2). (B) is correct.

124. Absent an ordinance creating rights to sunshine, Pauline has no legal rights. An easement by implication will not be created for light and air, nor does the blockage of light create an easement by necessity. (D) is correct. *See, e.g., Fontainbleau Hotel Corp. v. Forth-Five Twenty-Five, Inc.,* 114 So.2d 357 (Fla. 1959).

125. The *Restatement* allows recovery for damages for emotional distress caused by the defendant's intentional or willful conduct that is "extreme and outrageous." It is not enough that the defendant's conduct have been extreme, however. There is also a requirement that the plaintiff's emotional distress have been severe. *Rest.2d, Torts* § 46, Comment *j*. (C) is correct.

126. Knowledge of the falsity of the representation (A), and intent to induce reliance (B), are elements of an action for misrepresentation, but Perkins did not in fact rely on it or suffer any damages. (D) is correct.

127. The function of the judge on a motion for a directed verdict is to determine whether the case hinges on a question of law. The judge must not determine questions of fact, such as evaluating the relative credibility of witnesses, unless the evidence presented on the critical issues is so deficient as to be inadequate as a matter of law. (A) is correct and the others are incorrect for that reason.

128. Ignorance of a statute that creates a strict liability offense is no defense to a prosecution under the statute. (A) is incorrect. However, violation of the statute in itself does not make Trelawney liable for murder, for which the common law requirements include premeditation and deliberation. He lacked this mental state. This is a stronger

argument than lack of causation, since the statute contemplates that some person or persons other than the day-care worker will ultimately cause the harm to the child. (B) is correct and (C) is incorrect.

Finding vicarious liability on the part of Trelawney's employee would not relieve Trelawney of his own responsibility. (D) is incorrect.

129. A common carrier is not strictly liable for the safety of its passengers but has a duty of due care toward them. (C) is incorrect and (D) is correct.

Even a common carrier is not "required by law" to rescue its passenger from an assault by a third party. (A) is incorrect.

Perkins was under no obligation to take action to prevent the unexpected injury to herself. (B) is incorrect.

130. Battery is an intentional tort, for which vicarious liability is seldom applied. It does not state a cause of action against Delval Airline that Perkins suffered a harmful or offensive contact on the airline, or that she sustained permanent injury at the hands of Morton. (A) and (D) are incorrect. There is no reason to hold Delval liable for Morton's battery.

Vicarious liability could be imposed on the airline for acts of its agents. A battery is generally considered by be outside the scope of an agent's employment unless the employer knew of the agent's propensity to use violence and of the opportunity to do so on the job, but (C) was the answer chosen by the Bar Examiners. Many courts, however, might find liability either under the theory that a common carrier owes a special duty to its passengers to protect them from assault, or under the theory in (B) that the serving of liquor must be done responsibly. *See, Figueroa v. Evangelical Covenant Church,* 879 F.2d 1427 (7th Cir. 1989); *Toombs v. Manning,* 835 F.2d 453 (3rd Cir. 1987); *Matin v. Nelson,* 741 F. Supp. 690 (N.D. Ill. 1990); *Worcester Ins. Co. v. Fells Acres Day School, Inc.,* 558 N.E.2d 958 (Mass. 1990).

131. The presidential power of appointment does not give the President plenary power to protect his appointees. The appointees become officials of the United States government, not agents of the President, and are protected by federal and other laws. (B) is incorrect.

The U.S. Constitution explicitly provides for the division of authority between the state and federal governments and establishes procedures for resolving conflicts, so these matters are not nonjusticiable. (D) is incorrect.

The President's broadest power is his power to conduct foreign affairs, but it is not plenary. (A) is incorrect. The President may enter into executive agreements without ratification by Congress, and these have the force of federal law, including supremacy over state law. (C) is correct.

132. A plea bargain is admissible as impeachment because it shows the witness's interest or bias in favor of the prosecution. (A) is correct. This is a non-hearsay purpose, so (B) and (D) are incorrect.

133. (B) is correct. The contract was effectively modified.

134. Barrister's pre-existing promise to pay $10,000 for the books does not support Debbit's promise of the stacks or prevent Debbit from revoking this new offer. (A) is incorrect.

Holding an offer open requires consideration unless the offeror is a merchant who makes the promise in a signed writing. Debbit is not a merchant with respect to these goods. (C) is incorrect, and (B) is correct.

This is not a proper case for detrimental reliance. Under § 90 of the *Rest.2d, Contracts,* the reliance must be "substantial" and there must be "injustice" which can only be avoided by enforcing the promise. There was no substantial reliance or injustice to Barrister. (D) is incorrect.

135. A seller of property may be held liable on certain implied warranties, but these generally relate to buildings on the land, not to uses extending outside the property. A failure to disclose a matter substantially affecting the value of the land may be actionable in an action for misrepresentation. (A) is correct.

136. A new trial for juror misconduct may be only based on influences external to the courtroom proceedings, not matters such as misunderstanding instructions or reliance on stricken testimony. (D), which involves the entry of extraneous information not filtered through the courtroom admission process, is the correct answer. To be successful in

winning a new trial, Doxie will be required to show not only juror misconduct of this nature but also that the extraneous information colored the decision-making process and likely affected the outcome of the trial. *See, e.g., St. Louis Southwestern Railway Co. v. White,* 788 S.W.2d 483 (Ark. 1990).

137. Mistake of fact is a defense only when it negates the specific intent required for a particular crime and the defendant's mistake belief was reasonable. The standard is not a purely subjective belief, so (A) is incorrect.

Voluntary intoxication might have prevented Wilmont from forming the specific intent necessary for murder, but it will not prevent his prosecution for manslaughter on the ground that he was engaged in reckless and dangerous behavior. (B) is incorrect.

Wilmont should be convicted because of his recklessness. (D) is a better statement of the requirement as to his state of mind and mistake of fact than (C), so (D) is the correct answer.

138. A life tenant may convey his interest in the property, and a purported conveyance of Profitacre by Leon to Mona would be interpreted as a conveyance of Leon's life interest only, leaving Ralph's remainder interest undisturbed. The life tenant has a right to all rents and profits during his/her life but is also obligated to pay real estate taxes out of such income. (C) is the correct answer.

139. One co-tenant cannot bind another with respect to a boundary line dispute. Homer remained a tenant in common even during the period in which he was not exercising his right to possession. (D) is incorrect, and (B) is correct.

140. Merely owning guns and having them on one's property is not an inherently dangerous activity, so Grandmother will not be held strictly liable. (C) is incorrect.

Grandmother will not be held vicariously liable for the actions of her grandson, but she had a duty to supervise him and take due care to prevent him from harming others. (A) is incorrect.

Grandmother's duty of care toward Patrick was that of a landowner to a social guest/licensee. Generally, the duty to a licensee is to warn of known dangers, with no duty to inspect and discover dangers. However, the duty to a child visitor may be greater because one is charged with anticipating careless or dangerous conduct on the part of children, who are not expected to be capable of exercising the same degree of care as the average adult. (B) is incorrect, and (D) is correct.

141. Equity does not permit a party to "sleep on his rights" where the delay causes prejudice to the other party. Nonprejudicial delay, however does not bar equitable relief. Here there is no evidence of prejudice. (A) is incorrect.

Specific performance is available when the damage remedy is inadequate, which includes many cases where only nominal damages could be recovered at law. (D) is incorrect.

(B) is correct. The best defense is that specific performance is not available to enforce a contract to perform personal services and Joiner agreed to "personally" remodel Galley's kitchen.

142. Joiner may recover his expectancy damages of $3,000. However, he had a duty to mitigate damages after notice of the breach by Galley, and is not entitled to recover the $5,000 on either a reliance or restitutionary theory. (B) is correct.

143. The search occurred prior to the arrest and was the cause of the arrest; it was not "incident to" the arrest. (A) is incorrect.

Use of excessive force might give rise to police liability, but does not invalidate the arrest. (C) is incorrect.

Although the Supreme Court has found in recent years that public school children have lesser expectations of privacy on school grounds, this rationale has been used to uphold random searches, not searches targeted at a specific individual already under suspicion. (B) is incorrect, and (D) is correct.

144. The fact that Yancey was in custody triggered the *Miranda* rule, but Yancey received his *Miranda* warnings. (A) is incorrect.

The *Miranda* rule prohibits police interrogation after a custodial suspect has requested a lawyer, but Yancey was not subjected to police questioning beyond that point. (B) is incorrect.

The fact that Yancey invoked his right to counsel prohibits the police from listening in on conversations with his counsel, but not necessarily conversations with others. (B) and (C) are incorrect.

Yancey's parents were apparently not agents of the police and it is unclear whether they interrogated Yancey or just let him talk. However, the police arranged the meeting and taped it secretly, distinguishing this case from *Arizona v. Mauro*, 485 U.S. 520 (1987), in which the defendant's wife insisted on speaking with her husband over the objections of the police and the taping of the conversation was done openly. (D) is the correct answer.

145. It is not arbitrary or capricious to make an award based on merit, nor is it a denial of equal protection. (B) is incorrect. Congress may delegate the decision making with respect to the appropriate recipients of the award. (A) is incorrect.

Exercise of the spending power is not nonjusticiable, but it is subject to review only to see that it reasonably serves the general welfare and does not violate any specific constitutional prohibitions. (D) is incorrect, and (C) is correct.

146. An implied-in-fact contract involves conduct indicating assent or agreement. Agreement is not implied where the facts show the individual was unaware of the nature of the obligation. (A) is incorrect because Algernon was not aware he had been wrongly billed for taxes on Bathsheba's property. (B) is incorrect because Ryder was unconscious.

(D) is incorrect because helping one's mother with a relatively simple chore would not ordinarily imply a right to payment.

(C) is correct because Nabor was aware he was receiving a benefit to which he was not entitled without payment.

147. If mortgaged property is conveyed "subject to" the mortgage, the purchaser will lose his land if the mortgage is not paid, but he is not personally liable on the note. On the other hand, a purchaser who assumes the mortgage becomes personally liable to pay the mortgage and for any deficiency at a foreclosure sale. The original mortgagor also remains liable on the mortgage unless released by the mortgagee. In this case, Beam assumed and agreed to pay the mortgage but Carter did not. Ashton and Beam are liable for the deficiency, but Carter is not. (B) is the correct answer.

148. The *Restatement* provides that one who carries on an abnormally dangerous activity such as blasting is subject to liability for harm to the person or property of another resulting from the activity, even if he has exercised the utmost care to prevent the harm. (C) and (D) are incorrect, and (B) is correct.

Landco's liability arises from ownership of the land on which the abnormally dangerous activity is carried out, not its supervision and control of Poolco, so (A) is incorrect.

149. Higher usage charges for nonresidents are permitted under the Commerce Clause. (A) is incorrect.

Under the Article IV Privileges and Immunities Clause which requires comity for the rights of state citizenship, the interest protected must be fundamental. A hunting or fishing license is not a fundamental right. (B) is incorrect.

Due process is not implicated if the recipient of a government license is granted only a temporary permit and is given no reason to expect that the license will be renewed after its initial term. In such cases, the license does not create a property right beyond the period of its term. (D) is incorrect. (C) is correct.

150. Taxes on interstate commerce may be upheld unless discriminatory or unduly burdensome. This could be a valid "compensatory tax" designed to make interstate commerce share a burden already borne by intrastate commerce. (A) is incorrect.

The Privileges and Immunities Clause of the 14th Amendment is narrowly construed to protect only incidents of national citizenship, which include the right to enter public lands, but not all citizens have a right to do business on public lands, so the interest is not "fundamental." (B) is incorrect.

The Equal Protection Clause is not implicated because there is no discrimination based on a suspect category. (C) is incorrect.

The Supremacy Clause is the best argument. (D) is correct.

151. The attractive nuisance doctrine assumes that the child entered the property without the landowner's permission, so (C) is incorrect. The doctrine places a duty of reasonable care on the landowner, Davis, not on the child. The duty applicable to the landowner looks at such factors as whether he had reason to know that children were likely to trespass, and whether the burden of eliminating the danger was slight as compared to the risk to children involved.

The doctrine, despite its name, does not require that the child have been lured onto the property by the nuisance. (D) is incorrect. The doctrine does require, however, that the child's youth have prevented his realization of the danger. *Restatement 2d, Torts,* § 339(c). The age of the child and the nature of the hazard are relevant in this respect; most cases involve children between the ages of six and twelve, but there is no fixed age limit. The injured child will be barred from recovery if he could have been expected to apprehend the risk. (A) is correct. (B) is incorrect because it states the standard of care imposed on children generally, not in the attractive nuisance situation.

152. Wallman's and Witler's testimony is admissible, if at all, only to support Smith's identification. (A) is incorrect and (B) is correct.

153. Issues related to voting rights, including residency requirements, generally do present constitutional issues because they are fundamental interests protected by the due process and equal protection clauses. (B is incorrect.

Lengthy residency requirements for voters have been found unjustified, but substantial residency requirements for candidates may be justified on the basis that the state has a legitimate or even compelling interest in requiring that candidates understand and have a stake in the community. It is unclear how long a period may be justified on this basis. Five years may or may not be too long. *See, Hatcher v. Bell,* 521 S.W.2d 799 (Tenn.); *cf., Bay Area Women's Coalition v. San Francisco,* 78 Cal. App.3d 961, 144 Ca. Rptr. 591 (1978). There is a clearer basis for challenge, however.

A controversy that is appropriate for judicial determination must be "real and substantial," allowing for specific and conclusive relief, as distinguished from an advisory opinion on a hypothetical set of facts. Declaratory judgments are permitted where there is an actual controversy between adverse litigants. This case is not ripe, and presents no case or controversy at this time. It presents a hypothetical question concerning what would happen if Candidate were elected. If Candidate attempted to run and were not elected, a court would not have to decide the issue. Furthermore, Candidate has not named any specific adverse litigants who could vigorously present the case against Candidate's claim. (A) is correct.

154. The agreement between Oliver and Len was in substance a security agreement. Courts have found a deed to a lender with a promise to reconvey when the loan is repaid an "equitable mortgage." Extrinsic evidence may be admitted to show the intent of the parties despite the Statute of Frauds. To obtain possession, Len must bring a foreclosure proceeding. (D) is correct.

155. (A) states the rational basis test, which applies to statutes and regulations not implicating a fundamental right or protected class of persons.

(C), at the other extreme, states the strict scrutiny test. Classifications based on race are traditionally the only ones involving a suspect category requiring the strict scrutiny test.

Classifications based on sex are reviewed under an intermediate scrutiny standard. *Craig v. Boren,* 429 U.S. 190 (1976), held that gender classifications must serve important governmental objectives and be substantially related to those objectives. (D) is correct.

156. Even though the actual starting of the fire was not intentional, Defendant can be found guilty if he could have stopped the fire and intentionally did not do so. The fact that he started the fire imposed a duty on him to take corrective action. (C) and (D) are incorrect. Arson is a general intent crime, requiring either intent to burn or a wanton and reckless disregard for human safety. Simple negligence would not be enough. (B) is incorrect. (A) is correct.

157. A manufacturer may be liable for the manufacture and sale of a product that is suitable for its intended use but unreasonably dangerous if handled differently. Here the critical issue is whether proper warnings accompanied the sale of the product. The glasses, whether or not called "Safety Glasses," did not have to protect Grinder from all harm, so long as the warnings about their limitations were clear. (A) and (B) are incorrect, and (C) is correct. The glasses were not unreasonably dangerous when used for their intended, clearly specified use.

Workers' compensation laws would prevent Grinder from suing his employer for injuries resulting from this work-related accident, but would not prevent him from recovering from Glassco. Workers' compensation would not reduce or eliminate Glassco's liability. (D) is incorrect.

158. The *Restatement* recognizes that certain products are unavoidably unsafe for certain people while providing significant benefits for the majority of users. Such products are not deemed unreasonably dangerous if accompanied by adequate warnings of the risk and directions for use to minimize the risk. (D) is correct because Paul must show inadequate labeling in order to establish liability by Shampoo Company.

159. The plaintiff's misuse of a product may be a defense to a product liability claim. Where misuse of a product is foreseeable, however, strict liability may still apply. Paul's misuse was not unforeseeable, so (I) is not a defense.
(II) is incorrect because contributory negligence is not a defense to a strict liability claim unless the plaintiff knew of the danger and assumed the risk, which Paul did not.
(III) is incorrect because any user or consumer may be protected by strict liability rules; privity is not required.
Since neither (I), (II), nor (III) is a defense for Shampoo, (D) is correct.

160. Oscar and Paul were roommates, not strangers, and Oscar undertook to give Paul the shampoo. He cannot claim he had no duty not to behave negligently toward Paul regardless of the nature of Shampoo Company's liability, so (C) and (D) are incorrect.
Since Oscar is not the manufacturer, he need not prove that Paul knowingly and voluntarily assumed the risk. (B) is correct.
(A) is correct. Contributory negligence is Oscar's best defense.

161. To be guilty of conspiracy to commit battery or battery itself, the defendants need not have intended to hurt anyone. Battery is not a specific intent crime, and the general criminal intent required can be met by the commission of criminal negligence or the doing of an act that is malum in se. Pulling the fire alarm was probably one of these, and it set in motion forces that physically harmed people. The defendant need not have touched the plaintiff(s) directly so long as he was the cause of the indirect touching. However, the NCBE apparently thought this was a close call because they accepted both (B) and (D) as correct answers.
If there was a battery, there would also appear to have been a conspiracy here. The requirements of a plurality, an agreement for an unlawful purpose, and an overt act are met on these facts. Conspiracy does not merge into the crime that is the object of the conspiracy when that crime is completed.

162. *Webster v. Reproductive Health Services*, 492 U.S. 469 (1989), permitted the states to limit or prohibit the use of public funds and public facilities or employees to provide abortion services. (C) is a much more precise statement of the holding and rationale of *Webster* than (D). (C) is correct.

163. The recording act is a race-notice type statute. Belle's purchase cut off Ann's rights because Belle was a purchaser for value without notice of the deed to Ann, and Belle recorded first. Belle then had full power to convey to Cal, despite the recordation of Ann's deed. (B) is correct.

164. (A) is incorrect because Driver did not intend to cause an imminent harmful contact or the apprehension thereof.
Walker's defensive action was not independent of Driver's act, so (C) is incorrect.
The issue of Driver's negligence should go to the jury, not be decided on a motion for summary judgment. (D) is incorrect, and (B) is correct.

165. A strict liability crime occurs, despite a lack of intent, when the prohibited act takes place. There is no liability for "attempt" to commit a strict liability crime; there can be no attempt to commit a crime that does not require intent. (A) is incorrect.
Arson requires an intent to burn the dwelling of others or a reckless disregard for the safety of their place of habitation. (C) is incorrect because the jewelry store was not a dwelling, and Defendant had no intent to burn or reason to expect that his actions would cause a fire.

(D) is incorrect because attempting to frighten someone by playing a prank of this nature is not ordinarily a life-endangering act that is *malum in se*, leading to manslaughter liability.

Murder requires malice aforethought, but a person who acts without an intent to kill but with an intent to do great bodily injury and thereby causes another's death possesses malice aforethought. Defendant can be charged with murder. (B) is correct.

166. Happy Time's "good faith" promise does not require Happy Time to guarantee that sales won't decline or that another client of Happy Time's won't disparage Fizzy Cola. (A) and (B) are incorrect.

The parol evidence rule might bar evidence of an oral agreement for an exclusive distribution arrangement that should have been included in the written contract. (C) is incorrect. However, under the UCC, a written contract may be supplemented by evidence of trade usage. (D) is correct.

167. FRE 803(1) permits testimony regarding statement made by persons who were observing some event at the exact time there were making the statement, whether or not the declarant is unavailable at trial. This is a present sense impression. (A) is the correct answer.

168. Strict liability applies because Diggers was involved in an ultrahazardous activity, so neither Digger's care nor Paul's lack of care would decide the case. (A) and (D) are incorrect. A defense to strict liability is assumption of the risk, where the plaintiff knowingly and voluntarily proceeded in disregard of the danger, as Paul did. (C) is incorrect and (B) is correct.

169. Winters' testimony as to her affiliation with the church, like membership in any other organization, can be admitted where relevant to show bias. Her credibility is not being impeached because of her religious beliefs but rather because her church has an interest in the litigation. Her First Amendment rights will not be offended. (C) is correct.

170. The Full Faith and Credit Clause requires each state to recognize the public acts, records and judicial proceedings of every other state. This issue involves federal law, not the law of another state. (A) is incorrect.

The federal law does not attempt to regulate the field of radon testing, so Magenta does not have a basis to challenge the federal statute on Commerce Clause grounds. (D) is incorrect.

The correct analysis is under the Supremacy Clause. Because the federal statute does not require the use of testers on the EPA-approved list, there is no direct conflict with the Magenta licensing standards, and the state law promotes, rather than inhibits, the policy behind the federal law. (B) is incorrect.

(C) is correct.

171. The common law rule is that even if the contract states that no oral modifications will be recognized, the parties may alter their agreement by parol. If the contract is between a merchant and a non-merchant, a no-oral-modification clause on the merchant's form must be separately signed by the non-merchant. Bitz separately signed the clause, so the clause is valid. (C) is incorrect.

Despite the no-oral-modification clause, the Code allows the merchant to waive the requirement for modifications to be in writing. The waiver may be by conduct but is retractable upon reasonable notification "unless the retraction would be unjust in view of a material change of position in reliance on the waiver." (D) is correct.

172. Charitable trusts are liberally construed and may be reformed under the *cy pres* doctrine as necessary to ensure that the donor's charitable intent will be carried out. *Restatement, 2d, Trusts* § 399. Test apparently did not create a charitable trust, however, since the grant was by deed to the Church rather than into a trust. If there is no trust, the state official does not have a say in the disposition of the property. (D) is incorrect. Test in fact granted Blackacre to Church by deed, and Church had full rights to convey to Developer. (A) is correct.

173. Spousal immunity in a criminal case is a privilege in the witness spouse not to testify against her spouse. *Trammel v. California*, 445 U.S. 40 (1980). The privilege does not lie with the criminal defendant spouse. (C) is correct.

174. (A) is an accurate statement and thus the wrong answer because a promise to pay the debt of another is within the Statute of Frauds and requires a signed writing.

(B) is a correct statement of law and therefore the wrong answer.

(C) is an accurate statement and thus the wrong answer because consideration is required to make the contract enforceable.

(D) is correct because it is wrong.

175. Utility companies do not have a property right to rate increases, so the due process clause is not offended by the moratorium. (A) is incorrect.

(B) makes a true statement as a matter of general principles of law, but is too broad to apply specifically to this case, and there is a preliminary issue of justiciability.

The case is not ripe for judicial decision because Economy Electric is many months away from needing a rate increase and various factors such as future fuel prices are unknown. There is no specific and immediate set of facts for the decision-maker. (C) is correct.

176. Daniel's statement might be admitted as a statement of present intention or plan if the issue were whether he in fact subsequently made payments in accordance with his plan. That does not seem to be the reason for admitting this letter, however; the purpose is to prove that he owed back taxes. The exception does not serve to admit backward-looking statements such as Daniel's promise to his mother. (A) is incorrect.

Daniel's statement is an admission of his liability. (B) is correct. If the admission of liability is voluntary, not preceded by any claim or dispute or threat thereof, the rule excluding settlement offers or plea negotiations is not applicable. (C) is not the best answer because it is not clear that the authorities were aware of Daniel's tax liability and intended to prosecute before his statement was made

177. The answer to this question may depend on whether UCC Article 2 applies because Article 2 gives a right to demand assurances. Hoarda had reasonable grounds for insecurity because of the condition of the market, and was within his rights to request assurances on October 15 if the Code applies. U.C.C. § 2-609. Failure by Broker to supply adequate assurances with a reasonable time, not exceeding 30 days, could create an anticipatory repudiation, giving rise to all the remedies for repudiation. Broker's statement on October 17, while not an outright repudiation under other circumstances, probably falls short of providing assurances under these circumstances. If not covered by the Code, however, Broker has not repudiated and may perform within the contract term. (A) is the correct answer.

178. (C) is the best argument because it states the Code rule on anticipatory repudiation in § 2-610: "When either party repudiates the contract with respect to a performance not yet due the loss of which will substantially impair the value of the contract to the other, the aggrieved party may (a) for a commercially reasonable time await performance by the repudiating party; or (b) resort to any remedy for breach even though he has notified the repudiating party that he would await the latter's performance and has urged retraction; and (c) in either case suspend his own performance or proceed in accordance with the provisions of this Article on the seller's right to identify goods to the contract notwithstanding breach or to salvage unfinished goods."

179. A life estate may be conveyed or assigned. (A) is incorrect.

Since the property was mortgaged before the conveyance to Paul and Richard, Paul as the life tenant was obliged to pay only the mortgage interest, not the principal. (C) is incorrect.

The life tenant has a duty not to commit waste, which at common law included substantial changes in the use of the property even if such changes increased the value of the property. Ironically, Paul could be enjoined from committing "waste" under the common law rule even though Paul's purpose in building the larger office building was to make the property more profitable and even if Richard's proposed use of the property would also involve demolition of the current building. (B) is Richard's best argument.

180. FRE 608 permits opinion evidence about another witness's reputation for truth or veracity, or a direct opinion based on personal observation. Character may be impeached by specific instances of conduct only when character is directly is issue. Doppler has not put his character in issue here. (C) is correct.

181. Larceny is a taking from a person with a superior possessory interest in the property. Rita as manager had taken possession of the money, and Eddie no longer had the right to possession, as required for embezzlement. He had the intent to convert the property and physically carried it away as required for larceny. (A) is correct.

182. A criminal defendant is entitled to his *Miranda* rights when he is in custody and is questioned by the police or their agents or informers, but there must be interrogation, not merely a voluntary statement by the defendant. *Illinois v. Perkins*, 496 U.S. 292 (1990). Here there was no interrogation by the police informer. (D) is correct.

183. This was not a dying declaration unless there is a showing that Ronald believed he was dying imminently. (B) is incorrect.
    A statement concerning a past act does not come under the existing state of mind exception. (C) is incorrect.
    This statement was not an excited utterance because not made in the heat of the moment during the reported event. (D) is incorrect.
    The statement was against the declarant's pecuniary interest. (A) is correct.

184. A public employee may not be dismissed for the exercise of First Amendment rights so long as the speech was not unduly disruptive of the workplace, i.e., the danger to the employer's functions from the employee's remarks was minimal. *Rankin v. McPherson*, 483 U.S. 378 (1987). (B) is correct.

185. Both parties are merchants, so the contract is governed by UCC Article 2, which contains a statute of frauds provision for contracts involving goods with a price over $500.. Thus, Mitt will need to show a memorandum signed by the party to be charged, Slalome. Slalome's order was placed orally, and the only memorandum was signed by Mitt. However, § 2-201(2) contains an exception between merchants if within a reasonable time a writing in confirmation of the contract, sufficient against the sender, is received and the party receiving it has reason to know its contents and does not object to its contents within 10 days after it is received. (B) is correct, and (C) is incorrect for this reason. There are other exceptions to the writing requirement for specially manufactured goods and goods for which payment has been made and accepted or which have been received and accepted, but it is not necessary to fit the case within these exceptions because Mitt's memo, received and uncontested by Slalome, will suffice.

186. The preexisting duty rule does not apply here because Snoop had a duty to work for Artistic, not for Collecta. Snoop may collect on Collecta's promise, an offer that he accepted by performance. (D) is correct.

187. Cam's interest, like Cynthia's and Camelia's, was contingent upon surviving Well. Since he did not survive, his contingent interest was neither devisable nor inheritable. (B) recognizes the unborn widow problem, it does not deal with the fact that invalidating the remainder would apply equally to all Oren's children since none of these interests would vest until the end of Well's life. (D) is correct.

188. A false statement is a necessary element of defamation, but fault is also required. (C) is incorrect. Defamation is not a strict liability tort, so (A) is incorrect.
    A defamation action by a private plaintiff requires proof of negligence, which could be shown by Allen having doubts but not verifying the accuracy of his statement. It is not relevant that Allen was prompted to make the statement by the interviewer's question. (D) is incorrect, and (B) is correct.
    Slander is not actionable without proof of damages, unless it falls into the category of slander per se. Allen's statement does, because it related to Bradley's livelihood.

189. Prism may recover $75 because an infant has a right to avoid a contract made before the age of majority, or may ratify the contract in whole or in part by showing assent in any form after reaching majority. Once made as an adult, Starr's promise could not be repudiated without breach of contract. Starr will be required to pay the amount she agreed to, or the fair value of the goods (if this were a necessity). (C) is correct.

190. The contract will be enforced according to the terms agreed to by Starr after reaching her majority. Prism must prove that the condition precedent has been met. (D) is correct.

191. Carrol will lose as to both Beach and Daniel. As the easement holder, Carrol has an obligation to keep the easement in repair and does not have a right to contribution from either of the adjoining owners. (A) is correct.

192. A statement regarding one's intentions at the time the statement was made is admissible under the state of mind exception to the hearsay rule. This question is similar to *Mutual Life Insurance v. Hillmon,* 45 U.S. 285 (1891), in which a letter expressing intent to make a trip was found admissible to support the inference that the declarant's conduct was in accord with his intentions. (A) is correct.

193. (A) is incorrect because it proposes an impermissible content-based restriction on speech.
   In *Renton v. Playtime Theatres, Inc.*, 475 U.S. 41 (1986), the Supreme Court held that communities could apply time, place and manner-type zoning restrictions on adult bookstores in order to protect the community from the "secondary effects" of such businesses. (C) and (D) are incorrect.
   Zoning for adult theaters and bookstores is evaluated under the tests for content-neutral time, place and manner restrictions, i.e., "narrowly tailored to serve a significant governmental interest" and Leaving open "ample alternative channels for communication of the information." (B) is correct.

194. When the entrapment defense is raised, the defendant's past criminal record becomes relevant to prove predisposition under the majority rule. (A) is incorrect.
   The defendant bears the burden of persuasion on an affirmative defense such as entrapment, although the ultimate burden of proof remains on the prosecution. (B) is incorrect. (D) is correct.

195. Under pure comparative negligence, Pat's $100,000 in damages will be reduced by her own 30% fault, but she can sue either of the other responsible drivers for the full amount remaining ($70,000) because this jurisdiction allows joint and several liability. By requesting contribution from Drew, Donald can recover Drew's $40,000 share he paid Pat. (A) is correct.
   Pat's equal fault with Donald might be a problem under a "modified" comparative negligence statute, depending on whether the statute provided that the plaintiff cannot recover anything if her fault is *equal to or greater than* that of the defendant or if her negligence is *less than* that of the defendant, and whether her fault is compared to all the defendants in the aggregate or to each defendant individually. These problems need not be addressed in a pure comparative negligence jurisdiction.

196. Without joint and several liability, Pat may hold each defendant liable only for the percent of total damages attributable to that defendant's fault. (C) is correct.

197. An oral assignment for no consideration is valid. and Margin does not necessarily obtain an advantage over Bridey because his assignment was in writing and for value. However, when the obligor (Traviata) has paid the assignor (Dr. Pulmonary), payment is a defense against the assignee(s) unless the obligor had notice of the assignment. Traviata did not have notice of either assignment, so (A) and (B) are incorrect.
   Both Bridey and Margin retain any rights they previously had against Dr. Pulmonary. Bridey has no right to sue to recover a gift, but Margin may seek to enforce his legal rights against Dr. Pulmonary. (D) is correct.

198. (D) provides a true statement about the nature of informed consent, but does not deal with the basis of liability.
   (C) would be correct under the older battery theory of informed consent cases. However, negligence principles apply today in most informed consent cases. Both (A) and (B) relate to negligence issues, but (B) is the better answer because ultimately negligence cases turn on whether or not there was any compensable harm.

199. Home ownership is not an incident of national citizenship, so (B) is incorrect.
   There has been no "taking" of her property for public use, so (C) is incorrect.
   This is not an *ex post facto* law, which makes criminal an act that was not criminal when performed. (D) is incorrect.
   Owner's best argument, although it is not strong, would be based on equal protection. An equal protection challenge would be difficult because the Constitution requires merely that classifications made for tax purposes by rationally related to a legitimate government objective and that the tax be applied equally to persons or property of the same class. Owner may attempt to show that she is being treated differently than other property owners in the same category. *See, e.g., Minnegasco, Inc. v. County of Carver,* 447 N.W.2d 878 (Minn. 1989).

200. This information was compiled for purposes of litigation, not as part of a regularly conducted business activity. (C) is incorrect.

The exception for past recollection recorded requires that the declarant be available and testify that he made the record and has no present memory of the facts recorded. Even if Plaza Hotel could produce the employees who made the records, the memoranda themselves would not be admissible under this exception unless the adverse party requested their admission. (B) is correct.

July, 1998 MULTISTATE BAR EXAM

MBE III

The questions and letter answers contained herein have been publicly disclosed from the July, 1998 MBE and are reprinted herein with the permission of NCBE, the copyright owner. Permission to use the NCBE's questions does not constitute an endorsement by NCBE or otherwise signify that NCBE has reviewed or approved any aspect of these materials or the company or individuals who distribute these materials.

All questions, instructions and letter answers copyright ©1998-2009 by the National Conference of Bar Examiners. All rights reserved. All other material © 1996 - 2009 Celebration Bar Review

Celebration Bar Review MBE III

AM Book
Time—3 hours

<u>Directions</u>: Each of the questions or incomplete statements below is followed by four suggested answers or completions. You are to choose the <u>best</u> of the stated alternatives. Answer all questions according to the generally accepted view, except where otherwise noted.

For the purposes of this test, you are to assume that Articles 1 and 2 of the Uniform Commercial Code have been adopted. You are also to assume relevant application of Article 9 of the UCC concerning fixtures. The Federal Rules of Evidence are deemed to control. The terms "Constitution," "constitutional," and "unconstitutional" refer to the federal Constitution unless indicated to the contrary. You are to assume that there is no applicable statute unless otherwise specified; however, survival actions and claims for wrongful death should be assumed to be available where applicable. You should assume that joint and several liability, with pure comparative negligence, is the relevant rule unless otherwise indicated.

1. On July 15, in a writing signed by both parties, Fixtures, Inc., agreed to deliver to Druggist on August 15 five storage cabinets from inventory for a total price of $5,000 to be paid on delivery. On August 1, the two parties orally agreed to postpone the delivery date to August 20. On August 20, Fixtures tendered the cabinets to Druggist, who refused to accept or pay for them on the ground that they were not tendered on August 15, even though they otherwise met the contract specifications.

    Assuming that all appropriate defenses are seasonably raised, will Fixtures succeed in an action against Druggist for breach of contract?

    (A) Yes, because neither the July 15 agreement nor the August 1 agreement was required to be in writing.
    (B) Yes, because the August 1 agreement operated as a waiver of the August 15 delivery term.
    (C) No, because there was no consideration to support the August 1 agreement.
    (D) No, because the parol evidence rule will prevent proof of the August 1 agreement.

2. Beth wanted to make some money, so she decided to sell cocaine. She asked Albert, who was reputed to have access to illegal drugs, to supply her with cocaine so she could resell it. Albert agreed and sold Beth a bag of white powder. Beth then repackaged the white powder into smaller containers and sold one to Carol, an undercover police officer, who promptly arrested Beth. Beth immediately confessed and said that Albert was her supplier. Upon examination, the white powder was found not to be cocaine or any type of illegal substance.

    If Albert knew the white powder was not cocaine but Beth believed it was, which of the following is correct?

    (A) Both Albert and Beth are guilty of attempting to sell cocaine.
    (B) Neither Albert nor Beth is guilty of attempting to sell cocaine.
    (C) Albert is guilty of attempting to sell cocaine, but Beth is not.
    (D) Albert is not guilty of attempting to sell cocaine, but Beth is.

GO ON TO THE NEXT PAGE.

3. Neighbor, who lived next door to Homeowner, went into Homeowner's garage without permission and borrowed Homeowner's chain saw. Neighbor used the saw to clear broken branches from the trees on Neighbor's own property. After he had finished, Neighbor noticed several broken branches on Homeowner's trees that were in danger of falling on Homeowner's roof. While Neighbor was cutting Homeowner's branches, the saw broke.

In a suit for conversion by Homeowner against Neighbor, will Homeowner recover?

(A) Yes, for the actual damage to the saw.
(B) Yes, for the value of the saw before Neighbor borrowed it.
(C) No, because when the saw broke Neighbor was using it to benefit Homeowner.
(D) No, because Neighbor did not intend to keep the saw.

4. Homeowner hired Arsonist to set fire to Homeowner's house so that Homeowner could collect the insurance proceeds from the fire. After pouring gasoline around the house, Arsonist lit the fire with his cigarette lighter and then put the lighter in his pocket. As Arsonist was standing back admiring his work, the lighter exploded in his pocket. Arsonist suffered severe burns to his leg.

Arsonist brought an action against the manufacturer of the lighter based on strict product liability. Under applicable law, the rules of pure comparative fault apply in such actions.

Will Arsonist prevail?

(A) Yes, if the lighter exploded because of a defect caused by a manufacturing error.
(B) Yes, if Arsonist can establish that the lighter was the proximate cause of his injury.
(C) No, because the lighter was not being used for an intended or reasonably foreseeable purpose.
(D) No, because Arsonist was injured in the course of committing a felony by the device used to perpetrate the felony.

GO ON TO THE NEXT PAGE.

5. Susan owned Goldacre, a tract of land, in fee simple. By warranty deed, she conveyed Goldacre in fee simple to Ted for a recited consideration of "$10 and other valuable consideration." The deed was promptly and properly recorded. One week later, Susan and Ted executed a written document that stated that the conveyance of Goldacre was for the purpose of establishing a trust for the benefit of Benton, a child of Susan's. Ted expressly accepted the trust and signed the document with Susan. This written agreement was not authenticated to be eligible for recordation and there never was an attempt to record it.

    Ted entered into possession of Goldacre and distributed the net income from Goldacre to Benton at appropriate intervals.

    Five years later, Ted conveyed Goldacre in fee simple to Patricia by warranty deed. Patricia paid the fair market value of Goldacre, had no knowledge of the written agreement between Susan and Ted, and entered into possession of Goldacre.

    Benton made demand upon Patricia for distribution of income at the next usual time Ted would have distributed. Patricia refused. Benton brought an appropriate action against Patricia for a decree requiring her to perform the trust Ted had theretofore recognized.

    In such action, judgment should be for

    (A) Benton, because a successor in title to the trustee takes title subject to the grantor's trust.
    (B) Benton, because equitable interests are not subject to the recording act.
    (C) Patricia, because, as a bona fide purchaser, she took free of the trust encumbering Ted's title.
    (D) Patricia, because no trust was ever created since Susan had no title at the time of the purported creation.

6. In a federal investigation of Defendant for tax fraud, the grand jury seeks to obtain a letter written January 15 by Defendant to her attorney in which she stated: "Please prepare a deed giving my ranch to University but, in order to get around the tax law, I want it back-dated to December 15." The attorney refuses to produce the letter on the ground of privilege.

    Production of the letter should be

    (A) prohibited, because the statement is protected by the attorney-client privilege.
    (B) prohibited, because the statement is protected by the client's privilege against self-incrimination.
    (C) required, because the statement was in furtherance of crime or fraud.
    (D) required, because the attorney-client privilege belongs to the client and can be claimed only by her.

7. After being fired from his job, Mel drank almost a quart of vodka and decided to ride the bus home. While on the bus, he saw a briefcase he mistakenly thought was his own, and began struggling with the passenger carrying the briefcase. Mel knocked the passenger to the floor, took the briefcase, and fled. Mel was arrested and charged with robbery.

    Mel should be

    (A) acquitted, because he used no threats and was intoxicated.
    (B) acquitted, because his mistake negated the required specific intent.
    (C) convicted, because his intoxication was voluntary.
    (D) convicted, because mistake is no defense to robbery.

    GO ON TO THE NEXT PAGE.

8. A generally applicable state statute requires an autopsy by the county coroner in all cases of death that are not obviously of natural causes. The purpose of this law is to ensure the discovery and prosecution of all illegal activity resulting in death. In the 50 years since its enactment, the statute has been consistently enforced.

Mr. and Mrs. Long are sincere practicing members of a religion that maintains it is essential for a deceased person's body to be buried promptly and without any invasive procedures, including an autopsy. When the Longs' son died of mysterious causes and an autopsy was scheduled, the Longs filed an action in state court challenging the constitutionality of the state statute, and seeking an injunction prohibiting the county coroner from performing an autopsy on their son's body. In this action, the Longs claimed only that the application of this statute in the circumstances of their son's death would violate their right to the free exercise of religion as guaranteed by the First and Fourteenth Amendments. Assume that no federal statutes are applicable.

As applied to the Longs' case, the court should rule that the state's autopsy statute is

(A) constitutional, because a dead individual is not a person protected by the due process clause of the Fourteenth Amendment.
(B) constitutional, because it is a generally applicable statute and is rationally related to a legitimate state purpose.
(C) unconstitutional, because it is not necessary to vindicate a compelling state interest.
(D) unconstitutional, because it is not substantially related to an important state interest.

9. By the terms of a written contract signed by both parties on January 15, M.B. Ram, Inc., agreed to sell a specific ICB personal computer to Marilyn Materboard for $3,000, and Materboard agreed to pick up and pay for the computer at Ram's store on February 1. Materboard unjustifiably repudiated on February 1. Without notifying Materboard, Ram subsequently sold at private sale the same specific computer to Byte, who paid the same price ($3,000) in cash. The ICB is a popular product. Ram can buy from the manufacturer more units than it can sell at retail.

If Ram sues Materboard for breach of contract, Ram will probably recover

(A) nothing, because it received a price on resale equal to the contract price that Materboard had agreed to pay.
(B) nothing, because Ram failed to give Materboard proper notice of Ram's intention to resell.
(C) Ram's anticipated profit on the sale to Materboard plus incidental damages, if any, because Ram lost that sale.
(D) $3,000 (the contract price), because Materboard intentionally breached the contract by repudiation.

GO ON TO THE NEXT PAGE.

10. Anna owned Blackacre, which was improved with a dwelling. Beth owned Whiteacre, an adjoining unimproved lot suitable for constructing a dwelling. Beth executed and delivered a deed granting to Anna an easement over the westerly 15 feet of Whiteacre for convenient ingress and egress to a public street, although Anna's lot did abut another public street. Anna did not then record Beth's deed. After Anna constructed and started using a driveway within the described 15-foot strip in a clearly visible manner, Beth borrowed $10,000 cash from Bank and gave Bank a mortgage on Whiteacre. The mortgage was promptly and properly recorded. Anna then recorded Beth's deed granting the easement. Beth subsequently defaulted on her loan payments to Bank.

The recording act of the jurisdiction provides: "No conveyance or mortgage of real property shall be good against subsequent purchasers for value and without notice unless the same be recorded according to law."

In an appropriate foreclosure action as to Whiteacre, brought against Anna and Beth, Bank seeks, among other things, to have Anna's easement declared subordinate to Bank's mortgage, so that the easement will be terminated by completion of the foreclosure.

If Anna's easement is NOT terminated, it will be because

(A) the recording of the deed granting the easement prior to the foreclosure action protects Anna's rights.
(B) the easement provides access from Blackacre to a public street.
(C) Anna's easement is appurtenant to Blackacre and thus cannot be separated from Blackacre.
(D) visible use of the easement by Anna put Bank on notice of the easement.

11. A little more than five years ago, Len completed construction of a single-family home located on Homeacre, a lot that Len owned. Five years ago, Len and Tina entered into a valid five-year written lease of Homeacre that included the following language: "This house is rented as is, without certain necessary or useful items. The parties agree that Tina may acquire and install such items as she wishes at her expense, and that she may remove them if she wishes at the termination of this lease."

Tina decided that the house needed, and she paid cash to have installed, standard-sized combination screen/storm windows, a freestanding refrigerator to fit a kitchen alcove built for that purpose, a built-in electric stove and oven to fit a kitchen counter opening left for that purpose, and carpeting to cover the plywood living room floor.

Last month, by legal description of the land, Len conveyed Homeacre to Pete for $100,000. Pete knew of Tina's soon-expiring tenancy, but did not examine the written lease. As the lease expiration date approached, Pete learned that Tina planned to vacate on schedule, and learned for the first time that Tina claimed and planned to remove all of the above-listed items that she had installed.

Pete promptly brought an appropriate action to enjoin Tina from removing those items.

The court should decide that Tina may remove

(A) none of the items.
(B) only the refrigerator.
(C) all items except the carpet.
(D) all of the items.

GO ON TO THE NEXT PAGE.

12. The mineral alpha is added to bodies of fresh water to prevent the spread of certain freshwater parasites. The presence of those parasites threatens the health of the organisms living in rivers and streams throughout the country and imperils the freshwater commercial fishing industry. Alpha is currently mined only in the state of Blue.

    In order to raise needed revenue, Congress recently enacted a statute providing for the imposition of a $100 tax on each ton of alpha mined in the United States. Because it will raise the cost of alpha, this tax is likely to reduce the amount of alpha added to freshwater rivers and streams and, therefore, is likely to have an adverse effect on the interstate freshwater commercial fishing industry. The alpha producers in Blue have filed a lawsuit in federal court challenging this tax solely on constitutional grounds.

    Is this tax constitutional?

    (A) No, because only producers in Blue will pay the tax and, therefore, it is not uniform among the states and denies alpha producers the equal protection of the laws.
    (B) No, because it is likely to have an adverse effect on the freshwater commercial fishing industry and Congress has a responsibility under the commerce clause to protect, foster, and advance such interstate industries.
    (C) Yes, because the tax is a necessary and proper means of exercising federal authority over the navigable waters of the United States.
    (D) Yes, because the power of Congress to impose taxes is plenary, this tax does not contain any provisions extraneous to tax needs or purposes, and it is not barred by any prohibitory language in the Constitution.

13. Plaintiff sued Defendant for breach of a commercial contract in which Defendant had agreed to sell Plaintiff all of Plaintiff's requirements for widgets. Plaintiff called Expert Witness to testify as to damages. Defendant seeks to show that Expert Witness had provided false testimony as a witness in his own divorce proceedings.

    This evidence should be

    (A) admitted only if elicited from Expert Witness on cross-examination.
    (B) admitted only if the false testimony is established by clear and convincing extrinsic evidence.
    (C) excluded, because it is impeachment on a collateral issue.
    (D) excluded, because it is improper character evidence.

14. Karen was crossing Main Street at a crosswalk. John, who was on the sidewalk nearby, saw a speeding automobile heading in Karen's direction. John ran into the street and pushed Karen out of the path of the car. Karen fell to the ground and broke her leg.

    In an action for battery brought by Karen against John, will Karen prevail?

    (A) Yes, because John could have shouted a warning instead of pushing Karen out of the way.
    (B) Yes, if Karen was not actually in danger and John should have realized it.
    (C) No, because the driver of the car was responsible for Karen's injury.
    (D) No, if John's intent was to save Karen, not to harm her.

    GO ON TO THE NEXT PAGE.

15. Joe and Marty were coworkers. Joe admired Marty's wristwatch and frequently said how much he wished he had one like it. Marty decided to give Joe the watch for his birthday the following week.

    On the weekend before Joe's birthday, Joe and Marty attended a company picnic. Marty took his watch off and left it on a blanket when he went off to join in a touch football game. Joe strolled by, saw the watch on the blanket, and decided to steal it. He bent over and picked up the watch. Before he could pocket it, however, Marty returned. When he saw Joe holding the watch, he said, "Joe, I know how much you like that watch. I was planning to give it to you for your birthday. Go ahead and take it now." Joe kept the watch.

    Joe has committed

    (A) larceny.
    (B) attempted larceny.
    (C) embezzlement.
    (D) no crime.

16. Olivia, owner in fee simple of Richacre, a large parcel of vacant land, executed a deed purporting to convey Richacre to her nephew, Grant. She told Grant, who was then 19, about the deed and said that she would give it to him when he reached 21 and had received his undergraduate college degree. Shortly afterward Grant searched Olivia's desk, found and removed the deed, and recorded it.

    A month later, Grant executed an instrument in the proper form of a warranty deed purporting to convey Richacre to his fiancée, Bonnie. He delivered the deed to Bonnie, pointing out that the deed recited that it was given in exchange for "$1 and other good and valuable consideration," and that to make it valid Bonnie must pay him $1. Bonnie, impressed and grateful, did so. Together, they went to the recording office and recorded the deed. Bonnie assumed Grant had owned Richacre, and knew nothing about Grant's dealing with Olivia. Neither Olivia's deed to Grant nor Grant's deed to Bonnie said anything about any conditions.

    The recording act of the jurisdiction provides: "No conveyance or mortgage of real property shall be good against subsequent purchasers for value and without notice unless the same be recorded according to law."

    Two years passed. Grant turned 21, then graduated from college. At the graduation party, Olivia was chatting with Bonnie and for the first time learned the foregoing facts.

    The age of majority in the jurisdiction is 18 years.

    Olivia brought an appropriate action against Bonnie to quiet title to Richacre.

    The court will decide for

    (A) Olivia, because Grant's deed to Bonnie before Grant satisfied Olivia's conditions was void, as Bonnie had paid only nominal consideration.
    (B) Olivia, because her deed to Grant was not delivered.
    (C) Bonnie, because Grant has satisfied Olivia's oral conditions.
    (D) Bonnie, because the deed to her was recorded.

    GO ON TO THE NEXT PAGE.

17. Perry suffered a serious injury while participating in an impromptu basketball game at a public park. The injury occurred when Perry and Dever, on opposing teams, each tried to obtain possession of the ball when it rebounded from the backboard after a missed shot at the basket. During that encounter, Perry was struck and injured by Dever's elbow. Perry now seeks compensation from Dever.

    At the trial, evidence was introduced tending to prove that the game had been rough from the beginning, that elbows and knees had frequently been used to discourage interference by opposing players, and that Perry had been one of those making liberal use of such tactics.

    In this action, will Perry prevail?

    (A) Yes, if Dever intended to strike Perry with his elbow.
    (B) Yes, if Dever intended to cause a harmful or offensive contact with Perry.
    (C) No, because Perry impliedly consented to rough play.
    (D) No, unless Dever intentionally used force that exceeded the players' consent.

18. Water District is an independent municipal water-supply district incorporated under the applicable laws of the state of Green. The district was created solely to supply water to an entirely new community in a recently developed area of Green. That new community is racially, ethnically, and socioeconomically diverse, and the community has never engaged in any discrimination against members of minority groups.

    The five-member, elected governing board of the newly created Water District contains two persons who are members of racial minority groups. At its first meeting, the governing board of Water District adopted a rule unqualifiedly setting aside 25% of all positions on the staff of the District and 25% of all contracts to be awarded by the District to members of racial minority groups. The purpose of the rule was "to help redress the historical discrimination against these groups in this country and to help them achieve economic parity with other groups in our society." Assume that no federal statute applies.

    A suit by appropriate parties challenges the constitutionality of these set-asides.

    In this suit, the most appropriate ruling on the basis of applicable United States Supreme Court precedent would be that the set-asides are

    (A) unconstitutional, because they would deny other potential employees or potential contractors the equal protection of the laws.
    (B) unconstitutional, because they would impermissibly impair the right to contract of other potential employees or potential contractors.
    (C) constitutional, because they would assure members of racial minority groups the equal protection of the laws.
    (D) constitutional, because the function and activities of Water District are of a proprietary nature rather than a governmental nature and, therefore, are not subject to the usual requirements of the Fourteenth Amendment.

    GO ON TO THE NEXT PAGE.

Questions 19–20 are based on the following fact situation.

In a single writing, Painter contracted with Farmer to paint three identical barns on her rural estate for $2,000 each. The contract provided for Farmer's payment of $6,000 upon Painter's completion of the work on all three barns. Painter did not ask for any payment when the first barn was completely painted, but she demanded $4,000 after painting the second barn.

19. Is Farmer obligated to make the $4,000 payment?

    (A) No, because Farmer has no duty under the contract to pay anything to Painter until all three barns have been painted.
    (B) No, because Painter waived her right, if any, to payment on a per-barn basis by failing to demand $2,000 upon completion of the first barn.
    (C) Yes, because the contract is divisible.
    (D) Yes, because Painter has substantially performed the entire contract.

20. For this question only, assume that Farmer rightfully refused Painter's demand for payment.

    If Painter immediately terminates the contract without painting the third barn, what is Painter entitled to recover from Farmer?

    (A) Nothing, because payment was expressly conditioned on completion of all three barns.
    (B) Painter's expenditures plus anticipated "profit" in painting the first two barns, up to a maximum recovery of $4,000.
    (C) The reasonable value of Painter's services in painting the two barns, less Farmer's damages, if any, for Painter's failure to paint the third barn.
    (D) The amount that the combined value of the two painted barns has been increased by Painter's work.

GO ON TO THE NEXT PAGE.

21. The police in City notified local gas station attendants that a woman, known as Robber, recently had committed armed robberies at five City gas stations. The police said that Robber was approximately 75 years old, had white hair, and drove a vintage, cream-colored Ford Thunderbird. Attendants were advised to call police if they saw her, but not to attempt to apprehend her. Armed robbery is a felony under state law.

    Traveler was passing through City on a cross-country journey. Traveler was a 75-year-old woman who had white hair and drove a vintage, cream-colored Ford Thunderbird. When Traveler drove into Owner's gas station, Owner thought Traveler must be the robber wanted by the police. After checking the oil at Traveler's request, Owner falsely informed Traveler that she had a broken fan belt, that her car could not be driven without a new belt, that it would take him about an hour to replace it, and that she should stay in his office for consultation about the repair. Traveler was greatly annoyed that her journey was delayed, but she stayed in Owner's office while she waited for her car. Owner telephoned the police and, within the hour, the police came and questioned Traveler. The police immediately determined that Traveler was not Robber, and Traveler resumed her journey without further delay.

    In Traveler's action for false imprisonment against Owner, Traveler will

    (A) not prevail, if Owner reasonably believed that Traveler was Robber.
    (B) not prevail, because Traveler suffered no physical or mental harm.
    (C) prevail, if Traveler reasonably believed she could not leave Owner's premises.
    (D) prevail, because Owner lied to Traveler about the condition of her car.

22. In which of the following situations would Defendant's mistake most likely constitute a defense to the crime charged?

    (A) A local ordinance forbids the sale of alcoholic beverages to persons under 18 years of age. Relying on false identification, Defendant sells champagne to a 16-year-old high school student. Defendant is charged with illegal sale of alcoholic beverages.
    (B) Mistaking Defendant for a narcotics suspect, an undercover police officer attempts to arrest him. Defendant, unaware that the person who has grabbed him is an officer, hits him and knocks him unconscious. Defendant is charged with assault.
    (C) Defendant, aged 23, has sexual intercourse with a 15-year-old prostitute who tells Defendant that she is 18. Defendant is charged with the felony of statutory rape under a statute that makes sexual relations with a child under 16 a felony.
    (D) Relying on erroneous advice from his attorney that, if his wife has abandoned him for more than a year, he is free to marry, Defendant remarries and is subsequently charged with bigamy.

GO ON TO THE NEXT PAGE.

23. Powell, who was an asbestos insulation installer from 1955 to 1965, contracted asbestosis, a serious lung disorder, as a result of inhaling airborne asbestos particles on the job. The asbestos was manufactured and sold to Powell's employer by the Acme Asbestos Company. Because neither Acme nor anyone else discovered the risk to asbestos installers until 1966, Acme did not provide any warnings of the risks to installers until after that date.

    Powell brought an action against Acme based on strict liability in tort for failure to warn. The case is to be tried before a jury. The jurisdiction has not adopted a comparative fault rule in strict liability cases.

    In this action, an issue that is relevant to the case and is a question for the court to decide as a matter of law, rather than for the jury to decide as a question of fact, is whether

    (A) a satisfactory, safer, alternative insulation material exists under today's technology.
    (B) the defendant should be held to the standard of a prudent manufacturer who knew of the risks, regardless of whether the risks were reasonably discoverable before 1966.
    (C) the defendant should reasonably have known of the risks of asbestos insulation materials before 1966, even though no one else had discovered the risks.
    (D) the asbestos insulation materials to which the plaintiff was exposed were inherently dangerous.

24. PullCo sued Davidson, its former vice president, for return of $230,000 that had been embezzled during the previous two years. Called by PullCo as an adverse witness, Davidson testified that his annual salary had been $75,000, and he denied the embezzlement. PullCo calls banker Witt to show that, during the two-year period, Davidson had deposited $250,000 in his bank account.

    Witt's testimony is

    (A) admissible as circumstantial evidence of Davidson's guilt.
    (B) admissible to impeach Davidson.
    (C) inadmissible, because its prejudicial effect substantially outweighs its probative value.
    (D) inadmissible, because the deposits could have come from legitimate sources.

GO ON TO THE NEXT PAGE.

25. Alex and Betty, who were cousins, acquired title in fee simple to Blackacre, as equal tenants in common, by inheritance from Angela, their aunt. During the last 15 years of her lifetime, Angela allowed Alex to occupy an apartment in the house on Blackacre, to rent the other apartment in the house to various tenants, and to retain the rent. Alex made no payments to Angela; and since Angela's death 7 years ago, he has made no payments to Betty. For those 22 years, Alex has paid the real estate taxes on Blackacre, kept the building on Blackacre insured, and maintained the building. At all times, Betty has lived in a distant city and has never had anything to do with Angela, Alex, or Blackacre.

Recently, Betty needed money for the operation of her business and demanded that Alex join her in selling Blackacre. Alex refused.

The period of time to acquire title by adverse possession in the jurisdiction is 10 years. There is no other applicable statute.

Betty brought an appropriate action against Alex for partition. Alex asserted all available defenses and counterclaims.

In that action, the court should

(A) deny partition and find that title has vested in Alex by adverse possession.
(B) deny partition, confirm the tenancy in common, but require an accounting to determine if either Betty or Alex is indebted to the other on account of the rental payment, taxes, insurance premiums, and maintenance costs.
(C) grant partition and require, as an adjustment, an accounting to determine if either Betty or Alex is indebted to the other on account of the rental payments, taxes, insurance premiums, and maintenance costs.
(D) grant partition to Betty and Alex as equal owners, but without an accounting.

26. Plaintiff sued Defendant for illegal discrimination, claiming that Defendant fired him because of his race. At trial, Plaintiff called Witness, expecting him to testify that Defendant had admitted the racial motivation. Instead, Witness testified that Defendant said that he had fired Plaintiff because of his frequent absenteeism. While Witness is still on the stand, Plaintiff offers a properly authenticated secret tape recording he had made at a meeting with Witness in which Witness related Defendant's admissions of racial motivation.

The tape recording is

(A) admissible as evidence of Defendant's racial motivation and to impeach Witness's testimony.
(B) admissible only to impeach Witness's testimony.
(C) inadmissible, because it is hearsay not within any exception.
(D) inadmissible, because a secret recording is an invasion of Witness's right of privacy under the U.S. Constitution.

GO ON TO THE NEXT PAGE.

Questions 27–28 are based on the following fact situation.

On December 15, Lawyer received from Stationer, Inc., a retailer of office supplies, an offer consisting of its catalog and a signed letter stating, "We will supply you with as many of the items in the enclosed catalog as you order during the next calendar year. We assure you that this offer and the prices in the catalog will remain firm throughout the coming year."

27. For this question only, assume that no other correspondence passed between Stationer and Lawyer until the following April 15 (four months later), when Stationer received from Lawyer a faxed order for "100 reams of your paper, catalog item #101."

   Did Lawyer's April 15 fax constitute an effective acceptance of Stationer's offer at the prices specified in the catalog?

   (A) Yes, because Stationer had not revoked its offer before April 15.
   (B) Yes, because a one-year option contract had been created by Stationer's offer.
   (C) No, because under applicable law the irrevocability of Stationer's offer was limited to a period of three months.
   (D) No, because Lawyer did not accept Stationer's offer within a reasonable time.

28. For this question only, assume that on January 15, having at that time received no reply from Lawyer, Stationer notified Lawyer that effective February 1, it was increasing the prices of certain specified items in its catalog.

   Is the price increase effective with respect to catalog orders Stationer receives from Lawyer during the month of February?

   (A) No, because Stationer's original offer, including the price term, became irrevocable under the doctrine of promissory estoppel.
   (B) No, because Stationer is a merchant with respect to office supplies; and its original offer, including the price term, was irrevocable throughout the month of February.
   (C) Yes, because Stationer received no consideration to support its assurance that it would not increase prices.
   (D) Yes, because the period for which Stationer gave assurance that it would not raise prices was longer than three months.

GO ON TO THE NEXT PAGE.

29. State X enacted a statute "to regulate administratively the conduct of motor vehicle junkyard businesses in order to deter motor vehicle theft and trafficking in stolen motor vehicles or parts thereof." The statute requires a junkyard owner or operator "to permit representatives of the Department of Motor Vehicles or of any law enforcement agency upon request during normal business hours to take physical inventory of motor vehicles and parts thereof on the premises." The statute also states that a failure to comply with any of its requirements constitutes a felony.

Police officers assigned to Magnolia City's Automobile Crimes Unit periodically visited all motor vehicle junkyards in town to make the inspections permitted by the statute. Janet owned such a business in Magnolia City. One summer day, the officers asked to inspect the vehicles on her lot. Janet said, "Do I have a choice?" The officers told her she did not. The officers conducted their inspection and discovered three stolen automobiles.

Janet is charged with receiving stolen property. Janet moves pretrial to suppress the evidence relating to the three automobiles on the ground that the inspection was unconstitutional.

Her motion should be

(A) sustained, because the statute grants unbridled discretion to law enforcement officers to make warrantless searches.
(B) sustained, because the stated regulatory purpose of the statute is a pretext to circumvent the warrant requirement in conducting criminal investigations.
(C) denied, because the statute deals reasonably with a highly regulated industry.
(D) denied, because administrative searches of commercial establishments do not require warrants.

30. Current national statistics show a dramatic increase in the number of elementary and secondary school students bringing controlled substances (drugs) to school for personal use or distribution to others. In response, Congress enacted a statute requiring each state legislature to enact a state law that makes it a state crime for any person to possess, use, or distribute, within 1,000 feet of any elementary or secondary school, any controlled substance that has previously been transported in interstate commerce and that is not possessed, used, or distributed pursuant to a proper physician's prescription.

This federal statute is

(A) unconstitutional, because Congress has no authority to require a state legislature to enact any specified legislation.
(B) unconstitutional, because the possession, use, or distribution, in close proximity to a school, of a controlled substance that has previously been transported in interstate commerce does not have a sufficiently close nexus to such commerce to justify its regulation by Congress.
(C) constitutional, because it contains a jurisdictional provision that will ensure, on a case-by-case basis, that any particular controlled substance subject to the terms of this statute will, in fact, affect interstate commerce.
(D) constitutional, because Congress possesses broad authority under both the general welfare clause and the commerce clause to regulate any activities affecting education that also have, in inseverable aggregates, a substantial effect on interstate commerce.

GO ON TO THE NEXT PAGE.

31. Janet had a season ticket for the Scorpions' hockey games at Central Arena (Section B, Row 12, Seat 16). During the intermission between the first and second periods of a game between the Scorpions and the visiting Hornets, Janet solicited signatures for a petition urging that the coach of the Scorpions be fired.

    Central Arena and the Scorpions are owned by ABC, Inc., a privately owned entity. As evidenced by many prominently displayed signs, ABC prohibits all solicitations anywhere within Central Arena at any time and in any manner. ABC notified Janet to cease her solicitation of signatures.

    Janet continued to seek signatures on her petition during the Scorpions' next three home games at Central Arena. Each time, ABC notified Janet to cease such solicitation. Janet announced her intention to seek signatures on her petition again during the Scorpions' next home game at Central Arena. ABC wrote a letter informing Janet that her season ticket was canceled and tendering a refund for the unused portion. Janet refused the tender and brought an appropriate action to establish the right to attend all home games.

    In this action, the court will decide for

    (A) ABC, because it has a right and obligation to control activities on realty it owns and has invited the public to visit.
    (B) ABC, because Janet's ticket to hockey games created only a license.
    (C) Janet, because, having paid value for the ticket, her right to be present cannot be revoked.
    (D) Janet, because she was not committing a nuisance by her activities.

32. Company designed and built a processing plant for the manufacture of an explosive chemical. Engineer was retained by Company to design a filter system for the processing plant. She prepared an application for a permit to build the plant's filter system and submitted it to the state's Department of Environmental Protection (DEP). As required by DEP regulations, Engineer submitted a blueprint to the DEP with the application for permit. The blueprint showed the entire facility and was signed and sealed by her as a licensed professional engineer.

    After the project was completed, a portion of the processing plant exploded, injuring Plaintiff. During discovery in an action by Plaintiff against Engineer, it was established that the explosion was caused by a design defect in the processing plant that was unrelated to the filter system designed by Engineer.

    In that action, will Plaintiff prevail?

    (A) Yes, if Engineer signed, sealed, and submitted a blueprint that showed the design defect.
    (B) Yes, because all of the plant's designers are jointly and severally liable for the defect.
    (C) No, because Engineer owed no duty to Plaintiff to prevent the particular risk of harm.
    (D) No, if Engineer was an independent contractor.

    GO ON TO THE NEXT PAGE.

33. Several years ago, Bart purchased Goldacre, financing a large part of the purchase price by a loan from Mort that was secured by a mortgage. Bart made the installment payments on the mortgage regularly until last year. Then Bart persuaded Pam to buy Goldacre, subject to the mortgage to Mort. They expressly agreed that Pam would not assume and agree to pay Bart's debt to Mort. Bart's mortgage to Mort contained a due-on-sale clause stating, "If Mortgagor transfers his/her interest without the written consent of Mortgagee first obtained, then at Mortgagee's option the entire principal balance of the debt secured by this Mortgage shall become immediately due and payable." However, without seeking Mort's consent, Bart conveyed Goldacre to Pam, the deed stating in pertinent part " . . . , subject to a mortgage to Mort [giving details and recording data]."

Pam took possession of Goldacre and made several mortgage payments, which Mort accepted. Now, however, neither Pam nor Bart has made the last three mortgage payments. Mort has brought an appropriate action against Pam for the amount of the delinquent payments.

In this action, judgment should be for

(A) Pam, because she did not assume and agree to pay Bart's mortgage debt.
(B) Pam, because she is not in privity of estate with Mort.
(C) Mort, because Bart's deed to Pam violated the due-on-sale clause.
(D) Mort, because Pam is in privity of estate with Mort.

34. Congress recently enacted a statute imposing severe criminal penalties on anyone engaged in trading in the stock market who, in the course of that trading, takes "unfair advantage" of other investors who are also trading in the stock market. The statute does not define the term "unfair advantage." There have been no prosecutions under this new statute. The members of an association of law school professors that is dedicated to increasing the clarity of the language used in criminal statutes believe that this statute is unconstitutionally vague. Neither the association nor any of its members is currently engaged in, or intends in the future to engage in, trading in the stock market. The association and its members bring suit against the Attorney General of the United States in a federal district court, seeking an injunction against the enforcement of this statute on the ground that it is unconstitutional.

May the federal court determine the merits of this suit?

(A) Yes, because the suit involves a dispute over the constitutionality of a federal statute.
(B) Yes, because the plaintiffs seek real relief of a conclusive nature--an injunction against enforcement of this statute.
(C) No, because the plaintiffs do not have an interest in the invalidation of this statute that is adequate to ensure that the suit presents an Article III controversy.
(D) No, because a suit for an injunction against enforcement of a criminal statute may not be brought in federal court at any time prior to a bona fide effort to enforce that statute.

GO ON TO THE NEXT PAGE.

35. Rachel, an antique dealer and a skilled calligrapher, crafted a letter on very old paper. She included details that would lead knowledgeable readers to believe the letter had been written by Thomas Jefferson to a friend. Rachel, who had a facsimile of Jefferson's autograph, made the signature and other writing on the letter resemble Jefferson's. She knew that the letter would attract the attention of local collectors. When it did and she was contacted about selling it, she said that it had come into her hands from a foreign collector who wished anonymity, and that she could make no promises about its authenticity. As she had hoped, a collector paid her $5,000 for the letter. Later the collector discovered the letter was not authentic, and handwriting analysis established that Rachel had written the letter.

    In a jurisdiction that follows the common-law definition of forgery, Rachel has

    (A) committed both forgery and false pretenses.
    (B) committed forgery, because she created a false document with the intent to defraud, but has not committed false pretenses, since she made no representation as to the authenticity of the document.
    (C) not committed forgery, because the document had no apparent legal significance, but has committed false pretenses, since she misrepresented the source of the document.
    (D) not committed forgery, because the document had no apparent legal significance, and has not committed false pretenses, since she made no representation as to authenticity of the document.

36. Mom rushed her eight-year-old daughter, Child, to the emergency room at Hospital after Child fell off her bicycle and hit her head on a sharp rock. The wound caused by the fall was extensive and bloody.

    Mom was permitted to remain in the treatment room, and held Child's hand while the emergency room physician cleaned and sutured the wound. During the procedure, Mom said that she was feeling faint and stood up to leave the room. While leaving the room, Mom fainted and, in falling, struck her head on a metal fixture that protruded from the emergency room wall. She sustained a serious injury as a consequence.

    If Mom sues Hospital to recover damages for her injury, will she prevail?

    (A) Yes, because Mom was a public invitee of Hospital's.
    (B) Yes, unless the fixture was an obvious, commonly used, and essential part of Hospital's equipment.
    (C) No, unless Hospital's personnel failed to take reasonable steps to anticipate and prevent Mom's injury.
    (D) No, because Hospital's personnel owed Mom no affirmative duty of care.

    GO ON TO THE NEXT PAGE.

Questions 37–39 are based on the following fact situation.

Buyer, Inc., contracted in writing with Shareholder, who owned all of XYZ Corporation's outstanding stock, to purchase all of her stock at a specified price per share. At the time this contract was executed, Buyer's contracting officer said to Shareholder, "Of course, our commitment to buy is conditioned on our obtaining approval of the contract from Conglomerate, Ltd., our parent company." Shareholder replied, "Fine. No problem."

37. For this question only, assume that Conglomerate orally approved the contract, but that Shareholder changed her mind and refused to consummate the sale on two grounds: (1) when the agreement was made there was no consideration for her promise to sell; and (2) Conglomerate's approval of the contract was invalid.

If Buyer sues Shareholder for breach of contract, is Buyer likely to prevail?

(A) Yes, because Buyer's promise to buy, bargained for and made in exchange for Shareholder's promise to sell, was good consideration even though it was expressly conditioned on an event that was not certain to occur.
(B) Yes, because any possible lack of consideration for Shareholder's promise to sell was expressly waived by Shareholder when the agreement was made.
(C) No, because mutuality of obligation between the parties was lacking when the agreement was made.
(D) No, because the condition of Conglomerate's approval of the contract was an essential part of the agreed exchange and was not in a signed writing.

38. For this question only, assume the following facts. Shareholder subsequently refused to consummate the sale on the ground that Buyer had neglected to request Conglomerate's approval of the contract, which was true. Conglomerate's chief executive officer, however, is prepared to testify that Conglomerate would have routinely approved the contract if requested to do so. Buyer can also prove that it has made a substantial sale of other assets to finance the stock purchase, although it admittedly had not anticipated any such necessity when it entered into the stock purchase agreement.

If Buyer sues Shareholder for breach of contract, is Buyer likely to prevail?

(A) Yes, because the condition of Conglomerate's approval of the contract, being designed to protect only Buyer and Conglomerate, can be and has been waived by those entities.
(B) Yes, because Buyer detrimentally relied on Shareholder's commitment by selling off other assets to finance the stock purchase.
(C) No, because the express condition of Conglomerate's approval had not occurred prior to the lawsuit.
(D) No, because obtaining Conglomerate's approval of the contract was an event within Buyer's control and Buyer's failure to obtain it was itself a material breach of contract.

GO ON TO THE NEXT PAGE.

39. For this question only, assume the following facts. Shareholder is willing and ready to consummate the sale of her stock to Buyer, but the latter refuses to perform on the ground (which is true) that Conglomerate has firmly refused to approve the contract.

    If Shareholder sues Buyer for breach of contract and seeks to exclude any evidence of the oral condition requiring Conglomerate's approval, the court will probably

    (A) admit the evidence as proof of a collateral agreement.
    (B) admit the evidence as proof of a condition to the existence of an enforceable obligation, and therefore not within the scope of the parol evidence rule.
    (C) exclude the evidence on the basis of a finding that the parties' written agreement was a complete integration of their contract.
    (D) exclude the evidence as contradicting the terms of the parties' written agreement, whether or not the writing was a complete integration of the contract.

40. At Dove's trial for theft, Mr. Wong, called by the prosecutor, testified to the following: 1) that from his apartment window, he saw thieves across the street break the window of a jewelry store, take jewelry, and leave in a car; 2) that Mrs. Wong telephoned the police and relayed to them the license number of the thieves' car as Mr. Wong looked out the window with binoculars and read it to her; 3) that he has no present memory of the number, but that immediately afterward he listened to a playback of the police tape recording giving the license number (which belongs to Dove's car) and verified that she had relayed the number accurately.

    Playing the tape recording for the jury would be

    (A) proper, because it is recorded recollection.
    (B) proper, because it is a public record or report.
    (C) improper, because it is hearsay not within any exception.
    (D) improper, because Mrs. Wong lacked firsthand knowledge of the license number.

GO ON TO THE NEXT PAGE.

41. For ten years, Vacationer and Neighbor have owned summer vacation homes on adjoining lots. A stream flows through both lots. As a result of a childhood swimming accident, Vacationer is afraid of water and has never gone close to the stream.

    Neighbor built a dam on her property that has completely stopped the flow of the stream to Vacationer's property.

    In a suit by Vacationer against Neighbor, will Vacationer prevail?

    (A) Yes, if the damming unreasonably interferes with the use and enjoyment of Vacationer's property.
    (B) Yes, if Neighbor intended to affect Vacationer's property.
    (C) No, because Vacationer made no use of the stream.
    (D) No, if the dam was built in conformity with all applicable laws.

42. Corp, a corporation, owned Blackacre in fee simple, as the real estate records showed. Corp entered into a valid written contract to convey Blackacre to Barbara, an individual. At closing, Barbara paid the price in full and received an instrument in the proper form of a deed, signed by duly authorized corporate officers on behalf of Corp, purporting to convey Blackacre to Barbara. Barbara did not then record the deed or take possession of Blackacre.

    Next, George (who had no knowledge of the contract or the deed) obtained a substantial money judgment against Corp. Then, Barbara recorded the deed from Corp. Thereafter, George properly filed the judgment against Corp.

    A statute of the jurisdiction provides: "Any judgment properly filed shall, for ten years from filing, be a lien on the real property then owned or subsequently acquired by any person against whom the judgment is rendered."

    Afterward, Barbara entered into a valid written contract to convey Blackacre to Polly. Polly objected to Barbara's title and refused to close.

    The recording act of the jurisdiction provides: "Unless the same be recorded according to law, no conveyance or mortgage of real property shall be good against subsequent purchasers for value and without notice."

    Barbara brought an appropriate action to require Polly to complete the purchase contract.

    The court should decide for

    (A) Polly, because George's judgment was obtained before Barbara recorded the deed from Corp.
    (B) Polly, because even though Corp's deed to Barbara prevented George's judgment from being a lien on Blackacre, George's filed judgment poses a threat of litigation.
    (C) Barbara, because Barbara recorded her deed before George filed his judgment.
    (D) Barbara, because Barbara received the deed from Corp before George filed his judgment.

GO ON TO THE NEXT PAGE.

43. City enacted an ordinance banning from its public sidewalks all machines dispensing publications consisting wholly of commercial advertisements. The ordinance was enacted because of a concern about the adverse aesthetic effects of litter from publications distributed on the public sidewalks and streets. However, City continued to allow machines dispensing other types of publications on the public sidewalks. As a result of the City ordinance, 30 of the 300 sidewalk machines that were dispensing publications in City were removed.

    Is this City ordinance constitutional?

    (A) Yes, because regulations of commercial speech are subject only to the requirement that they be rationally related to a legitimate state goal, and that requirement is satisfied here.
    (B) Yes, because City has a compelling interest in protecting the aesthetics of its sidewalks and streets, and such a ban is necessary to vindicate this interest.
    (C) No, because it does not constitute the least restrictive means with which to protect the aesthetics of City's sidewalks and streets.
    (D) No, because there is not a reasonable fit between the legitimate interest of City in preserving the aesthetics of its sidewalks and streets and the means it chose to advance that interest.

44. Plaintiff's estate sued Defendant Stores claiming that Guard, one of Defendant's security personnel, wrongfully shot and killed Plaintiff when Plaintiff fled after being accused of shoplifting. Guard was convicted of manslaughter for killing Plaintiff. At his criminal trial Guard, who was no longer working for Defendant, testified that Defendant's security director had instructed him to stop shoplifters "at all costs." Because Guard's criminal conviction is on appeal, he refuses to testify at the civil trial. Plaintiff's estate then offers an authenticated transcript of Guard's criminal trial testimony concerning the instructions of Defendant's security director.

    This evidence is

    (A) admissible as a statement of an agent of a party-opponent.
    (B) admissible, because the instruction from the security director is not hearsay.
    (C) admissible, although hearsay, as former testimony.
    (D) inadmissible, because it is hearsay not within any exception.

GO ON TO THE NEXT PAGE.

45. Mrs. Pence sued Duarte for shooting her husband from ambush. Mrs. Pence offers to testify that, the day before her husband was killed, he described to her a chance meeting with Duarte on the street in which Duarte said, "I'm going to blow your head off one of these days."

    The witness's testimony concerning her husband's statement is

    (A) admissible, to show Duarte's state of mind.
    (B) admissible, because Duarte's statement is that of a party-opponent.
    (C) inadmissible, because it is improper evidence of a prior bad act.
    (D) inadmissible, because it is hearsay not within any exception.

46. The state of Brunswick enacted a statute providing for the closure of the official state records of arrest and prosecution of all persons acquitted of a crime by a court or against whom criminal charges were filed and subsequently dropped or dismissed. The purpose of this statute is to protect these persons from further publicity or embarrassment relating to those state proceedings. However, this statute does not prohibit the publication of such information that is in the possession of private persons.

    A prominent businessman in Neosho City in Brunswick was arrested and charged with rape. Prior to trial, the prosecutor announced that new information indicated that the charges should be dropped. He then dropped the charges without further explanation, and the records relating thereto were closed to the public pursuant to the Brunswick statute.

    The Neosho City *Times* conducted an investigation to determine why the businessman was not prosecuted, but was refused access to the closed official state records. In an effort to determine whether the law enforcement agencies involved were properly doing their duty, the *Times* filed suit against appropriate state officials to force opening of the records and to invalidate the statute on constitutional grounds.

    Which of the following would be most helpful to the state in defending the constitutionality of this statute?

    (A) The fact that the statute treats in an identical manner the arrest and prosecution records of all persons who have been acquitted of a crime by a court or against whom criminal charges were filed and subsequently dropped or dismissed.
    (B) The argument that the rights of the press are no greater than those of citizens generally.
    (C) The fact that the statute only prohibits public access to these official state records and does not prohibit the publication of information they contain that is in the possession of private persons.
    (D) The argument that the state may seal official records owned by the state on any basis its legislature chooses.

    GO ON TO THE NEXT PAGE.

47. Nora, executive director of an equal housing opportunity organization, was the leader of a sit-in at the offices of a real estate management company. The protest was designed to call attention to the company's racially discriminatory rental practices. When police demanded that Nora desist from trespassing on the company's property, she refused and was arrested. In Nora's trial for trespass, the prosecution peremptorily excused all nonwhites from the jury, arguing to the court that even though Nora was white, minority groups would automatically support Nora because of her fight against racism in housing accommodations.

If Nora is convicted of trespass by an all-white jury and appeals, claiming a violation of her constitutional rights, the court should

(A) affirm the conviction, because Nora was not a member of the class discriminated against.
(B) affirm the conviction, because peremptory challenge of the nonwhites did not deny Nora the right to an impartial jury.
(C) reverse the conviction, because racially based peremptory challenges violate equal protection of the law.
(D) reverse the conviction, because Nora was denied the right to have her case heard by a fair cross section of the community.

48. Arthur's estate plan included a revocable trust established 35 years ago with ABC Bank as trustee. The principal asset of the trust has always been Blackacre, a very profitable, debt-free office building. The trust instrument instructs the trustee to pay the net income to Arthur for life, and, after the death of Arthur, to pay the net income to his wife, Alice, for life; and, after her death, "to distribute the net trust estate as she may appoint by will, or in default of her exercise of this power of appointment, to my son (her stepson), Charles."

Arthur died 30 years ago survived by Alice and Charles. Arthur had not revoked or amended the trust agreement. A few years after Arthur's death, Alice remarried; she then had a child, Marie; was widowed for a second time; and, last year, died. Her will contained only one dispositive provision: "I give my entire estate to my daughter, Marie, and I intentionally make no provision for my stepson, Charles." Marie is now 22 years old. The common-law Rule Against Perpetuities is unmodified by statute in the jurisdiction. There are no other applicable statutes.

Charles brought an appropriate action against Marie to determine who was entitled to the net trust estate and thus to Blackacre.

If the court rules for Marie, it will be because

(A) Alice's life estate and general power of appointment merge into complete ownership in Alice.
(B) the Rule Against Perpetuities does not apply to general powers of appointment.
(C) the jurisdiction deems "entire estate" to be a reference to Blackacre or to Alice's general power of appointment.
(D) Alice intended that Charles should not benefit by reason of her death.

GO ON TO THE NEXT PAGE.

Questions 49–50 are based on the following fact situation.

Tenant rented a commercial building from Landlord, and operated a business in it. The building's large front window was smashed by vandals six months before expiration of the Tenant-Landlord lease. Tenant, who was obligated thereunder to effect and pay for repairs in such cases, promptly contracted with Glazier to replace the window for $2,000, due 30 days after satisfactory completion of the work. Landlord was then unaware of the Tenant-Glazier contract. Glazier was aware that the building was under lease, but dealt entirely with Tenant.

Sixty days after Glazier's satisfactory completion of the window replacement, and prior to the expiration of Tenant's lease, Tenant, then insolvent, ceased doing business and vacated the building. In so doing, Tenant forfeited under the lease provisions its right to the return of a $2,000 security deposit with Landlord. The deposit had been required, however, for the express purpose (as stated in the lease) of covering any damage to the leased property except ordinary wear and tear. The only such damage occurring during Tenant's occupancy was the smashed window. Glazier's $2,000 bill for the window replacement is wholly unpaid.

49. Assuming that Glazier has no remedy *quasi in rem* under the relevant state mechanic's lien statute, which of the following would provide Glazier's best chance of an effective remedy *in personam* against Landlord?

    (A) An action in quasi contract for the reasonable value of a benefit unofficiously and non-gratuitously conferred on Landlord.
    (B) An action based on promissory estoppel.
    (C) An action based on an implied-in-fact contract.
    (D) An action as third-party intended beneficiary of the Tenant-Landlord lease.

50. For this question only, assume the following facts. Upon vacating the building, Tenant mailed a $1,000 check to Glazier bearing on its face the following conspicuous notation: "This check is in full and final satisfaction of your $2,000 window replacement bill." Without noticing this notation, Glazier cashed the check and now sues Tenant for the $1,000 difference.

    If Tenant's only defense is accord and satisfaction, is Tenant likely to prevail?

    (A) No, because Glazier failed to notice Tenant's notation on the check.
    (B) No, because the amount owed by Tenant to Glazier was liquidated and undisputed.
    (C) Yes, because by cashing the check Glazier impliedly agreed to accept the $1,000 as full payment of its claim.
    (D) Yes, because Glazier failed to write a reservation-of-rights notation on the check before cashing it.

GO ON TO THE NEXT PAGE.

51. Defendant is on trial for robbing a bank in State A. She testified that she was in State B at the time of the robbery. Defendant calls her friend, Witness, to testify that two days before the robbery Defendant told him that she was going to spend the next three days in State B.

    Witness's testimony is

    (A) admissible, because the statement falls within the present sense impression exception to the hearsay rule.
    (B) admissible, because a statement of plans falls within the hearsay exception for then-existing state of mind.
    (C) inadmissible, because it is offered to establish an alibi by Defendant's own statement.
    (D) inadmissible, because it is hearsay not within any exception.

52. The legislature of State X is debating reforms in the law governing insanity. Two reforms have been proposed. Proposal A would eliminate the insanity defense altogether. Proposal B would retain the defense but place on the defendant the burden of proving insanity by a preponderance of the evidence. Opponents of the reforms argue that the proposals would be unconstitutional under the due process clause of the United States Constitution.

    Which of the proposed reforms would be unconstitutional?

    (A) Both proposals.
    (B) Neither proposal.
    (C) Proposal A only.
    (D) Proposal B only.

53. A federal statute appropriated $7 million for a nationwide essay contest on "How the United States Can Best Stop Drug Abuse." The statute indicates that its purpose is to generate new, practical ideas for eliminating drug abuse in the United States.

    Contest rules set forth in the statute provide that winning essays are to be selected on the basis of the "originality, aptness, and feasibility of their ideas." The statute expressly authorizes a first prize of $1 million, 50 second prizes of $100,000 each, and 100 third prizes of $10,000 each. It also states that judges for the contest are to be appointed by the President of the United States with the advice and consent of the Senate, and that all residents of the United States who are not employees of the federal government are eligible to enter and win the contest. A provision of the statute authorizes any taxpayer of the United States to challenge its constitutionality.

    In a suit by a federal taxpayer to challenge the constitutionality of the statute, the court should

    (A) refuse to decide its merits, because the suit involves policy questions that are inherently political and, therefore, nonjusticiable.
    (B) hold the statute unconstitutional, because it does not provide sufficient guidelines for awarding the prize money appropriated by Congress and, therefore, unconstitutionally delegates legislative power to the contest judges.
    (C) hold the statute unconstitutional, because its relationship to legitimate purposes of the spending power of Congress is too tenuous and conjectural to satisfy the necessary and proper clause of Article I.
    (D) hold the statute constitutional, because it is reasonably related to the general welfare, it states concrete objectives, and it provides adequate criteria for conducting the essay contest and awarding the prize money.

GO ON TO THE NEXT PAGE.

54. Fran, who was driving at an excessive speed, applied her brakes to stop at a traffic light. Due to damp, fallen leaves, her car skidded and came to a halt perpendicular to the roadway. Sid, who was also driving at an excessive speed and was immediately behind Fran, saw Fran's car perpendicular to the roadway. Although Sid had sufficient distance to come to a slow, controlled stop, he decided not to slow down but, rather, to swerve to the left in an effort to go around Fran's car. Due to oncoming traffic, the space was insufficient and Sid's car collided with Fran's car, severely injuring Fran.

    Fran filed a personal injury action against Sid in a jurisdiction in which contributory negligence is a bar to recovery.

    Will Fran prevail?

    (A) Yes, if the jury finds that Sid was more than 50% at fault.
    (B) Yes, if the jury finds that Sid had the last clear chance.
    (C) No, if the jury finds that Fran's conduct was in any way a legal cause of the accident.
    (D) No, if the jury finds that, in speeding, Fran assumed the risk.

55. Sal owned five adjoining rectangular lots, numbered 1 through 5 inclusive, all fronting on Main Street. All of the lots are in a zone limited to one- and two-family residences under the zoning ordinance. Two years ago, Sal conveyed Lots 1, 3, and 5. None of the three deeds contained any restrictions. Each of the new owners built a one-family residence.

    One year ago, Sal conveyed Lot 2 to Peter. The deed provided that each of Peter and Sal, their respective heirs and assigns, would use Lots 2 and 4 respectively only for one-family residential purposes. The deed was promptly and properly recorded. Peter built a one-family residence on Lot 2.

    Last month, Sal conveyed Lot 4 to Betty. The deed contained no restrictions. The deed from Sal to Peter was in the title report examined by Betty's lawyer. Betty obtained a building permit and commenced construction of a two-family residence on Lot 4.

    Peter, joined by the owners of Lots 1, 3, and 5, brought an appropriate action against Betty to enjoin the proposed use of Lot 4, or, alternatively, damages caused by Betty's breach of covenant.

    Which is the most appropriate comment concerning the outcome of this action?

    (A) All plaintiffs should be awarded their requested judgment for injunction because there was a common development scheme, but award of damages should be denied to all.
    (B) Peter should be awarded appropriate remedy, but recovery by the other plaintiffs is doubtful.
    (C) Injunction should be denied, but damages should be awarded to all plaintiffs, measured by diminution of market value, if any, suffered as a result of the proximity of Betty's two-family residence.
    (D) All plaintiffs should be denied any recovery or relief because the zoning preempts any private scheme of covenants.

GO ON TO THE NEXT PAGE.

56. Kelly County, in the state of Green, is located adjacent to the border of the state of Red. The communities located in Kelly County are principally suburbs of Scarletville, a large city located in Red, and therefore there is a large volume of traffic between that city and Kelly County. While most of that traffic is by private passenger automobiles, some of it is by taxicabs and other kinds of commercial vehicles.

An ordinance of Kelly County, the stated purpose of which is to reduce traffic congestion, provides that only taxicabs registered in Kelly County may pick up or discharge passengers in the county. The ordinance also provides that only residents of Kelly County may register taxicabs in that county.

Which of the following is the proper result in a suit brought by Scarletville taxicab owners challenging the constitutionality of this Kelly County ordinance?

(A) Judgment for Scarletville taxicab owners, because the fact that private passenger automobiles contribute more to the traffic congestion problem in Kelly County than do taxicabs indicates that the ordinance is not a reasonable means by which to solve that problem.
(B) Judgment for Scarletville taxicab owners, because the ordinance unduly burdens interstate commerce by insulating Kelly County taxicab owners from out-of-state competition without adequate justification.
(C) Judgment for Kelly County, because the ordinance forbids taxicabs registered in other counties of Green as well as in states other than Green to operate in Kelly County and, therefore, it does not discriminate against interstate commerce.
(D) Judgment for Kelly County, because Scarletville taxicab owners do not constitute a suspect class and the ordinance is reasonably related to the legitimate governmental purpose of reducing traffic congestion.

57. Paul sued Donna for breach of contract. Paul's position was that Joan, whom he understood to be Donna's agent, said: "On behalf of Donna, I accept your offer." Donna asserted that Joan had no actual or apparent authority to accept the offer on Donna's behalf.

Paul's testimony concerning Joan's statement is

(A) admissible, provided the court first finds by a preponderance of the evidence that Joan had actual or apparent authority to act for Donna.
(B) admissible, upon or subject to introduction of evidence sufficient to support a finding by the jury that Joan had actual or apparent authority to act for Donna.
(C) inadmissible, if Joan does not testify and her absence is not excused.
(D) inadmissible, because it is hearsay not within any exception.

GO ON TO THE NEXT PAGE.

58. A city ordinance requires a taxicab operator's license to operate a taxicab in King City. The ordinance states that the sole criteria for the issuance of such a license are driving ability and knowledge of the geography of King City. An applicant is tested by the city for these qualifications with a detailed questionnaire, written and oral examinations, and a practical behind-the-wheel demonstration.

    The ordinance does not limit the number of licenses that may be issued. It does, however, allow any citizen to file an objection to the issuance of a particular license, but only on the ground that an applicant does not possess the required qualifications. City licensing officials are also authorized by the ordinance to determine, in their discretion, whether to hold an evidentiary hearing on an objection before issuing a license.

    Sandy applies for a taxicab operator's license and is found to be fully qualified after completing the usual licensing process. Her name is then posted as a prospective licensee, subject only to the objection process. John, a licensed taxicab driver, files an objection to the issuance of such a license to Sandy solely on the ground that the grant of a license to Sandy would impair the value of John's existing license. John demands a hearing before a license is issued to Sandy so that he may have an opportunity to prove his claim. City licensing officials refuse to hold such a hearing, and they issue a license to Sandy. John petitions for review of this action by city officials in an appropriate court, alleging that the Constitution requires city licensing officials to grant his request for a hearing before issuing a license to Sandy.

    In this case, the court should rule for

    (A) John, because the due process clause of the Fourteenth Amendment requires all persons whose property may be adversely affected by governmental action to be given an opportunity for a hearing before such action occurs.
    (B) John, because the determination of whether to hold a hearing may not constitutionally be left to the discretion of the same officials whose action is being challenged.
    (C) city officials, because John had the benefit of the licensing ordinance and, therefore, may not now question actions taken under it.
    (D) city officials, because the licensing ordinance does not give John any property interest in being free of competition from additional licensees.

59. Homer lived on the second floor of a small convenience store/gas station that he owned. One night he refused to sell Augie a six-pack of beer after hours, saying he could not violate the state laws. Augie became enraged and deliberately drove his car into one of the gasoline pumps, severing it from its base. There was an ensuing explosion causing a ball of fire to go from the underground gasoline tank into the building. As a result, the building burned to the ground and Homer was killed.

    In a common-law jurisdiction, if Augie is charged with murder and arson, he should be

    (A) convicted of both offenses.
    (B) convicted of involuntary manslaughter and acquitted of arson.
    (C) convicted of arson and involuntary manslaughter.
    (D) acquitted of both offenses.

GO ON TO THE NEXT PAGE.

60. Bye Bye telegraphed Vendor on June 1, "At what price will you sell 100 of your QT-Model garbage-disposal units for delivery around June 10?" Thereafter, the following communications were exchanged:

   1. Telegram from Vendor received by Bye Bye on June 2: "You're in luck. We have only 100 QT's, all on clearance at 50% off usual wholesale of $120 per unit, for delivery at our shipping platform on June 12."
   2. Letter from Bye Bye received in U.S. mail by Vendor on June 5: "I accept. Would prefer to pay in full 30 days after invoice."
   3. Telegram from Vendor received by Bye Bye on June 6: "You must pick up at our platform and pay C.O.D."
   4. Letter from Bye Bye received in U.S. mail by Vendor on June 9: "I don't deal with people who can't accommodate our simple requests."
   5. Telegram from Bye Bye received by Vendor on June 10, after Vendor had sold and delivered all 100 of the QT's to another buyer earlier that day: "Okay. I'm over a barrel and will pick up the goods on your terms June 12."

Bye Bye now sues Vendor for breach of contract.

Which of the following arguments will best serve Vendor's defense?

(A) Vendor's telegram received on June 2 was merely a price quotation, not an offer.
(B) Bye Bye's letter received on June 5 was not an acceptance because it varied the terms of Vendor's initial telegram.
(C) Bye Bye's use of the mails in response to Vendor's initial telegram was an ineffective method of acceptance.
(D) Bye Bye's letter received on June 9 was an unequivocal refusal to perform that excused Vendor even if the parties had previously formed a contract.

61. At a party, Diane and Victor agreed to play a game they called "spin the barrel." Victor took an unloaded revolver, placed one bullet in the barrel, and spun the barrel. Victor then pointed the gun at Diane's head and pulled the trigger once. The gun did not fire. Diane then took the gun, pointed it at Victor, spun the barrel, and pulled the trigger once. The gun fired, and Victor fell over dead.

A statute in the jurisdiction defines murder in the first degree as an intentional and premeditated killing or one occurring during the commission of a common-law felony, and murder in the second degree as all other murder at common law. Manslaughter is defined as a killing in the heat of passion upon an adequate legal provocation or a killing caused by gross negligence.

The most serious crime for which Diane can properly be convicted is

(A) murder in the first degree, because the killing was intentional and premeditated and, in any event, occurred during commission of the felony of assault with a deadly weapon.
(B) murder in the second degree, because Diane's act posed a great threat of serious bodily harm.
(C) manslaughter, because Diane's act was grossly negligent and reckless.
(D) no crime, because Victor and Diane voluntarily agreed to play a game and each assumed the risk of death.

GO ON TO THE NEXT PAGE.

62. Abel owned Blackacre in fee simple. Three years ago, Abel and Betty agreed to a month-to-month tenancy with Betty paying Abel rent each month. After six months of Betty's occupancy, Abel suggested to Betty that she could buy Blackacre for a monthly payment of no more than her rent. Abel and Betty orally agreed that Betty would pay $25,000 in cash, the annual real estate taxes, the annual fire insurance premiums, and the costs of maintaining Blackacre, plus the monthly mortgage payments that Abel owed on Blackacre. They further orally agreed that within six years Betty could pay whatever mortgage balances were then due and Abel would give her a warranty deed to the property. Betty's average monthly payments did turn out to be about the same as her monthly rent.

Betty fully complied with all of the obligations she had undertaken. She made some structural modifications to Blackacre. Blackacre is now worth 50% more than it was when Abel and Betty made their oral agreement. Betty made her financing arrangements and was ready to complete the purchase of Blackacre, but Abel refused to close. Betty brought an appropriate action for specific performance against Abel to enforce the agreement.

The court should rule for

(A) Abel, because the agreements were oral and violated the statute of frauds.
(B) Abel, subject to the return of the $25,000, because the arrangement was still a tenancy.
(C) Betty, because the doctrine of part performance applies.
(D) Betty, because the statute of frauds does not apply to oral purchase and sale agreements between landlords and tenants in possession.

63. A statute of State X permits a person's name to appear on the general election ballot as a candidate for statewide public office if the person pays a $100 filing fee and provides proof from the State Elections Board that he or she was nominated in the immediately preceding primary election by one of the state's two major political parties. It also permits the name of an independent candidate or a candidate of a smaller party to appear on the general election ballot if that person pays a filing fee of $1,000, and submits petitions signed by at least 3% of the voters who actually cast ballots for the office of governor in the last State X election. State X maintains that these filing requirements are necessary to limit the size of the election ballot, to eliminate frivolous candidacies, and to help finance the high cost of elections.

Historically, very few of State X's voters who are members of racial minority groups have been members of either of the two major political parties. Recently, a new political party has been formed by some of these voters.

Which of the following constitutional provisions would be most helpful to the new political party as a basis for attacking the constitutionality of this statute of State X?

(A) The First Amendment.
(B) The Thirteenth Amendment.
(C) The Fourteenth Amendment.
(D) The Fifteenth Amendment.

GO ON TO THE NEXT PAGE.

64. Defendant is on trial for the murder of his father. Defendant's defense is that he shot his father accidentally. The prosecutor calls Witness, a police officer, to testify that on two occasions in the year prior to this incident, he had been called to Defendant's home because of complaints of loud arguments between Defendant and his father, and had found it necessary to stop Defendant from beating his father.

The evidence is

(A) inadmissible, because it is improper character evidence.
(B) inadmissible, because Witness lacks firsthand knowledge of who started the quarrels.
(C) admissible to show that Defendant killed his father intentionally.
(D) admissible to show that Defendant is a violent person.

65. Alex and Brenda owned in fee simple Greenacre as tenants in common, each owning an undivided one-half interest. Alex and Brenda joined in mortgaging Greenacre to Marge by a properly recorded mortgage that contained a general warranty clause. Alex became disenchanted with land-owning and notified Brenda that he would no longer contribute to the payment of installments due Marge. After the mortgage was in default and Marge made demand for payment of the entire amount of principal and interest due, Brenda tendered to Marge, and Marge deposited, a check for one-half of the amount due Marge. Brenda then demanded a release of Brenda's undivided one-half interest. Marge refused to release any interest in Greenacre. Brenda promptly brought an action against Marge to quiet title to an undivided one-half interest in Greenacre.

In such action, Brenda should

(A) lose, because Marge's title had been warranted by an express provision of the mortgage.
(B) lose, because there was no redemption from the mortgage.
(C) win, because Brenda is entitled to marshalling.
(D) win, because the cotenancy of the mortgagors was in common and not joint.

GO ON TO THE NEXT PAGE.

Questions 66–68 are based on the following fact situation.

The police had, over time, accumulated reliable information that Jason operated a large cocaine-distribution network, that he and his accomplices often resorted to violence, and that they kept a small arsenal of weapons in his home.

One day, the police received reliable information that a large brown suitcase with leather straps containing a supply of cocaine had been delivered to Jason's home and that it would be moved to a distribution point the next morning. The police obtained a valid search warrant to search for and seize the brown suitcase and the cocaine and went to Jason's house.

The police knocked on Jason's door and called out, "Police. Open up. We have a search warrant." After a few seconds with no response, the police forced the door open and entered. Hearing noises in the basement, the police ran down there and found Jason with a large brown suitcase with leather straps. They seized the suitcase and put handcuffs on Jason. A search of his person revealed a switchblade knife and a .45-caliber pistol. Jason cursed the police and said, "You never would have caught me with the stuff if it hadn't been for that lousy snitch Harvey!"

The police then fanned out through the house, looking in every room and closet. They found no one else, but one officer found an Uzi automatic weapon in a box on a closet shelf in Jason's bedroom.

In addition to charges relating to the cocaine in the suitcase, Jason is charged with unlawful possession of weapons.

Jason moves pretrial to suppress the use as evidence of the weapons seized by the police and of the statement he made.

66. As to the switchblade knife and the .45-caliber pistol, Jason's motion to suppress should be

(A) granted, because the search and seizure were the result of illegal police conduct in executing the search warrant.
(B) granted, because the police did not inform Jason that he was under arrest and did not read him his Miranda rights.
(C) denied, because the search and seizure were incident to a lawful arrest.
(D) denied, because the police had reasonable grounds to believe that there were weapons in the house.

67. As to Jason's statement, his motion to suppress should be

(A) granted, because the entry by forcing open the door was not reasonable.
(B) granted, because the police failed to read Jason his Miranda rights.
(C) denied, because the statement was volunteered.
(D) denied, because the statement was the product of a lawful public safety search.

68. As to the Uzi automatic weapon, Jason's motion to suppress should be

(A) granted, because the search exceeded the scope needed to find out if other persons were present.
(B) granted, because once the object of the warrant—the brown suitcase—had been found and seized, no further search of the house is permitted.
(C) denied, because the police were lawfully in the bedroom and the weapon was immediately identifiable as being subject to seizure.
(D) denied, because the police were lawfully in the house and had probable cause to believe that weapons were in the house.

GO ON TO THE NEXT PAGE.

69. Plaintiff is suing Doctor for medical malpractice occasioned by allegedly prescribing an incorrect medication, causing Plaintiff to undergo substantial hospitalization. When Doctor learned of the medication problem, she immediately offered to pay Plaintiff's hospital expenses. At trial, Plaintiff offers evidence of Doctor's offer to pay the costs of his hospitalization.

    The evidence of Doctor's offer is

    (A) admissible as a nonhearsay statement of a party.
    (B) admissible, although hearsay, as a statement against interest.
    (C) inadmissible, because it is an offer to pay medical expenses.
    (D) inadmissible, because it is an offer to compromise.

70. Sam and two of his friends were members of a teenage street gang. While they were returning from a dance late one evening, their car collided with a car driven by an elderly woman. After an argument, Sam attacked the elderly woman with his fists and beat her to death. Sam's two friends watched, and when they saw the woman fall to the ground they urged Sam to flee. Sam was eventually apprehended and tried for manslaughter, but the jury could not decide on a verdict.

    If Sam's companions are subsequently tried as accomplices to manslaughter, they should be

    (A) acquitted, because Sam was not convicted of the offense.
    (B) acquitted, because they did not assist or encourage Sam to commit the crime.
    (C) convicted, because they urged him to flee.
    (D) convicted, because they made no effort to intervene.

71. Employer retained Doctor to evaluate medical records of prospective employees. Doctor informed Employer that Applicant, a prospective employee, suffered from AIDS. Employer informed Applicant of this and declined to hire her.

    Applicant was shocked by this news and suffered a heart attack as a result. Subsequent tests revealed that Applicant in fact did not have AIDS. Doctor had negligently confused Applicant's file with that of another prospective employee.

    If Applicant sued Doctor for damages, on which of the following causes of action would Applicant recover?

    I. Invasion of privacy.
    II. Negligent misrepresentation.
    III. Negligent infliction of emotional distress.

    (A) III only.
    (B) I and II only.
    (C) II and III only.
    (D) I, II, and III.

    GO ON TO THE NEXT PAGE.

Questions 72–73 are based on the following fact situation.

Gourmet, a famous chef, entered into a written agreement with his friend Deligor, a well-known interior decorator respected for his unique designs, in which Deligor agreed, for a fixed fee, to design the interior of Gourmet's new restaurant, and, upon Gourmet's approval of the design plan, to decorate and furnish the restaurant accordingly. The agreement was silent as to assignment or delegation by either party. Before beginning the work, Deligor sold his decorating business to Newman under an agreement in which Deligor assigned to Newman, and Newman agreed to complete, the Gourmet-Deligor contract. Newman, also an experienced decorator of excellent repute, advised Gourmet of the assignment, and supplied him with information confirming both Newman's financial responsibility and past commercial success.

72. Is Gourmet obligated to permit Newman to perform the Gourmet-Deligor agreement?

    (A) Yes, because the agreement contained no prohibition against assignment or delegation.
    (B) Yes, because Gourmet received adequate assurances of Newman's ability to complete the job.
    (C) No, because Deligor's duties were of a personal nature, involving his reputation, taste, and skill.
    (D) No, because Deligor's purported delegation to Newman of his obligations to Gourmet effected a novation.

73. If Gourmet allows Newman to perform and approves his design plan, but Newman fails without legal excuse to complete the decorating as agreed, against whom does Gourmet have an enforceable claim for breach of contract?

    (A) Deligor only, because Deligor's agreement with Newman did not discharge his duty to Gourmet, and Newman made no express promise to Gourmet.
    (B) Newman only, because Deligor's duty to Gourmet was discharged when Deligor obtained a skilled decorator (Newman) to perform the Gourmet-Deligor contract.
    (C) Newman only, because Gourmet was an intended beneficiary of the Deligor-Newman agreement, and Deligor's duty to Gourmet was discharged when Gourmet permitted Newman to do the work and approved Newman's design.
    (D) Either Deligor, because his agreement with Newman did not discharge his duty to Gourmet; or Newman, because Gourmet was an intended beneficiary of the Deligor-Newman agreement.

74. Plaintiff sued Defendant Auto Manufacturing for his wife's death, claiming that a defective steering mechanism on the family car caused it to veer off the road and hit a tree when his wife was driving. Defendant claims that the steering mechanism was damaged in the collision and offers testimony that the deceased wife was intoxicated at the time of the accident.

    Testimony concerning the wife's intoxication is

    (A) admissible to provide an alternate explanation of the accident's cause.
    (B) admissible as proper evidence of the wife's character.
    (C) inadmissible, because it is improper to prove character evidence by specific conduct.
    (D) inadmissible, because it is substantially more prejudicial than probative.

GO ON TO THE NEXT PAGE.

75. Otis owned in fee simple Lots 1 and 2 in an urban subdivision. The lots were vacant and unproductive. They were held as a speculation that their value would increase. Otis died and, by his duly probated will, devised the residue of his estate (of which Lots 1 and 2 were part) to Lena for life with remainder in fee simple to Rose. Otis's executor distributed the estate under appropriate court order, and notified Lena that future real estate taxes on Lots 1 and 2 were Lena's responsibility to pay.

    Except for the statutes relating to probate and those relating to real estate taxes, there is no applicable statute.

    Lena failed to pay the real estate taxes due for Lots 1 and 2. To prevent a tax sale of the fee simple, Rose paid the taxes and demanded that Lena reimburse her for same. When Lena refused, Rose brought an appropriate action against Lena to recover the amount paid.

    In such action, Rose should recover

    (A) the amount paid, because a life tenant has the duty to pay current charges.
    (B) the present value of the interest that the amount paid would earn during Lena's lifetime.
    (C) nothing, because Lena's sole possession gave the right to decide whether or not taxes should be paid.
    (D) nothing, because Lena never received any income from the lots.

76. During an altercation between Oscar and Martin at a company picnic, Oscar suffered a knife wound in his abdomen and Martin was charged with assault and attempted murder. At his trial, Martin seeks to offer evidence that he had been drinking at the picnic and was highly intoxicated at the time of the altercation.

    In a jurisdiction that follows the common-law rules concerning admissibility of evidence of intoxication, the evidence of Martin's intoxication should be

    (A) admitted without limitation.
    (B) admitted subject to an instruction that it pertains only to the attempted murder charge.
    (C) admitted subject to an instruction that it pertains only to the assault charge.
    (D) excluded altogether.

77. Plaintiff Construction Co. sued Defendant Development Co. for money owed on a cost-plus contract that required notice of proposed expenditures beyond original estimates. Defendant asserted that it never received the required notice. At trial Plaintiff calls its general manager, Witness, to testify that it is Plaintiff's routine practice to send cost overrun notices as required by the contract. Witness also offers a photocopy of the cost overrun notice letter to Defendant on which Plaintiff is relying, and which he has taken from Plaintiff's regular business files.

    On the issue of giving notice, the letter copy is

    (A) admissible, though hearsay, under the business record exception.
    (B) admissible, because of the routine practices of the company.
    (C) inadmissible, because it is hearsay not within any exception.
    (D) inadmissible, because it is not the best evidence of the notice.

GO ON TO THE NEXT PAGE.

78. Plaintiff sued Defendant under an age discrimination statute, alleging that Defendant refused to hire Plaintiff because she was over age 65. Defendant's defense was that he refused to employ Plaintiff because he reasonably believed that she would be unable to perform the job. Defendant seeks to testify that Employer, Plaintiff's former employer, advised him not to hire Plaintiff because she was unable to perform productively for more than four hours a day.

The testimony of Defendant is

(A) inadmissible, because Defendant's opinion of Plaintiff's abilities is not based on personal knowledge.
(B) inadmissible, because Employer's statement is hearsay not within any exception.
(C) admissible as evidence that Plaintiff would be unable to work longer than four hours per day.
(D) admissible as evidence of Defendant's reason for refusing to hire Plaintiff.

79. A federal statute provides that the cities in which certain specified airports are located may regulate the rates and services of all limousines that serve those airports, without regard to the origin or destination of the passengers who use the limousines.

The cities of Redville and Greenville are located adjacent to each other in different states. The airport serving both of them is located in Redville and is one of those airports specified in the federal statute. The Redville City Council has adopted a rule that requires any limousines serving the airport to charge only the rates authorized by the Redville City Council.

Airline Limousine Service has a lucrative business transporting passengers between Greenville and the airport in Redville, at much lower rates than those required by the Redville City Council. It transports passengers in interstate traffic only; it does not provide local service within Redville. The new rule adopted by the Redville City Council will require Airline Limousine Service to charge the same rates as limousines operating only in Redville.

Must Airline Limousine Service comply with the new rule of the Redville City Council?

(A) Yes, because the airport is located in Redville and, therefore, its city council has exclusive regulatory authority over all transportation to and from the airport.
(B) Yes, because Congress has authorized this form of regulation by Redville and, therefore, removed any constitutional impediments to it that may have otherwise existed.
(C) No, because the rule would arbitrarily destroy a lucrative existing business and, therefore, would amount to a taking without just compensation.
(D) No, because Airline Limousine Service is engaged in interstate commerce and this rule is an undue burden on that commerce.

GO ON TO THE NEXT PAGE.

80. While approaching an intersection with the red light against him, Motorist suffered a heart attack that rendered him unconscious. Motorist's car struck Child, who was crossing the street with the green light in her favor. Under the state motor vehicle code, it is an offense to drive through a red traffic light.

Child sued Motorist to recover for her injuries. At trial it was stipulated that (1) immediately prior to suffering the heart attack, Motorist had been driving within the speed limit, had seen the red light, and had begun to slow his car; (2) Motorist had no history of heart disease and no warning of this attack; (3) while Motorist was unconscious, his car ran the red light.

On cross motions for directed verdicts on the issue of liability at the conclusion of the proofs, the court should

(A) grant Child's motion, because Motorist ran a red light in violation of the motor vehicle code.
(B) grant Child's motion, because, in the circumstances, reasonable persons would infer that Motorist was negligent.
(C) grant Motorist's motion, because he had no history of heart disease or warning of the heart attack.
(D) deny both motions and submit the case to the jury, to determine whether, in the circumstances, Motorist's conduct was that of a reasonably prudent person.

81. In a jurisdiction without a Dead Man's Statute, Parker's estate sued Davidson claiming that Davidson had borrowed from Parker $10,000, which had not been repaid as of Parker's death. Parker was run over by a truck. At the accident scene, while dying from massive injuries, Parker told Officer Smith to "make sure my estate collects the $10,000 I loaned to Davidson."

Smith's testimony about Parker's statement is

(A) inadmissible, because it is more unfairly prejudicial than probative.
(B) inadmissible, because it is hearsay not within any exception.
(C) admissible as an excited utterance.
(D) admissible as a statement under belief of impending death.

GO ON TO THE NEXT PAGE.

Questions 82–83 are based on the following fact situation.

Landholder was land-rich by inheritance but money-poor, having suffered severe losses on bad investments, but still owned several thousand acres of unencumbered timberland. He had a large family, and his normal, fixed personal expenses were high. Pressed for cash, he advertised a proposed sale of standing timber on a choice 2,000-acre tract. The only response was an offer by Logger, the owner of a large, integrated construction enterprise, after inspection of the advertised tract.

82. For this question only, assume the following facts. Logger offered to buy, sever, and remove the standing timber from the advertised tract at a cash price 70% lower than the regionally prevailing price for comparable timber rights. Landholder, by then in desperate financial straits and knowing little about timber values, signed and delivered to Logger a letter accepting the offer.

If, before Logger commences performance, Landholder's investment fortunes suddenly improve and he wishes to get out of the timber deal with Logger, which of the following legal concepts affords his best prospect of effective cancellation?

(A) Bad faith.
(B) Equitable estoppel.
(C) Unconscionability.
(D) Duress.

83. For this question only, assume the following facts. Logger offered a fair price for the timber rights in question, and Landholder accepted the offer. The 2,000-acre tract was an abundant wild-game habitat and had been used for many years, with Landholder's permission, by area hunters. Logger's performance of the timber contract would destroy this habitat. Without legal excuse and over Landholder's strong objection, Logger repudiated the contract before commencing performance. Landholder could not afford to hire a lawyer and take legal action, and made no attempt to assign any cause of action he might have had against Logger.

If Logger is sued for breach of the contract by Landholder's next-door neighbor, whose view of a nearby lake is obscured by the standing timber, the neighbor will probably

(A) lose, as only an incidental beneficiary, if any, of the Logger-Landholder contract.
(B) lose, as a maintainer of nuisance litigation.
(C) prevail, as a third-party intended beneficiary of the Logger-Landholder contract.
(D) prevail, as a surrogate for Landholder in view of his inability to enforce the contract.

GO ON TO THE NEXT PAGE.

84. A federal statute with inseverable provisions established a new five-member National Prosperity Board with broad regulatory powers over the operation of the securities, banking, and commodities industries, including the power to issue rules with the force of law. The statute provides for three of the board members to be appointed by the President with the advice and consent of the Senate. They serve seven-year terms and are removable only for good cause. The other two members of the board were designated in the statute to be the respective general counsel of the Senate and House of Representatives Committees on Government Operations. The statute stipulated that they were to serve on the board for as long as they continued in those positions.

Following all required administrative procedures, the board issued an elaborate set of rules regulating the operations of all banks, securities dealers, and commodities brokers. The Green Light Securities Company, which was subject to the board's rules, sought a declaratory judgment that the rules were invalid because the statute establishing the board was unconstitutional.

In this case, the court should rule that the statute establishing the National Prosperity Board is

(A) unconstitutional, because all members of federal boards having broad powers that are quasi-legislative in nature, such as rulemaking, must be appointed by Congress.
(B) unconstitutional, because all members of federal boards exercising executive powers must be appointed by the President or in a manner otherwise consistent with the appointments clause of Article II.
(C) constitutional, because the necessary and proper clause authorizes Congress to determine the means by which members are appointed to boards created by Congress under its power to regulate commerce among the states.
(D) constitutional, because there is a substantial nexus between the power of Congress to legislate for the general welfare and the means specified by Congress in this statute for the appointment of board members.

GO ON TO THE NEXT PAGE.

85. By a writing, Oner leased his home, Blackacre, to Tenn for a term of three years, ending December 31 of last year, at the rent of $1,000 per month. The lease provided that Tenn could sublet and assign.

    Tenn lived in Blackacre for one year and paid the rent promptly. After one year, Tenn leased Blackacre to Agrit for one year at a rent of $1,000 per month.

    Agrit took possession of Blackacre and lived there for six months but, because of her unemployment, paid no rent. After six months, on June 30 Agrit abandoned Blackacre, which remained vacant for the balance of that year. Tenn again took possession of Blackacre at the beginning of the third and final year of the term but paid Oner no rent.

    At the end of the lease term, Oner brought an appropriate action against both Tenn and Agrit to recover $24,000, the unpaid rent.

    In such action Oner is entitled to a judgment

    (A) against Tenn individually for $24,000, and no judgment against Agrit.
    (B) against Tenn individually for $18,000, and against Agrit individually for $6,000.
    (C) against Tenn for $12,000, and against Tenn and Agrit jointly and severally for $12,000.
    (D) against Tenn individually for $18,000, and against Tenn and Agrit jointly and severally for $6,000.

86. In a trial to a jury, Owner proved that Power Company's negligent maintenance of a transformer caused a fire that destroyed his restaurant. The jury returned a verdict for Owner in the amount of $450,000 for property loss and $500,000 for emotional distress. The trial judge entered judgment in those amounts. Power Company appealed that part of the judgment awarding $500,000 for emotional distress.

    On appeal, the judgment should be

    (A) affirmed, because Power Company negligently caused Owner's emotional distress.
    (B) affirmed, because harm arising from emotional distress is as real as harm caused by physical impact.
    (C) reversed, because the law does not recognize a claim for emotional distress incident to negligently caused property loss.
    (D) reversed, unless the jury found that Owner suffered physical harm as a consequence of the emotional distress caused by his property loss.

    GO ON TO THE NEXT PAGE.

87. Bill owned in fee simple Lot 1 in a properly approved subdivision, designed and zoned for industrial use. Gail owned the adjoining Lot 2 in the same subdivision. The plat of the subdivision was recorded as authorized by statute.

Twelve years ago, Bill erected an industrial building wholly situated on Lot 1 but with one wall along the boundary common with Lot 2. The construction was done as authorized by a building permit, validly obtained under applicable statutes, ordinances, and regulations. Further, the construction was regularly inspected and passed as being in compliance with all building code requirements.

Lot 2 remained vacant until six months ago, when Gail began excavation pursuant to a building permit authorizing the erection of an industrial building situated on Lot 2 but with one wall along the boundary common with Lot 1. The excavation caused subsidence of a portion of Lot 1 that resulted in injury to Bill's building. The excavation was not done negligently or with any malicious intent to injure. In the jurisdiction, the time to acquire title by adverse possession or rights by prescription is 10 years.

Bill brought an appropriate action against Gail to recover damages resulting from the injuries to the building on Lot 1.

In such lawsuit, judgment should be for

(A) Bill, if, but only if, the subsidence would have occurred without the weight of the building on Lot 1.
(B) Bill, because a right for support, appurtenant to Lot 1, had been acquired by adverse possession or prescription.
(C) Gail, because Lots 1 and 2 are urban land, as distinguished from rural land and, therefore, under the circumstances Bill had the duty to protect any improvements on Lot 1.
(D) Gail, because the construction and the use to be made of the building were both authorized by the applicable law.

88. Defendant is charged with murder in connection with a carjacking incident during which Defendant allegedly shot Victim while attempting to steal Victim's car. The prosecutor calls Victim's four-year-old son, whose face was horribly disfigured by the same bullet, to testify that Defendant shot his father and him.

The son's testimony should be

(A) admitted, provided the prosecutor first provides evidence that persuades the judge that the son is competent to testify despite his tender age.
(B) admitted, provided there is sufficient basis for believing that the son has personal knowledge and understands his obligation to testify truthfully.
(C) excluded, because it is insufficiently probative in view of the son's tender age.
(D) excluded, because it is more unfairly prejudicial than probative.

GO ON TO THE NEXT PAGE.

89. A federal statute provides that the United States Supreme Court has authority to review any case filed in a United States Court of Appeals, even though that case has not yet been decided by the court of appeals.

The Environmental Protection Agency (EPA), an agency in the executive branch of the federal government, issued an important environmental rule. Although the rule had not yet been enforced against them, companies that would be adversely affected by the rule filed a petition for review of the rule in a court of appeals, seeking a declaration that the rule was invalid solely because it was beyond the statutory authority of the EPA. The companies made no constitutional claim. A statute specifically provides for direct review of EPA rules by a court of appeals without any initial action in a district court.

The companies have filed a petition for a writ of certiorari in the Supreme Court requesting immediate review of this case by the Supreme Court before the court of appeals has actually decided the case. The EPA acknowledges that the case is important enough to warrant Supreme Court review and that it should be decided promptly, but it asks the Supreme Court to dismiss the petition on jurisdictional grounds.

The best constitutional argument in support of the EPA's request is that

(A) the case is not within the original jurisdiction of the Supreme Court as defined by Article III, and it is not a proper subject of that court's appellate jurisdiction because it has not yet been decided by any lower court.
(B) the case is appellate in nature, but it is beyond the appellate jurisdiction of the Supreme Court, because Article III states that its jurisdiction extends only to cases arising under the Constitution.
(C) Article III precludes federal courts from reviewing the validity of any federal agency rule in any proceeding other than an action to enforce the rule.
(D) Article III provides that all federal cases, except those within the original jurisdiction of the Supreme Court, must be initiated by an action in a federal district court.

GO ON TO THE NEXT PAGE.

90. Patron ate a spicy dinner at Restaurant on Sunday night. He enjoyed the food and noticed nothing unusual about the dinner.

    Later that evening, Patron had an upset stomach. He slept well through the night, went to work the next day, and ate three meals. His stomach discomfort persisted, and by Tuesday morning he was too ill to go to work.

    Eventually, Patron consulted his doctor, who found that Patron was infected with a bacterium that can be contracted from contaminated food. Food can be contaminated when those who prepare it do not adequately wash their hands.

    Patron sued Restaurant for damages. He introduced testimony from a health department official that various health code violations had been found at Restaurant both before and after Patron's dinner, but that none of Restaurant's employees had signs of bacterial infection when they were tested one month after the incident.

    Restaurant's best argument in response to Patron's suit would be that

    (A) no one else who ate at Restaurant on Sunday complained about stomach discomfort.
    (B) Restaurant instructs its employees to wash their hands carefully and is not responsible if any employee fails to follow these instructions.
    (C) Patron has failed to establish that Restaurant's food caused his illness.
    (D) Patron assumed the risk of an upset stomach by choosing to eat spicy food.

91. In a jurisdiction that has abolished the felony-murder rule, but otherwise follows the common law of murder, Sally and Ralph, both armed with automatic weapons, went into a bank to rob it. Ralph ordered all the persons in the bank to lie on the floor. When some were slow to obey, Sally, not intending to hit anyone, fired about 15 rounds into the air. One of these ricocheted off a stone column and struck and killed a customer in the bank.

    Sally and Ralph were charged with murder of the customer.

    Which of the following is correct?

    (A) Sally can be convicted of murder, because she did the act of killing, but Ralph cannot be convicted of either murder or manslaughter.
    (B) Neither can be guilty of murder, but both can be convicted of manslaughter based upon an unintentional homicide.
    (C) Sally can be convicted only of manslaughter, but Ralph cannot be convicted of murder or manslaughter.
    (D) Both can be convicted of murder.

    GO ON TO THE NEXT PAGE.

92. In recent years, several large corporations incorporated and headquartered in State A have suddenly been acquired by out-of-state corporations that have moved all of their operations out of State A. Other corporations incorporated and headquartered in State A have successfully resisted such attempts at acquisition by out-of-state corporations, but they have suffered severe economic injury during those acquisition attempts.

In an effort to preserve jobs in State A and to protect its domestic corporations against their sudden acquisition by out-of-state purchasers, the legislature of State A enacts a statute governing acquisitions of shares in all corporations incorporated in State A. This statute requires that any acquisition of more than 25% of the voting shares of a corporation incorporated in State A that occurs over a period of less than one year must be approved by the holders of record of a majority of the shares of the corporation as of the day before the commencement of the acquisition of those shares. The statute expressly applies to acquisitions of State A corporations by both in-state and out-of-state entities.

Assume that no federal statute applies.

Is this statute of State A constitutional?

(A) No, because one of the purposes of the statute is to prevent out-of-state entities from acquiring corporations incorporated and headquartered in State A.

(B) No, because the effect of the statute will necessarily be to hinder the acquisition of State A corporations by other corporations, many of whose shareholders are not residents of State A and, therefore, it will adversely affect the interstate sale of securities.

(C) Yes, because the statute imposes the same burden on both in-state and out-of-state entities wishing to acquire a State A corporation, it regulates only the acquisition of State A corporations, and it does not create an impermissible risk of inconsistent regulation on this subject by different states.

(D) Yes, because corporations exist only by virtue of state law and, therefore, the negative implications of the commerce clause do not apply to state regulations governing their creation and acquisition.

GO ON TO THE NEXT PAGE.

93. A written construction contract began with the following recital: "This Agreement, between Land, Inc. (hereafter called `Owner'), and Builder, Inc., and Boss, its President (hereafter called `Contractor'), witnesseth:" The signatures to the contract appeared in the following format:

> LAND, INC.
> By /s/ Oscar Land
> President
>
> BUILDER, INC.
> By /s/ George Mason
>
> Vice President
> /s/ Mary Boss,

President

> Mary Boss

Builder, Inc., became insolvent and defaulted. Land, Inc., sued Boss individually for the breach, and at the trial Boss proffered evidence from the pre-contract negotiations that only Builder, Inc., was to be legally responsible for performing the contract.

If the court finds the contract to be completely integrated, is Boss's proffered evidence admissible?

(A) Yes, because the writing is ambiguous as to whether or not Boss was intended individually to be a contracting party.
(B) Yes, because the evidence would contradict neither the recital nor the form of Boss's signature.
(C) No, because the legal effect of Boss's signature cannot be altered by evidence of prior understandings.
(D) No, because of the application of the "four corners" rule, under which the meaning of a completely integrated contract must be ascertained solely from its own terms.

94. When Parents were told that their child, Son, should repeat second grade, they sought to have him evaluated by a psychologist. The psychologist, who charged $300, determined that Son had a learning disability. Based upon the report, the school board placed Son in special classes. At an open meeting of the school board, Parents asked that the $300 they had paid to the psychologist be reimbursed by the school district. A reporter attending the meeting wrote a newspaper article about this request, mentioning Son by name.

In a privacy action brought by Son's legal representative against the newspaper, the plaintiff will

(A) recover, because the story is not newsworthy.
(B) recover, because Son is under the age of consent.
(C) not recover, if the story is a fair and accurate report of what transpired at the meeting.
(D) not recover, if Parents knew that the reporter was present.

GO ON TO THE NEXT PAGE.

95. On trial for murdering her husband, Defendant testified she acted in self-defense. Defendant calls Expert, a psychologist, to testify that under hypnosis Defendant had described the killing, and that in Expert's opinion Defendant had been in fear for her life at the time of the killing.

   Is Expert's testimony admissible?

   (A) Yes, because Expert was able to ascertain that Defendant was speaking truthfully.
   (B) Yes, because it reports a prior consistent statement by a witness (Defendant) subject to examination concerning it.
   (C) No, because reliance on information tainted by hypnosis is unconstitutional.
   (D) No, because it expresses an opinion concerning Defendant's mental state at the time of the killing.

96. The legislature of State X enacts a statute that it believes reconciles the state's interest in the preservation of human life with a woman's right to reproductive choice. That statute permits a woman to have an abortion on demand during the first trimester of pregnancy but prohibits a woman from having an abortion after that time unless her physician determines that the abortion is necessary to protect the woman's life or health.

   If challenged on constitutional grounds in an appropriate court, this statute will probably be held

   (A) constitutional, because the state has made a rational policy choice that creates an equitable balance between the compelling state interest in protecting fetal life and the fundamental right of a woman to reproductive choice.
   (B) constitutional, because recent rulings by the United States Supreme Court indicate that after the first trimester a fetus may be characterized as a person whose right to life is protected by the due process clause of the Fourteenth Amendment.
   (C) unconstitutional, because the state has, without adequate justification, placed an undue burden on the fundamental right of a woman to reproductive choice prior to fetal viability.
   (D) unconstitutional, because a statute unqualifiedly permitting abortion at one stage of pregnancy, and denying it at another with only minor exceptions, establishes an arbitrary classification in violation of the equal protection clause of the Fourteenth Amendment.

GO ON TO THE NEXT PAGE.

97. Olive owned Blackacre, a single-family residence. Fifteen years ago, Olive conveyed a life estate in Blackacre to Lois.

Fourteen years ago, Lois, who had taken possession of Blackacre, leased Blackacre to Trent for a term of 15 years at the monthly rental of $500.

Eleven years ago, Lois died intestate leaving Ron as her sole heir.

Trent regularly paid rent to Lois and, after Lois's death, to Ron until last month.

The period in which to acquire title by adverse possession in the jurisdiction is 10 years.

In an appropriate action, Trent, Olive, and Ron each asserted ownership of Blackacre.

The court should hold that title in fee simple is in

(A) Olive, because Olive held a reversion and Lois has died.
(B) Ron, because Lois asserted a claim adverse to Olive when Lois executed a lease to Trent.
(C) Ron, because Trent's occupation was attributable to Ron, and Lois died 11 years ago.
(D) Trent, because of Trent's physical occupancy and because Trent's term ended with Lois's death.

98. While browsing in a clothing store, Alice decided to take a purse without paying for it. She placed the purse under her coat and took a couple of steps toward the exit. She then realized that a sensor tag on the purse would set off an alarm. She placed the purse near the counter from which she had removed it.

Alice has committed

(A) no crime, because the purse was never removed from the store.
(B) no crime, because she withdrew from her criminal enterprise.
(C) only attempted larceny, because she intended to take the purse out of the store.
(D) larceny, because she took the purse from its original location and concealed it with the intent to steal.

GO ON TO THE NEXT PAGE.

Questions 99-100 are based on the following fact situation.

Adam's car sustained moderate damage in a collision with a car driven by Basher. The accident was caused solely by Basher's negligence. Adam's car was still drivable after the accident. Examining the car the next morning, Adam could see that a rear fender had to be replaced. He also noticed that gasoline had dripped onto the garage floor. The collision had caused a small leak in the gasoline tank.

Adam then took the car to Mechanic, who owns and operates a body shop, and arranged with Mechanic to repair the damage. During their discussion Adam neglected to mention the gasoline leakage. Thereafter, while Mechanic was loosening some of the damaged material with a hammer, he caused a spark, igniting vapor and gasoline that had leaked from the fuel tank. Mechanic was severely burned.

Mechanic has brought an action to recover damages against Adam and Basher. The jurisdiction has adopted a pure comparative negligence rule in place of the traditional common-law rule of contributory negligence.

99. In this action, will Mechanic obtain a judgment against Basher?

(A) No, unless there is evidence that Basher was aware of the gasoline leak.
(B) No, if Mechanic would not have been harmed had Adam warned him about the gasoline leak.
(C) Yes, unless Mechanic was negligent in not discovering the gasoline leak himself.
(D) Yes, if Mechanic's injury was a proximate consequence of Basher's negligent driving.

100. In this action, will Mechanic obtain a judgment against Adam?

(A) No, because it was Mechanic's job to inspect the vehicle and repair whatever needed repair.
(B) No, unless Adam was aware of the risk that the gasoline leak represented.
(C) Yes, if a reasonable person in Adam's position would have warned Mechanic about the gasoline leak.
(D) Yes, because the car was unreasonably dangerous when Adam delivered it to Mechanic.

STOP

PM Book
Time—3 hours

101. At 11:00 p.m., John and Marsha were accosted in the entrance to their apartment building by Dirk, who was armed as well as masked. Dirk ordered the couple to take him into their apartment. After they entered the apartment, Dirk forced Marsha to bind and gag her husband John and then to open a safe which contained a diamond necklace. Dirk then tied her up and fled with the necklace. He was apprehended by apartment building security guards. Before the guards could return to the apartment, but after Dirk was arrested, John, straining to free himself, suffered a massive heart attack and died.

    Dirk is guilty of

    (A) burglary, robbery, and murder.
    (B) robbery and murder only.
    (C) burglary and robbery only.
    (D) robbery only.

102. Plaintiff sued Defendant for injuries suffered in a car accident allegedly caused by brakes that had been negligently repaired by Defendant. At a settlement conference, Plaintiff exhibited the brake shoe that caused the accident and pointed out the alleged defect to an expert, whom Defendant had brought to the conference. No settlement was reached. At trial, the brake shoe having disappeared, Plaintiff seeks to testify concerning the condition of the shoe.

    Plaintiff's testimony is

    (A) admissible, because Defendant's expert had been able to examine the shoe carefully.
    (B) admissible, because Plaintiff had personal knowledge of the shoe's condition.
    (C) inadmissible, because the brake shoe was produced and examined as a part of settlement negotiations.
    (D) inadmissible, unless Plaintiff establishes that the disappearance was not his fault.

GO ON TO THE NEXT PAGE.

Questions 103–104 are based on the following fact situation.

Fixtures, Inc., in a signed writing, contracted with Apartments for the sale to Apartments of 50 identical sets of specified bathroom fixtures, 25 sets to be delivered on March 1, and the remaining 25 sets on April 1. The agreement did not specify the place of delivery, or the time or place of payment.

103. Which of the following statements is correct?

(A) Fixtures must tender 25 sets to Apartments at Apartments' place of business on March 1, but does not have to turn them over to Apartments until Apartments pays the contract price for the 25 sets.
(B) Fixtures has no duty to deliver the 25 sets on March 1 at Fixtures' place of business unless Apartments tenders the contract price for the 25 sets on that date.
(C) Fixtures must deliver 25 sets on March 1, and Apartments must pay the contract price for the 25 sets within a reasonable time after their delivery.
(D) Fixtures must deliver 25 sets on March 1, but Apartments' payment is due only upon the delivery of all 50 sets.

104. For this question only, make the following assumptions. On March 1, Fixtures tendered 24 sets to Apartments and explained, "One of the 25 sets was damaged in transit from the manufacturer to us, but we will deliver a replacement within 5 days."

Which of the following statements is correct?

(A) Apartments is entitled to accept any number of the 24 sets, reject the rest, and cancel the contract both as to any rejected sets and the lot due on April 1.
(B) Apartments is entitled to accept any number of the 24 sets and to reject the rest, but is not entitled to cancel the contract as to any rejected sets or the lot due on April 1.
(C) Apartments must accept the 24 sets but is entitled to cancel the rest of the contract.
(D) Apartments must accept the 24 sets and is not entitled to cancel the rest of the contract.

GO ON TO THE NEXT PAGE.

105. Defendant is on trial for nighttime breaking and entering of a warehouse. The warehouse owner had set up a camera to take infrared pictures of any intruders. After an expert establishes the reliability of infrared photography, the prosecutor offers the authenticated infrared picture of the intruder to show the similarities to Defendant.

The photograph is

(A) admissible, provided an expert witness points out to the jury the similarities between the person in the photograph and Defendant.
(B) admissible, allowing the jury to compare the person in the photograph and Defendant.
(C) inadmissible, because there was no eyewitness to the scene available to authenticate the photograph.
(D) inadmissible, because infrared photography deprives a defendant of the right to confront witnesses.

106. Olivia owned Blackacre, her home. Her daughter, Dawn, lived with her and always referred to Blackacre as "my property." Two years ago, Dawn, for a valuable consideration, executed and delivered to Bruce an instrument in the proper form of a warranty deed purporting to convey Blackacre to Bruce in fee simple, reserving to herself an estate for two years in Blackacre. Bruce promptly and properly recorded his deed.

One year ago, Olivia died and by will, duly admitted to probate, left her entire estate to Dawn.

One month ago, Dawn, for a valuable consideration, executed and delivered to Carl an instrument in the proper form of a warranty deed purporting to convey Blackacre to Carl, who promptly and properly recorded the deed. Dawn was then in possession of Blackacre and Carl had no actual knowledge of the deed to Bruce. Immediately thereafter, Dawn gave possession to Carl.

The recording act of the jurisdiction provides: "No conveyance or mortgage of real property shall be good against subsequent purchasers for value and without notice unless the same be recorded according to law."

Last week, Dawn fled the jurisdiction. Upon learning the facts, Carl brought an appropriate action against Bruce to quiet title to Blackacre.

If Carl wins, it will be because

(A) Dawn had nothing to convey to Bruce two years ago.
(B) Dawn's deed to Bruce was not to take effect until after Dawn's deed to Carl.
(C) Carl was first in possession.
(D) Dawn's deed to Bruce was not in Carl's chain of title.

GO ON TO THE NEXT PAGE.

107. Grace, while baby-sitting one night, noticed that Sam, who lived next door, had left his house but that the door did not close completely behind him. Grace said to Roy, the 11-year-old boy she was baby-sitting with, "Let's play a game. You go next door and see if you can find my portable television set, which I lent to Sam, and bring it over here." Grace knew that Sam had a portable television set and Grace planned to keep the set for herself. Roy thought the set belonged to Grace, went next door, found the television set, and carried it out the front door. At that moment, Sam returned home and discovered Roy in his front yard with the television set. Roy explained the "game" he and Grace were playing. Sam took back his television set and called the police.

Grace is

(A) not guilty of larceny or attempted larceny, because Roy did not commit any crime.
(B) not guilty of larceny but guilty of attempted larceny, because she never acquired possession of the television set.
(C) guilty of larceny as an accessory to Roy.
(D) guilty of larceny by the use of an innocent agent.

108. The warden of State Prison prohibits the photographing of the face of any prisoner without the prisoner's consent. Photographer, a news photographer, wanted to photograph Mobster, a notorious organized crime figure incarcerated at State Prison. To circumvent the warden's prohibition, Photographer flew over the prison exercise yard and photographed Mobster. Prisoner, who was imprisoned for a technical violation of a regulatory statute, happened to be standing next to Mobster when the photograph was taken.

When the picture appeared in the press, Prisoner suffered severe emotional distress because he believed that his business associates and friends would think he was consorting with gangsters. Prisoner suffered no physical harm as the result of his emotional distress. Prisoner brought an action against Photographer for intentional or reckless infliction of emotional distress.

What is the best argument that Photographer can make in support of a motion for summary judgment?

(A) No reasonable person could conclude that Photographer intended to photograph Prisoner.
(B) Prisoner did not suffer any physical injury arising from the emotional distress.
(C) As a news photographer, Photographer was privileged to take photographs that others could not.
(D) No reasonable person could conclude that Photographer's conduct was extreme and outrageous as to Prisoner.

GO ON TO THE NEXT PAGE.

109. The vaccination of children against childhood contagious diseases (such as measles, diphtheria and whooping cough) has traditionally been a function of private doctors and local and state health departments. Because vaccination rates have declined in recent years, especially in urban areas, the President proposes to appoint a Presidential Advisory Commission on Vaccination which would be charged with conducting a national publicity campaign to encourage vaccination as a public health measure. No federal statute authorizes or prohibits this action by the President. The activities of the Presidential Advisory Commission on Vaccination would be financed entirely from funds appropriated by Congress to the Office of the President for "such other purposes as the President may think appropriate."

May the President constitutionally create such a commission for this purpose?

(A) Yes, because the President has plenary authority to provide for the health, safety, and welfare of the people of the United States.
(B) Yes, because this action is within the scope of executive authority vested in the President by the Constitution, and no federal statute prohibits it.
(C) No, because the protection of children against common diseases by vaccination is a traditional state function and, therefore, is reserved to the states by the Tenth Amendment.
(D) No, because Congress has not specifically authorized the creation and support of such a new federal agency.

110. Defendant is on trial for extorting $10,000 from Victim. An issue is the identification of the person who made a telephone call to Victim. Victim is prepared to testify that the caller had a distinctive accent like Defendant's, but that he cannot positively identify the voice as Defendant's. Victim recorded the call but has not brought the tape to court, although its existence is known to Defendant.

Victim's testimony is

(A) inadmissible, because Victim cannot sufficiently identify the caller.
(B) inadmissible, because the tape recording of the conversation is the best evidence.
(C) admissible, because Defendant waived the "best evidence" rule by failing to subpoena the tape.
(D) admissible, because Victim's lack of certainty goes to the weight to be given Victim's testimony, not to its admissibility.

GO ON TO THE NEXT PAGE.

111. Owner owned Greenacre, a tract of land, in fee simple. Owner executed an instrument in the proper form of a deed, purporting to convey Greenacre to Purchaser in fee simple. The instrument recited that the conveyance was in consideration of "$5 cash in hand paid and for other good and valuable consideration." Owner handed the instrument to Purchaser and Purchaser promptly and properly recorded it.

    Two months later, Owner brought an appropriate action against Purchaser to cancel the instrument and to quiet title. In support, Owner proved that no money in fact had been paid by Purchaser, notwithstanding the recitation, and that no other consideration of any kind had been supplied by Purchaser.

    In such action, Owner should

    (A) lose, because any remedy Owner might have had was lost when the instrument was recorded.
    (B) lose, because the validity of conveyance of land does not depend upon consideration being paid, whether recited or not.
    (C) prevail, because the recitation of consideration paid may be contradicted by parol evidence.
    (D) prevail, because recordation does not make a void instrument effective.

112. Vintner is the owner of a large vineyard and offers balloon rides to visitors who wish to tour the grounds from the air. During one of the rides, Vintner was forced to make a crash landing on his own property. Without Vintner's knowledge or consent, Trespasser had entered the vineyard to camp for a couple of days. Trespasser was injured when he was hit by the basket of the descending balloon.

    If Trespasser sues Vintner to recover damages for his injuries, will Trespasser prevail?

    (A) No, unless the crash landing was made necessary by negligence on Vintner's part.
    (B) No, unless Vintner could have prevented the injury to Trespasser after becoming aware of Trespasser's presence.
    (C) Yes, because even a trespasser may recover for injuries caused by an abnormally dangerous activity.
    (D) Yes, if the accident occurred at a place which Vintner knew was frequented by intruders.

    GO ON TO THE NEXT PAGE.

113. Matt and his friend Fred were watching a football game at Matt's home when they began to argue. Fred became abusive, and Matt asked him to leave. Fred refused, walked into the kitchen, picked up a knife, and said he would cut Matt's heart out. Matt pulled a gun from under the sofa, walked to his front door, opened it, and again told Fred to leave. Fred again refused. Instead, he walked slowly toward Matt, brandishing the knife in a threatening manner. Matt, rather than running out the door himself, shot in Fred's direction, intending only to scare him. However, the bullet struck Fred, killing him instantly.

    Charged with murder, Matt should be

    (A) convicted, because the use of deadly force was unreasonable under the circumstances.
    (B) convicted, because he had a clear opportunity and duty to retreat.
    (C) acquitted, because he did not intend to kill Fred.
    (D) acquitted, because he was acting in self-defense and had no duty to retreat.

114. Central City in the state of Green is a center for businesses that assemble personal computers. Components for these computers are manufactured elsewhere in Green and in other states, then shipped to Central City, where the computers are assembled. An ordinance of Central City imposes a special license tax on all of the many companies engaged in the business of assembling computers in that city. The tax payable by each such company is a percentage of the company's gross receipts.

    The Green statute that authorizes municipalities to impose this license tax has a "Green content" provision. To comply with this provision of state law, the Central City license tax ordinance provides that the tax paid by any assembler of computers subject to this tax ordinance will be reduced by a percentage equal to the proportion of computer components manufactured in Green.

    Assembler is a company that assembles computers in Central City and sells them from its offices in Central City to buyers throughout the United States. All of the components of its computers come from outside the state of Green. Therefore, Assembler must pay the Central City license tax in full without receiving any refund. Other Central City computer assemblers use components manufactured in Green in varying proportions and, therefore, are entitled to partial reductions of their Central City license tax payments.

    Following prescribed procedure, Assembler brings an action in a proper court asking to have Central City's special license tax declared unconstitutional on the ground that it is inconsistent with the negative implications of the commerce clause.

    In this case, the court should rule

    (A) against Assembler, because the tax falls only on companies resident in Central City and, therefore, does not discriminate against or otherwise adversely affect interstate commerce.
    (B) against Assembler, because the commerce clause does not interfere with the right of a state to foster and support businesses located within its borders by encouraging its residents to purchase the products of those businesses.
    (C) for Assembler, because any tax on a company engaged in interstate commerce, measured in whole or in part by its gross receipts, is a per se violation of the negative implications of the commerce clause.
    (D) for Assembler, because the tax improperly discriminates against interstate commerce by treating in-state products more favorably than out-of-state products.

    GO ON TO THE NEXT PAGE.

115. Hannah, who was homeless, broke into the basement of a hotel and fell asleep. She was awakened by a security guard, who demanded that she leave. As Hannah was leaving, she cursed the security guard. Angered, the guard began to beat Hannah on her head with his flashlight. After the second blow, Hannah grabbed a fire extinguisher and sprayed the guard in his face, causing him to lose his sight in one eye.

The jurisdiction defines aggravated assault as assault with intent to cause serious bodily injury.

The most serious crime for which Hannah could properly be convicted is

(A) aggravated assault.
(B) burglary.
(C) assault.
(D) trespass.

116. On March 1, Mechanic contracted to repair Textiles' knitting machine and to complete the job by March 6. On March 2, Textiles contracted to manufacture and deliver specified cloth to Knitwear on March 15. Textiles knew that it would have to use the machine then under repair to perform this contract. Because the Knitwear order was for a rush job, Knitwear and Textiles included in their contract a liquidated damages clause, providing that Textiles would pay $5,000 for each day's delay in delivery after March 15.

Mechanic was inexcusably five days late in repairing the machine, and, as a result, Textiles was five days late in delivering the cloth to Knitwear. Textiles paid $25,000 to Knitwear as liquidated damages and now sues Mechanic for $25,000. Both Mechanic and Textiles knew when making their contract on March 1 that under ordinary circumstances Textiles would sustain little or no damages of any kind as a result of a five-day delay in the machine repair.

Assuming that the $5,000 liquidated damages clause in the Knitwear-Textiles contract is valid, which of the following arguments will serve as Mechanic's best defense to Textiles' action?

(A) Time was not of the essence in the Mechanic-Textiles contract.
(B) Mechanic had no reason to foresee on March 1 that Knitwear would suffer consequential damages in the amount of $25,000.
(C) By entering into the Knitwear contract while knowing that its knitting machine was being repaired, Textiles assumed the risk of any delay loss to Knitwear.
(D) In all probability, the liquidated damages paid by Textiles to Knitwear are not the same amount as the actual damages sustained by Knitwear in consequence of Textiles' late delivery of the cloth.

GO ON TO THE NEXT PAGE.

117. Plaintiff sued Defendant for personal injuries suffered in a train-automobile collision. Plaintiff called an eyewitness, who testified that the train was going 20 miles per hour. Defendant then offers the testimony of an experienced police accident investigator that, based on his training and experience and on his examination of the physical evidence, it is his opinion that the train was going between 5 and 10 miles per hour.

    Testimony by the investigator is

    (A) improper, because there cannot be both lay and expert opinion on the same issue.
    (B) improper, because the investigator is unable to establish the speed with a sufficient degree of scientific certainty.
    (C) proper, because a police accident investigator has sufficient expertise to express an opinion on speed.
    (D) proper, because Plaintiff first introduced opinion evidence as to speed.

118. Farmer owns a small farm with several head of cattle, which are kept in a fenced grazing area. One day the cattle were frightened by a thunderstorm, an occasional occurrence in the area. The cattle broke through the fence, entered onto Neighbor's property, and severely damaged Neighbor's crops. Under the law of the state, landowners are not required to erect fences to prevent the intrusion of livestock.

    If Neighbor sues Farmer to recover for the damage done to his crops, will Neighbor prevail?

    (A) Yes, because Farmer's cattle caused the damage to Neighbor's crops.
    (B) Yes, if Farmer's cattle had panicked during previous thunderstorms.
    (C) No, unless the fence was negligently maintained by Farmer.
    (D) No, because the thunderstorm was a force of nature.

119. Ven owned Goldacre, a tract of land, in fee simple. Ven and Pur entered into a written agreement under which Pur agreed to buy Goldacre for $100,000, its fair market value. The agreement contained all the essential terms of a real estate contract to sell and buy, including a date for closing. The required $50,000 down payment was made. The contract provided that in the event of Pur's breach, Ven could retain the $50,000 deposit as liquidated damages.

    Before the date set for the closing in the contract, Pur died. On the day that Addy was duly qualified as administratrix of the estate of Pur, which was after the closing date, Addy made demand for return of the $50,000 deposit. Ven responded by stating that he took such demand to be a declaration that Addy did not intend to complete the contract and that Ven considered the contract at an end. Ven further asserted that Ven was entitled to retain, as liquidated damages, the $50,000. The reasonable market value of Goldacre had increased to $110,000 at that time.

    Addy brought an appropriate action against Ven to recover the $50,000. In answer, Ven made no affirmative claim but asserted that he was entitled to retain the $50,000 as liquidated damages as provided in the contract.

    In such lawsuit, judgment should be for

    (A) Addy, because the provision relied upon by Ven is unenforceable.
    (B) Addy, because the death of Pur terminated the contract as a matter of law.
    (C) Ven, because the court should enforce the express agreement of the contracting parties.
    (D) Ven, because the doctrine of equitable conversion prevents termination of the contract upon the death of a party.

GO ON TO THE NEXT PAGE.

120. An ordinance of Central City requires every operator of a taxicab in the city to have a license and permits revocation of that license only for "good cause." The Central City taxicab operator's licensing ordinance conditions the issuance of such a license on an agreement by the licensee that the licensee "not display in or on his or her vehicle any bumper sticker or other placard or sign favoring a particular candidate for any elected municipal office." The ordinance also states that it imposes this condition in order to prevent the possible imputation to the city council of the views of its taxicab licensees and that any licensee who violates this condition shall have his or her license revoked.

Driver, the holder of a Central City taxicab operator's license, decorates his cab with bumper stickers and other signs favoring specified candidates in a forthcoming election for municipal offices. A proceeding is initiated against him to revoke his taxicab operator's license on the sole basis of that admitted conduct.

In this proceeding, does Driver have a meritorious defense based on the United States Constitution?

(A) No, because he accepted the license with knowledge of the condition and, therefore, has no standing to contest it.
(B) No, because a taxicab operator's license is a privilege and not a right and, therefore, is not protected by the due process clause of the Fourteenth Amendment.
(C) Yes, because such a proceeding threatens Driver with a taking of property, his license, without just compensation.
(D) Yes, because the condition imposed on taxicab operators' licenses restricts political speech based wholly on its content, without any adequate governmental justification.

121. Pat had been under the care of a cardiologist for three years prior to submitting to an elective operation that was performed by Surgeon. Two days thereafter, Pat suffered a stroke, resulting in a coma, caused by a blood clot that lodged in her brain. When it appeared that she had entered a permanent vegetative state, with no hope of recovery, the artificial life-support system that had been provided was withdrawn, and she died a few hours later. The withdrawal of artificial life support had been requested by her family, and duly approved by a court. Surgeon was not involved in that decision, or in its execution.

The administrator of Pat's estate thereafter filed a wrongful death action against Surgeon, claiming that Surgeon was negligent in having failed to consult a cardiologist prior to the operation. At the trial the plaintiff offered evidence that accepted medical practice would require examination of the patient by a cardiologist prior to the type of operation that Surgeon performed.

In this action, the plaintiff should

(A) prevail, if Surgeon was negligent in failing to have Pat examined by a cardiologist prior to the operation.
(B) prevail, if the blood clot that caused Pat's death was caused by the operation which Surgeon performed.
(C) not prevail, absent evidence that a cardiologist, had one examined Pat before the operation, would probably have provided advice that would have changed the outcome.
(D) not prevail, because Surgeon had nothing to do with the withdrawal of artificial life support, which was the cause of Pat's death.

GO ON TO THE NEXT PAGE.

122. At Devlin's trial for burglary, Jaron supported Devlin's alibi that they were fishing together at the time of the crime. On cross-examination, Jaron was asked whether his statement on a credit card application that he had worked for his present employer for the last five years was false. Jaron denied that the statement was false.

The prosecutor then calls Wilcox, the manager of the company for which Jaron works, to testify that although Jaron had been first employed five years earlier and is now employed by the company, there had been a three-year period during which he had not been so employed.

The testimony of Wilcox is

(A) admissible, in the judge's discretion, because Jaron's credibility is a fact of major consequence to the case.
(B) admissible, as a matter of right, because Jaron "opened the door" by his denial on cross-examination.
(C) inadmissible, because whether Jaron lied in his application is a matter that cannot be proved by extrinsic evidence.
(D) inadmissible, because the misstatement by Jaron could have been caused by misunderstanding of the application form.

123. Owen owned Blackacre in fee simple, as the land records showed, when he contracted to sell Blackacre to Bryer. Two weeks later, Bryer paid the agreed price and received a warranty deed. A week thereafter, when neither the contract nor the deed had been recorded and while Owen remained in possession of Blackacre, Cred properly filed her money judgment against Owen. She knew nothing of Bryer's interest.

A statute in the jurisdiction provides: "Any judgment properly filed shall, for ten years from filing, be a lien on the real property then owned or subsequently acquired by any person against whom the judgment is rendered."

The recording act of the jurisdiction provides: "No conveyance or mortgage of real property shall be good against subsequent purchasers for value and without notice unless the same be recorded according to law."

Cred brought an appropriate action to enforce her lien against Blackacre in Bryer's hands.

If the court decides for Bryer, it will most probably be because

(A) the doctrine of equitable conversion applies.
(B) the jurisdiction's recording act does not protect creditors.
(C) Owen's possession gave Cred constructive notice of Bryer's interest.
(D) Bryer was a purchaser without notice.

GO ON TO THE NEXT PAGE.

124. A written construction contract, under which Contractor agreed to build a new house for Owner at a fixed price of $200,000, contained the following provision:

> Prior to construction or during the course thereof, this contract may be modified by mutual agreement of the parties as to "extras" or other departures from the plans and specifications provided by Owner and attached hereto. Such modifications, however, may be authorized only in writing, signed by both parties.

During construction, Contractor incorporated into the structure overhanging gargoyles and other "extras" orally requested by Owner for orally agreed prices in addition to the contract price. Owner subsequently refused to pay anything for such extras, aggregating $30,000 at the agreed prices, solely on the ground that no written, signed authorization for them was ever effected.

If Contractor sues Owner on account of the "extras," which, if any, of the following will effectively support Owner's defense?

I. The parol evidence rule.
II. The preexisting duty rule.
III. Failure of an express condition.
IV. The statute of frauds.

(A) I and III only.
(B) I and IV only.
(C) II and IV only.
(D) Neither I, II, III, nor IV.

125. Scott held up a drugstore at 10:30 at night, and drove away. His car broke down in an isolated area just outside the small city in which the crime occurred. Scott walked to the nearest house and asked Henry, the homeowner, if he could stay until the next morning, explaining that he had been searching for his sister's home and had run out of gas. Henry agreed to let him sleep on a couch in the basement. During the course of the night, Henry began to doubt the story Scott had told him. Early the next morning, Henry called the police and said he was suspicious and frightened of a stranger whom he had allowed to stay the night. The police went immediately to the house to assist Henry and walked through the open front door. They found Scott and Henry drinking coffee in the kitchen. When they saw Scott, they realized he matched the description of the drugstore robber. They arrested Scott and in his jacket they found drugs taken during the robbery.

Scott moves to suppress the evidence of the drugs.

If the court finds that the police did not have probable cause to believe Scott was the robber until they saw him inside Henry's house and realized he matched the description, the court should

(A) grant the motion, because, as a guest, Scott has sufficient standing to contest the entry of the house without a warrant.
(B) grant the motion, because, as a guest, Scott has sufficient standing to contest the lack of probable cause at the time of the entry.
(C) deny the motion, because Scott had no ownership or other possessory interest in the premises.
(D) deny the motion, because the police had the permission of the owner to enter the house.

GO ON TO THE NEXT PAGE.

126. Susan entered a guilty plea to a charge of embezzlement. Her attorney hired a retired probation officer as a consultant to gather information for the preparation of a sentencing plan for Susan that would avoid jail. For that purpose, the consultant interviewed Susan for three hours.

Thereafter, the prosecution undertook an investigation of Susan's possible involvement in other acts of embezzlement. The consultant was subpoenaed to testify before a grand jury. The consultant refused to answer any questions concerning her conversation with Susan. The prosecution has moved for an order requiring her to answer those questions.

The motion should be

(A) denied, on the basis of the attorney-client privilege.
(B) denied, in the absence of probable cause to believe the interview developed evidence relevant to the grand jury's inquiry.
(C) granted, because the consultant is not an attorney.
(D) granted, because exclusionary evidentiary rules do not apply in grand jury proceedings.

127. Agitator, a baseball fan, has a fierce temper and an extremely loud voice. Attending a baseball game in which a number of calls went against the home team, Agitator repeatedly stood up, brandished his fist, and angrily shouted, "Kill the umpires." The fourth time he engaged in this conduct, many other spectators followed Agitator in rising from their seats, brandishing fists, and shouting, "Kill the umpires."

The home team lost the game. Although no violence ensued, spectators crowded menacingly around the umpires after the game. As a result, the umpires were able to leave the field and stadium only with the help of a massive police escort.

For his conduct, Agitator was charged with inciting to riot and was convicted in a jury trial in state court. He appealed. The state supreme court reversed his conviction. In its opinion, the court discussed in detail decisions of the United States Supreme Court dealing with the First Amendment free speech clause as incorporated into the Fourteenth Amendment. At the end of that discussion, however, the court stated that it "need not resolve how, on the basis of these cases," the United States Supreme Court would decide Agitator's case. "Instead," the court stated, "this court has always given the free-speech guarantee of the state's constitution the broadest possible interpretation. As a result, we hold that in this case, where no riot or other violence actually occurred, the state constitution does not permit this conviction for incitement to riot to stand."

The United States Supreme Court grants a writ of certiorari to review this decision of the state supreme court.

In this case, the United States Supreme Court should

(A) affirm the state supreme court's decision, because Agitator's ballpark shout is commonplace hyperbole that cannot, consistently with the First and Fourteenth Amendments, be punished.
(B) remand the case to the state supreme court with directions that it resolve the First and Fourteenth Amendment free-speech issue that it discussed in such detail.
(C) dismiss the writ as improvidently granted, because the state supreme court's decision rests on an independent and adequate state law ground.
(D) reverse the decision of the state supreme court, because incitement to violent action is not speech protected by the First and Fourteenth Amendments.

GO ON TO THE NEXT PAGE.

128. The day after Seller completed the sale of his house and moved out, one of the slates flew off the roof during a windstorm. The slate struck Pedestrian, who was on the public sidewalk. Pedestrian was seriously injured.

The roof is old and has lost several slates in ordinary windstorms on other occasions.

If Pedestrian sues Seller to recover damages for his injuries, will Pedestrian prevail?

(A) Yes, because the roof was defective when Seller sold the house.
(B) Yes, if Seller should have been aware of the condition of the roof and should have realized that it was dangerous to persons outside the premises.
(C) No, because Seller was neither the owner nor the occupier of the house when Pedestrian was injured.
(D) No, if Pedestrian knew that in the past slates had blown off the roof during windstorms.

Questions 129–130 are based on the following fact situation.

On April 1, Owner and Buyer signed a writing in which Owner, "in consideration of $100 to be paid to Owner by Buyer," offered Buyer the right to purchase Greenacre for $100,000 within 30 days. The writing further provided, "This offer will become effective as an option only if and when the $100 consideration is in fact paid." On April 20, Owner, having received no payment or other communication from Buyer, sold and conveyed Greenacre to Citizen for $120,000. On April 21, Owner received a letter from Buyer enclosing a cashier's check for $100 payable to Owner and stating, "I am hereby exercising my option to purchase Greenacre and am prepared to close whenever you're ready."

129. Which of the following, if proved, best supports Buyer's suit against Owner for breach of contract?

(A) Buyer was unaware of the sale to Citizen when Owner received the letter and check from Buyer on April 21.
(B) On April 15, Buyer decided to purchase Greenacre, and applied for and obtained a commitment from Bank for a $75,000 loan to help finance the purchase.
(C) When the April 1 writing was signed, Owner said to Buyer, "Don't worry about the $100; the recital of `$100 to be paid' makes this deal binding."
(D) Owner and Buyer are both professional dealers in real estate.

130. For this question only, assume that, for whatever reason, Buyer prevails in the suit against Owner.

Which of the following is Buyer entitled to recover?

(A) Nominal damages only, because the remedy of specific performance was not available to Buyer.
(B) The fair market value, if any, of an assignable option to purchase Greenacre for $100,000.
(C) $20,000, plus the amount, if any, by which the fair market value of Greenacre on the date of Owner's breach exceeded $120,000.
(D) The amount, if any, by which the fair market value of Greenacre on the date of Owner's breach exceeded $100,000.

GO ON TO THE NEXT PAGE.

131. Alpha and Beta owned Greenacre, a large farm, in fee simple as tenants in common, each owning an undivided one-half interest. For five years Alpha occupied Greenacre and conducted farming operations. Alpha never accounted to Beta for any income but Alpha did pay all real estate taxes when the taxes were due and kept the buildings located on Greenacre insured against loss from fire, storm, and flood. Beta lived in a distant city and was interested only in realizing a profit from the sale of the land when market conditions produced the price Beta wanted.

    Alpha died intestate survived by Hera, Alpha's sole heir. Thereafter Hera occupied Greenacre but was inexperienced in farming operations. The result was a financial disaster. Hera failed to pay real estate taxes for two years. The appropriate governmental authority held a tax sale to recover the taxes due. At such sale Beta was the only bidder and obtained a conveyance from the appropriate governmental authority upon payment of an amount sufficient to discharge the amounts due for taxes, plus interest and penalties, and the costs of holding the tax sale. The amount paid was one-third of the reasonable market value of Greenacre.

    Thereafter Beta instituted an appropriate action against Hera to quiet title in and to recover possession of Greenacre. Hera asserted all defenses available to Hera.

    Except for the statutes related to real estate taxes and tax sales, there is no applicable statute.

    In this lawsuit, Beta is entitled to a decree quieting title so that Beta is the sole owner in fee simple of Greenacre

    (A) because Beta survived Alpha.
    (B) because Hera defaulted in the obligations undertaken by Alpha.
    (C) unless Hera pays Beta one-half of the reasonable market value of Greenacre.
    (D) unless Hera pays Beta one-half of the amount Beta paid for the tax deed.

132. Eighteen-year-old Kenneth and his 14-year-old girlfriend, Emma, made plans to meet in Kenneth's apartment to have sexual intercourse, and they did so. Emma later told her mother about the incident. Kenneth was charged with statutory rape and conspiracy to commit statutory rape.

    In the jurisdiction, the age of consent is 15, and the law of conspiracy is the same as at common law.

    Kenneth was convicted of both charges and given consecutive sentences. On appeal, he contends that his conspiracy conviction should be reversed.

    That conviction should be

    (A) affirmed, because he agreed with Emma to commit the crime.
    (B) reversed, because Emma could not be a conspirator to this crime.
    (C) reversed, because the crime is one that can only be committed by agreement and thus Wharton's Rule bars conspiracy liability.
    (D) reversed, because one cannot conspire with a person too young to consent.

                                   GO ON TO THE NEXT PAGE.

133. Sam decided to kill his boss, Anna, after she told him that he would be fired if his work did not improve. Sam knew Anna was scheduled to go on a business trip on Monday morning. On Sunday morning, Sam went to the company parking garage and put a bomb in the company car that Anna usually drove. The bomb was wired to go off when the car engine started. Sam then left town. At 5 a.m. Monday, Sam, after driving all night, was overcome with remorse and had a change of heart. He called the security officer on duty at the company and told him about the bomb. The security officer said he would take care of the matter. An hour later, the officer put a note on Anna's desk telling her of the message. He then looked at the car but could not see any signs of a bomb. He printed a sign saying "DO NOT USE THIS CAR," put it on the windshield, and went to call the police. Before the police arrived, Lois, a company vice president, got into the car and started the engine. The bomb went off, killing her.

The jurisdiction defines murder in the first degree as any homicide committed with premeditation and deliberation or any murder in the commission of a common-law felony. Second-degree murder is defined as all other murder at common law. Manslaughter is defined by the common law.

Sam is guilty of

(A) murder in the first degree, because, with premeditation and deliberation, he killed whoever would start the car.
(B) murder in the second degree, because he had no intention of killing Lois.
(C) manslaughter, because at the time of the explosion, he had no intent to kill, and the death of Lois was in part the fault of the security officer.
(D) only attempted murder of Anna, because the death of Lois was the result of the security officer's negligence.

134. The state of Green imposes a tax on the "income" of each of its residents. As defined in the taxing statute, "income" includes the fair rental value of the use of any automobile provided by the taxpayer's employer for the taxpayer's personal use. The federal government supplies automobiles to some of its employees who are resident in Green so that they may perform their jobs properly. A federal government employee supplied with an automobile for this purpose may also use it for the employee's own personal business.

Assume there is no federal legislation on this subject.

May the state of Green collect this tax on the fair rental value of the personal use of the automobiles furnished by the federal government to these employees?

(A) No, because such a tax would be a tax on the United States.
(B) No, because such a tax would be a tax upon activities performed on behalf of the United States, since the automobiles are primarily used by these federal employees in the discharge of their official duties.
(C) Yes, because the tax is imposed on the employees rather than on the United States, and the tax does not discriminate against persons who are employed by the United States.
(D) Yes, because an exemption from such state taxes for federal employees would be a denial to others of the equal protection of the laws.

GO ON TO THE NEXT PAGE.

135. Orderly, a male attendant who worked at Hospital, had sexual relations with Patient, a severely retarded person, in her room at Hospital.

In a tort action brought on Patient's behalf against Hospital, Patient will

(A) not prevail, if Orderly's actions were outside the scope of his employment.
(B) not prevail, if Patient initiated the relationship with Orderly and encouraged his actions.
(C) prevail, if Orderly was an employee of Hospital.
(D) prevail, if Hospital failed to use reasonable care to protect Patient from such conduct.

136. Passenger is suing Defendant for injuries suffered in the crash of a small airplane, alleging that Defendant had owned the plane and negligently failed to have it properly maintained. Defendant has asserted in defense that he never owned the plane or had any responsibility to maintain it. At trial, Passenger calls Witness to testify that Witness had sold to Defendant a liability insurance policy on the plane.

The testimony of Witness is

(A) inadmissible, because the policy itself is required under the original document rule.
(B) inadmissible, because of the rule against proof of insurance where insurance is not itself at issue.
(C) admissible to show that Defendant had little motivation to invest money in maintenance of the airplane.
(D) admissible as some evidence of Defendant's ownership of or responsibility for the airplane.

137. Opal owned several vacant lots in ABC Subdivision. She obtained a $50,000 loan from a lender, Bank, and executed and delivered to Bank a promissory note and mortgage describing Lots 1, 2, 3, 4, and 5. The mortgage was promptly and properly recorded.

Upon payment of $10,000, Opal obtained a release of Lot 2 duly executed by Bank. She altered the instrument of release to include Lot 5 as well as Lot 2 and recorded it. Opal thereafter sold Lot 5 to Eva, an innocent purchaser, for value.

Bank discovered that the instrument of release had been altered and brought an appropriate action against Opal and Eva to set aside the release as it applied to Lot 5. Opal did not defend against the action, but Eva did.

The recording act of the jurisdiction provides: "No unrecorded conveyance or mortgage of real property shall be good against subsequent purchasers for value without notice, who shall first record."

The court should rule for

(A) Eva, because Bank was negligent in failing to check the recordation of the release.
(B) Eva, because she was entitled to rely on the recorded release.
(C) Bank, because Eva could have discovered the alteration by reasonable inquiry.
(D) Bank, because the alteration of the release was ineffective.

GO ON TO THE NEXT PAGE.

Questions 138–139 are based on the following fact situation.

Jones, a marijuana farmer, had been missing for several months. The sheriff's department received an anonymous tip that Miller, a rival marijuana farmer, had buried Jones in a hillside about 200 yards from Miller's farmhouse. Sheriff's deputies went to Miller's farm. They cut the barbed wire that surrounded the hillside and entered, looking for the grave. They also searched the adjacent fields on Miller's farm that were within the area enclosed by the barbed wire and discovered clothing that belonged to Jones hanging on a scarecrow. Miller observed their discovery and began shooting. The deputies returned the fire. Miller dashed to his pickup truck to escape. Unable to start the truck, he fled across a field toward the barn. A deputy tackled him just as he entered the barn.

As Miller attempted to get up, the deputy pinned his arms behind his back. Another deputy threatened, "Tell us what you did with Jones or we will shut you down and see your family on relief." Miller responded that he had killed Jones in a fight but did not report the incident because he did not want authorities to enter his land and discover his marijuana crop. Instead, he buried him behind the barn. Miller was thereafter charged with murder.

138. If Miller moves to suppress his admission about killing his neighbor, the court should

(A) grant the motion, because Miller did not voluntarily waive his right to silence.
(B) grant the motion, because the statement was the product of the warrantless entry and search of Miller's farm.
(C) deny the motion, because the deputy was in hot pursuit when he questioned Miller.
(D) deny the motion, because Miller was questioned during a police emergency search.

139. If Miller moves to exclude the introduction of Jones's clothing into evidence, the court should

(A) grant the motion, because the deputies had not obtained a warrant.
(B) grant the motion, because the deputies' conduct in its entirety violated Miller's right to due process of law.
(C) deny the motion, because Miller had no expectation of privacy in the fields around his farmhouse.
(D) deny the motion, because the clothing was not Miller's property.

GO ON TO THE NEXT PAGE.

140. Passenger departed on an ocean liner knowing that it would be a rough voyage due to predicted storms. The ocean liner was not equipped with the type of lifeboats required by the applicable statute.

Passenger was swept overboard and drowned in a storm so heavy that even a lifeboat that conformed to the statute could not have been launched.

In an action against the operator of the ocean liner brought by Passenger's representative, will Passenger's representative prevail?

(A) Yes, because the ocean liner was not equipped with the statutorily required lifeboats.
(B) Yes, because in these circumstances common carriers are strictly liable.
(C) No, because the storm was so severe that it would have been impossible to launch a statutorily required lifeboat.
(D) No, because Passenger assumed the risk by boarding the ocean liner knowing that it would be a rough voyage.

141. The King City zoning ordinance contains provisions restricting places of "adult entertainment" to two specified city blocks within the commercial center of the city. These provisions of the ordinance define "adult entertainment" as "live or filmed nudity or sexual activity, real or simulated, of an indecent nature."

Sam proposes to operate an adult entertainment establishment outside the two-block area zoned for such establishments but within the commercial center of King City. When his application for permission to do so is rejected solely because it is inconsistent with provisions of the zoning ordinance, he sues the appropriate officials of King City, seeking to enjoin them from enforcing the adult entertainment provisions of the ordinance against him. He asserts that these provisions of the ordinance violate the First Amendment as made applicable to King City by the Fourteenth Amendment.

In this case, the court hearing Sam's request for an injunction would probably hold that the adult entertainment provisions of the King City zoning ordinance are

(A) constitutional, because they do not prohibit adult entertainment everywhere in King City, and the city has a substantial interest in keeping the major part of its commercial center free of uses it considers harmful to that area.
(B) constitutional, because adult entertainment of the kind described in these provisions of the King City ordinance is not protected by the free speech guarantee of the First and Fourteenth Amendments.
(C) unconstitutional, because they prohibit in the commercial area of the city adult entertainment that is not "obscene" within the meaning of the First and Fourteenth Amendments.
(D) unconstitutional, because zoning ordinances that restrict freedom of speech may be justified only by a substantial interest in preserving the quality of a community's residential neighborhoods.

GO ON TO THE NEXT PAGE.

Questions 142–143 are based on the following fact situation.

On June 1, Seller and Buyer contracted in writing for the sale and purchase of Seller's cattle ranch (a large single tract), and to close the transaction on December 1.

142. For this question only, assume the following facts. On October 1, Buyer told Seller, "I'm increasingly unhappy about our June 1 contract because of the current cattle market, and do not intend to buy your ranch unless I'm legally obligated to do so."

If Seller sues Buyer on October 15 for breach of contract, Seller will probably

(A) win, because Buyer committed a total breach by anticipatory repudiation on October 1.
(B) win, because Buyer's October 1 statement created reasonable grounds for Seller's insecurity with respect to Buyer's performance.
(C) lose, because the parties contracted for the sale and conveyance of a single tract, and Seller cannot bring suit for breach of such a contract prior to the agreed closing date.
(D) lose, because Buyer's October 1 statement to Seller was neither a repudiation nor a present breach of the June 1 contract.

143. For this question only, assume the following facts. Buyer unequivocally repudiated the contract on August 1. On August 15, Seller urged Buyer to change her mind and proceed with the scheduled closing on December 1. On October 1, having heard nothing further from Buyer, Seller sold and conveyed his ranch to Rancher without notice to Buyer. On December 1, Buyer attempted to close under the June 1 contract by tendering the full purchase price to Seller. Seller rejected the tender.

If Buyer sues Seller for breach of contract, Buyer will probably

(A) win, because Seller failed seasonably to notify Buyer of any pending sale to Rancher.
(B) win, because Seller waived Buyer's August 1 repudiation by urging her to retract it on August 15.
(C) lose, because Buyer did not retract her repudiation before Seller materially changed his position in reliance thereon by selling the ranch to Rancher.
(D) lose, because acceptance of the purchase price by Seller was a concurrent condition to Seller's obligation to convey the ranch to Buyer on December 1.

GO ON TO THE NEXT PAGE.

144. Owner owned a hotel, subject to a mortgage securing a debt Owner owed to Lender One. Owner later acquired a nearby parking garage, financing a part of the purchase price by a loan from Lender Two, secured by a mortgage on the parking garage. Two years thereafter, Owner defaulted on the loan owed to Lender One, which caused the full amount of that loan to become immediately due and payable. Lender One decided not to foreclose the mortgage on Owner's hotel at that time, but instead brought an action, appropriate under the laws of the jurisdiction and authorized by the mortgage loan documents, for the full amount of the defaulted loan. Lender One obtained and properly filed a judgment for that amount.

A statute of the jurisdiction provides: "Any judgment properly filed shall, for ten years from filing, be a lien on the real property then owned or subsequently acquired by any person against whom the judgment is rendered."

There is no other applicable statute, except the statute providing for judicial foreclosure of mortgages, which places no restriction on deficiency judgments.

Lender One later brought an appropriate action for judicial foreclosure of its first mortgage on the hotel and of its judgment lien on the parking garage. Lender Two was joined as a party defendant, and appropriately counterclaimed for foreclosure of its mortgage on the parking garage, which was also in default. All procedures were properly followed and the confirmed foreclosure sales resulted as follows:

Lender One purchased the hotel for $100,000 less than its mortgage balance.

Lender One purchased the parking garage for an amount that is $200,000 in excess of Lender Two's mortgage balance.

The $200,000 surplus arising from the bid paid by Lender One for the parking garage should be paid

(A) $100,000 to Lender One and $100,000 to Owner.
(B) $100,000 to Lender Two and $100,000 to Owner.
(C) $100,000 to Lender One and $100,000 to Lender Two.
(D) $200,000 to Owner.

GO ON TO THE NEXT PAGE.

145. Kontractor agreed to build a power plant for a public utility. Subbo agreed with Kontractor to lay the foundation for $200,000. Subbo supplied goods and services worth $150,000, for which Kontractor made progress payments aggregating $100,000 as required by the subcontract. Subbo then breached by refusing unjustifiably to perform further. Kontractor reasonably spent $120,000 to have the work completed by another subcontractor.

    Subbo sues Kontractor for the reasonable value of benefits conferred, and Kontractor counterclaims for breach of contract.

    Which of the following should be the court's decision?

    (A) Subbo recovers $50,000, the benefit conferred on Kontractor for which Subbo has not been paid.
    (B) Subbo recovers $30,000, the benefit Subbo conferred on Kontractor minus the $20,000 in damages incurred by Kontractor.
    (C) Kontractor recovers $20,000, the excess over the contract price that was paid by Kontractor for the performance it had bargained to receive from Subbo.
    (D) Neither party recovers anything, because Subbo committed a material, unexcused breach and Kontractor received a $50,000 benefit from Subbo for which Subbo has not been paid.

146. The Rapido is a sports car manufactured by the Rapido Motor Co. The Rapido has an excellent reputation for mechanical reliability with one exception, that the motor may stall if the engine has not had an extended warm-up. Driver had just begun to drive her Rapido in city traffic without a warm-up when the engine suddenly stalled. A car driven by Troody rear-ended Driver's car. Driver suffered no external physical injuries as a result of the collision. However, the shock of the crash caused her to suffer a severe heart attack.

    Driver brought an action against the Rapido Motor Co. based on strict liability in tort. During the trial, the plaintiff presented evidence of an alternative engine design of equal cost that would eliminate the stalling problem without impairing the functions of the engine in any way. The defendant moves for a directed verdict at the close of the evidence.

    This motion should be

    (A) denied, because the jury could find that an unreasonably dangerous defect in the engine was a proximate cause of the collision.
    (B) denied, if the jury could find that the Rapido was not crashworthy.
    (C) granted, because Troody's failure to stop within an assured clear distance was a superseding cause of the collision.
    (D) granted, if a person of normal sensitivity would not have suffered a heart attack under these circumstances.

GO ON TO THE NEXT PAGE.

147. Pedestrian died from injuries caused when Driver's car struck him. Executor, Pedestrian's executor, sued Driver for wrongful death. At trial, Executor calls Nurse to testify that two days after the accident, Pedestrian said to Nurse, "The car that hit me ran the red light." Fifteen minutes thereafter, Pedestrian died.

    As a foundation for introducing evidence of Pedestrian's statement, Executor offers to the court Doctor's affidavit that Doctor was the intern on duty the day of Pedestrian's death and that several times that day Pedestrian had said that he knew he was about to die.

    Is the affidavit properly considered by the court in ruling on the admissibility of Pedestrian's statement?

    (A) No, because it is hearsay not within any exception.
    (B) No, because it is irrelevant since dying declarations cannot be used except in prosecutions for homicide.
    (C) Yes, because, though hearsay, it is a statement of then-existing mental condition.
    (D) Yes, because the judge may consider hearsay in ruling on preliminary questions.

148. John is a licensed barber in State A. The State A barber licensing statute provides that the Barber Licensing Board may revoke a barber license if it finds that a licensee has used his or her business premises for an illegal purpose.

    John was arrested by federal narcotics enforcement agents on a charge of selling cocaine in his barbershop in violation of federal laws. However, the local United States Attorney declined to prosecute and the charges were dropped.

    Nevertheless, the Barber Licensing Board commenced a proceeding against John to revoke his license on the ground that John used his business premises for illegal sales of cocaine. At a subsequent hearing before the board, the only evidence against John was affidavits by unnamed informants, who were not present or available for cross-examination. Their affidavits stated that they purchased cocaine from John in his barbershop. Based solely on this evidence, the board found that John used his business premises for an illegal purpose and ordered his license revoked.

    In a suit by John to have this revocation set aside, his best constitutional argument is that

    (A) John's inability to cross-examine his accusers denied him a fair hearing and caused him to be deprived of his barber license without due process of law.
    (B) the administrative license revocation proceeding was invalid, because it denied full faith and credit to the dismissal of the criminal charges by the United States Attorney.
    (C) Article III requires a penalty of the kind imposed on John to be imposed by a court rather than an administrative agency.
    (D) the existence of federal laws penalizing the illegal sale of cocaine preempts state action relating to drug trafficking of the kind involved in John's case.

GO ON TO THE NEXT PAGE.

149. Driver was driving his car near Owner's house when Owner's child darted into the street in front of Driver's car. As Driver swerved and braked his car to avoid hitting the child, the car skidded up into Owner's driveway and stopped just short of Owner, who was standing in the driveway and had witnessed the entire incident. Owner suffered serious emotional distress from witnessing the danger to his child and to himself. Neither Owner nor his property was physically harmed.

    If Owner asserts a claim for damages against Driver, will Owner prevail?

    (A) Yes, because Driver's entry onto Owner's land was unauthorized.
    (B) Yes, because Owner suffered serious emotional distress by witnessing the danger to his child and to himself.
    (C) No, unless Driver was negligent.
    (D) No, unless Owner's child was exercising reasonable care.

150. Vendor owned Greenacre, a tract of land, in fee simple. Vendor entered into a valid written agreement with Purchaser under which Vendor agreed to sell and Purchaser agreed to buy Greenacre by installment purchase. The contract stipulated that Vendor would deliver to Purchaser, upon the payment of the last installment due, "a warranty deed sufficient to convey the fee simple." The contract contained no other provision that could be construed as referring to title.

    Purchaser entered into possession of Greenacre. After making 10 of the 300 installment payments obligated under the contract, Purchaser discovered that there was outstanding a valid and enforceable mortgage on Greenacre, securing the payment of a debt in the amount of 25% of the purchase price Purchaser had agreed to pay. There was no evidence that Vendor had ever been late in payments due under the mortgage and there was no evidence of any danger of insolvency of Vendor. The value of Greenacre now is four times the amount due on the debt secured by the mortgage.

    Purchaser quit possession of Greenacre and demanded that Vendor repay the amounts Purchaser had paid under the contract. After Vendor refused the demand, Purchaser brought an appropriate action against Vendor to recover damages for Vendor's alleged breach of the contract.

    In such action, should damages be awarded to Purchaser?

    (A) No, because the time for Vendor to deliver marketable title has not arrived.
    (B) No, because Purchaser assumed the risk by taking possession.
    (C) Yes, because in the absence of a contrary express agreement, an obligation to convey marketable title is implied.
    (D) Yes, because the risk of loss assumed by Purchaser in taking possession relates only to physical loss.

GO ON TO THE NEXT PAGE.

151. The state of Red sent three of its employees to a city located in the state of Blue to consult with a chemical laboratory there about matters of state business. While in the course of their employment, the three employees of Red negligently released into local Blue waterways some of the chemical samples they had received from the laboratory in Blue.

    Persons in Blue injured by the release of the chemicals sued the three Red state employees and the state of Red in Blue state courts for the damages they suffered. After a trial in which all of the defendants admitted jurisdiction of the Blue state court and fully participated, plaintiffs received a judgment against all of the defendants for $5 million, which became final.

    Subsequently, plaintiffs sought to enforce their Blue state court judgment by commencing a proper proceeding in an appropriate court of Red. In that enforcement proceeding, the state of Red argued, as it had done unsuccessfully in the earlier action in Blue state court, that its liability is limited by a law of Red to $100,000 in any tort case. Because the three individual employees of Red are able to pay only $50,000 of the judgment, the only way the injured persons can fully satisfy their Blue state court judgment is from the funds of the state of Red.

    Can the injured persons recover the full balance of their Blue state court judgment from the state of Red in the enforcement proceeding they filed in a court of Red?

    (A) Yes, because the final judgment of the Blue court is entitled to full faith and credit in the courts of Red.
    (B) Yes, because a limitation on damage awards against Red for tortious actions of its agents would violate the equal protection clause of the Fourteenth Amendment.
    (C) No, because the Tenth Amendment preserves the right of a state to have its courts enforce the state's public policy limiting its tort liability.
    (D) No, because the employees of Red were negligent and, therefore, their actions were not authorized by the state of Red.

152. Martha's high school teacher told her that she was going to receive a failing grade in history, which would prevent her from graduating. Furious, she reported to the principal that the teacher had fondled her, and the teacher was fired. A year later, still unable to get work because of the scandal, the teacher committed suicide. Martha, remorseful, confessed that her accusation had been false.

    If Martha is charged with manslaughter, her best defense would be that she

    (A) committed no act that proximately caused the teacher's death.
    (B) did not intend to cause the teacher's death.
    (C) did not act with malice.
    (D) acted under extreme emotional distress.

153. Plaintiff sued Defendant for personal injuries arising out of an automobile accident.

    Which of the following would be ERROR?

    (A) The judge allows Defendant's attorney to ask Defendant questions on cross-examination that go well beyond the scope of direct examination by Plaintiff, who has been called as an adverse witness.
    (B) The judge refuses to allow Defendant's attorney to cross-examine Defendant by leading questions.
    (C) The judge allows cross-examination about the credibility of a witness even though no question relating to credibility has been asked on direct examination.
    (D) The judge, despite Defendant's request for exclusion of witnesses, allows Plaintiff's eyewitness to remain in the courtroom after testifying, even though the eyewitness is expected to be recalled for further cross-examination.

    GO ON TO THE NEXT PAGE.

154. Phil is suing Dennis for injuries suffered in an automobile collision. At trial Phil's first witness, Wanda, testified that, although she did not see the accident, she heard her friend Frank say just before the crash, "Look at the crazy way old Dennis is driving!" Dennis offers evidence to impeach Frank by asking Wanda, "Isn't it true that Frank beat up Dennis just the day before the collision?"

The question is

(A) proper, because it tends to show the possible bias of Frank against Dennis.
(B) proper, because it tends to show Frank's character.
(C) improper, because Frank has no opportunity to explain or deny.
(D) improper, because impeachment cannot properly be by specific instances.

155. Thirty years ago Able, the then-record owner of Greenacre, a lot contiguous to Blueacre, in fee simple, executed and delivered to Baker an instrument in writing which was denominated "Deed of Conveyance." In pertinent part it read, "Able does grant to Baker and her heirs and assigns a right-of-way for egress and ingress to Blueacre." If the quoted provision was sufficient to create an interest in land, the instrument met all other requirements for a valid grant. Baker held record title in fee simple to Blueacre, which adjoined Greenacre.

Twelve years ago Charlie succeeded to Able's title in fee simple in Greenacre and seven years ago Dorcas succeeded to Baker's title in fee simple in Blueacre by a deed which made no mention of a right-of-way or driveway. At the time Dorcas took title, there existed a driveway across Greenacre which showed evidence that it had been used regularly to travel between Main Road, a public road, and Blueacre. Blueacre did have frontage on Side Road, another public road, but this means of access was seldom used because it was not as convenient to the dwelling situated on Blueacre as was Main Road. The driveway originally was established by Baker.

Dorcas has regularly used the driveway since acquiring title. The period of time required to acquire rights by prescription in the jurisdiction is ten years.

Six months ago Charlie notified Dorcas that Charlie planned to develop a portion of Greenacre as a residential subdivision and that Dorcas should cease any use of the driveway. After some negotiations, Charlie offered to permit Dorcas to construct another driveway to connect with the streets of the proposed subdivision. Dorcas declined this offer on the ground that travel from Blueacre to Main Road would be more circuitous.

Dorcas brought an appropriate action against Charlie to obtain a definitive adjudication of the respective rights of Dorcas and Charlie. In such lawsuit Charlie relied upon the defense that the location of the easement created by the grant from Able to Baker was governed by reasonableness and that Charlie's proposed solution was reasonable.

Charlie's defense should

(A) fail, because the location had been established by the acts of Baker and Able.
(B) fail, because the location of the easement had been fixed by prescription.
(C) prevail, because the reasonableness of Charlie's proposal was established by Dorcas's refusal to suggest any alternative location.
(D) prevail, because the servient owner is entitled to select the location of a right-of-way if the grant fails to identify its location.

GO ON TO THE NEXT PAGE.

Questions 156–157 are based on the following fact situation.

Computers, Inc., contracted in writing with Bank to sell and deliver to Bank a mainframe computer using a new type of magnetic memory, then under development but not perfected by Computers, at a price substantially lower than that of a similar computer using current technology. The contract's delivery term was "F.O.B. Bank, on or before July 31."

156. For this question only, assume that Computers tendered the computer to Bank on August 15, and that Bank rejected it because of the delay.

If Computers sues Bank for breach of contract, which of the following facts, if proved, will best support a recovery by Computers?

(A) The delay did not materially harm Bank.
(B) Computers believed, on the assumption that Bank was getting a "super deal" for its money, that Bank would not reject because of the late tender of delivery.
(C) Computers' delay in tender was caused by a truckers' strike.
(D) A usage in the relevant trade allows computer sellers a 30-day leeway in a specified time of delivery, unless the usage is expressly negated by the contract.

157. For this question only, assume the following facts. After making the contract with Bank, Computers discovered that the new technology it intended to use was unreliable and that no computer manufacturer could yet build a reliable computer using that technology. Computers thereupon notified Bank that it was impossible for Computers or anyone else to build the contracted-for computer "in the present state of the art."

If Bank sues Computers for failure to perform its computer contract, the court will probably decide the case in favor of

(A) Computers, because its performance of the contract was objectively impossible.
(B) Computers, because a contract to build a machine using technology under development imposes only a duty on the builder to use its best efforts to achieve the result contracted for.
(C) Bank, because the law of impossibility does not apply to merchants under the applicable law.
(D) Bank, because Computers assumed the risk, in the given circumstances, that the projected new technology would not work reliably.

158. Defendant was charged with attempted murder of Victor in a sniping incident in which Defendant allegedly shot at Victor from ambush as Victor drove his car along an expressway. The prosecutor offers evidence that seven years earlier Defendant had fired a shotgun into a woman's home and that Defendant had once pointed a handgun at another driver while driving on the street.

This evidence should be

(A) excluded, because such evidence can be elicited only during cross-examination.
(B) excluded, because it is improper character evidence.
(C) admitted as evidence of Defendant's propensity toward violence.
(D) admitted as relevant evidence of Defendant's identity, plan, or motive.

GO ON TO THE NEXT PAGE.

159. Art, who owned Blackacre in fee simple, conveyed Blackacre to Bea by warranty deed. Celia, an adjoining owner, asserted title to Blackacre and brought an appropriate action against Bea to quiet title to Blackacre. Bea demanded that Art defend Bea's title under the deed's covenant of warranty, but Art refused. Bea then successfully defended at her own expense.

Bea brought an appropriate action against Art to recover Bea's expenses incurred in defending against Celia's action to quiet title to Blackacre.

In this action, the court should decide for

(A) Bea, because in effect it was Art's title that was challenged.
(B) Bea, because Art's deed to her included the covenant of warranty.
(C) Art, because the title Art conveyed was not defective.
(D) Art, because Celia may elect which of Art or Bea to sue.

160. Alex contracted for expensive cable television service for a period of six months solely to view the televised trial of Clark, who was on trial for murder in a court of the state of Green.

In the midst of the trial, the judge prohibited any further televising of Clark's trial because he concluded that the presence of television cameras was disruptive.

Alex brought an action in a federal district court against the judge in Clark's case asking only for an injunction that would require the judge to resume the televising of Clark's trial. Alex alleged that the judge's order to stop the televising of Clark's trial deprived him of property—his investment in cable television service—without due process of law.

Before Alex's case came to trial, Clark's criminal trial concluded in a conviction and sentencing. There do not appear to be any obvious errors in the proceeding that led to the result in Clark's case. After Clark's conviction and sentencing, the defendant in Alex's case moved to dismiss that suit.

The most proper disposition of this motion by the federal court would be to

(A) defer action on the motion until after any appellate proceedings in Clark's case have concluded, because Clark might appeal, his conviction might be set aside, he might be tried again, and television cameras might be barred from the new trial.
(B) defer action on the motion until after the Green Supreme Court expresses a view on its proper disposition, because the state law of mootness governs suits in federal court when the federal case is inexorably intertwined with a state proceeding.
(C) grant the motion, because the subject matter of the controversy between Alex and the defendant has ceased to exist and there is no strong likelihood that it will be revived.
(D) deny the motion, because Alex has raised an important constitutional question—whether his investment in cable service solely to view Clark's trial is property protected by the due process clause of the Fourteenth Amendment.

GO ON TO THE NEXT PAGE.

161. Traveler was a passenger on a commercial aircraft owned and operated by Airline. The aircraft crashed into a mountain, killing everyone on board. The flying weather was good.

    Traveler's legal representative brought a wrongful death action against Airline. At trial, the legal representative offered no expert or other testimony as to the cause of the crash.

    On Airline's motion to dismiss at the conclusion of the legal representative's case, the court should

    (A) grant the motion, because the legal representative has offered no evidence as to the cause of the crash.
    (B) grant the motion, because the legal representative has failed to offer evidence negating the possibility that the crash may have been caused by mechanical failure that Airline could not have prevented.
    (C) deny the motion, because the jury may infer that the aircraft crashed due to Airline's negligence.
    (D) deny the motion, because in the circumstances common carriers are strictly liable.

162. Company wanted to expand the size of the building it owned that housed Company's supermarket by adding space for a coffeehouse. Company's building was located in the center of five acres of land owned by Company and devoted wholly to parking for its supermarket customers.

    City officials refused to grant a required building permit for the coffeehouse addition unless Company established in its store a child care center that would take up space at least equal to the size of the proposed coffeehouse addition, which was to be 20% of the existing building. This action of City officials was authorized by provisions of the applicable zoning ordinance.

    In a suit filed in state court against appropriate officials of City, Company challenged this child care center requirement solely on constitutional grounds. The lower court upheld the requirement even though City officials presented no evidence and made no findings to justify it other than a general assertion that there was a shortage of child care facilities in City. Company appealed.

    The court hearing the appeal should hold that the requirement imposed by City on the issuance of this building permit is

    (A) constitutional, because the burden was on Company to demonstrate that there was no rational relationship between this requirement and a legitimate governmental interest, and Company could not do so because the requirement is reasonably related to improving the lives of families and children residing in City.
    (B) constitutional, because the burden was on Company to demonstrate that this requirement was not necessary to vindicate a compelling governmental interest, and Company could not do so on these facts.
    (C) unconstitutional, because the burden was on City to demonstrate that this requirement was necessary to vindicate a compelling governmental interest, and City failed to meet its burden under that standard.
    (D) unconstitutional, because the burden was on City to demonstrate a rough proportionality between this requirement and the impact of Company's proposed action on the community, and City failed to do so.

GO ON TO THE NEXT PAGE.

163. Ollie owned a large tract of land known as Peterhill. During Ollie's lifetime, Ollie conveyed the easterly half (East Peterhill), situated in the municipality of Hawthorn, to Abel, and the westerly half (West Peterhill), situated in the municipality of Sycamore, to Betty. Each of the conveyances, which were promptly and properly recorded, contained the following language:

> The parties agree for themselves and their heirs and assigns that the premises herein conveyed shall be used only for residential purposes; that each lot created within the premises herein conveyed shall contain not less than five acres; and that each lot shall have not more than one single-family dwelling. This agreement shall bind all successor owners of all or any portion of Peterhill and any owner of any part of Peterhill may enforce this covenant.

After Ollie's death, Abel desired to build houses on one-half acre lots in the East Peterhill tract as authorized by current applicable zoning and building codes in Hawthorn. The area surrounding East Peterhill in Hawthorn was developed as a residential community with homes built on one-half acre lots. West Peterhill was in a residential area covered by the Sycamore zoning code, which allowed residential development only on five-acre tracts of land.

In an appropriate action brought by Betty to enjoin Abel's proposed construction on one-half acre lots, the court will find the quoted restriction to be

(A) invalid, because of the change of circumstance in the neighborhood.
(B) invalid, because it conflicts with the applicable zoning code.
(C) valid, but only so long as the original grantees from Ollie own their respective tracts of Peterhill.
(D) valid, because the provision imposed an equitable servitude.

164. At Defendant's murder trial, Defendant calls Witness as his first witness to testify that Defendant has a reputation in their community as a peaceable and truthful person. The prosecutor objects on the ground that Witness's testimony would constitute improper character evidence.

The court should

(A) admit the testimony as to peaceableness, but exclude the testimony as to truthfulness.
(B) admit the testimony as to truthfulness, but exclude the testimony as to peaceableness.
(C) admit the testimony as to both character traits.
(D) exclude the testimony as to both character traits.

GO ON TO THE NEXT PAGE.

165. The governor of the state of Green proposes to place a Christmas nativity scene, the components of which would be permanently donated to the state by private citizens, in the Green Capitol Building rotunda where the Green Legislature meets annually. The governor further proposes to display this state-owned nativity scene annually from December 1 to December 31, next to permanent displays that depict the various products manufactured in Green. The governor's proposal is supported by all members of both houses of the legislature.

If challenged in a lawsuit on establishment clause grounds, the proposed nativity scene display would be held

(A) unconstitutional, because the components of the nativity scene would be owned by the state rather than by private persons.
(B) unconstitutional, because the nativity scene would not be displayed in a context that appeared to depict and commemorate the Christmas season as a primarily secular holiday.
(C) constitutional, because the components of the nativity scene would be donated to the state by private citizens rather than purchased with state funds.
(D) constitutional, because the nativity scene would be displayed alongside an exhibit of various products manufactured in Green.

166. Two police officers in uniform were on foot patrol in a neighborhood frequented by drug sellers. They saw Sandra, who, when she saw them, turned around and started to walk quickly away. The police ran after her and shouted, "Stop and don't take another step, lady!" Sandra turned, looked at the police, and stopped. She put her arms up in the air. As the police approached, she threw a small object into nearby bushes. The police retrieved the object, which turned out to be a small bag of cocaine, and then arrested Sandra.

Sandra is charged with possession of the cocaine. She moves pretrial to suppress its use as evidence on the ground that it was obtained as the result of an illegal search and seizure.

Her motion should be

(A) granted, because the police did not know the item was cocaine until after they had seized it.
(B) granted, because the police acquired the cocaine as the result of an unlawful seizure.
(C) denied, because the police had probable cause to seize the package.
(D) denied, because Sandra voluntarily discarded the contraband.

GO ON TO THE NEXT PAGE.

167. In a federal civil trial, Plaintiff wishes to establish that, in a state court, Defendant had been convicted of fraud, a fact that Defendant denies.

    Which mode of proof of the conviction is LEAST likely to be permitted?

    (A) A certified copy of the judgment of conviction, offered as a self-authenticating document.
    (B) Testimony of Plaintiff, who was present at the time of the sentence.
    (C) Testimony by a witness to whom Defendant made an oral admission that he had been convicted.
    (D) Judicial notice of the conviction, based on the court's telephone call to the clerk of the state court, whom the judge knows personally.

168. Three years ago Adam conveyed Blackacre to Betty for $50,000 by a deed that provided: "By accepting this deed, Betty covenants for herself, her heirs and assigns, that the premises herein conveyed shall be used solely for residential purposes and, if the premises are used for nonresidential purposes, Adam, his heirs and assigns, shall have the right to repurchase the premises for the sum of one thousand dollars ($1,000)." In order to pay the $50,000 purchase price for Blackacre, Betty obtained a $35,000 mortgage loan from the bank. Adam had full knowledge of the mortgage transaction. The deed and mortgage were promptly and properly recorded in proper sequence. The mortgage, however, made no reference to the quoted language in the deed.

    Two years ago Betty converted her use of Blackacre from residential to commercial without the knowledge or consent of Adam or of the bank. Betty's commercial venture failed, and Betty defaulted on her mortgage payments to the bank. Blackacre now has a fair market value of $25,000.

    The bank began appropriate foreclosure proceedings against Betty. Adam properly intervened, tendered $1,000, and sought judgment that Betty and the bank be ordered to convey Blackacre to Adam, free and clear of the mortgage.

    The common-law Rule Against Perpetuities is unmodified by statute.

    If the court rules against Adam, it will be because

    (A) the provision quoted from the deed violates the Rule Against Perpetuities.
    (B) the Bank had no actual knowledge of, and did not consent to, the violation of the covenant.
    (C) the rights reserved by Adam were subordinated, by necessary implication, to the rights of the bank as the lender of the purchase money.
    (D) the consideration of $1,000 was inadequate.

GO ON TO THE NEXT PAGE.

169. Loyal, aged 60, who had no plans for early retirement, had worked for Mutate, Inc., for 20 years as a managerial employee-at-will when he had a conversation with the company's president, George Mutant, about Loyal's post-retirement goal of extensive travel around the United States. A month later, Mutant handed Loyal a written, signed resolution of the company's Board of Directors stating that when and if Loyal should decide to retire, at his option, the company, in recognition of his past service, would pay him a $2,000-per-month lifetime pension. (The company had no regularized retirement plan for at-will employees.) Shortly thereafter, Loyal retired and immediately bought a $30,000 recreational vehicle for his planned travels. After receiving the promised $2,000 monthly pension from Mutate, Inc., for six months, Loyal, now unemployable elsewhere, received a letter from Mutate, Inc., advising him that the pension would cease immediately because of recessionary budget constraints affecting in varying degrees all managerial salaries and retirement pensions.

In a suit against Mutate, Inc., for breach of contract, Loyal will probably

(A) win, because he retired from the company as bargained-for consideration for the Board's promise to him of a lifetime pension.
(B) win, because he timed his decision to retire and to buy the recreational vehicle in reasonable reliance on the Board's promise to him of a lifetime pension.
(C) lose, because the Board's promise to him of a lifetime pension was an unenforceable gift promise.
(D) lose, because he had been an employee-at-will throughout his active service with the company.

170. Congress wishes to enact legislation prohibiting discrimination in the sale or rental of housing on the basis of the affectional preference or sexual orientation of the potential purchaser or renter. Congress wishes this statute to apply to all public and private vendors and lessors of residential property in this country, with a few narrowly drawn exceptions.

The most credible argument for congressional authority to enact such a statute would be based upon the

(A) general welfare clause of Article I, Section 8, because the conduct the statute prohibits could reasonably be deemed to be harmful to the national interest.
(B) commerce clause of Article I, Section 8, because, in inseverable aggregates, the sale or rental of almost all housing in this country could reasonably be deemed to have a substantial effect on interstate commerce.
(C) enforcement clause of the Thirteenth Amendment, because that amendment clearly prohibits discrimination against the class of persons protected by this statute.
(D) enforcement clause of the Fourteenth Amendment, because that amendment prohibits all public and private actors from engaging in irrational discrimination.

GO ON TO THE NEXT PAGE.

171. Because of Farmer's default on his loan, the bank foreclosed on the farm and equipment that secured the loan. Among the items sold at the resulting auction was a new tractor recently delivered to Farmer by the retailer. Shortly after purchasing the tractor at the auction, Pratt was negligently operating the tractor on a hill when it rolled over due to a defect in the tractor's design. He was injured as a result. Pratt sued the auctioneer, alleging strict liability in tort. The jurisdiction has not adopted a comparative fault rule in strict liability cases.

    In this suit, the result should be for the

    (A) plaintiff, because the defendant sold a defective product that injured the plaintiff.
    (B) plaintiff, if the defendant failed to inspect the tractor for defects prior to sale.
    (C) defendant, because he should not be considered a "seller" for purposes of strict liability in tort.
    (D) defendant, because the accident was caused in part by Pratt's negligence.

172. In exchange for a valid and sufficient consideration, Goodbar orally promised Walker, who had no car and wanted a minivan, "to pay to anyone from whom you buy a minivan within the next six months the full purchase-price thereof." Two months later, Walker bought a used minivan on credit from Minivanity Fair, Inc., for $8,000. At the time, Minivanity Fair was unaware of Goodbar's earlier promise to Walker, but learned of it shortly after the sale.

    Can Minivanity Fair enforce Goodbar's promise to Walker?

    (A) Yes, under the doctrine of promissory estoppel.
    (B) Yes, because Minivanity Fair is an intended beneficiary of the Goodbar-Walker contract.
    (C) No, because Goodbar's promise to Walker is unenforceable under the suretyship clause of the statute of frauds.
    (D) No, because Minivanity Fair was neither identified when Goodbar's promise was made nor aware of it when the minivan-sale was made.

GO ON TO THE NEXT PAGE.

173. Plaintiff sued Defendant for injuries sustained in an automobile collision. During Plaintiff's hospital stay, Doctor, a staff physician, examined Plaintiff's X rays and said to Plaintiff, "You have a fracture of two vertebrae, C4 and C5." Intern, who was accompanying Doctor on her rounds, immediately wrote the diagnosis on Plaintiff's hospital record. At trial, the hospital records custodian testifies that Plaintiff's hospital record was made and kept in the ordinary course of the hospital's business.

The entry reporting Doctor's diagnosis is

(A) inadmissible, because no foundation has been laid for Doctor's competence as an expert.
(B) inadmissible, because Doctor's opinion is based upon data that are not in evidence.
(C) admissible as a statement of then-existing physical condition.
(D) admissible as a record of regularly conducted business activity.

174. A city owns and operates a large public auditorium. It leases the auditorium to any group that wishes to use it for a meeting, lecture, concert, or contest. Each user must post a damage deposit and pay rent, which is calculated only for the actual time the building is used by the lessee. Reservations are made on a first-come, first-served basis.

A private organization that permits only males to serve in its highest offices rented the auditorium for its national convention. The organization planned to install its new officers at that convention. It broadly publicized the event, inviting members of the general public to attend the installation ceremony at the city auditorium. No statute or administrative rule prohibits the organization from restricting its highest offices to men.

An appropriate plaintiff sues the private organization seeking to enjoin it from using the city auditorium for the installation of its new officers. The sole claim of the plaintiff is that the use of this auditorium by the organization for the installation ceremony is unconstitutional because the organization disqualifies women from serving in its highest offices.

Will the plaintiff prevail?

(A) Yes, because the Fourteenth Amendment prohibits such an organization from discriminating against women in any of its activities to which it has invited members of the general public.
(B) Yes, because the organization's use of the city auditorium for this purpose subjects its conduct to the provisions of the Fourteenth Amendment.
(C) No, because the freedom of association protected by the Fourteenth Amendment prohibits the city from interfering in any way with the organization's use of city facilities.
(D) No, because this organization is not a state actor and, therefore, its activities are not subject to the provisions of the Fourteenth Amendment.

GO ON TO THE NEXT PAGE.

175. Adam owns Townacres in fee simple, and Bess owns the adjoining Greenacres in fee simple. Adam has kept the lawns and trees on Townacres trimmed and neat. Bess "lets nature take its course" at Greenacres. The result on Greenacres is a tangle of underbrush, fallen trees, and standing trees that are in danger of losing limbs. Many of the trees on Greenacres are near Townacres. In the past, debris and large limbs have been blown from Greenacres onto Townacres. By local standards Greenacres is an eyesore that depresses market values of real property in the vicinity, but the condition of Greenacres violates no applicable laws or ordinances.

    Adam demanded that Bess keep the trees near Townacres trimmed. Bess refused.

    Adam brought an appropriate action against Bess to require Bess to abate what Adam alleges to be a nuisance. In the lawsuit, the only issue is whether the condition of Greenacres constitutes a nuisance.

    The strongest argument that Adam can present is that the condition of Greenacres

    (A) has an adverse impact on real estate values.
    (B) poses a danger to the occupants of Townacres.
    (C) violates community aesthetic standards.
    (D) cannot otherwise be challenged under any law or ordinance.

176. Breeder bought a two-month-old registered boar at auction from Pigstyle for $800. No express warranty was made. Fifteen months later, tests by experts proved conclusively that the boar had been born incurably sterile. If this had been known at the time of the sale, the boar would have been worth no more than $100.

    In an action by Breeder against Pigstyle to avoid the contract and recover the price paid, the parties stipulate that, as both were and had been aware, the minimum age at which the fertility of a boar can be determined is about 12 months.

    Which of the following will the court probably decide?

    (A) Breeder wins, because the parties were mutually mistaken as to the boar's fertility when they made the agreement.
    (B) Breeder wins, because Pigstyle impliedly warranted that the boar was fit for breeding.
    (C) Pigstyle wins, because Breeder assumed the risk of the boar's sterility.
    (D) Pigstyle wins, because any mistake involved was unilateral, not mutual.

GO ON TO THE NEXT PAGE.

177. Homeowner owns a house on a lake. Neighbor owns a house across a driveway from Homeowner's property. Neighbor's house sits on a hill and Neighbor can see the lake from his living room window.

    Homeowner and Neighbor got into an argument and Homeowner erected a large spotlight on his property that automatically comes on at dusk and goes off at sunrise. The only reason Homeowner installed the light was to annoy Neighbor. The glare from the light severely detracts from Neighbor's view of the lake.

    In a suit by Neighbor against Homeowner, will Neighbor prevail?

    (A) Yes, because Homeowner installed the light solely to annoy Neighbor.
    (B) Yes, if, and only if, Neighbor's property value is adversely affected.
    (C) No, because Neighbor's view of the lake is not always obstructed.
    (D) No, if the spotlight provides added security to Homeowner's property.

178. On May 1, 1987, a car driven by Debra struck Peggy, a pedestrian. On July 1, 1987, with regard to this incident, Debra pleaded guilty to reckless driving (a misdemeanor) and was sentenced to 30 days in jail and a fine of $1,000. She served the sentence and paid the fine. On April 1, 1988, Peggy died as a result of the injuries she suffered in the accident. On March 1, 1991, a grand jury indicted Debra on a charge of manslaughter of Peggy. On May 15, 1991, trial had not begun and Debra filed a motion to dismiss the indictment on the ground of double jeopardy in that her conviction of reckless driving arose out of the same incident, and on the ground that the three-year statute of limitations for manslaughter had run.

    Debra's motion should be

    (A) granted only on double jeopardy grounds.
    (B) granted only on statute of limitations grounds.
    (C) granted on either double jeopardy grounds or statute of limitations grounds.
    (D) denied on both grounds.

GO ON TO THE NEXT PAGE.

179. Defendant is on trial for participating in a drug sale. The prosecution calls Witness, an undercover officer, to testify that, when Seller sold the drugs to Witness, Seller introduced Defendant to Witness as "my partner in this" and Defendant shook hands with Witness but said nothing.

Witness's testimony is

(A) inadmissible, because there is no evidence that Seller was authorized to speak for Defendant.
(B) inadmissible, because the statement of Seller is hearsay not within any exception.
(C) admissible as a statement against Defendant's penal interest.
(D) admissible as Defendant's adoption of Seller's statement.

180. State Y has a state employee grievance system that requires any state employee who wishes to file a grievance against the state to submit that grievance for final resolution to a panel of three arbitrators chosen by the parties from a statewide board of 13 arbitrators. In any given case, the grievant and the state alternate in exercising the right of each party to eliminate five members of the board, leaving a panel of three members to decide their case. At the present time, the full board is composed of seven male arbitrators and six female arbitrators.

Ellen, a female state employee, filed a sexual harassment grievance against her male supervisor and the state. Anne, the state's attorney, exercised all of her five strikes to eliminate five of the female arbitrators. At the time she did so, Anne stated that she struck the five female arbitrators solely because she believed women, as a group, would necessarily be biased in favor of another woman who was claiming sexual harassment. Counsel for Ellen eliminated four males and one female arbitrator, all solely on grounds of specific bias or conflicts of interest. As a result, the panel was all male.

When the panel ruled against Ellen on the merits of her case, she filed an action in an appropriate state court, challenging the panel selection process as a gender-based denial of equal protection of the laws.

In this case, the court should hold that the panel selection process is

(A) unconstitutional, because the gender classification used by the state's attorney in this case does not satisfy the requirements of intermediate scrutiny.
(B) unconstitutional, because the gender classification used by the state's attorney in this case denies the grievant the right to a jury made up of her peers.
(C) constitutional, because the gender classification used by the state's attorney in this case satisfies the requirements of the strict scrutiny test.
(D) constitutional, because the gender classification used by the state's attorney in this case satisfies the requirements of the rational basis test.

GO ON TO THE NEXT PAGE.

181. Theresa owned Blueacre, a tract of land, in fee simple. Theresa wrote and executed, with the required formalities, a will that devised Blueacre to "my daughter, Della, for life with remainder to my descendants *per stirpes*." At the time of writing the will, Theresa had a husband and no descendants living other than her two children, Della and Seth.

    Theresa died and the will was duly admitted to probate. Theresa's husband predeceased her. Theresa was survived by Della, Seth, four grandchildren, and one great-grandchild. Della and Seth were Theresa's sole heirs at law.

    Della and Seth brought an appropriate action for declaratory judgment as to title of Blueacre. Guardians *ad litem* were appointed and all other steps were taken so that the judgment would bind all persons interested whether born or unborn.

    In that action, if the court rules that Della has a life estate in the whole of Blueacre and that the remainder is contingent, it will be because the court chose one of several possible constructions and that the chosen construction

    (A) related all vesting to the time of writing of the will.
    (B) related all vesting to the death of Theresa.
    (C) implied a condition that remaindermen survive Della.
    (D) implied a gift of a life estate to Seth.

182. Driver negligently drove his car into Pedestrian, breaking her leg. Pedestrian's leg was put in a cast, and she used crutches to get about. While shopping at Market, her local supermarket, Pedestrian nonnegligently placed one of her crutches on a banana peel that had been negligently left on the floor by the manager of Market's produce department. Pedestrian's crutch slipped on the peel, and she fell to the floor, breaking her arm. Had Pedestrian stepped on the banana peel at a time when she did not have to use crutches, she would have regained her balance.

    Pedestrian sued Driver and Market for her injuries.

    Pedestrian will be able to recover from

    (A) Driver, for her broken leg only.
    (B) Driver, for both of her injuries.
    (C) Market, for both of her injuries.
    (D) Driver, for her broken leg only, and Market, for her broken arm only.

    GO ON TO THE NEXT PAGE.

183. FBI agents, without a warrant and without permission of Mexican law enforcement or judicial officers, entered Mexico, kidnapped Steven, an American citizen wanted in the United States for drug smuggling violations, and forcibly drove him back to Texas. Thereafter, the agents, again without a warrant, broke into the Texas home of Joan, wanted as a confederate of Steven, and arrested her.

Steven and Joan were both indicted for narcotics violations. Both moved to dismiss the indictment on the ground that their arrests violated the Fourth Amendment.

The court should

(A) grant the motions of both Steven and Joan.
(B) grant the motion of Steven and deny the motion of Joan.
(C) grant the motion of Joan and deny the motion of Steven.
(D) deny the motions of both Steven and Joan.

184. Gourmet purchased the front portion of the land needed for a restaurant he desired to build and operate, but the back portion was the subject of a will dispute between Hope and Faith (two sisters). Hope's attorney advised her that her claim was doubtful. Gourmet, knowing only that the unresolved dispute existed, agreed in a signed writing to pay Hope $6,000, payable $1,000 annually, in exchange for a quitclaim deed (a deed containing no warranties) from Hope, who promptly executed such a deed to Gourmet and received Gourmet's first annual payment. Shortly thereafter, the probate court handed down a decision in Faith's favor, ruling that Hope had no interest in the land. This decision has become final. Gourmet subsequently defaulted when his second annual installment came due.

In an action against Gourmet for breach of contract, Hope will probably

(A) lose, because she was aware at the time of the agreement with Gourmet that her claim to the property quitclaimed was doubtful.
(B) lose, because Hope suffered no legal detriment in executing the quitclaim deed.
(C) win, because Gourmet bargained for and received in exchange a quitclaim deed from Hope.
(D) win, because Gourmet, by paying the first $1,000 installment, is estopped to deny that his agreement with Hope is an enforceable contract.

GO ON TO THE NEXT PAGE.

185. Athlete, a professional football player, signed a written consent for his team's physician, Doctor, to perform a knee operation. After Athlete was under a general anesthetic, Doctor asked Surgeon, a world famous orthopedic surgeon, to perform the operation. Surgeon's skills were superior to Doctor's, and the operation was successful.

In an action for battery by Athlete against Surgeon, Athlete will

(A) prevail, because Athlete did not agree to allow Surgeon to perform the operation.
(B) prevail, because the consent form was in writing.
(C) not prevail, because Surgeon's skills were superior to Doctor's.
(D) not prevail, because the operation was successful.

186. Senator makes a speech on the floor of the United States Senate in which she asserts that William, a federal civil servant with minor responsibilities, was twice convicted of fraud by the courts of State X. In making this assertion, Senator relied wholly on research done by Frank, her chief legislative assistant. In fact, it was a different man named William and not William the civil servant, who was convicted of these crimes in the state court proceedings. This mistake was the result of carelessness on Frank's part.

No legislation affecting the appointment or discipline of civil servants or the program of the federal agency for which William works was under consideration at the time Senator made her speech about William on the floor of the Senate.

William sues Senator and Frank for defamation. Both defendants move to dismiss the complaint.

As a matter of constitutional law, the court hearing this motion should

(A) grant it as to Frank, because he is protected by the freedom of speech guarantee against defamation actions by government officials based on his mere carelessness; but deny it as to Senator, because, as an officer of the United States, she is a constituent part of the government and, therefore, has no freedom of speech rights in that capacity.
(B) grant it as to both defendants, because Senator is immune to suit for any speech she makes in the Senate under the speech or debate clause of Article I, Section 6, and Frank may assert Senator's immunity for his assistance to her in preparing the speech.
(C) deny it as to both defendants, because any immunity of Senator under the speech or debate clause does not attach to a speech that is not germane to pending legislative business, and Frank is entitled to no greater immunity than the legislator he was assisting.
(D) deny it as to Frank, because he is not a legislator protected by the speech or debate clause; but grant it as to Senator, because she is immune from suit for her speech by virtue of that clause.

GO ON TO THE NEXT PAGE.

187. Six years ago, Oscar, owner of Blackacre in fee simple, executed and delivered to Albert an instrument in the proper form of a warranty deed, purporting to convey Blackacre to "Albert and his heirs." At that time, Albert was a widower who had one child, Donna.

Three years ago, Albert executed and delivered to Bea an instrument in the proper form of a warranty deed, purporting to convey Blackacre to "Bea." Donna did not join in the deed. Bea was and still is unmarried and childless.

The only possibly applicable statute in the jurisdiction states that any deed will be construed to convey the grantor's entire estate, unless expressly limited.

Last month, Albert died, never having remarried. Donna is his only heir.

Blackacre is now owned by

(A) Donna, because Albert's death ended Bea's life estate *pur autre vie*.
(B) Bea in fee simple pursuant to Albert's deed.
(C) Donna and Bea as tenants in common of equal shares.
(D) Donna and Bea as joint tenants, because both survived Albert.

188. Smart approached Johnson and inquired about hiring someone to kill his girlfriend's parents. Unknown to Smart, Johnson was an undercover police officer who pretended to agree to handle the job and secretly taped subsequent conversations with Smart concerning plans and payment. A few days before the payment was due, Smart changed his mind and called the plan off. Nevertheless, Smart was charged with solicitation to commit murder.

Smart should be

(A) acquitted, because he withdrew before payment and commission of the act.
(B) acquitted, because no substantial acts were performed.
(C) convicted, because the offense was completed before his attempt to withdraw.
(D) convicted, because Johnson agreed to commit the offense.

GO ON TO THE NEXT PAGE.

189. Retailer, a dry goods retailer, telephoned Manufacturer, a towel manufacturer, and offered to buy for $5 each a minimum of 500 and a maximum of 1,000 large bath towels, to be delivered in 30 days. Manufacturer orally accepted this offer and promptly sent the following letter to Retailer, which Retailer received two days later: "This confirms our agreement today by telephone to sell you 500 large bath towels for 30-day delivery. /s/ Manufacturer." Twenty-eight days later, Manufacturer tendered to Retailer 1,000 (not 500) conforming bath towels, all of which Retailer rejected because it had found a better price term from another supplier. Because of a glut in the towel market, Manufacturer cannot resell the towels except at a loss.

In a suit by Manufacturer against Retailer, which of the following will be the probable decision?

(A) Manufacturer can enforce a contract for 1,000 towels, because Retailer ordered and Manufacturer tendered that quantity.
(B) Manufacturer can enforce a contract for 500 towels, because Manufacturer's letter of confirmation stated that quantity term.
(C) There is no enforceable agreement, because Retailer never signed a writing.
(D) There is no enforceable agreement, because Manufacturer's letter of confirmation did not state a price term.

190. Doctor, a resident of the city of Greenville in the state of Green, is a physician licensed to practice in both Green and the neighboring state of Red. Doctor finds that the most convenient place to treat her patients who need hospital care is in the publicly owned and operated Redville Municipal Hospital of the city of Redville in the state of Red, which is located just across the state line from Greenville. For many years Doctor had successfully treated her patients in that hospital. Early this year she was notified that she could no longer treat patients in the Redville hospital because she was not a resident of Red, and a newly adopted rule of Redville Municipal Hospital, which was adopted in conformance with all required procedures, stated that every physician who practices in that hospital must be a resident of Red.

Which of the following constitutional provisions would be most helpful to Doctor in an action to challenge her exclusion from the Redville hospital solely on the basis of this hospital rule?

(A) The bill of attainder clause.
(B) The privileges and immunities clause of Article IV.
(C) The due process clause of the Fourteenth Amendment.
(D) The ex post facto clause.

GO ON TO THE NEXT PAGE.

191. Martin, the owner in fee simple of Orchardacres, mortgaged Orchardacres to Marie to secure the payment of the loan she made to him. The loan was due at the end of the growing season of the year in which it was made. Martin maintained and operated an orchard on the land, which was his sole source of income. Halfway through the growing season, Martin experienced severe health and personal problems and, as a result, left the state; his whereabouts were unknown. Marie learned that no one was responsible for the cultivation and care of the orchard on Orchardacres. She undertook to provide, through employees, the care of the orchard and the harvest for the remainder of the growing season. The net profits were applied to the debt secured by the mortgage on Orchardacres.

During the course of the harvest, Paul, a business invitee, was injured by reason of a fault in the equipment used. Under applicable tort case law, the owner of the premises would be liable for Paul's injuries. Paul brought an appropriate action against Marie to recover damages for the injuries suffered, relying on this aspect of tort law.

In such lawsuit, judgment should be for

(A) Paul, if, but only if, the state is a title theory state, because in other jurisdictions a mortgagee has no title interest but only a lien.
(B) Paul, because Marie was a mortgagee in possession.
(C) Marie, because she acted as agent of the owner only to preserve her security interest.
(D) Marie, if, but only if, the mortgage expressly provided for her taking possession in the event of danger to her security interest.

192. Actor, a well-known movie star, was drinking Vineyard wine at a nightclub. A bottle of the Vineyard wine, with its label plainly showing, was on the table in front of Actor. An amateur photographer asked Actor if he could take his picture and Actor said, "Yes." Subsequently, the photographer sold the photo to Vineyard. Vineyard, without Actor's consent, used the photo in a wine advertisement in a nationally circulated magazine. The caption below the photo stated, "Actor enjoys his Vineyard wine."

If Actor sues Vineyard to recover damages as a result of Vineyard's use of the photograph, will Actor prevail?

(A) No, because Actor consented to being photographed.
(B) No, because Actor is a public figure.
(C) Yes, because Vineyard made commercial use of the photograph.
(D) Yes, unless Actor did, in fact, enjoy his Vineyard wine.

GO ON TO THE NEXT PAGE.

193. At Defendant's trial for sale of drugs, the government called Witness to testify, but Witness refused to answer any questions about Defendant and was held in contempt of court. The government then calls Officer to testify that, when Witness was arrested for possession of drugs and offered leniency if he would identify his source, Witness had named Defendant as his source.

The testimony offered concerning Witness's identification of Defendant is

(A) admissible as a prior inconsistent statement by Witness.
(B) admissible as an identification of Defendant by Witness after having perceived him.
(C) inadmissible, because it is hearsay not within any exception.
(D) inadmissible, because Witness was not confronted with the statement while on the stand.

194. Buyer mailed a signed order to Seller that read: "Please ship us 10,000 widgets at your current price." Seller received the order on January 7 and that same day mailed to Buyer a properly stamped, addressed, and signed letter stating that the order was accepted at Seller's current price of $10 per widget. On January 8, before receipt of Seller's letter, Buyer telephoned Seller and said, "I hereby revoke my order." Seller protested to no avail. Buyer received Seller's letter on January 9. Because of Buyer's January 8 telephone message, Seller never shipped the goods.

Under the relevant and prevailing rules, is there a contract between Buyer and Seller as of January 10?

(A) No, because the order was an offer that could be accepted only by shipping the goods; and the offer was effectively revoked before shipment.
(B) No, because Buyer never effectively agreed to the $10 price term.
(C) Yes, because the order was, for a reasonable time, an irrevocable offer.
(D) Yes, because the order was an offer that Seller effectively accepted before Buyer attempted to revoke it.

GO ON TO THE NEXT PAGE.

195. As Seller, an encyclopedia salesman, approached the grounds on which Hermit's house was situated, he saw a sign that said, "No salesmen. Trespassers will be prosecuted. Proceed at your own risk." Although Seller had not been invited to enter, he ignored the sign and drove up the driveway toward the house. As he rounded a curve, a powerful explosive charge buried in the driveway exploded, and Seller was injured.

Can Seller recover damages from Hermit for his injuries?

(A) Yes, if Hermit was responsible for the explosive charge under the driveway.
(B) Yes, unless Hermit, when he planted the charge, intended only to deter, not to harm, a possible intruder.
(C) No, because Seller ignored the sign, which warned him against proceeding further.
(D) No, if Hermit reasonably feared that intruders would come and harm him or his family.

196. Adam owned Blackacre. Adam entered into a written three-year lease of Blackacre with Bertha. Among other provisions, the lease prohibited Bertha from "assigning this lease, in whole or in part, and from subletting Blackacre, in whole or in part." In addition to a house, a barn, and a one-car garage, Blackacre's 30 acres included several fields where first Adam, and now Bertha, grazed sheep.

During the following months, Bertha:

I. By a written agreement allowed her neighbor Charles exclusive use of the garage for storage, under lock and key, of his antique Packard automobile for two years, charging him $240.
II. Told her neighbor Doris that Doris could use the fields to practice her golf as long as she did not disturb Bertha's sheep.

Which, if any, of Bertha's actions constituted a violation of the lease?

(A) I only.
(B) II only.
(C) Both I and II.
(D) Neither I nor II.

GO ON TO THE NEXT PAGE.

197. Defendant is charged with murder. The evidence shows that she pointed a gun at Victim and pulled the trigger. The gun discharged, killing Victim. The gun belonged to Victim.

Defendant testifies that Victim told her, and she believed, that the "gun" was a stage prop that could fire only blanks, and that she fired the gun as part of rehearsing a play with Victim at his house.

If the jury believes Defendant's testimony and finds that her mistaken belief that the gun was a prop was reasonable, they should find her

(A) guilty of murder.
(B) guilty of manslaughter.
(C) guilty of either murder or manslaughter.
(D) not guilty of murder or manslaughter.

198. Del's sporting goods shop was burglarized by an escaped inmate from a nearby prison. The inmate stole a rifle and bullets from a locked cabinet. The burglar alarm at Del's shop did not go off because Del had negligently forgotten to activate the alarm's motion detector.

Shortly thereafter, the inmate used the rifle and ammunition stolen from Del in a shooting spree that caused injury to several people, including Paula.

If Paula sues Del for the injury she suffered, will Paula prevail?

(A) Yes, if Paula's injury would have been prevented had the motion detector been activated.
(B) Yes, because Del was negligent in failing to activate the motion detector.
(C) No, because the storage and sale of firearms and ammunition is not an abnormally dangerous activity.
(D) No, unless there is evidence of circumstances suggesting a high risk of theft and criminal use of firearms stocked by Del.

GO ON TO THE NEXT PAGE.

199. A statute of the state of Texona prohibits any retailer of books, magazines, pictures, or posters from "publicly displaying or selling to any person any material that may be harmful to minors because of the violent or sexually explicit nature of its pictorial content." Violation of this statute is a misdemeanor.

Corner Store displays publicly and sells magazines containing violent and sexually explicit pictures. The owner of this store is prosecuted under the above statute for these actions.

In defending against this prosecution in a Texona trial court, the argument that would be the best defense for Corner Store is that the statute violates the

(A) First Amendment as it is incorporated into the Fourteenth Amendment, because the statute is excessively vague and overbroad.
(B) First Amendment as it is incorporated into the Fourteenth Amendment, because a state may not prohibit the sale of violent or sexually explicit material in the absence of proof that the material is utterly without any redeeming value in the marketplace of ideas.
(C) equal protection of the laws clause, because the statute irrationally treats violent and sexually explicit material that is pictorial differently from such material that is composed wholly of printed words.
(D) equal protection of the laws clause, because the statute irrationally distinguishes between violent and sexually explicit pictorial material that may harm minors and such material that may harm only adults.

200. In an arson prosecution the government seeks to rebut Defendant's alibi that he was in a jail in another state at the time of the fire. The government calls Witness to testify that he diligently searched through all the records of the jail and found no record of Defendant's having been incarcerated there during the time Defendant specified.

The testimony of Witness is

(A) admissible as evidence of absence of an entry from a public record.
(B) admissible as a summary of voluminous documents.
(C) inadmissible, because it is hearsay not within any exception.
(D) inadmissible, because the records themselves must be produced.

STOP

IF YOU FINISH BEFORE TIME IS CALLED, CHECK YOUR WORK ON THIS TEST.

MBE ANSWER KEY

Subject	test item	key
CONTRACTS	1	B
CRIM LAW	2	D
TORTS	3	B
TORTS	4	A
REAL PROP	5	C
EVIDENCE	6	C
CRIM LAW	7	B
CONST LAW	8	B
CONTRACTS	9	C
REAL PROP	10	D
REAL PROP	11	D
CONST LAW	12	D
EVIDENCE	13	A
TORTS	14	B
CRIM LAW	15	A
REAL PROP	16	B
TORTS	17	D
CONST LAW	18	A
CONTRACTS	19	A
CONTRACTS	20	C
TORTS	21	C
CRIM LAW	22	B
TORTS	23	B
EVIDENCE	24	A
REAL PROP	25	C
EVIDENCE	26	B
CONTRACTS	27	A
CONTRACTS	28	B
CRIM LAW	29	C
CONST LAW	30	A
REAL PROP	31	B
TORTS	32	C
REAL PROP	33	A
CONST LAW	34	C
CRIM LAW	35	C
TORTS	36	C
CONTRACTS	37	A
CONTRACTS	38	A
CONTRACTS	39	B

Subject	#	Answer
EVIDENCE	40	A
TORTS	41	A
REAL PROP	42	D
CONST LAW	43	D
EVIDENCE	44	D
EVIDENCE	45	D
CONST LAW	46	C
CRIM LAW	47	C
REAL PROP	48	C
CONTRACTS	49	A
CONTRACTS	50	B
EVIDENCE	51	B
CRIM LAW	52	B
CONST LAW	53	D
TORTS	54	B
REAL PROP	55	B
CONST LAW	56	B
EVIDENCE	57	B
CONST LAW	58	D
CRIM LAW	59	A
CONTRACTS	60	D
CRIM LAW	61	B
REAL PROP	62	C
CONST LAW	63	C
EVIDENCE	64	C
REAL PROP	65	B
CRIM LAW	66	C
CRIM LAW	67	C
CRIM LAW	68	A
EVIDENCE	69	C
CRIM LAW	70	B
TORTS	71	A
CONTRACTS	72	C
CONTRACTS	73	D
EVIDENCE	74	A
REAL PROP	75	D
CRIM LAW	76	A,B*
EVIDENCE	77	B
EVIDENCE	78	D
CONST LAW	79	B
TORTS	80	C
EVIDENCE	81	B
CONTRACTS	82	C
CONTRACTS	83	A

CONST LAW	84	B
REAL PROP	85	A
TORTS	86	C
REAL PROP	87	A
EVIDENCE	88	B
CONST LAW	89	A
TORTS	90	C
CRIM LAW	91	D
CONST LAW	92	C
CONTRACTS	93	A
TORTS	94	C
EVIDENCE	95	D
CONST LAW	96	C
REAL PROP	97	C
CRIM LAW	98	D
TORTS	99	D
TORTS	100	C
CRIM LAW	101	A
EVIDENCE	102	B
CONTRACTS	103	B
CONTRACTS	104	D
EVIDENCE	105	B
REAL PROP	106	D
CRIM LAW	107	D
TORTS	108	D
CONST LAW	109	B
EVIDENCE	110	D
REAL PROP	111	B
TORTS	112	B
CRIM LAW	113	D
CONST LAW	114	D
CRIM LAW	115	D
CONTRACTS	116	B
EVIDENCE	117	C
TORTS	118	A,C*
REAL PROP	119	A
CONST LAW	120	D
TORTS	121	C
EVIDENCE	122	C
REAL PROP	123	B
CONTRACTS	124	D
CRIM LAW	125	D
CRIM LAW	126	A
CONST LAW	127	C

Subject	#	Answer
TORTS	128	B
CONTRACTS	129	A
CONTRACTS	130	D
REAL PROP	131	D
CRIM LAW	132	B
CRIM LAW	133	A
CONST LAW	134	C
TORTS	135	D
EVIDENCE	136	D
REAL PROP	137	D
CRIM LAW	138	A
CRIM LAW	139	C
TORTS	140	C
CONST LAW	141	A
CONTRACTS	142	D
CONTRACTS	143	C
REAL PROP	144	A
CONTRACTS	145	C
TORTS	146	A
EVIDENCE	147	D
CONST LAW	148	A
TORTS	149	C
REAL PROP	150	A
CONST LAW	151	A
CRIM LAW	152	A
EVIDENCE	153	D
EVIDENCE	154	A
REAL PROP	155	A
CONTRACTS	156	D
CONTRACTS	157	D
EVIDENCE	158	B
REAL PROP	159	C
CONST LAW	160	C
TORTS	161	C
CONST LAW	162	D
REAL PROP	163	D
EVIDENCE	164	A
CONST LAW	165	B
CRIM LAW	166	B
EVIDENCE	167	D
REAL PROP	168	A
CONTRACTS	169	B
CONST LAW	170	B
TORTS	171	C

CONTRACTS	172	B
EVIDENCE	173	D
CONST LAW	174	D
REAL PROP	175	B
CONTRACTS	176	C
TORTS	177	A
CRIM LAW	178	D
EVIDENCE	179	D
CONST LAW	180	A
REAL PROP	181	C
TORTS	182	B
CRIM LAW	183	D
CONTRACTS	184	C
TORTS	185	A
CONST LAW	186	B
REAL PROP	187	B
CRIM LAW	188	C
CONTRACTS	189	B
CONST LAW	190	B
REAL PROP	191	B
TORTS	192	C
EVIDENCE	193	C
CONTRACTS	194	D
TORTS	195	A
REAL PROP	196	A
CRIM LAW	197	D
TORTS	198	D
CONST LAW	199	A
EVIDENCE	200	A

*Immediately following the administration of an MBE, preliminary scoring is conducted to identify any unanticipated item functioning or unusual response patterns. For example, an item might be flagged if a large number of applicants who did well on the test overall selected an option other than the key on that item. Flagged items are then reviewed by the MBE Drafting Committees to assure there are no ambiguities and that they have been keyed correctly. If a content problem is identified, an item may be rekeyed, double-keyed, or eliminated from scoring by having all four options keyed correct. In a typical administration of the MBE, more than one option may be scored as correct on two or three of the 200 items.

Please Note: The explanations that follow are not prepared by the National Conference but are the editorial work of Celebration Bar Review. In some cases, we are unable to explain why the Examiners chose a particular answer over another. Students should use the following explanations as a starting point in their review of the subjects rather than a definitive explanation of any particular choice.

Answer to Question 1

(A) is incorrect because the July 15 agreement was required to be in writing. It involved a sale of goods for more than $500, so the statute of frauds in UCC Article 2 applies.

(B) is the correct answer. The parties may waive performance of an obligation stated in the original contract.

(C) is incorrect because Article 2 does not require consideration for modification of a contract for the sale of goods so long as the modification is in good faith.

(D) is incorrect because proof of a subsequent oral agreement is not barred by the parol evidence rule. Only prior or contemporaneous agreements are covered by the parol evidence rule.

Answer to Question 2

Attempt is an intentional crime. The defendant must intend to commit the crime or at least to do the act he or she is attempting to perform. The defendant need not know the act is criminal so long as he intended to commit the act and it is a crime. If the defendant thinks he is committing a crime but the act he desires to accomplish is not a crime, there is no attempt. If the defendant knows the act is not a crime, there can be no attempt.

(D) is the correct answer because Albert knew the white powder was not cocaine and that no crime was being committed. He did not have the requisite intent to sell cocaine and thus cannot be found guilty of attempt to sell it. Beth, however, is guilty of attempt because her intended act was criminal. Factual impossibility, i.e., the defendant cannot accomplish the intended crime because of facts unknown to her at the time of the act, is not a defense.

Answer to Question 3

The tort of conversion or trespass to chattels is committed when the defendant exercises dominion over the plaintiff's personal property, interfering with the plaintiff's possessory interest in the property. It is irrelevant that the defendant was acting in good faith or intended to return the chattel after using it, so (C) and (D) are incorrect.

Where there has been a conversion of personal property, the remedy is to award the plaintiff actual damages. (A) does not explain how such damages are to be measured, however, so (B) is a better answer. The measure of damages when an item of personal property is completely destroyed as a result of a conversion is the fair market value of the item before the conversion. Here the saw is broken and we are not told that it can be repaired, so (B) is the best answer.

Answer to Question 4

(A) is the correct answer.

(C) is incorrect because the purpose for which the lighter was being used is not relevant. It is the manner in which the lighter was used that must have been foreseeable. Here, the lighter was not even being used when it exploded. Arsonist used the lighter and then put it in his pocket, where it exploded. The same injury could have occurred if he had used the lighter to light a cigarette and then put the lighter in his pocket, or perhaps even if he had not used the lighter.

(D) is incorrect because it is not a defense to a strict liability action that the plaintiff was committing a felony using the defective device.

Answer to Question 5

(A) is incorrect because Patricia took title to the land without knowledge or notice of the trust. She did not agree to accept the duties of a trustee. A trustee or successor trustee must voluntarily agree to perform the duties of a trustee of the trust.

(B) is an incorrect statement of law. A trust affecting land can and should be recorded to give notice to others holding interests in the land.

The correct answer is (C). Patricia was a bona fide purchaser without actual or constructive notice of the trust interest on the property.

(D) is incorrect because the trust and the deed were intended to be part of the same transaction, even though not executed simultaneously. Sue had title at the time of executing the deed and intended to make the transfer to Ted subject to the trust. Ted's ownership in trust need not have been noted on the deed for the trust to be effective. Susan might have had a problem of proof if Ted had asserted absolute ownership of the property, but Ted did not deny the existence of the trust.

Answer to Question 6

(A) is incorrect because there is an exception to the attorney-client privilege for statements made to perpetrate a fraud in the future.

(B) is incorrect because the privilege against self-incrimination protects witnesses from being compelled to answer questions that might tend to incriminate them and protects criminal defendants from being compelled to take the stand. It does not apply to oral or written statements made voluntarily before the investigation began.

(C) is the correct answer. If the purpose of the client's communication to the lawyer is to plan or perpetrate a future crime or fraud, the attorney-client privilege does not arise.

(D) is incorrect. Although the attorney-client privilege belongs to the client and may be waived only by the client, it can and must be claimed by the attorney on the client's behalf unless it has been waived by the client.

Answer to Question 7

(A) is incorrect because it is not necessary to use threats to commit robbery. Robbery is a larceny committed with force or intimidation, and Mel used force, grabbing the briefcase away from the passenger with a struggle and knocking the passenger to the floor. (A) is also incorrect and (C) is incorrect because voluntary intoxication is not a defense to criminal charges generally. The facts do not show that the intoxication negated Mel's ability to form the necessary specific intent to steal.

Mistake of fact may be a defense when it negates the existence of a mental state essential to the crime charged. Robbery is a specific intent crime. If the defendant takes another's property believing that it is his when in fact it is not, he is not guilty of larceny or robbery. Thus, (D) is incorrect.

The correct answer is (B). Mel's mistaken belief that the briefcase was his own property negated the specific intent required, the intent to deprive another of his property.

Answer to Question 8

(A) is incorrect because Mr. and Mrs. Long are the real parties whose interests are at stake here, not their son.

As this statute is generally applicable to all, there are no equal protection concerns that might raise the standard of review to require a compelling state interest. Even though the Longs raise First Amendment free exercise concerns, no constitutional protection exists where the person would violate a criminal statute in exercising his religious rights. In *Employment Division, Dept. of Human Resources of Oregon v. Smith*, 494 U.S. 872 (1990), the Court held that generally applicable, religion-neutral laws that have the effect of burdening a particular religious practice need not be justified by a compelling governmental interest, declining to extend *Sherbert v. Verner,* to "free exercise" claims against neutral criminal laws of general applicability. *Smith* has been applied to claims that autopsies violate certain religious beliefs. See *Yang v. Sturner,* 750 F. Supp. 558 (R.I. 1990). Thus, (C) is incorrect.

(D) is incorrect because a requirement that the statute be substantially related to an important state interest is the intermediate standard that applies to gender-based discrimination, discrimination based on illegitimacy, or forms of speech that are not fully protected by the First Amendment.

(B) is the correct answer. The basic test for whether a statute meets substantive due process standards is whether it is rationally related to a legitimate state purpose. The statute also passes muster under the First Amendment's free exercise clause because it is a generally applicable law not directed at particular religious practices.

Answer to Question 9

(A) is incorrect. When a buyer breaches a contract for the sale of goods governed by UCC Article 2, the seller has several remedies, including reselling the goods to a third party and suing for the difference between the contract price and the resale price, plus any incidental damages such as costs of the sale. However, there is a different measure of damages for anticipatory repudiation by the buyer, as set out in (C). Even using resale price minus contract price as the measure of damages, which nets even here, Ram would probably still recover something, as incidental damages would be allowed.

If the seller intends to resell at a private sale, he must give the buyer notification of such intent.

The correct answer is (C). The measure of damages for repudiation by the buyer is the difference between the market price and the contract price, or the seller's anticipated profit if the market price is less than the contract price. UCC §2-708.

(D) is incorrect. Under Article 2, even where a party intentionally breaches or repudiates the contract, the other party is entitled to recovery only so much as will make him whole (restitution) or give him the benefit of his bargain (expectancy damages).

Answer to Question 10

(A) is incorrect. This recording statute in this jurisdiction is the notice type, so the prior recording of Bank's mortgage did not give it priority over Anna's interest unless Bank lacked notice of Anna's interest.

(B) is incorrect because the easement is not an easement by necessity since Blackacre abuts another public street and thus the easement is not strictly necessary for access to Blackacre.

(C) is incorrect. An easement appurtenant can be extinguished by foreclosure of a prior mortgage on the servient estate.

The correct answer is (D). Although Bank did not have record notice of Anna's prior interest, it was put on inquiry notice by Anna's visible use of the easement.

Answer to Question 11

(D) is the correct answer. Tina may remove all of the items she installed, per the terms of the lease. The terms of the lease govern what items the tenant may remove at the end of the tenancy, regardless of whether the items might otherwise be deemed fixtures or necessary to habitability. Pete knew of the existence of the lease at the time of the conveyance of Homeacre to him, and thus was on inquiry notice of the terms of the lease in this regard.

Answer to Question 12

The fact that alpha is mined only in the state of Blue does not deny alpha producers the equal protection of the law. In the future the mineral might be mined in other states as well, and in that event the tax would apply to them. Furthermore, there does not appear to be any discriminatory intent against alpha producers in the state of Blue. (A) is incorrect.

Congress may have the power to protect and advance interstate industries, but it does not have an affirmative duty to do so. (B) is incorrect.

The term "navigable waters" operates in statutes like the Clean Water Act as shorthand for "waters over which federal authority may properly be asserted." However, the tax will have only an indirect effect on rivers and streams that is not related to their navigability. The tax cannot be justified as a means of exercising federal authority over navigable waters when that is not its purpose.

The correct answer is (D). The tax can be justified under the plenary taxing power and it does not run afoul of any constitutional prohibitions on Congressional power.

Answer to Question 13

(A) is the correct answer. Fed. Rule 608(b) permits inquiry on cross-examination into specific instances of conduct involving honesty or dishonesty of the witness. No extrinsic evidence is permitted under this rule, so (B) is incorrect.

(C) is incorrect. When a witness's prior statement deals with a collateral matter, extrinsic evidence will not be admitted on the collateral matter; the examiner must take the witness's answer on cross-examination. Expert's divorce case is not merely a collateral issue; it is completely irrelevant to the present case.

(D) is incorrect because Expert's credibility is always relevant to his testimony on the stand. Expert's character for truthfulness may be attacked on cross-examination by reference to specific prior acts, although extrinsic evidence thereof is not permitted.

Answer to Question 14

(A) is incorrect because it goes to the reasonableness of John's conduct but this is not a negligence action. The fact that John could have shouted a warning is not relevant to Karen's recovery for battery.

The correct answer is (B). John's best argument is that he had a privilege to attempt to rescue Karen. This privilege could not be invoked, however, if Karen was not in danger and John should have realized it.

(C) is incorrect because Karen can sue John even if she could also sue the driver of the car. The driver of the car, by placing Karen in danger, may be held liable for injuries caused by John while attempting to rescue her, but Karen may choose to sue John for those injuries directly.

(D) is incorrect because John's motive is irrelevant, so long as he intended to touch Karen in a way that would be harmful or offensive and was not privileged. A hard push is a battery even if done for a benevolent motive.

Answer to Question 15

Joe has committed larceny, not merely an attempt to commit larceny, so (A) is correct and (B) and (D) are incorrect. We are told that Joe had intent to steal. Joe has committed a trespassory taking against one rightfully in possession, but it is a close question whether there has been asportation or carrying away since Joe only picked the watch up and did not put it in his pocket. Since asportation is a technical requirement that can be satisfied by a very slight movement, the better answer is that this requirement has been met. It is irrelevant that Marty intended to give him the watch; a gift is not complete until delivered, so at the moment Joe decided to steal the watch and picked it up, the watch was still Marty's, not Joe's.

Embezzlement is conversion after the defendant obtained lawful possession. Since Joe took the watch and intended to steal it before Marty actually made the gift, Joe was not in lawful possession when he picked up the watch, and thus (C) is incorrect.

Answer to Question 16

Nominal consideration is valid consideration, and the deed also recites "other good and valuable consideration." "Good consideration" is generally interpreted as love and affection. No consideration would have been necessary for Grant to make a valid transfer to Bonnie if he had good title to the property, and the deed is not void for citing nominal consideration, which Bonnie paid. (A) is incorrect.

The correct answer is (B). The deed was actually stolen from Olivia since Grant took it before Olivia intended to deliver it to him. The recording acts do not protect fraudulent transactions. Although Grant has now met Olivia's conditions, the deed must first be properly delivered by Olivia to Grant, so (C) is incorrect.

This jurisdiction has a notice-type recording statute. Bonnie did not have actual or constructive notice of the problem with the deed, so recording should protect her if she is deemed a bona fide purchaser. It is questionable whether Bonnie was a BFP, however. She did not intend to purchase the property; it was essentially a gift from Grant. Although consideration is not necessary for property to be transferred by deed, the recording act in most states does not protect donees. The consideration paid need not equal the value of the land, but it must be more than nominal consideration for the recording act to protect the purchaser.

Answer to Question 17

Participating in an impromptu basketball game, knowing that the game will be rough, constitutes an implied assumption of the risk by Perry. Assumption of the risk bars a plaintiff's recovery unless the defendant intentionally used force that exceeded the players' consent. (D) is thus the best answer.

(A) is the wrong choice because intentional touching with the elbow was within the players' implied consent in this game.

(B) is incorrect because what would otherwise be a battery may be comprehended within Perry's implied consent.

(C) is not the best choice because it does not state the exception to the rule. (D) is a more complete statement of the applicable law.

Answer to Question 18

The correct answer is (A). Voluntary "affirmative action" programs which attempt to promote racial equality without a showing of past discriminatory intent were struck down in *United Steel Workers of America v. Weber*, 443 U.S. 193 (1979) and the *University of California Regents v. Bakke*, 438 U.S. 265 (1978), because the effect is to deny equal protection of the laws to those who have not been unfairly advantaged in the past.

(B) is incorrect because potential employees and contractors do not have existing contract rights that would be impaired by this action.

(C) is incorrect because racial minority groups are adequately assured of equal protection by not being discriminated against in ongoing practices; racial quotas are not appropriate except to correct the lingering effects of a prior history of discrimination.

(D) is incorrect because municipal water districts are treated as state actors for purposes of the Fourteenth Amendment. See *Saboff v. St. John's River Water Management District*, 200 F.3d 1356 (11th Cir. 2000); *Smith v. Salt River Project*, 109 F.3d 586 (9th Cir. 1997).

Answer to Question 19

(A) is the correct answer. The contract is not divisible; under its express terms, Painter must complete work on all three barns to receive any payment.

Because the contract is indivisible, Painter had no right to demand payment after painting the first or second barns so there could be no waiver of such right, and (B) is incorrect.

(C) is factually incorrect; it is not a divisible contract since it does not call for payment of $2,000 after each of the barns is completed.

(D) is incorrect. Not having painted an entire barn leaves Painter far short of substantial performance. This is a significant part of the performance that Farmer contracted for.

Answer to Question 20

Even where the contract is not divisible and the breaching party has not substantially performed, the breaching party may recover the reasonable value of his actual performance so (A) is incorrect.

(B) is incorrect because Painter would be entitled to his profit or expectancy damages only if he were not in breach.

The correct answer is (C). Painter is entitled to the reasonable value of his services minus Farmer's damages for Painter's failure to paint the third barn, such as any increased cost of another painter.

(D) is incorrect. This is not a case of unjust enrichment. The parties bargained for Farmer to receive the increased value of painted barns. Painter can be made whole by receiving payment for his services.

Answer to Question 21

False imprisonment is an intentional tort. If the defendant intentionally confined the plaintiff without her consent, the tort of false imprisonment has been committed, regardless of whether the defendant had a reasonable belief that he was privileged to do so. (A) is incorrect. Owner would have had a defense if making a lawful arrest, but since it was in fact unlawful, Owner has no defense. There can usually be no liability for false imprisonment unless the person confined is aware of her confinement. So, if Traveler reasonably believed she could not leave the Owner's gas station, then she may have an action. Therefore (C) is correct.

The nature of false imprisonment lies in the confinement of the plaintiff, not in physical or mental harm, so (B) is incorrect.

Answer to Question 22

Ignorance or mistake of fact is a defense when it negates the existence of a mental state essential to the crime charged. (A) is incorrect because the alcoholic beverage sale law creates a strict liability offense; Defendant's mistake of fact creating lack of knowledge or intent does not negate the crime.

Statutory rape is also a strict liability offense, so (C) is incorrect for the same reason.

Mistake of law is not a defense to a general intent crime, but may negate specific intent. Erroneous advice from a private attorney regarding the law does not give Defendant a mistake of law defense, however, so (D) is incorrect.

The correct answer is (B). Defendant had a right to use nondeadly force to resist an unlawful arrest. Even if he did not know this was an attempted arrest by a police officer, Defendant had a right to use reasonable force to repel what appeared to be an attack on him. Unless the amount of force Defendant used was unreasonable under the circumstances, he has a defense to the crime of assault.

Answer to Question 23

The defendant in a strict liability failure-to-warn case is required to warn only of dangers that were known or reasonably should have been known to the defendant at the time of delivering the product. (A) is incorrect because today's technology is not relevant where the failure to warn occurred decades ago.

(B) is correct because the standard to which the defendant should be held is a question of law for the court. This standard is relevant even if the defendant argues that the state of the art was such that most manufacturers did not know of the danger because a duty to warn may be imposed even where the defendant cannot be charged with knowledge of the risk, so long as the risk was reasonably discoverable.

(C) is incorrect because, although this is a relevant question, the issue of whether the defendant should have known of the risks of asbestos at that point in time is a fact issue that would go to the jury.

(D) is incorrect because, although the danger posed by the insulation materials is relevant to the application of strict liability and the duty to warn, it is a fact question that should be posed to the jury. Asbestos itself may be deemed an obvious danger of which there is no duty to warn, but the extent to which these insulation materials posed an actual risk to the plaintiff as a result of their asbestos content would be a fact question for the jury.

Answer to Question 24

(A) is the correct answer. The evidence of Davidson's bank deposits is admissible as circumstantial evidence of his embezzlement since the amount appears inconsistent with his income.

Evidence of the bank deposits is admissible substantively, not merely to impeach Davidson, so (B) is not the best choice.

(C) is incorrect because the probative value of this evidence in an embezzlement case is clear. The probative value should outweigh any prejudicial effect.

The fact that the deposits could have come from legitimate sources does not affect the admissibility of this evidence. The jury may consider various possible explanations and rule on this issue of fact. (D) is thus incorrect.

Answer to Question 25

Obtaining title by adverse possession requires that the possession be hostile or adverse, i.e., with the owner's knowledge but without the owner's consent. In this case, Alex's possession was never hostile to Angela, since he had been living in the house with Angela's knowledge and consent since before he and Betty took title from Angela. If possession commences in a permissive manner, it does not become adverse until there is explicit notification that the possession is henceforth adverse. Alex's possession continued in the same manner after Angela's death, presumably with Betty's consent unless she made her objections known. Even if Betty had objected after Angela's death, this period has lasted only 7 years. Thus, Alex has not acquired sole title by adverse possession against Betty, and (A) is incorrect.

A cotenant has the right to seek involuntary partition by court action. Where one tenant pays more than his share of costs of maintaining the property, he is generally entitled to contribution from the other cotenant(s). Although Alex is not liable to Betty for the fair rental value of his own use and occupancy of the property, he is liable to account for rental payments received from other tenants, as well as the property expenses he paid from such income from the property. The correct answer is (C). The court should grant Betty's request for partition as a matter of right and require an accounting of the income and expenses on the property during Alex's management.

(B) is incorrect because it does not allow the partition.

(D) is incorrect because it does not allow the accounting.

Answer to Question 26

A witness's prior inconsistent statements are admissible to impeach his credibility, but they are not admissible substantively unless given under oath. If the prior statement by Witness had been made under oath, it would be admissible substantively as non-hearsay under the Federal Rules of Evidence. (A) is thus incorrect. The tape recording is not admissible substantively because it was not made under oath.

The correct answer is (B). Prior inconsistent statements are not hearsay when offered only to impeach credibility.

(C) is incorrect because this is a prior inconsistent statement by the witness. Although out-of-court statements by the witness on the stand are hearsay generally, prior inconsistent statements are not hearsay if offered only to impeach credibility or if made under oath.

(D) is incorrect. Absent a statute penalizing unauthorized tape recordings, there is no exclusionary rule for recordings made by private parties without state action.

Answer to Question 27

The rule at common law is that an offer remains in effect for the stated length of time or for a reasonable time, but the offeror retains the power to revoke the offer at any time, even if the offer states that it will be held open for a specified period of time, unless there was consideration for holding the offer open. If the offeror is a merchant, however, UCC §2-205 provides that the offer is irrevocable if the merchant makes an assurance in a signed writing that the offer will not be revoked, but the period of irrevocability under this section cannot exceed 90 days.

(A) is the correct answer. Stationer's offer became revocable because the period of irrevocability under Article 2 expired, and there was no consideration to make the offer irrevocable longer under the common law rule. However, Stationer's offer did not expire automatically at the end of 90 days, so (C) is incorrect. The offer remained in effect for its stated period of one year under common law rules, but Stationer had the power to revoke it after the 90 days expired.

There was no consideration to make the offer an irrevocable option contract, so (B) is incorrect.

(D) is incorrect because Stationer's offer stated a period of time that it would be held open. Where the offer states a period, under the common law it remains open for that period unless earlier revoked. Lawyer would have a reasonable time to accept if the offer had not stated a definite period.

Answer to Question 28

(A) is factually incorrect. Lawyer has not relied on Stationer's promise to his detriment, so there is no basis for promissory estoppel.

The correct answer is (B). Because Stationer is a merchant, the UCC's irrevocable offer rule applies. Stationer made an assurance in a signed writing that the offer would be held open for one year; this assurance is enforceable without consideration for 90 days. Thus, the offer made in December was still irrevocable in February.

(C) would be correct under common law rules, but the Code's irrevocable offer rule applies because Stationer is a merchant. The irrevocable offer rule requires a signed writing to hold the offer open for 90 days, but not consideration.

(D) is incorrect. Stationer's offer stating that it would be held open for longer than three months does not automatically terminate upon the expiration of the Code's 90 days. After that point, the common law rules apply, and the offer may remain open for its stated period, for a reasonable period, or until revoked.

Answer to Question 29

(A) is incorrect. The fact that officers periodically visit all motor vehicle junkyards in town means that they are not exercising "unbridled discretion" to single out particular proprietors.

(B) is incorrect because this argument would be a substantive due process challenge to the statute. The court is unlikely to find that the stated legislative purpose is a "pretext" to circumvent the warrant requirement where there is a substantial government interest in the regulatory scheme pursuant to which the inspection is made. See *New York v. Burger, infra.*

(C) is the correct answer. *In New York v. Burger,* 479 U.S. 812 (1987), the Court held that a warrantless search of an automobile junkyard pursuant to a state statute fell within the warrant exception for administrative inspections of pervasively regulated industries even though the purpose of the statute was not merely to aid in the discovery of regulatory violations but also to aid in the discovery of stolen property.

(D) is incorrect because it is too broad a statement of the rule of law. The administrative search exception applies to highly regulated industries, not to all commercial establishments.

Answer to Question 30

The correct answer is (A). Congress cannot use the commerce power to force states to regulate. *New York v. U.S.,* 505 U.S. 1041 (1992). Congress can encourage the states to regulate by use of the spending power, but cannot directly require them to regulate.

A federal law prohibiting possession of firearms in school zones was held to exceed Congress' Commerce Clause authority in *United States v. Lopez,* 514 U.S. 549 (1995), because possession of a gun in a local school zone in itself was found in no sense an economic activity that might, through repetition elsewhere, have a substantial effect on interstate commerce, and the statute did not impose any requirement of a finding on a case-by-case basis that the firearms in question had a nexus with interstate commerce. The statute in question does require an inquiry into the nexus of the controlled substance with interstate commerce, which might make it sustainable under *Lopez,* so (B) is incorrect, but the fact that the federal commerce power might extend to this situation does not give Congress the authority to force the states to enact such legislation, and thus (C) is also incorrect.

(D) is incorrect because Congress only possesses power to spend, not regulate, under the general welfare clause. The congressional commerce power does not extend to requiring states to legislate.

Answer to Question 31

While the statements in (A) are generally true, the obligations of ABC toward the public in general would not necessarily justify its action against Janet as a licensee.

The correct answer is (B). Janet's ticket gives her a license to enter Central Arena. A license is a right granted by the owner of property permitting the license holder to enter and/or use the owner's land for a particular purpose. A license is revocable if the licensee violates the terms of admission to the licensor's facilities.

Thus, (C) is incorrect. Because Janet paid value, her right cannot be unreasonably revoked, but ABC acted reasonably in giving Janet warnings and offering to refund the unused value of her ticket.

ABC need not and could not show that Janet is committing a nuisance by her actions on ABC's property. A nuisance is created by the defendant's use of his own property in a way that interferes with the plaintiff's use of his property. It is not an ambulatory tort. (D) is incorrect.

Answer to Question 32

(A) is incorrect. Engineer's signature on the blueprint submitted to DEP would make Engineer liable to Company for defects in the design, and might subject Engineer to sanctions from the state for any regulatory violations. It does not make Engineer liable to Plaintiff, however, absent a duty to Plaintiff.

The correct answer is (C). Engineer owed no duty to Plaintiff with respect to harm from other parts of the plant that were unrelated to the filter system designed by Engineer.

(D) is incorrect because regardless of whether Engineer was an employee or an independent contractor with respect to Company, Engineer could be sued for her design of a defective filter system. If she were an independent contractor, Plaintiff could only sue Engineer unless Company had a nondelegable duty. In any event, the issue here is whether Engineer can be held liable for a defect for which she was not directly responsible. Being an employee would not make her liable for the actions of other employees of Company.

Answer to Question 33

The correct answer is (A). Bart's conveyance to Pam "subject to" the mortgage, without an assumption of the mortgage by Pam, leaves Bart solely liable on the mortgage note. Mort has no action against Pam.

Bart's deed to Pam may have violated the due-on-sale clause, but Mort did not exercise its option to make the entire principal balance immediately due and payable. By accepting mortgage payments from Pam, Mort waived its right to accelerate the loan. Furthermore, if Mort exercised the due-on-sale clause, the entire remaining principal balance would have been due from Bart; Mort would not have a right to collect delinquent monthly payments from Pam. Thus, (C) is incorrect.

Pam is not in direct privity of estate with Mort here; however, Mort acquires a right to sue as a third-party beneficiary so (B) and (D) are both incorrect.

Answer to Question 34

(A) is incorrect because it is not enough that the court have jurisdiction over the subject matter of the litigation. The issues must be raised in the context of an actual case or controversy brought by a party or parties with a direct and substantial interest in the outcome, which is lacking here.

(B) is incorrect because, while the fact that the parties seek real injunctive relief indicates that the court is not merely being asked for an advisory opinion, the relief sought is not sufficient in itself to give the plaintiffs standing.

The correct answer is (C). These plaintiffs do not have standing to challenge the statute because they have not alleged any real or potential harm to themselves specifically. They do not currently trade in the stock market, nor do they intend to do so. Their interest is purely academic.

(D) is incorrect as a matter of law. The mere existence of a criminal statute is generally insufficient to satisfy the case or controversy requirement. *Poe v. Ullman*, 367 U.S. 497 (1961). However, if the complaint seeks a declaration that a statute is unconstitutional and no state prosecution is pending, then the federal court may hear the claim, if there is a "real threat" of prosecution under the statute. This is an issue of ripeness; there must either be a substantial likelihood that the government will soon prosecute under the statute or some way in which the existence of the statute presently interferes with the plaintiff's rights.

Answer to Question 35

Rachel has not committed forgery, which requires the creation of a false document with intent to defraud as to a fact or transaction of legal significance. Thus, (A) and (B) are incorrect.

(C) is the correct answer. Rachel took actions in creating the letter with intent to deceive a purchaser as to the provenance of the letter, thus committing the crime of false pretenses. Although she made no express warranty of authenticity, she intended her actions in creating the likeness of a letter from Thomas Jefferson to deceive a purchaser as to the nature and source of the document. Thus, both (B) and (D) are incorrect.

Answer to Question 36

(A) is incorrect because it does not completely state the basis for Hospital's liability here. The fact that Mom was an invitee does not mean Hospital was strictly liable for any injuries she might incur on the property. There must have been some further oversight by Hospital.

(D) is incorrect because it is untrue that the hospital owed Mom no affirmative duty of care. The owner or possessor of real property owes a business or public invitee a duty to protect the invitee against known defects and those which the invitor could have discovered with the exercise of reasonable care. Even though Child was the person needed Hospital's services, Hospital's duty to invitees extended to Mom, who accompanied Child.

The correct answer is (C). Hospital owed Mom a duty of reasonable care.

Answer to Question 37

(A) is the correct answer. A conditional promise is not illusory so long as the condition is not an act that is totally within the promisor's discretion and the promisor does not know that the condition cannot occur.

(B) is incorrect because a court will not enforce as a bilateral contract an agreement that lacks consideration. This requirement cannot be waived.

(C) is incorrect because there was consideration for Shareholder's promise in Buyer's conditional promise, and thus there was mutuality of consideration.

(D) is incorrect because there is no statute of frauds requirement for this agreement to be in writing, and if there were, it would not be necessary for a preliminary condition to the enforceability of the contract to be in writing.

Answer to Question 38

The correct answer is (A). The condition has been waived by Buyer's failure to request Conglomerate's approval while proceeding as if Buyer intended to perform the contract. Conglomerate has indicated it had no objections to the sale, thus waiving its own approval requirement. Because the express condition has been waived, (C) is incorrect.

(B) is incorrect because Shareholder did not do anything to justify a belief by Buyer that the sale would go through without Conglomerate's approval.

(D) is incorrect. Obtaining the parent company's approval was not legally within Buyer's control.

Answer to Question 39

Where there is a condition precedent, the evidence of its existence is neither admitted as proof of a collateral agreement nor excluded on the ground that the parties' written agreement was a complete integration. (A) and (C) are incorrect.

(B) is the correct answer. A condition precedent to the existence of a contract may be shown by parol evidence. The condition does not change the terms of the agreement, but merely shows that the agreement would have no binding effect unless the condition occurred.

(D) is incorrect. Parol evidence is always admissible to show that no contract was in fact made, or that the terms are not enforceable.

Answer to Question 40

The correct answer is (A). The police tape qualifies under the recorded recollection exception to the hearsay rule. A witness who takes the stand may testify that he made an out-of-court statement that was recorded when his memory was fresh but he currently does not have independent memory of the contents of the recording.

(B) is incorrect because the tape is not a public record. It is not a record made by a public official or filed with a public agency according to law.

(C) is incorrect because there is an available hearsay exception, the recorded recollection exception.

(D) is incorrect because Mrs. Wong need not have had first-hand knowledge of the license plate number in order for the recorded recollection exception to apply. Two or more persons may have cooperated in the recording of the statement, such as by the observer relaying information to a recorder, so long as each testifies as to his or her part in making the record.

Answer to Question 41

(A) is the correct answer. A substantial and unreasonable interference with the use and enjoyment of neighboring property constitutes an actionable tort. The plaintiff's intent to affect the defendant's property is irrelevant, so (B) is incorrect.

The plaintiff is not entitled to deprive the defendant of potential uses of his property, regardless of whether the defendant actually makes such use of the property, so (C) is incorrect.

(D) is incorrect because compliance with all applicable laws would not be a defense if Neighbor in fact were causing a substantial interference with the use and enjoyment of Vacationer's property.

Answer to Question 42

The correct answer is (D). The judgment lien statute specifies that the lien is effective when filed against property "then owned" by the person against whom the judgment is rendered. Corp did not own Blackacre when George obtained his judgment, due to the prior conveyance to Barbara. Her recordation of the deed was not necessary to effect the transfer of title from Corp, so (A) and (C) are incorrect.

(B) is incorrect because a potential threat of litigation would not be sufficient to excuse Polly from performing the contract to purchase Blackacre when Barbara can convey good title to the property.

Answer to Question 43

The correct answer is (D). In *City of Cincinnati v. Discovery Network, Inc.*, 507 U.S. 410 (1993), the Court struck down a city ordinance that prohibited news racks that displayed "commercial handbills," but did not prohibit news racks that displayed newspapers or magazines, on the basis that there was no "reasonable" relationship between the ordinance and the city's legitimate interests in maintaining clean streets.

(A) is incorrect because a rational relationship to a legitimate state goal is not the standard for regulation of commercial speech under *Central Hudson Gas v. Public Service Commission*, 447 U.S. 557 (1980). The four-part *Central Hudson* test requires that the regulation directly advance the state's legitimate interest and be no broader than necessary to do so.

(B) is incorrect because the state interest in regulating commercial speech need not be "compelling."

(C) is incorrect because the regulation need not be the "least" restrictive means of furthering the state's interest.

Answer to Question 44

(A) is incorrect because a party-opponent is traditionally bound by the statements of an agent only if the agent had authority to make a statement on that subject on behalf of the principal. It is unlikely that Guard was authorized to speak about Defendant's instructions on the apprehension of shoplifters. The Federal Rules are broader, however, permitting vicarious admissions regarding the employment, provided the agent is still working for the employer at the time of making the statement. Guard was not still working for Defendant at the time of making this statement, so the statement is not a vicarious admission of Defendant's.

(B) is incorrect. The security director's instruction is not hearsay if offered to prove the effect on Guard, the listener. In a criminal case, however, it is irrelevant that Guard thought he was under instructions to kill if necessary. Such instructions would not justify Guard's action. Furthermore, there is a double hearsay problem here; there must be a basis for the admission of Guard's statement as well as the security director's.

(C) is incorrect because the former testimony exception applies only when the parties in the two actions are the same so that the party against whom the evidence is now offered had a chance to cross-examine the declarant in the former proceeding. Identical parties are not present here. Defendant Stores would not have been able to cross-examine the Guard at his criminal trial. Furthermore, there is another level of hearsay here that is not subject to the former testimony exception.

The correct answer is (D). It's double hearsay and neither level fits within a hearsay exception..

Answer to Question 45

The problem here is one of double hearsay. Mr. Pence's statement as well as Duarte's must be examined under the hearsay rules.

(B) is incorrect because it does not explain how Mr. Pence's statement could be admitted, even if Duarte's assertion is admissible to show his state of mind (intent) at the time.

(C) is incorrect because it does not explain how Mr. Pence's statement could be admitted, even if Duarte's statement is an admission of a party-opponent.

(D) is the correct answer. Mrs. Pence's statement concerns double hearsay. Even though there may be rules permitting the admission of Duarte's statement, Mrs. Pence's testimony is inadmissible unless there is also an exception or exclusion from the operation of the hearsay rule for her husband's statement to her. Her husband's statement does not fall within any hearsay exceptions. It is not a dying declaration since he relayed Duarte's statement the day before he was shot.

Answer to Question 46

The correct answer is (C).

Answer to Question 47

(A) is incorrect because racially-based peremptory challenges are impermissible even if those potential jurors who are stricken are not of the same race as the defendant. *Powers v. Ohio,* 499 U.S. 400 (1991).

(B) is incorrect because exclusion of nonwhites from the jury constitutes a *per se* denial of an impartial jury regardless of Nora's race, and probably also acted to prejudice the trial as a matter of fact in this case.

The correct answer is (C). The Equal Protection Clause bars racial discrimination in the selection of juries. The Fourteenth Amendment to the United States Constitution prohibits both the defendant and the prosecutor from exercising peremptory challenges based solely on race.

Answer to Question 48

The Rule Against Perpetuities applies to all non-reversionary future interests, including powers of appointment, so (B) is incorrect.

(C) is the correct answer. Alice's "entire estate" could be deemed to include the power of appointment and her gift of the entire estate to Marie would be the exercise of the power.

(D) is incorrect because Alice's intent not to benefit Charles does not automatically mean that Marie can take under the power of appointment.

Answer to Question 49

(A) is the correct answer. Glazier conferred a benefit on Landlord without intending a gift, for which Glazier rightfully should be compensated.

(B) is incorrect because Landlord had made no promises to Glazier upon which Glazier relied to his detriment.

(C) is incorrect. An implied in fact contract exists where the parties' dealings with each other show intent to contract, even though there is no express agreement. Landlord and Glazier had had no dealings from which a contract might be implied.

(D) is incorrect. Glazier was not an intended beneficiary of the Tenant-Landlord lease. His involvement with the property was not expressly contemplated at the time Tenant and Landlord entered into the lease contract. Neither Tenant nor Landlord owed Glazier any payments at the time of making the contract, and extinguishing such debt was not the purpose of the lease.

Answer to Question 50

If the drawer of a check writes "in full satisfaction" of a particular obligation on the check, there is an offer of an accord and satisfaction as to the compromise amount. Cashing the check will likely bind the payee who endorsed the check, regardless of whether he noticed the endorsement or wrote a reservation-of-rights notation on the check before cashing it. (A) and (D) are incorrect.

Consideration for an accord can be found only if there a bona fide dispute as to the amount owed. (B) is correct and (C) is incorrect because there was no dispute as to the amount Tenant owed to Glazier.

Answer to Question 51

(A) is incorrect because Defendant's statement was not a present sense impression, which means a statement about something the declarant is observing at the time. Defendant's statement of intent to spend the next three days in State B was not an observation of a present event.

(B) is the correct answer. Defendant's statement of intent to spend the next three days in State B falls within the then-existing state of mind exception to the hearsay rule. Because there is an applicable hearsay exception, (D) is incorrect.

(C) is incorrect because it is not improper for the defendant to establish an alibi with her own statements made before the alleged crime.

Answer to Question 52

The correct answer is (B). Both proposals are constitutional.

Proposal A is constitutional because the Due Process Clause does not bar states from making changes in their substantive criminal law that have the effect of making it easier for the prosecution to obtain convictions. There is no "due process" right to have evidence of intoxication taken into consideration, for instance, and a state may exclude evidence of the defendant's intoxicated condition in determining the existence of a mental state that is an element of the offense. *Montana v. Egelhoff,* 518 U.S. 37 (1996). The same principle would permit a state to exclude evidence of insanity.

Proposal B is constitutional because a state may presume that the defendant is competent and require him to prove incompetency by a preponderance of the evidence, *Medina v. California,* 505 U.S. 47 (1992). The state may not, however, require that the defendant prove his incompetency by the higher standard of clear and convincing evidence. *Cooper v. Oklahoma,* 517 U.S. 348 (1996).

Answer to Question 53

(A) is incorrect. This is not an inherently political question because it does not deal with the internal governance or constitutionally committed powers of any branch of the government.

(B) is incorrect. Congress may vest substantial discretion in the President and his subordinates regarding the manner in which laws are executed and money is spent. Such delegation of power is constitutionally permissible unless there are absolutely no standards specified for its exercise, which is not the case here.

(C) is incorrect because the Congressional power to spend for the general welfare is broad. It is not limited to the enumerated powers of Congress and is limited only by the specific prohibition against establishment of religion in the First Amendment.

The correct answer is (D). The essay contest is reasonably related to the general welfare, the statute states concrete objects and provides adequate criteria for conducting the essay contest and awarding the prize money.

Answer to Question 54

This is not a comparative negligence jurisdiction, so (A) is incorrect. Fran could recover if she were 49% at fault in a comparative negligence jurisdiction, but not in a contributory negligence jurisdiction.

In a contributory negligence jurisdiction, the plaintiff's contributory negligence in any degree generally constitutes a complete bar to her recovery. However, most states mitigate the harshness of this result by allowing the plaintiff to recover despite her own negligence if she can establish that the defendant had the last clear chance to avoid causing the plaintiff's injury. Thus, (B), which takes last clear chance into consideration, is a better answer than (C), which would apply the strict contributory negligence doctrine.

(D) is incorrect because assumption of the risk is inapplicable. Fran did not know of or consent to Sid's active negligence in speeding as well.

Answer to Question 55

(A) is incorrect because there was no common scheme here. There are a number of factors in determining a common scheme, but it is significant that Sal conveyed only one lot with the restriction in the deed and there are apparently no development plans showing such a restriction.

(B) is the correct answer. Peter can enforce the restriction against Betty because the restriction was imposed on the land that Sal retained when he conveyed to Peter. This is not a common scheme but a case of reliance. A restriction can be enforced where the grantor indicates that the land will be restricted according to a common plan and the purchaser relies on this representation. See *Stewart Transp. Co. v. Ashe,* 269 Md. 74, 304 A.2d 788 (1973). Only Peter, not the other purchasers, relied on Sal's representation about the restriction.

The usual method of enforcement of a common scheme is by injunctive relief. Money damages may be available where injunctive relief is denied based on a balancing of the interests. Since Betty has only begun construction, equitable relief would probably be available if the common scheme is deemed enforceable. Thus, (C) is not the best answer.

(D) is incorrect because zoning does not preempt private covenants that would impose more restrictive requirements than are allowed under the applicable zoning ordinance.

Answer to Question 56

(A) is incorrect because this argument is based solely on substantive due process, which is not likely to be a winning argument for the taxicab owners. The state need not adopt a solution to all aspects of the problem at once, and the ordinance in question may be a rational way to address part of the congestion problem. While the taxicab owners should probably raise the substantive due process argument, it is not the most likely basis for a judgment in their favor.

The correct answer is (B). This is a stronger basis for judgment for the Scarlettville taxicab owners. The Court will permit a considerable amount of state regulation if there is a valid reason for the state's regulation, and that regulation is as burdensome on local residents as it is on out-of-state business. However, laws which favor local businesses or economic interests on their face or in their application, or discriminate against out-of-state interests, are likely to be held unconstitutional no matter what the state justification may be.

(C) is incorrect because the fact that the ordinance discriminates against other counties of Green does not mean it does not also discriminate against interstate commerce.

(D) is incorrect because substantive due process is not the most likely basis for the disposition of this action since there are commerce clause concerns.

Answer to Question 57

Whether Joan had actual or apparent authority to accept the offer on Donna's behalf is ultimately a fact question that should go to the jury, so (A) is incorrect. The court needs only to find sufficient evidence to support such a finding by the jury and then can allow the statement in under the rule for admissions by a person authorized by a party-opponent to make statements on the subject. (B) is the correct answer.

An admission by a party-opponent or his authorized agent is admissible even if the declarant is available, so (C) is incorrect.

An admission by a party-opponent or his authorized agent is treated as non-hearsay under the Federal Rules, so (D) is incorrect.

Answer to Question 58

(A) is incorrect because John's due process rights would protect him from the revocation of his own license without notice and a hearing, but not every government action that might adversely affect his income from the licensed activity is protected by procedural due process.

(B) is incorrect. The issue is John's right to a hearing on a competitor's license. Since he does not have such a right, he cannot challenge the officials' exercise of discretion.

(C) is incorrect because it is too broad a statement of the power of the licensing authorities. John may challenge certain actions that directly affect his right to use his own license.

The correct answer is (D). John's license gives him a property right in continuing to make a living through the use of his license but does not give him a property interest in a certain level of income or in freedom from competition by other licensees.

Answer to Question 59

The correct answer is (A). Augie is guilty of both murder and arson, as charged.

Augie could be found guilty of involuntary manslaughter because his conduct amounted to criminal negligence at least. However, Augie should be convicted of murder rather than merely manslaughter because his act of running into the gasoline pumps shows intent to do great bodily harm, or wanton and willful disregard of an unreasonable human risk.

Furthermore, Augie is guilty of arson because the building that burned was Homer's dwelling, as required at common law, and Augie had the required intent, at least reckless disregard for Homer's safety.

Answer to Question 60

(A) is not the best defense for Vendor because Vendor's June 2 telegram would probably be found to be an offer under the facts of this case. It was an answer to an inquiry from Bye Bye, and the communication went only to Bye Bye. Under these circumstances, the language could be found to constitute an offer without the express use of that term.

(B) is not the best defense because under Article 2, a definite and seasonable expression of acceptance operates as an acceptance even though it states different terms from the offer, unless acceptance is expressly made conditional on assent to the new terms. Bye Bye's letter was clearly an acceptance.

Article 2 of the UCC has changed the traditional rule that an acceptance must be by the same means by which the offer was made. Under Article 2, an acceptance can be by any medium reasonable under the circumstances. Thus, (C) is incorrect.

(D) is the correct answer. Anticipatory repudiation must be clear and unequivocal. Although it may be a fact issue whether Bye Bye's letter was a repudiation, it is Vendor's best argument.

Answer to Question 61

Diane cannot be convicted of first-degree murder because playing Russian roulette is not considered intentional and premeditated murder. Furthermore, Diane did not commit the killing during the felony of assault with a deadly weapon because she neither attempted to commit a battery on Victor nor intended to cause apprehension of receiving an immediate battery. (A) is incorrect.

The correct answer is (B). Diane's act in pulling the trigger posed a great threat of serious bodily harm to Victor. There was a greater likelihood of such harm than would be posed by mere negligence or recklessness, so (C) is incorrect.

(D) is incorrect because the assumption of the risk doctrine does not extend to criminal acts.

Answer to Question 62

The correct answer is (C). Although the Statute of Frauds requires contracts for the conveyance of land to be in writing to be enforceable, specific performance may be awarded on the ground of part performance where the parties' actions are sufficient to demonstrate that they actually entered an agreement to convey the land. Betty has met the usual requirements for such a showing: she made a down payment, occupied the property and made improvements to it as if she were the owner. These facts take the oral agreement out of the Statute of Frauds, so (A) is incorrect.

The arrangement thus became a purchase contract rather than a mere tenancy, so (B) is incorrect. There is no exception to the Statute of Frauds for agreements between landlords and tenants in possession for purchase of the property, so (D) is incorrect.

Answer to Question 63

(A) is incorrect because the First Amendment by its own terms applies only to federal government encroachment. Freedom of association, including the right of individuals to associate for the advancement of political beliefs, is protected against infringement by the states through the Fourteenth Amendment.

(B) is incorrect. The Thirteenth Amendment outlaws slavery or involuntary servitude, except as punishment for a crime. While Congress may have discretion in determining what kind of protective legislation to enact pursuant to the Thirteenth Amendment, it appears that the amendment's independent scope is limited to the eradication of the incidents or badges of slavery and does not reach other acts of discrimination. See *The Civil Rights Cases*, 109 U.S. 3, 23-25 (1883). In the realm of voting, the Thirteenth Amendment offers no protections not already provided under the Fourteenth or Fifteenth amendments. See *Mobile v. Bolden*, 446 U.S. 55 (1980); *Washington v. Finlay*, 664 F.2d 913 (1981). Furthermore, Congress has the power to regulate individual conduct to prevent various forms of racial discrimination under the Thirteenth Amendment, so the Thirteenth Amendment is generally invoked only where there is no state action. These facts do not involve a Congressional attempt to regulate discriminatory private behavior. In fact, there is no Congressional action at issue here at all, only a state statute. The Thirteenth Amendment does not operate independently of Congressional action.

The correct answer is (C). The Fourteenth Amendment protects from state infringement the First Amendment rights to association through the political process, including the process of forming new political parties and placing candidates on the ballot. However, states have power to regulate their elections under the Tenth Amendment. The state may impose reasonable burdens upon candidates or parties to show that they have some degree of political support before their names are placed upon the ballot. This is usually accomplished by requiring signatures of voters on nominating petitions, and the payment of a filing fee. Both of these requirements are constitutional so long as a reasonably diligent candidate with political support in the community can comply with them. *American Party v. White*, 415 U.S. 767 (1974). *Jenness v. Fortson*, 403 U.S. 431 (1971), upheld a state requirement that a candidate file a petition signed by five percent of the voters registered at the previous election. However, in *Williams v. Rhodes*, 393 U.S. 23 (1968), the Court struck down ballot access requirements that were more onerous for new or independent parties than for the Republican and Democratic parties and made it virtually impossible for a new political party to be on the ballot. A filing fee was held unconstitutional in *Bullock v. Carter*, 405 U.S. 134 (1972), because it was so large that it effectively barred access to the ballot. While it is not clear that the requirements in the State X statute would have this effect, the Fourteenth Amendment would be the most helpful constitutional provision to use in attacking the statute.

(D) is incorrect. The Fifteenth Amendment prohibits only purposefully discriminatory denial or abridgement by the government of the freedom to vote on account of race, color, or previous condition of servitude. See *City of Mobile v. Bolden*, 446 U.S. 55 (1980). Racially discriminatory intent in denying the right to vote must be shown, and the Fifteenth Amendment has not been extended to ballot access cases.

Answer to Question 64

Character may be in issue only in limited circumstances in a criminal case, such as when the defendant raises an entrapment defense and the prosecution attempts to show that the defendant was predisposed to commit the crime. Proof that a criminal defendant has committed other crimes, whether or not convicted of them, is generally inadmissible but may be admitted to prove intent or absence of mistake or accident when the defendant denies having the required mental state. Character evidence is thus not always inadmissible, but it would not be admissible here to show that Defendant is a violent person. (D) is incorrect. Evidence of Defendant's prior arguments with his father would be admissible to raise an inference of intent, to rebut Defendant's claim of accident. Thus, (C) is correct, and (A) is incorrect.

(B) is incorrect because it is not relevant who started the quarrels.

Answer to Question 65

(A) is incorrect because a general warranty clause in the mortgage would not affect Brenda's right of redemption.

(B) is the correct answer. Brenda should lose because she did not pay the entire amount so, she did not effectively redeem the mortgage. Payment of half is insufficient.

Marshalling is used to protect junior mortgagees or subsequent purchasers, requiring the mortgagee to foreclose first on portions of the property that have not been subsequently mortgaged or conveyed. Brenda and Alex have identical interests, so marshalling is not available, and (C) is incorrect.

(D) is incorrect. Whether the tenancy was in common or joint does not affect Marge's right to foreclose on the property or Brenda's obligation to pay the entire amount due in order to redeem the property.

Answer to Question 66

(A) is incorrect. There was no illegal police conduct in executing the warrant. The police satisfied the "knock and announce" requirement before entering the house. They are allowed to break and enter if necessary to execute the warrant, and may enter any part of the house where they believe suspects might be found.

Fifth Amendment Miranda rights are not imposed on police officers conducting a search under the Fourth Amendment, so (B) is incorrect.

The correct answer is (C). The narrowest and most certain ground on which the search can be justified is a search incident to arrest. The police had a clear right to search his person immediately upon arresting him.

Although the police had reasonable grounds to believe that there were weapons in the house, these were not included in the search warrant and there was no exigency beyond searching his person and his wingspan that would justify a warrantless search for weapons. (D) is incorrect.

Answer to Question 67

(A) is incorrect. Forcing the door open is not an unreasonable means of executing the search warrant.

(B) is incorrect. The reading of Miranda rights is required before police interrogation begins, but the lack thereof does not prohibit admission of a volunteered statement. The correct answer is (C).

(D) is incorrect. The police here were not conducting a public safety search, which would entail a search for weapons that might have been disposed of in a public place where the suspect was taken into custody. See *New York v. Quarles,* 467 U.S. 649 (1984). There is no concern here for public safety from a weapon in Jason's house, where there are no passersby to pick it up.

Answer to Question 68

When the police lawfully arrest a suspect in his home, they may conduct a limited sweep of other parts of the house if there is a reasonable belief that another person is hiding there and poses a danger to the officers. This means that a general search of areas large enough for a person to hide is permitted, but small enclosed areas are beyond the scope. While opening closet doors would be permissible, the police could not open a box on a closet shelf in this search for hidden persons. (C) is incorrect.

(D) is incorrect. *Chimel v. California* held that a search of the entire home for weapons was not incidental to the suspect's arrest. Since these items were not specified in the search warrant, only weapons that might be within Jason's reach could justifiably be seized.

The correct answer is (A). The search of a box on a closet shelf clearly exceeded the scope of any search for hidden persons in the house. (B) is close, but it does not completely state the rule that a search of the house for other persons believed to be hiding there is permissible upon execution of a search warrant if there is an articulable and reasonable belief that such persons might be found.

Answer to Question 69

The correct answer is (C). An offer to pay medical expenses and costs of hospitalization is inadmissible for policy reasons under Fed. R. Ev. 409.

Doctor's offer was not an offer to settle Plaintiff's claim so it was not an offer to compromise under Fed. R. Ev. 408, and (D) is thus incorrect.

Regardless of the potential admissibility of the offer under the rules of hearsay, the offer to pay medical expenses is inadmissible under Rule 409, so (A) and (B) are incorrect.

Answer to Question 70

The correct answer is (B). An accomplice is generally someone who aids or encourages the commission of a crime, but at common law one may become an accessory after the fact by concealing the felon, aiding in his escape, or destroying or altering evidence. Sam's two friends did none of these, so they should be acquitted.

(C) is incorrect because more is required to become an accessory after the fact than merely urging the principal to flee.

(D) is incorrect because bystanders do not have a duty to intervene to prevent the commission of a crime.

Answer to Question 71

Doctor will not be held liable for invasion of privacy. He communicated the information only to Employer, with whom Applicant was applying for a job. In conducting the examination of her records and reporting to Employer, Doctor did not intrude upon Applicant's seclusion, publish materials obtained unlawfully, or give unreasonable publicity to her private life. Thus, (B) and (D) may be eliminated because they include this cause of action.

(C) is incorrect because it includes negligent misrepresentation. This cause of action would not be available to Applicant as a plaintiff because Doctor did not supply erroneous information to Applicant on which Applicant relied to her detriment.

The correct answer is (A). The only viable cause of action for Applicant is negligent infliction of emotional distress. Doctor's negligence caused emotional distress and resulting physical injury to Applicant.

Answer to Question 72

An express prohibition on delegation in the original contract is only one circumstance that would prevent delegation of Deligor's duties. Whether or not the contract prohibits delegation, delegation of duties requiring personal taste and skill is not permitted. (A) is incorrect.

(B) is incorrect. Because the duties are a matter of personal taste and skill, Gourmet is not required to accept assurances that Newman will perform as well as Deligor.

The correct answer is (C). When a contract calls for the exercise of personal skill, the duties cannot be delegated, and an attempted delegation constitutes a breach of contract.

(D) is incorrect. A novation requires a promise by the obligee, here Gourmet, to accept the substituted performance of the delegate.

Answer to Question 73

Gourmet is an intended beneficiary of the Deligor-Newman agreement. An intended beneficiary acquires a right to sue the promisor under the third-party beneficiary contract, but the third-party contract does not discharge the duty the promisee owed to the third-party beneficiary. The beneficiary may receive only one recovery, but may proceed against either the promisor or promisee. (A) is incorrect.

When a contract calls for the exercise of personal skill, the duties cannot be delegated, and an attempted delegation constitutes a breach of contract. Delegation of one's duties under a contract, even if permitted, does not relieve the delegating party of his obligations under the contract. Thus, (B) is incorrect.

Only a novation, including a clear promise by the obligee to release the delegator in exchange for the liability of the delegate, will release the delegator. Even though Gourmet allowed Newman to perform, Gourmet did not expressly release Deligor, so (C) is incorrect.

(D) is the correct answer. Gourmet may proceed against either Deligor or Newman because Gourmet did not release Deligor, and as an intended beneficiary of the Deligor-Newman agreement, Gourmet acquired a right to sue Newman.

Answer to Question 74

(A) is the correct answer. The wife's character is not at issue in this case and the purpose of the testimony about her intoxication is not to prove her character but merely to explain the cause of the accident.

(B) and (C) are incorrect because the testimony is not being offered to prove the wife's character. Only her intoxication on this particular occasion is at issue, not her propensity for drunkenness.

(D) is incorrect. The testimony is germane to the central issue in this case -- the cause of the accident.

Answer to Question 75

(A) is incorrect because the life tenant must pay current charges only to the extent of income received or receivable from the property. If there is no income, the remainderman may pay such charges in order to preserve her property interest but may not recover such charges from the life tenant, with or without interest. (B) is also incorrect.

A life tenant is obligated to pay annual real estate taxes assessed against the property to the extent that she receives actual or imputed income from the property. If the property is not capable of producing income, the life tenant is not obligated to pay ordinary property taxes out of her own pocket. Lena did not receive income from the property, so (D) is the correct answer. The duty to pay taxes is not left to the life tenant's discretion, so (C) is incorrect.

Answer to Question 76

Intoxication is a defense at common law only where it negates the existence of a specific element of the crime charged, particularly specific intent. Both assault and attempted murder are specific intent crimes, and intoxication could negate the required intent, so (D) is incorrect.

The question thus is whether a limiting instruction is required. The examiners decided after the test was administered that either (A) or (B) is the correct answer.

Answer to Question 77

The letter is being introduced for a non-hearsay purpose, to show notice to Plaintiff where notice is a legally relevant issue. Because it is non-hearsay, both (A) and (C) are incorrect.

The correct answer is (B). Proof of a routine practice in the business world is admissible to raise the inference that the routine procedure was followed in the instant case.

(D) is incorrect because the best evidence rule would not block the introduction of the copy of the letter. The original was allegedly mailed to Plaintiff and Plaintiff denies receiving it. Thus, the original cannot be produced, and the next best form of proof is the copy from Defendant's files.

Answer to Question 78

(B) is incorrect because the statement is being introduced for the non-hearsay purpose of showing the effect of Plaintiff's statement on Defendant's state of mind.

(C) is incorrect because Defendant's belief as to Plaintiff's inability to perform is not credible evidence of her abilities since not based on personal knowledge. Nevertheless, the evidence is not rendered inadmissible for lack of personal knowledge because it is not being admitted to show her abilities, so (A) is also incorrect.

The correct answer is (D). Defendant is entitled to attempt to prove the basis for his belief that Plaintiff would be unable to perform the job.

Answer to Question 79

(A) is incorrect because the federal commerce power extends to this type of regulation. The Supreme Court found in *United States v. Yellow Cab,* 332 U.S. 218 (1947), that ordinary local taxicab services that only incidentally serviced airport traffic were not in interstate commerce. However, airport limousine services that primarily service airport traffic, particularly in interstate areas, have been considered part of interstate commerce for some time. In *Executive Town & Country Services, Inc. v. Atlanta,* 789 F.2d 1523 (1986), the Eleventh Circuit addressed a similar regulatory scheme for airport limousines. The court found that airport limousine services that exclusively transported airport passengers were sufficiently engaged in interstate commerce to warrant commerce clause analysis. See also, *Charter Limousine, Inc. v. Dade County,* 678 F.2d 589 (5th Cir. 1982).

(D) is incorrect because there is no undue burden on interstate commerce here. In *Executive Town & Country Services, Inc.,* the court found that, while rate regulations might force interstate travelers to choose between more expensive, luxurious limousine services and a less expensive and perhaps less comfortable mode of transportation such as local taxicabs, there was no evidence that interstate travelers would have to alter their plans or would be affected in any other significant way by the minimum fare regulations. Any burden that these regulations might impose on interstate commerce was found, at most, incidental and not in excess of the putative benefits to be gained by the city.

(C) is incorrect. There is no evidence that the regulation would destroy Airline Limousine Service. The company would be required to charge more for its services, not less, so it could not lose money unless its business volume of declined substantially. Many customers would probably still prefer to pay higher rates for luxury services. Furthermore, possible future revenues are not vested property rights for Takings Clause purposes. The fact that the value of a going concern may be affected by a regulation that constitutes a valid exercise of the commerce clause does not generally support a takings claim. See *American Trucking Assoc. v. U.S.*, 344 U.S. 298 (1953). The question provides insufficient facts to conclude that there would be a taking without just compensation.

The correct answer is (B). The Congressional power to regulate matters affecting interstate commerce is sufficient to justify this form of regulation. Congress can authorize state regulation in cases where commerce clause principles developed by the courts would otherwise prohibit the state action.

Answer to Question 80

If Motorist had been conscious and in control of the vehicle at the time his car ran the red light, the code violation would constitute negligence per se. However, violations of this nature may be excused by circumstances such as the fact that Motorist was unconscious and had not intended to run the red light before he passed out. Thus, (A) is incorrect.

Under the circumstances, reasonable persons could not conclude that Motorist was negligent, so (B) is incorrect. Without a conscious violation of a criminal law, there is no evidence of negligence by Motorist.

Because there is no evidence of negligence, the court must grant Motorist's motion for a directed verdict and should not submit the case to the jury. Thus, (C) is correct and (D) is incorrect.

Answer to Question 81

(A) is incorrect. This is the test for counterweights to relevancy under Federal Evidence Rule 403. The balancing of interests under this test is within the judge's discretion, and these facts do not clearly show that the judge must exclude this evidence.

The correct answer is (B). Smith's testimony about Parker's statement is inadmissible. It is hearsay because the declarant, Parker, made the statement out of court and it is being offered to prove the truth of the matter asserted, that Davidson owes money to Parker's estate. There are no applicable exceptions, as this is not an excited utterance or a dying declaration, discussed below, and the residual exception does not apply because there is most likely more probative evidence the estate could put forth to prove the debt than Parker's statement.

Parker's statement is not admissible as an excited utterance because it is not sufficiently related to the exciting event, i.e., the event of being run over by the truck. Thus, (C) is incorrect.

(D) is also incorrect because a statement under belief of impending death, i.e., a dying declaration, must relate to the causes and circumstances of what the declarant believes to be his impending death. Parker's statement was unrelated to the causes or circumstances of the accident.

Answer to Question 82

This contract is governed by Article 2 because it concerns timber to be severed from realty. UCC §2-207. Article 2 imposes an obligation of good faith in every sales transaction. Good faith is defined as honesty in fact in the transaction in question. There is no indication that Logger's actions were not in good faith, i.e., not honest. Thus, (A) is not Landholder's best argument for cancellation.

Equitable estoppel estops a party from denying his utterances or acts when he is guilty of a misrepresentation of existing fact or concealment upon which the other party justifiably relies to his detriment. There is no evidence here that Logger was guilty of misrepresentation. Thus, (B) is incorrect.

Article 2 permits a court to refuse to enforce a contract on the ground of unconscionability where the contract is unduly one-sided or harsh to one party at the time it is made, usually because of unequal bargaining positions. Although Landholder was probably as knowledgeable or sophisticated as Logger, Landholder was in "desperate financial straits" and thus agreed to terms that were overly harsh. When Landholder changes his mind about the need and desirability of going forward with this contract, he can ask a court to cancel or refuse to enforce the contract. (C) is his best argument.

(D) is incorrect. Logger did not apply force or threats of force in negotiating with Landholder. Any pressures Landholder felt were due to circumstances not caused by Logger.

Answer to Question 83

(A) is the correct answer. The neighbor is at most an incidental beneficiary since it was not the promisee's intent for the neighbor to benefit from the contract. Incidental beneficiaries gain no rights to sue under the contract. Nevertheless, the neighbor may attempt to raise an argument that his view is obscured without being accused of maintaining nuisance litigation, so (B) is incorrect.

(C) is incorrect. The neighbor is not an intended beneficiary of the Logger-Landholder contract.

(D) is incorrect. The neighbor has no legal status by which to sue as a "surrogate" for Landholder.

Answer to Question 84

(A) is incorrect because Congress frequently vests substantial discretion in the President and his subordinates regarding the manner in which laws are executed, and in many instances the members of the executive branch make legislative policy determinations. Such delegation of power is constitutionally permissible unless there are absolutely no standards specified for its exercise, or if the Congressional power is nondelegable. Thus rulemaking is often an executive function but whether rulemaking is considered an executive or quasi-legislative function is not determinative; separation-of-powers analysis does not turn on the labeling of an activity. *Mistretta* v. *United States*, 488 U.S. 361, 393 (1989).

The correct answer is (B). The Appointments Clause provides that Congress may vest the appointment of inferior officers in the President. When a federal board exercises executive powers, the members must be appointed in a manner consistent with the Appointments Clause. Congress may not participate in the activities of the board without violating the separation of powers doctrine. Because the structure of the Constitution does not permit Congress to execute the laws, Congress cannot permit the execution of the laws to be vested in an officer answerable only to Congress. See *Metropolitan Washington Airports Authority v. Citizens for the Abatement of Aircraft Noise,* 501 U.S. 252 (1991).

Under the necessary and proper clause, Congress has the authority to exercise powers not specifically enumerated in the Constitution, so long as these powers are appropriate to the exercise of specifically delegated powers, including the federal commerce power. However, the creation of the board violates the separation of powers and thus oversteps Congressional authority, as discussed above.

Congress does not possess the power to legislate for the general welfare, although it has power to spend for the general welfare. Therefore, (D) is incorrect.

Answer to Question 85

When a tenant for years conveys less than his entire estate, there is a sublease rather than an assignment of the tenant's interest. The subtenant is not in privity of estate with the landlord, and the obligation to pay rent is not directly enforceable against the subtenant by the landlord. (A) is the correct answer. The others are all incorrect because they would allow Oner to proceed against Agrit, either individually or jointly with Tenn. Tenn may collect from Agrit the portion due (one year's rent) from Agrit, but Oner may not.

Answer to Question 86

(A) is incorrect because, although negligence and causation has been proved, the law imposes limitations on recovery for mental suffering or emotional distress not arising from physical harm to the plaintiff.

(B) is incorrect because the law is somewhat cautious about awarding damages for emotional distress that was not caused by physical impact.

(C) is the correct answer. The law does not recognize a claim for emotional distress incident to negligently caused property damage, regardless of whether the plaintiff also suffered physical harm as a consequence of the emotional distress. Where there has been no physical impact, the plaintiff must show both that he was physically endangered and suffered physical consequences from the emotional distress. Thus, (D) is incorrect.

Answer to Question 87

(A) is the correct answer. A possessor of land has the right to lateral support for his property in its natural condition. Neighbors cannot use their land in such a way that the possessor's land subsides, if it would have subsided in its natural state. If development on the possessor's land contributed to the subsidence, then the neighbor is not liable. Thus, Bill can recover only if the subsidence of Lot 1 caused by Gail's building would have occurred even if Bill did not have a building on Lot 1.

The right to lateral support applies to every landholder; it need not be acquired by adverse possession with respect to improvements, so (B) is incorrect.

The difference between urban land and rural land actually relates to whether the land has been "artificially altered." When support is withdrawn from artificially altered land, the usual strict liability standard is typically replaced with a negligence standard. This does not shift the duty to Bill. Gail had a duty to take precautions against foreseeable subsidence and damage to the building on Bill's land.

(D) is incorrect because compliance with applicable zoning laws and building codes is not sufficient to protect a neighbor from liability for subsidence.

Answer to Question 88

The standard for competency of a very young witness is the same as for any witness, i.e., personal knowledge of the subject matter of his testimony and understanding of the requirement to tell the truth. There is no separate competency inquiry, so (A) is incorrect and (B) is correct.

Victim's son's testimony would clearly be probative, so (C) and (D) are incorrect.

Answer to Question 89

The correct answer is (A). The case is not within the original jurisdiction of the Supreme Court. Article III, §2(2) of the Constitution confers original jurisdiction on the Supreme Court in all cases affecting ambassadors, other public ministers and consuls, and cases in which a state is a party. Congress may neither enlarge nor contract that jurisdiction. *Marbury v. Madison*, 1 Cranch 137 (1803).

The judicial power of the Supreme Court extends to all cases in law and equity arising under not merely the Constitution, but also the laws of the United States, and treaties made under their authority. Thus, (B) is incorrect.

(D) is incorrect because Article III does not specify the mechanics of the Supreme Court's appellate jurisdiction. Article III creates only the Supreme Court, and gives Congress plenary power to establish lower federal courts and prescribe their jurisdiction as well as the Supreme Court's appellate jurisdiction over them.

Answer to Question 90

(A) is a good argument for Restaurant but it is not the best argument because it is only a partial response. The lack of complaints by others would not necessarily disprove that Patron was infected at Restaurant.

Restaurant could be held vicariously liable for a failure of its employees to wash their hands, despite Restaurant's instructions, so (B) is incorrect.

The best answer is (C). The burden is on Patron to make a causal connection between his illness and any health code violations at Restaurant, and in fact that he contracted the illness at Restaurant. The lack of other complaints from customers and the absence of signs of bacterial infection in Restaurant's employees when tested would deprive Patron of key elements of proof.

(D) is incorrect as a factual matter. It was not the spicy food that caused Patron's upset stomach, so this would not help Restaurant.

Answer to Question 91

(D) is the correct answer. Both can be convicted of murder.

In the absence of a felony-murder statute, Sally can be convicted of second-degree murder under the depraved heart theory. Since she did not aim the gun at anyone, she might not be found guilty of first-degree murder, but firing the weapon repeatedly inside the bank shows a willful and wanton disregard of risk to human life. Since she can be convicted of murder, (B) and (C) are incorrect.

Ralph can be convicted of murder on a theory of accomplice liability, in the absence of a felony-murder statute. At common law, one who was present at the scene of a felony and stood ready to aid in its commission can be found guilty as a principal and is punishable to the same extent as the perpetrator. Ralph might argue that he only intended to rob, not to kill, but the use of automatic weapons raises a presumption of intent to kill.

Answer to Question 92

(A) is incorrect. Although one of the instigating factors for this legislation may have been acquisitions by out-of-state corporations, the statute expressly applies to acquisitions by both in-state and out-of-state entities, so there is no discrimination on the face of the statute. If a discriminatory effect could be proven, the answer would be different.

(B) is incorrect. In *CTS Corp. v. Dynamics Corp. of America,* 481 U.S. 69 (1987), the Supreme Court found that an Indiana state law dealing with tender offers did not discriminate against interstate commerce since it had the same effect on tender offers whether or not the offeror was an Indiana domiciliary or resident. That the act might apply most often to out-of-state entities who launch most hostile tender offers was found irrelevant, since a claim of discrimination is not established by the mere fact that the burden of a state regulation falls on some interstate companies.

The correct answer is (C). These factors should be sufficient to protect this statute from challenge under the *Pike v. Bruce Church* balancing test for state regulation under the dormant commerce clause and *CTS Corp, supra.*

(D) is incorrect because, although corporations are creatures of state law, their impact on interstate commerce is clear enough to invoke the dormant or negative implications of the commerce clause.

Answer to Question 93

This question deals with the parol evidence rule, which excludes evidence of statements made by either of the parties prior to or contemporaneous with the signing of a contract that vary or contradict the writing, where the parties intended that the writing be a complete and final expression of their agreement.

(A) is the correct answer. Parol evidence is admissible where there is ambiguity in the written agreement, even if the agreement is deemed completely integrated. Here the recital indicates that Boss is also a party, whereas the signature lines show her signing merely as a representative of Builder.

Evidence that only Builder was intended to be responsible would contradict the recital, which refers to "Builder, Inc., and Boss." Thus, (B) is incorrect.

(C) is incorrect. The effect of the evidence will be to explain the capacity in which Boss signed, not to contradict the writing.

(D) is incorrect because when there is an ambiguity in the language on the face of the instrument, parol evidence may be used to explain it.

Answer to Question 94

(A) is incorrect as a factual matter. Parents' request was made at an open school board meeting and concerned the use of public funds. It was not solely a matter of private concern to Parents, and could appropriately be deemed newsworthy.

(B) is incorrect because Son or his representative(s) need not consent to the release of his name in connection with a story of legitimate public concern.

(D) is also incorrect because Parents' knowledge or consent, whether implied or express, is irrelevant.

(C) is the correct answer. If the story was a fair and accurate report of what transpired at the meeting, Son cannot complain that the publicity placed him in a false light or otherwise exceeded the scope of a reporter's privilege to report on matters of legitimate public interest.

Answer to Question 95

(A) is incorrect. Expert has no independent proof of Defendant's truthfulness under hypnosis, which is not generally excepted scientific evidence.

Prior consistent statements of the witness on the stand are admissible substantively only if they are offered to rebut a charge of recent fabrication by the witness. Thus, (B) is incorrect.

(C) is an incorrect statement of the law. In *Rock v. Arkansas,* 483 U.S. 44 (1987), the Supreme Court held that a state evidentiary rule excluding an accused's hypnotically refreshed testimony from admission as evidence at the accused's trial violated the accused's constitutional right to testify on his or her own behalf as guaranteed by the Fifth Amendment privilege against self-incrimination, the Sixth Amendment right to compulsory process and to conduct one's own defense, and the Fourteenth Amendment right to due process, where the state rule (1) per se prohibited the admission at trial of any accused's hypnotically refreshed testimony on the ground that such testimony is always unreliable, and (2) did not allow a trial court to consider whether post-hypnosis testimony may be admissible in a particular case.

(D) is the correct answer. In a criminal case, expert opinion is not permitted as to whether the defendant had the mental state constituting an element of the crime charged or of his defense.

Answer to Question 96

(A) is incorrect because a general prohibition on abortions, absent serious health reasons, in the second trimester, goes beyond the state's interest in protecting the health of the mother and there would be as yet no legitimate state interest in protecting fetal life, prior to a showing of viability. While the woman's liberty interest in the abortion decision remains constant throughout her pregnancy, the state's regulatory interest grows over the term of the pregnancy. According to the Court in *Roe v. Wade*, the state's interest in protecting fetal life becomes "compelling," and thereby capable of surviving strict scrutiny, when the fetus becomes viable. In *Roe*, strict scrutiny was triggered by the woman's substantive due process right to decide the outcome of her pregnancy.

(B) is incorrect because fetal viability, not the end of the first trimester, is the point at which the fetus may be characterized as a person whose right to life may be protected.

The correct answer is (C). Fetal viability is the point at which the constitutional interest shifts from the woman's right to privacy and right to reproductive choice to the state's right to regulate abortion. The Court in *Casey* held that even before viability, the state may advance its interest in fetal life by, for example, persuading women to carry their children to term, as long as it does not place an "undue burden" on the execution of the woman's decision. *Casey*, 505 U.S. at 876-78.

(D) is incorrect because arbitrary classifications that invoke the equal protection clause involve distinctions between one person and another. A classification of this nature involving stages of pregnancy might raise substantive due process issues, but not equal protection.

Answer to Question 97

It is true that Olive held a reversionary interest because she conveyed less than fee simple to Lois and there was no other remainderman after Lois' life estate. However, Olive has been divested of this interest by adverse possession.

(B) is incorrect because Lois did not assert a claim adverse to Olive merely by executing a lease to Trent. When Lois died, however, Ron's continuing to allow Trent to occupy the property and make payments to Ron was inconsistent with Olive's reversionary interest.

(C) is the correct answer. Ron, as Lois's sole heir, is Lois's successor in interest to the property acquired by adverse possession. Ron's continuing to accept the rental payments was an act of dominion over the property that was adverse to Olive and vested title in Ron when it continued for over ten years.

(D) is incorrect because Trent was only asserting his rights as a tenant under the lease in continuing to occupy the property, not rights of ownership. Also, the term of a lease does not end automatically with the landlord's death; the landlord's interest belongs to her estate if she held the property in fee simple. The only reason the lease would terminate here was that Lois's rights in the property ended with her death and thus her estate had nothing more to lease out. The fact that Ron continued to act as a landlord made him the adverse possessor, not Trent.

Answer to Question 98

Asportation, for purposes of larceny, requires only a slight movement of the article. It is not necessary that the purse have been removed from the store, so (A) is incorrect, nor is it relevant that she intended to take the purse out of the store and failed to do so, so (C) is incorrect. Taking the purse from its original location and concealing it with intent to steal would be sufficient to satisfy the asportation requirement, so (D) is the correct answer.

Withdrawal is not at issue here. This was not part of a conspiracy. The larceny had already been committed, so (B) is incorrect.

Answer to Question 99

(A) is incorrect. Basher's liability for the consequences of his negligence does not depend on his knowledge of those consequences.

(B) is incorrect because one who is negligent must also take responsibility for the foreseeable intervening negligence of another, even assuming that Adam had a duty to warn Mechanic and breached that duty.

(C) is incorrect because it states that Basher is definitely liable unless Mechanic was contributorily negligent. It does not state the preliminary issue with respect to Basher's liability, a showing of proximate cause between Basher's negligence and Mechanic's injury. The correct answer is (D). Mechanic must show that his injury was a proximate cause of Basher's negligent driving.

Answer to Question 100

(A) is incorrect because the gas leak posed an unreasonable risk of harm to Mechanic before he could reasonably find it and repair it. Adam created this risk to Mechanic by giving him the car to work on without warning him of this known risk.

(B) is incorrect because an awareness of the risk posed by gasoline leaks is the sort of knowledge with which any reasonable person would be charged. His awareness of the existence of the leak is all that would need to be proven.

The correct answer is (C). If Mechanic can show that Adam had a duty to warn Mechanic and breached that duty, Mechanic may recover from Adam.

(D) is incorrect because this is not a product liability case; Adam was not in the direct chain of distribution from the manufacturer.

Answer to Question 101

(A) is the correct answer and the others are incorrect because Dirk is guilty of all three crimes.

Dirk is guilty of burglary because he entered John and Marsha's dwelling in the nighttime with intent to commit a felony therein. Although he did not physically break in, there was a constructive breaking since he forced John and Marsha to let him in under duress.

Dirk is guilty of robbery because he committed larceny by force and intimidation.

Dirk is guilty of murder because most states recognize the doctrine of felony-murder, and burglary is an inherently dangerous felony to which the doctrine would be applied. A killing during and as a result of a dangerous felony, even if unintentional, can be punished as murder under the felony-murder rule. Although Dirk had been apprehended before John died, John had not yet been released from the dangerous (to him) condition Dirk placed him in and died as a result thereof.

Answer to Question 102

(A) is incorrect because the fact that Defendant's expert had examined the brake shoe would allow Defendant's expert to testify about its condition, not Plaintiff.

The correct answer is (B). The fundamental requirement for witness testimony is that the witness have personal knowledge of the subject matter of his testimony.

(C) is incorrect because Rule 408 does not require the exclusion of any evidence otherwise discoverable merely because it is presented in the course of compromise negotiations.

(D) is incorrect because the proponent of documentary evidence must establish that the loss of the original is not his fault where the best evidence rule applies, but the brake shoe is physical evidence, not documentary evidence needed to prove the contents.

Answer to Question 103

Article 2 of the UCC provides for what should happen when delivery and payment terms are not specified in a contract for the sale of goods.

In the absence of a specified place for delivery, §2-308 provides that the place for delivery of the goods is generally the seller's place of business. Thus, (A) is incorrect.

Where the time for payment is left open, payment is due at the time and place at which the buyer is to receive the goods, here, the seller's place of business. §2-310. Thus, (B) is correct, and (C) is incorrect.

When the seller has the right to make delivery in lots, the seller can demand payment for each lot if payment can be so apportioned. §2-307. Thus, (D) is incorrect.

Answer to Question 104

Generally, Article 2 provides that if the goods delivered under a contract fail to conform to the contract in any respect, the buyer may reject the whole, accept the whole, or accept any commercial unit(s) and reject the rest. §2-601. However, there are particular rules with respect to installment contracts, which permit shipment in separate lots. In an installment contract, the buyer may reject any non-conforming installment if the nonconformity substantially impairs the value of that installment and cannot be cured, but if the nonconformity does not impair the whole contract and the seller gives adequate assurance of its cure, the buyer must accept that installment. §2-612. Here, Fixtures has given adequate assurances of cure, so Apartments is obligated to accept the 24 sets in this lot. (A) and (B) are incorrect.

The nonconformity as to the first installment does not substantially impair the entire contract, so Apartments does not have a right to cancel the entire contract. §2-711. (C) is thus incorrect.

(D) is the correct answer. The nonconformity in the first lot does not substantially impair the whole contract and Fixtures has given adequate assurances of cure as to the first lot, so Apartments must accept the 24 sets in this installment and has no right to cancel the rest of the contract.

Answer to Question 105

(A) is incorrect because expert testimony is not needed to point out similarities between a person and a photograph. Lay witnesses and the jury members themselves can reach their own opinions on this matter without the assistance of expert testimony.

(B) is the correct answer. The jury members may compare the person in the photograph with Defendant and determine whether they think Defendant is in the photograph.

(C) is incorrect because, while the photograph must be authenticated, it may be done by authentication of the process or system by which such photographs are taken and handled. There need not have been an eyewitness at the scene.

(D) is incorrect. The photograph is a form of non-testimonial recording. The Sixth Amendment does not apply to non-testimonial evidence.

Answer to Question 106

Although Dawn had nothing to convey to Bruce when she executed the deed to him, the doctrine of after-acquired title or estoppel by deed holds that when Dawn subsequently acquired title, it inured immediately to Bruce. However, in most jurisdictions the difficulty of finding this deed in the land recording system causes Carl's subsequent purchase to prevail over the fact that Bruce's deed was previously recorded.

(B) is incorrect because Dawn granted Bruce fee simple. The life estate in Dawn would not change the operation of the after-acquired title doctrine. Title vested in Bruce despite the fact that immediate possession did not.

(C) is incorrect. The recording statute here is a race-notice type statute. It is relevant that Carl had no actual or record notice of Bruce's deed and it is relevant when Carl recorded, but it is not relevant that Carl was first in possession.

(D) is the correct answer. Dawn's deed to Bruce was not in Carl's chain of title because there was no preceding deed from Olivia to Dawn. Thus, the deed to Bruce, although recorded, was nearly undiscoverable under the recording systems in most states, and most courts will not protect Bruce against a subsequent purchaser who records. If Carl wins, it will be for this reason.

Answer to Question 107

It is possible to commit a crime such as larceny through the use of an innocent agent. The fact that Roy did not intend to commit larceny and thus was not guilty of a crime does not negate Grace's guilt. Thus, (A) is incorrect.

Grace is not an accessory to Roy because Grace had intent to steal and Roy did not, so Roy is not the principal. Thus, (C) is incorrect.

Removal of the property from Sam's home satisfied the asportation requirement for larceny; it is not necessary that Grace have actually obtained possession. It is enough that Grace interfered with Sam's possessory interest by exercising dominion and control through her agent. Thus, (B) is incorrect.

The correct answer is (D). Grace intended to steal and exercised dominion over the television through her agent, Roy, who caused its asportation, so Grace committed larceny through the use of an innocent agent.

Answer to Question 108

The Restatement of Torts 2d §46 provides: "One who, by extreme and outrageous conduct, intentionally or recklessly causes severe emotional distress to another, is subject to liability for such emotional distress, and if bodily harm results from it, for such bodily harm." Intent to photograph Prisoner would not be required if Photographer acted in reckless disregard of the probable consequences of his behavior, so (A) is incorrect.

Physical injury is not a necessary element of the cause of action for intentional or reckless infliction of emotional distress, so (B) is incorrect.

The *New York Times* rule of privilege to report newsworthy events and about public figures has been applied to invasion of privacy cases but not to intentional torts such as infliction of emotional distress. If the tort is proven, no news privilege would protect Photographer.

The correct answer is (D). Photographer's best argument is that, under all the circumstances, his conduct was not extreme and outrageous.

Answer to Question 109

The President does not have plenary authority to provide for the health and welfare of the people of the United States. His power must stem from the Constitution, which specifically directs him only to execute the laws of the United States and to be the Commander in Chief of the Army and Navy. (A) is incorrect.

(B) is the correct answer. While the President has specific authority under Article II of the Constitution to execute laws passed by Congress, he also has some inherent authority to act in domestic affairs, without specific legislative authority, by virtue of the fact that he is the Chief Executive. *Youngstown Sheet & Tube Co. v. Sawyer,* 343 U.S. 579 (1952), suggested that, in the face of national emergencies, the President may possess some inherent power to deal with a crisis in the domestic field except where specifically prohibited by Congress. The Court did not uphold the executive order for seizure of the steel mills issued in *Youngstown,* however, and this fact pattern does not involve a national emergency. What makes this action by the President legal is the fact that it is much narrower in scope than the action challenged in *Youngstown.* Here the President merely proposes an advisory commission that would conduct a national publicity campaign using funds already appropriated for Presidential use.

(C) is incorrect because the activities of the commission will be solely promotional and educational. There is no legislative or regulatory authority being asserted that would infringe on states' rights.

(D) is incorrect because a commission is not a federal agency that requires permanent funding. The President may fund it from funds already appropriated for use by the Office of the President.

Answer to Question 110

Victim has personal knowledge of the voice he heard, so he may testify as to how it sounded and its likeness to Defendant's voice. Victim's lack of certainty goes to the weight of the evidence, not its admissibility, so (A) is incorrect, and (D) is correct.

The best evidence rule is inapplicable here because it is the sound of Defendant's voice, not the content of the words on the recording, which is at issue. Thus, (B) and (C) are incorrect.

Answer to Question 111

(A) is incorrect because recordation does not cure defects in the underlying transaction between a grantor and grantee of a deed.

(B) is the correct answer. An absolute conveyance is not usually affected by the grantee's failure to pay the recited consideration unless the transaction was fraudulent. Nonpayment may give the grantor a vendor's lien against the property for the unpaid amount, but here the recited consideration was only $5 so a lien is unlikely.

The recitation in this case indicates that the consideration was "in hand paid" so parol evidence conflicting with the terms of the writing would not be allowed. Whether or not the recitation of consideration can be contradicted by parol evidence here, (C) is incorrect because the nonpayment of recited consideration does not make the instrument void, so proving the nonpayment would not mean Owner would prevail. Courts are very reluctant to set aside deeds for nonpayment of consideration, generally requiring a showing of fraud, which Owner has not alleged.

(D) is incorrect because the instrument is not void.

Answer to Question 112

(A) is incorrect because negligence on Vintner's part would not render him liable to Trespasser without a duty toward Trespasser.

(B) is the correct answer. The duty of a landholder to a discovered trespasser is to use ordinary care to avoid injury to him. If Vintner could not have prevented the injury to Trespasser with the use of ordinary care after discovering his presence, Trespasser will not prevail.

(C) is incorrect because the operation of balloon rides is probably not an abnormally dangerous activity. Whether an activity is abnormally dangerous requires consideration of a number of factors, including a high degree of risk of harm, inability to eliminate the risk by the exercise of reasonable care, and inappropriateness of the activity to the place where it is carried on. These factors would not seem to weigh in favor of strict liability in this case.

(D) is incorrect because it is not enough that Vintner knew or should have known of the presence of trespassers; it is also necessary that Vintner have been negligent.

Answer to Question 113

Fred made threats to kill Matt and brandished a knife at him in a threatening manner. Under the circumstances, Matt was justified in using deadly force to counter the perceived attack. (A) is incorrect.

Matt had no duty to retreat from his own home. Thus, (B) is incorrect.

Although Matt may not have intended to kill Fred, firing a gun in Fred's direction was willful and wanton conduct that would justify a conviction of murder on a depraved heart theory. (C) is incorrect.

The correct answer is (D). Matt acted reasonably within the scope of the self-defense doctrine and had no duty to retreat from his home.

Answer to Question 114

National Labor Relations Board v. Jones & Laughlin Steel Corp., 301 U.S. 1 (1937), held that although the production of steel was a local activity, such production had a substantial effect upon interstate commerce, and therefore was subject to federal labor laws. (A) is incorrect because components of the computers assembled in Central City by Assembler come from outside the state of Green, and the computers are sold throughout the

United States, so the tax on Assembler and others clearly affects interstate commerce.

(B) is incorrect because the commerce clause forbids a state from attempting to foster local businesses by discriminating against out-of-state products or favoring local products. A state tax on interstate commercial activity violates the commerce clause unless it "is applied to an activity with a substantial nexus to the taxing State, is fairly apportioned, does not discriminate against interstate commerce, and is fairly related to the services or benefits provided by the State." *Complete Auto Transit, Inc. v. Brady*, 430 U.S. 274, 279 (1977).

(C) is incorrect because gross receipts tax is not a per se violation of the commerce clause. The Supreme Court has upheld the use of a gross receipts tax that is properly apportioned. See *American Manufacturing Co. v. St. Louis,* 250 U.S. 459 (1919). Taxes on gross receipts are unconstitutional on due process grounds when they are not apportioned, because they subject the interstate business to the possibility of multiple taxation. *Armco, Inc. v. Hardesty*, 467 U.S. 638 (1984).

The correct answer is (D). A tax must not discriminate against interstate commerce. A tax which favors local commerce over out-of-state or interstate commerce is almost automatically invalid, unless it is a true compensatory tax designed solely to make interstate commerce bear a burden already borne by intrastate commerce. This tax clearly favors in-state products over out-of-state products.

Answer to Question 115

In most jurisdictions, assault and/or battery can be committed by a touching with a harmful substance such as a chemical spray. Whether Hannah intended to cause serious bodily injury with the spray from the fire extinguisher is more uncertain. With respect to either crime, however, it appears that she has the defense of self-defense, since she was she was being beaten on the head with a hard object and did not use excessive force in attempting to fight off this attack. Thus, (A) and (C) are incorrect.

Hannah was not guilty of burglary when she broke into the hotel because she did not intend to commit a felony when she entered. Thus, (B) is incorrect.

(D) is the correct answer. Hannah committed a trespass, which is an intended and nonconsensual/unprivileged entry of another's land. However, she committed none of the other offenses.

Answer to Question 116

(A) is incorrect because the contract called for performance by a specific date, and Mechanic was in breach by not completing his performance by that date.

The correct answer is (B). If there was no reason at the time of making the contract to anticipate damages in the amount provided for, the liquidated damages clause would be unenforceable. On March 1, Textiles had not yet entered the contract with Knitwear and under ordinary circumstances a delay of the kind that was caused by Mechanic would not have caused Textile to sustain damages.

While (C) in effect is a true statement, it is not the way Mechanic's defense should be framed. Mechanic's defense should be framed in terms of the foreseeability of consequential damages to Textiles when the contract between them was signed on March 1.

A liquidated damages clause will be enforced, and not construed as an unenforceable "penalty," if the amount of damages stipulated is either reasonable in relation to the actual damages suffered or seemed reasonable in relation to the amount of damages anticipated when the contract was made. The liquidated damages amount need not be the same as the actual damage amount if reasonable in relation to anticipated damages at the time the contract was entered. Regardless of whether the liquidated damages clause in favor of Knitwear is valid, this would not constitute a defense to Mechanic under his separate contract with Textiles, so (D) is incorrect.

Answer to Question 117

(A) is incorrect because this topic is appropriate for both lay and expert opinion. The lay eyewitness is testifying from personal knowledge of the event, and the expert is reconstructing the event from the physical evidence.

The fact that the expert witness has given a range of possible speeds does not mean his testimony lacks a sufficient degree of scientific certainty. This goes only to the weight that may be given to the testimony by the factfinder, not its admissibility. Thus, (B) is incorrect.

(C) is the correct answer. The police accident investigator is an appropriate expert on this issue.

(D) is incorrect because Plaintiff need not have first introduced opinion evidence as to speed for Defendant to be able do so.

Answer to Question 118

Under the *Restatement of Torts, 2d,* §504, the possessor of livestock is strictly liable for damage done by the animals' trespass. Thus, (A) is correct.

Farmer's prior knowledge or reason to know of the animals' propensity to panic during thunderstorms is not required, so (B) is incorrect.

Some jurisdictions require that the plaintiff in an action for trespass by livestock have built a fence to prevent intrusions on his property by cattle; other jurisdictions impose a duty on those keeping cattle to fence them in. This jurisdiction does not have such a requirement, but if Farmer undertook to build a fence, he could be found liable for negligent maintenance.

Section 504(3)(c) of the Restatement 2d says that strict liability under this section does not extend to harm "brought about by the unexpectable operation of a force of nature." The illustration in the official Comments indicates that where lightning strikes the fence and destroys part of it, so the defendant's cattle escape, the defendant will not be held liable. The thunderstorm did not create the breach in the fence in this case, however; this was done by the defendant's livestock. Therefore, Farmer cannot use the "force of nature" defense and will be held strictly liable.

Answer to Question 119

(A) is the correct answer. A liquidated damages clause will not be enforced but will be construed as an unenforceable "penalty" if the amount of damages stipulated is neither reasonable in relation to the actual damages suffered nor reasonably related to the amount of damages anticipated when the contract was made. The $50,000 down payment was 50% of the purchase price, clearly a huge penalty, and there are probably no actual damages since the market price of Goldacre has risen and Ven could presumably sell it to someone else for more than the contract price with Pur.

A court will not enforce a penalty regardless of the fact that it is part of an express agreement. Thus, (C) is incorrect.

(B) is an incorrect statement of the law. When a purchaser under a contract for the sale of real estate dies before the closing, the doctrine of equitable conversion treats the heirs as the owners of the real property. The heirs can be forced to pay the rest of the purchase price out of the estate funds. The contract does not automatically terminate.

This action does not involve the doctrine of equitable conversion, however. Neither party is attempting to enforce the contract for the sale of Goldacre. (D) is incorrect as a matter of law because the doctrine does not "prevent" termination of the contract if the seller and the purchaser's heirs agree not to enforce it, and it is incorrect on the facts of this case because Ven did not make a claim for the rest of the purchase price.

Answer to Question 120

The government may not condition the issuance of a license upon a surrender of First Amendment rights, so (A) is incorrect. Under the doctrine of "unconstitutional conditions," the government may not require a person to give up a constitutional right in exchange for a discretionary benefit conferred by the government where the property taken has little or no relationship to the benefit. Even though Driver accepted the condition against displaying political signs on his cab and clearly violated that condition, the fundamental nature of his right to free speech gives him standing to contest the condition when the issue becomes ripe, i.e., when he is faced with imminent revocation of his license on this basis.

(B) is incorrect because a license involving the right to practice a line of work is treated as a property right, not a privilege, under the Due Process Clause.

(C) is incorrect. Driver does not have a good defense based on the "takings" or "just compensation" clause. In *Penn Central Transportation Co. v. New York City*, 438 U.S. 104 (1978), the Supreme Court surveyed some of the general principles governing the Takings Clause, pointing out that among the factors that have particular significance in determining whether a particular government restriction upon the use of property amounts to a taking are "the character of the governmental action. A 'taking' may more readily be found when the interference with property can be characterized as a physical invasion by government, see, *e.g., United States v. Causby*, 328 U.S. 256 (1946), than when interference arises from some public program adjusting the benefits and burdens of economic life to promote the common good." 438 U.S. at 124. See *Hilton Washington Corp. v. District of Columbia*, 250 U.S. App. D.C. 47 (1985) [regulation of taxicab stands in front of hotels found no taking].

The correct answer is (D). This ordinance is a content-based regulation of free speech and must meet strict scrutiny standards. Political speech is the most highly protected form of speech. In *Lehman v.*

Shaker Heights, 418 U.S. 298 (1974), the Supreme Court upheld a city ordinance prohibiting political advertisements on vehicles in the city transit system. The Court found that the city had not created a public forum by allowing commercial advertisements, that the city had a legitimate interest in appearing to favor certain candidates, and that the passengers were a captive audience that had a right to be free from having speech imposed on them.

The case of taxicab advertising is somewhat different because the taxicab is not city property and those who view the advertisements from outside the cab are not a captive audience and would see the ads only fleetingly.

Answer to Question 121

(A) is incorrect because the failure to consult a cardiologist, even though a negligent act, would not result in liability for Surgeon unless such consultation would have prevented or changed the outcome of the operation. The correct answer is (C).

(B) is incorrect because Surgeon will not be liable for Pat's death unless the blood clot was preventable by the exercise of due care.

(D) is incorrect because the withdrawal of life support would not have been the cause of Pat's death without the earlier injury from the operation by Surgeon.

Answer to Question 122

Fed. Rule 608 permits inquiry on cross-examination at the discretion of the court in the form of questions into specific instances of the witness's conduct involving honesty or dishonesty. No extrinsic evidence of such acts is permitted. Thus, while the question to Jaron about the statement on his credit card application was properly admitted within the judge's discretion, the testimony of Wilcox about the facts of Jaron's employment was unpermitted extrinsic evidence. (A) is incorrect.

(B) is incorrect because it involves the rule for admissibility of character evidence. Jaron's character is not in issue in this case beyond the usual concern for the veracity of all witnesses.

The correct answer is (C). Specific instances of the witness's conduct involving honesty or dishonesty cannot be proved by extrinsic evidence such as Wilcox's testimony. Counsel must accept the witness's answer and the trier of fact may infer the reasons for the instances of conduct in question. The possibility of other explanations does not change the rule, so (D) is incorrect.

Answer to Question 123

The doctrine of equitable conversion would treat Blackacre as belonging to Bryer from the time of the contract of sale. There is a split of opinion as to whether the vendor's interest in an executory land sale contract is an interest in real estate or personalty, but a slight majority allows a judgment lien to attach to the vendor's interest. These jurisdictions nonetheless hold that the purchaser is protected until the purchaser gets actual notice that a lien has been docketed. Here, however, the contract is no longer executory. Bryer has paid the price and received the deed before Cred filed her judgment. Nevertheless, Bryer would lose to a subsequent purchaser for value and without notice during the period before Bryer records. (A) is incorrect because the doctrine of equitable conversion in itself would be insufficient to allow Bryer to prevail over Cred without recording or taking possession.

(B) is the correct answer. Judgment creditors are not "subsequent purchasers for value" under the recording act; they generally do not rely on the land records in extending credit. Since Cred is not protected by the statute, it is unnecessary to determine whether either party had notice of the other, so (C) and (D) are incorrect.

Owen's continued possession would not in any way give Cred constructive notice of Bryer's interest, so (C) is incorrect. If Bryer had been in possession, Cred would probably have been charged with notice of that fact. By permitting Owen to remain in possession after ownership had passed to Bryer and before the deed was recorded, Bryer failed to put a subsequent purchaser on notice of Bryer's claim.

Being a purchaser without notice may cut off prior unrecorded interests, but we do not know when Cred obtained her money judgment against Owen except that she filed it after Bryer took title. A vendor who conveys title to a third person or imposes an encumbrance on the property after contracting to sell it may be liable to the original vendee for damages (if the value of the property exceeds the purchase price) if his interest is cut off by a BFP. Cred appears to be the BFP here, not Bryer, so (D) is incorrect.

Answer to Question 124

The parol evidence rule does not bar proof of subsequent oral agreements between the parties, so this rule will not support Owner's defense.

The preexisting duty rule will not provide a defense for Owner because Contractor was under no duty to provide the "extras" requested by Owner. Thus, Owner's promise to pay for such modifications of the contract was supported by consideration.

Failure of an express condition is not an appropriate defense for Owner because the writing requirement for modifications is a limitation, not a condition.

The statute of frauds does not require that all the terms of a contract for the conveyance of real estate be in writing, only the essential terms. The oral agreement for the "extras" could be enforceable without a writing.

(D) is the correct answer. None of these arguments would support Owner's refusal to pay for the extras.

Answer to Question 125

An overnight guest in another's home has a reasonable expectation of privacy and thus standing to object to search of the home in violation of the Fourth Amendment. *Minnesota v. Olson,* 495 U.S. 91 (1990). Although Scott had standing to object to the search, there was no violation of the Fourth Amendment despite the lack of a warrant or probable cause to arrest or search at the time of the entry into Henry's house. If the owner of the house consented to the entry by the police, there was no Fourth Amendment violation, so (A), (B), and (C) are incorrect.

The correct answer is (D). Henry's consent for the police to enter the house to look for Scott rendered their entry permissible under the Fourth Amendment because Henry was the owner of the house. Once inside, their identification and arrest of Scott was valid.

Answer to Question 126

(A) is the correct answer. The attorney-client privilege is not limited to communications between the client and the attorney. Communications between a client and her lawyer's representatives are also privileged.

(B) is incorrect because a grand jury investigation need not be based on probable cause. So long as the information requested is possibly relevant to the grand jury's legitimate purpose of returning and indictment, there is no other threshold evidentiary requirement. See *U.S. v. Scott,* 784 F.2d 787, 792 (7th Cir.), *cert. denied,* 476 U.S. 1145 (1986).

Consultant is a representative of Susan's lawyer and communications between Susan and the consultant about the case are privileged, so (C) is incorrect.

The exclusionary rule does not apply in grand jury proceedings, but (D) is incorrect because the attorney-client privilege is applicable in grand jury proceedings. Under the Federal Rules, privileges apply "at all stages of all actions, cases, and proceedings." Fed. R. Evid. 1101(c).

Answer to Question 127

The U.S. Supreme Court will not review a case from a state court if the opinion rests upon an independent and adequate state ground, even if federal issues were also addressed, because the Supreme Court decision must be dispositive of the litigation. The U.S. Supreme Court cannot affect the outcome of a case that is controlled by a principle of state law, even if there is a point of federal law discussed in the opinion, unless the federal standard was expressly incorporated into state law as the basis for the state court's decision. This does not appear to be the case here.

The correct answer is (C). The state supreme court's ruling was based on an interpretation of the state constitution, an independent and adequate state ground. It is irrelevant that the state court also discussed, without deciding, federal constitutional issues, so (B) is incorrect.

(A) is incorrect because the U.S. Supreme Court cannot affirm on federal grounds when the state supreme court based its decision on the state constitution and not on the federal Constitution.

(D) is incorrect because, while "fighting words" may not be protected speech under the First Amendment to the U.S. Constitution, the state court could interpret the state constitution more broadly without being inconsistent with the federal constitution.

Answer to Question 128

The fact that the roof was defective when Seller sold the house might give rise to a cause of action by the purchaser if the defect is one that should have been disclosed. However, this theory would not help Pedestrian, and the fact that the roof was defective would not in itself render Seller liable to Pedestrian without negligence, so (A) is incorrect.

The correct answer is (B). The general rule is that there is no liability on the part of a seller to the buyer or to third persons for any condition present at the time possession was surrendered to the buyer. There are exceptions, however. If the land was sold with dangerous conditions known to the seller, the mere transfer of title may not terminate the seller's responsibility, especially where the danger was created by the seller's negligence. The seller may remain liable for foreseeable injuries, including to persons outside the premises, at least until the buyer has had a reasonable opportunity to discover the dangerous condition and repair it.

Seller's duty to Pedestrian was not that of a landholder, since he did not own the house at the time of the injury, and Pedestrian was injured outside the property on a public sidewalk. However, Seller can be liable on a negligence theory to any foreseeable plaintiff injured by his negligence, so (C) is incorrect.

(D) is too narrow. Pedestrian need not have known of the danger to be barred from recovery.

Answer to Question 129

The correct answer is (A). Although the offer had not yet become irrevocable for the 30-day period because Buyer had not paid the required consideration, Buyer possessed the power to accept the offer until it was expressly revoked or until Buyer became aware of facts that clearly showed Seller no longer wished to enter into the deal.

Promissory estoppel would not be a substitute for consideration here, so (B) is incorrect. The common law rule is that an offer may be withdrawn prior to acceptance unless consideration has been given to keep it open. Some courts might find that the offer was rendered irrevocable because Buyer relied on it to his detriment, but this is a minority position. Furthermore, Buyer has not truly incurred a detriment; obtaining a commitment does not necessarily obligate Buyer to take the loan.

(C) is incorrect. Nonpayment of recited consideration may give rise to a contractual claim. However, the parol evidence rule prevents proof of prior or contemporaneous oral agreements where there is a writing that reflects the parties' final agreement. Evidence of oral statements may be introduced to explain ambiguities in the terms of the writing, but not to contradict those terms. The written memorandum was clear that the consideration of $100 needed to be paid, so a contemporaneous oral agreement that it need not be paid could not be shown to contradict the written term.

There are no special rules applicable to professional dealers in real estate with respect to these issues. Article 2 of the UCC contains special rules for merchants that apply to the sale of goods, but these do not apply to real estate, so (D) is incorrect.

Answer to Question 130

Specific performance is not available to Buyer because the property has been legally conveyed to Citizen, but Buyer can nevertheless recover full contract damages, so (A) is incorrect.

Buyer is not entitled to recover Owner's profit on the sale to Citizen, so (C) is incorrect. Buyer is entitled only to his expectancy damages, which are generally the market price less the consideration promised by the non-breaching party. In other words, Buyer's expectancy damages are the market value on the date of breach minus the contract price. (D) is the correct answer.

Answer to Question 131

(A) is incorrect because a tenancy in common does not carry rights of survivorship. When Alpha died, his interest passed to Hera, his heir.

Hera's default does not terminate his interest, so (B) is incorrect.

(C) is incorrect because Hera need only pay her contribution toward the taxes and costs of sale, not half the market value of Greenacre.

The correct answer is (D). A fiduciary duty exists between Beta and Hera, Alpha's heir, so that Beta will not be allowed to extinguish Hera's interest by purchasing the property at the tax sale. Hera must pay only one-half the amount needed to purchase the property at the sale and obtain the tax deed; this is the amount of Hera's required contribution to retain a one-half interest in the property.

Answer to Question 132

(B) is correct. A person cannot commit the crime of conspiracy by himself or with someone who belongs in a legislatively protected class that the substantive offense was made criminal in order to protect. Emma is a minor protected by the statutory rape statute. She cannot be convicted of the substantive offense or of conspiracy to commit it. Kenneth could be convicted of statutory rape but not of conspiracy to commit it because Emma would not be treated as his co-conspirator.

(A) is incorrect because their agreement as a factual matter alone is insufficient.

(C) is incorrect because it inaccurately states the Wharton Rule, which would preclude conspiracy liability where the only parties to the agreement are those necessary to the substantive offense.

(D) is incorrect because it does not state the rule as clearly as (B). Emma is too young to consent to sex with Kenneth under the statutory rape law, but is not too young to enter into an agreement in the nature of a conspiracy.

Answer to Question 133

This is an example of transferred intent. Although Sam had no intention of killing Lois, he intended to kill Anna and killed Lois instead by the same premeditated and deliberate act. (A) is correct and (B) is incorrect because intent may be transferred.

(C) is incorrect because Sam had set in motion a sequence of events that led to Lois' death, and he intended to kill when he embarked on this conduct. His change of mind is not effective so long as the circumstances he created were still capable of killing someone. (C) and (D) are also incorrect because any negligence of the security officer in attempting to respond to the situation would be a foreseeable consequence of Sam's acts, not a superseding cause that would cut off Sam's criminal liability.

Answer to Question 134

(A) is incorrect because the immunity of instrumentalities and agents of the federal government to taxation by the states does not extend to private activities of federal employees.

(B) is incorrect because the tax applies to only to the value of personal use of the automobiles. A tax on the full value of the automobiles, including their use for official purposes on behalf of the U.S. government, would be problematic.

The correct answer is (C). State income taxes on federal employees are valid. *Graves v. O'Keefe*, 306 U.S. 466 (1939). A tax on personal use of an automobile provided by the taxpayer's employer would be valid as against employees of the federal government in the same manner as employees of other entities.

(D) is incorrect because a distinction between federal employees and others would not involve a suspect category and could be sustainable under a rational basis test.

Answer to Question 135

Orderly committed a criminal act. Thus, vicarious liability would not ordinarily be imposed on his employer for such act. (A) is merely another way of saying that Hospital could be vicariously liable, so (A) is incorrect.

Because Orderly's status as an employee of Hospital is not sufficient to impose liability on Hospital, (C) is incorrect.

The correct answer is (D). Hospital's liability here is direct, not vicarious. It is the duty of an employer in the hiring and retention of employees. If Hospital was negligent in hiring and supervising Orderly, and could have protected Patient from such conduct with the exercise of reasonable care, Hospital can be held liable. Hospitals have a duty to screen and monitor their staff to prevent sexual misconduct with patients. *O'Shea v. Phillips,* 746 So.2d 1105 (Fla. App. 1999).

Answer to Question 136

(A) is incorrect because the best evidence rule is inapplicable where it is the existence of a document rather than its precise terms that is relevant. Here the existence of the liability insurance policy issued to Defendant is offered to disprove Defendant's statement that he did not own the plane or have responsibility to maintain it.

(B) is incorrect because the fact of insurance coverage may be admitted on a number of other issues, such as ownership of the vehicle involved, which is a fact in issue in this case.

(C) is incorrect because this would be an attempt to use the fact of insurance coverage to prove Defendant's negligence, which is not allowed.

(D) is the correct answer. Defendant has denied ownership of the plane, and the liability policy on the plane is some evidence of Defendant's ownership of the plane.

Answer to Question 137

Opal's fraudulent alteration of the release voided the instrument of release as to Lot 5. Neither Bank nor Eva had a duty to check the record for altered instruments, so (A) and (C) are incorrect.

The recording act will not protect even a BFP such as Eva from a void instrument, so (B) is incorrect.

The correct answer is (D). The recordation acts do not protect subsequent purchasers without notice of a forged or altered instrument. There can be no bona fide holder of title under such an instrument because the instrument is void in its inception.

Answer to Question 138

(A) is the correct answer. Miller had been seized—he had been significantly deprived of his freedom, and at that point his *Miranda* rights attached. He was not informed of his right to remain silent so he will not be deemed to have waived that right voluntarily.

(B) is incorrect because the fruit of the poisonous tree doctrine does not apply. The search was not illegal since it was in an open field.

(C) is incorrect as a factual matter. The deputy was not in hot pursuit but in fact had seized Miller when he interrogated him.

(D) is incorrect because there was no police emergency.

Answer to Question 139

The correct answer is (C). One does not have a privacy interest in fields beyond the curtilage immediately surrounding the home. Such areas are deemed open fields even if the owner has erected a fence. No warrant was necessary to search a public area, so (A) is incorrect.

(D) is incorrect because standing to raise a search and seizure issue belongs to the party whose person or property is searched. Miller would have standing if the area searched was within the zone in which he had an expectation of privacy. Generally, only the person who owns the items seized has standing to object to their seizure, but Jones had no expectation of privacy to assert in the clothing, either because it had been abandoned or it was in plain view.

Answer to Question 140

(A) is incorrect because failure to comply with a statutorily mandated safety requirement is only evidence of negligence in most jurisdictions, not negligence per se.

(B) is incorrect because common carriers are not held strictly liable. Most courts require the highest degree of care to be exercised by carriers and may hold a carrier liable for the slightest negligence, but do not impose strict liability for all injuries or damages that may occur.

The correct answer is (C). Although violation of a regulatory statute is either negligence per se or evidence of negligence, the violation must be shown to have contributed to the harm. In other words, if there is no causal relationship between the statutory violation and the harm Passenger suffered, Passenger's representative will not prevail. Thus, (A) is incorrect because it does not take the causation problem into effect.

Assumption of the risk doctrine is applied in statutory violation cases. However, (D) is incorrect because Passenger did not assume the risk that there would not be adequate lifeboats to deal with the type of storms that could be expected.

Answer to Question 141

The correct answer is (A). In *Young v. American Mini Theatres, Inc.*, 427 U.S. 50 (1976), the Court permitted a zoning ordinance to regulate the location of theaters based upon the "adult" content of the movies shown at the theaters because the state objective of avoiding the violence sometimes associated with adult theaters was a valid state purpose for content-based regulation, so long as the viewing public had reasonable access to the product. See also *City of Renton v. Playtime Theatres*, 475 U.S. 41 (1986) (upheld city zoning ordinance prohibiting adult movie theaters from locating within 1,000 feet of any residential property, church, park or school; ample land area was still available for use as adult theater sites.)

(B) is incorrect because adult entertainment is not wholly without First Amendment protection; in these cases the Court in effect applies an intermediate level of scrutiny or balancing of interests.

(C) is incorrect. In *Young v. American Mini Theatres, supra,* the Court upheld the zoning ordinance despite a lack of showing that the movies were obscene.

(D) is incorrect because the Court looks only for a legitimate state purpose in controlling the location of such enterprises, and it has found a legitimate state purpose in similar cases where adult entertainment was not totally prohibited but only confined to a certain part of the city.

Answer to Question 142

The doctrine of anticipatory repudiation allows a party to a contract to treat it as a breach immediately when the other party repudiates his promise before the time for performance arises. Without the doctrine, the promisee would be required to wait for the date set for performance before suing for breach. For the doctrine to apply, however, the repudiation by the promisor must be clear and unequivocal, and it is not clear that Buyer's statement was a complete repudiation. Market conditions might have improved between October 1 and December 1. Thus, (A) is incorrect.

(B) states the rule of anticipatory repudiation under Article 2 of the UCC, but Article 2 is not applicable here because the contract involves the sale of real estate, not goods.

The fact that the sale is not an installment contract under Article 2 of the Code is also irrelevant, so (C) is incorrect.

(D) is the correct answer. Buyer's statement was not a total repudiation and thus cannot be treated as a present breach of the contract. Seller must wait until December 1 to see if Buyer fails to perform.

Answer to Question 143

A promisor who repudiates a contract has the right to retract the repudiation until the promisee acts in reliance on the repudiation. Buyer could retract her repudiation until Seller acted in reliance on the repudiation or notified Buyer that he accepted her repudiation. The fact that Seller did not notify Buyer that he accepted the repudiation does not mean the contract was still in effect after Seller changed his position in reliance on the repudiation, so (A) is incorrect.

When a party repudiates the contract before his performance is due, the aggrieved party may await performance for a commercially reasonable time, *or* resort to any available remedies for breach, *even though* he has notified the repudiating party that he would await the latter's performance and has urged retraction. UCC §2-610(b). Thus, Seller did not waive Buyer's repudiation, and (B) is incorrect.

The correct answer is (C). Buyer did not retract her repudiation before Seller materially changed his position in reliance on such repudiation.

(D) is incorrect because the promisee need not perform any conditions precedent to the promisor's obligation in order to treat the contract as terminated after a repudiation. So long as Seller was ready and able to perform absent the repudiation, he was entitled to treat his obligations under the contract as terminated.

Answer to Question 144

Lender One is entitled to have the full amount of its debt satisfied from both properties due to its mortgage on the hotel and its lien on the parking garage. The $100,000 deficiency on the hotel sale can be satisfied from the surplus on the parking garage. The mortgagor is entitled to any surplus after both mortgage debts are paid off. (A) is the correct answer. Lender Two's security interest has been satisfied from the proceeds of the foreclosure sale on the parking garage. The amount Lender One paid was more than sufficient to satisfy Lender Two's debt. Lender Two is not entitled to any portion of the surplus, which belongs to the mortgagor once all the debts secured by the mortgage are satisfied. Thus, (B) and (C) are incorrect.

Owner is not entitled to any of the surplus until the debts secured by the mortgaged properties are paid off, so (D) is incorrect.

Answer to Question 145

Subbo is the party in breach. If one of the parties has partially performed at the time of a breach by the other party, the performing party can recover for work done at the contract rate, plus expectancy damages for the work not yet performed. The breaching party is generally entitled to nothing, so (A) is incorrect. The UCC is not applicable here because this is a contract for services, not primarily for the sale of goods.

The correct answer is (C). Kontractor can recover $20,000, the excess of its expenses as a result of the breach in obtaining the services that Subbo promised to provide. Subbo's out-of-pocket expense or the value of the benefit Subbo conferred on Kontractor is not recoverable under the majority rule, so (B) and (D) are incorrect.

Answer to Question 146

(A) is the correct answer. Driver has put on sufficient evidence to support a finding of liability on the basis of defective design.

(B) is incorrect because the plaintiff has not put on any evidence that the Rapido was not crashworthy, i.e., that Driver's injuries were caused by the Rapido's inability to withstand the crash.

(C) is incorrect because Troody's failure to stop when the Rapido suddenly stalled in traffic was a foreseeable intervening cause, not a superseding cause.

(D) is incorrect because it was foreseeable that some physical harm would come to Driver as a result of being rear-ended by Troody. Troody must take the plaintiff as he finds her and is liable for any injuries that are not extraordinary in hindsight.

Answer to Question 147

Fed. R. Ev. 104 provides that preliminary questions on the admissibility of evidence are determined by the judge, and in making this determination the judge is not bound by the rules of evidence except with respect to privileges. (D) is correct and (A) is incorrect because the hearsay rules will not prevent the affidavit from being considered by the judge on this preliminary question.

(B) is incorrect. The Federal Rules expand the dying declaration exception to include civil cases. Thus, the judge can and should consider the affidavit to determine if the statement was made while Pedestrian believed his death was imminent.

Declarations of a mental state are not admissible to show past conduct, so (C) is incorrect.

Answer to Question 148

The correct answer is (A). John's license is a property right that cannot be taken away without due process of law, including the right to examine his accusers.

(B) is incorrect. The Full Faith and Credit Clause does not require the states to give up all their sovereignty over certain local issues, such as whether a crime has been committed in the jurisdiction or whether a conveyance of local real estate is valid. Furthermore, a dismissal of charges by the federal authorities is not a "public act" or a "judicial proceeding" within the purview of the Full Faith and Credit Clause

(C) is incorrect. The revocation of a license granted under state authority may be effected by the state licensing authority under administrative procedures so long as basic due process rights are upheld.

(D) is incorrect because it is unlikely a court would find that Congress intended to preempt the field of drug trafficking; state criminal enforcement would also be permitted. Even if Congress intended to preempt the field in terms of judicial criminal enforcement, a court would likely find that administrative enforcement was outside the scope of the federal preemption.

Answer to Question 149

(A) is incorrect because, although Driver's entry onto Owner's land was unauthorized, it was unintentional. Furthermore, Driver may have had a privilege to enter Owner's property to avoid hitting the child. This could also be called justification on the ground of necessity.

(B) is incorrect because Driver did not intentionally cause emotional distress to Owner or his child, and Owner cannot recover for negligent infliction of emotional distress because there was no physical impact or injury to either Owner or his child. Even though Owner was within the zone of danger with respect to possible injury to himself, most courts require a substantial illness as a manifestation of the emotional injury before recovery is allowed. Owner cannot recover for the trauma of seeing the danger to his child because the "bystander" rule of *Dillon v. Legg* requires that the third-party victim, here, Owner's child, have suffered a critical injury or death.

The correct answer is (C).

The facts do not specify the age of the child, but in some states a child under the age of seven is incapable of contributory negligence. In any event, any negligence of Owner's child would not bar Owner's recovery because the child's contributory negligence will not be imputed to his parent under the modern rule. Thus, (D) is incorrect.

Answer to Question 150

(A) is the correct answer. The vendor's title is not required to be in marketable condition until the time of closing. In long-term installment contracts, some courts will give the purchaser an immediate right of rescission if a title problem is discovered and the vendor is unable to provide reasonable assurances that a cure will be effected, but the traditional rule would force the purchaser to make payments even for years with no assurance that the vendor will be able to cure the title problems by the time the last installment payment is made.

(B) is incorrect because Purchaser's taking possession would not change the contract requirement for Vendor to deliver a warranty deed.

It is true that in every contract for the sale of real estate, there is an implied covenant for the seller to convey marketable title unless the parties agree otherwise. If there is no provision in the contract for the purchaser to take subject to encumbrances, then the existence of a mortgage on the property would be considered a breach of the obligation to convey marketable title. However, (C) is incorrect because the time for providing marketing title has not arrived, so there has as yet been no breach.

The doctrine of equitable conversion operates to pass the risk of loss on real property to the purchaser after an enforceable contract of sale has been signed. While the type of risk contemplated is usually physical risk such as from fire, courts have recognized that the doctrine may also apply to legal changes such as zoning changes or eminent domain actions. See *Mohave County v. Mohave-Kingman Estates, Inc.*, 120 Ariz. 417, 586 P.2d 978 (1978). Taking possession does not change the seller's obligation to deliver the title promised, however. Thus, (D) is incorrect.

Answer to Question 151

The correct answer is (A). Article IV, § 1 of the Constitution (the Full Faith and Credit Clause) requires that "Full Faith and Credit shall be given in each State to the public acts, records and judicial proceedings of every other State." The final judgment in Blue can be enforced in Red up to its full unsatisfied dollar amount, despite the limitations on recovery in Red. Although the public policy of Red may disapprove of such large judgments, the situs of the tort and the plaintiffs is in State B, which has a stronger interest in recovery for its citizens if a court should apply an interests analysis to this conflict of laws. See *Ohlhaver v. Narron*, 195 F.2d 676 (4th Cir. 1952); *Rosenthal v. Warren*, 475 F.2d 438 (2nd Cir. 1973).

(B) is incorrect because the Equal Protection Clause applies to "persons" who are "citizens" of the United States. It does not protect states.

(C) is incorrect because the Tenth Amendment involves the rights of the states vis-à-vis the federal government, not other states.

(D) is incorrect. The judgment established the liability of the state of Red for the actions of its employees while on state business, and this issue is subject to the full faith and credit guarantee.

Answer to Question 152

(A) is correct. There is a causation problem because the teacher's act of suicide would be treated as an independent superseding cause of the teacher's death.

(B) and (C) are incorrect because intent to cause the teacher's death, or malice aforethought, would not be required for a manslaughter conviction. Martha merely needed to act with a willful and wanton disregard of human risk.

(D) is incorrect because her distress at her failing grade was not legally sufficient provocation and would not have justified her lying about the teacher.

Answer to Question 153

Cross-examination is generally limited to the subject matters raised on direct examination and any matters relating to the credibility of the witness. Because Plaintiff called Defendant to the stand, Defendant is on direct examination when being questioned by Plaintiff's lawyer and is on cross-examination when being questioned by his own counsel. However, the tests for relevancy are broader on cross-examination and the court may permit inquiry into other matters if counsel proceeds under the rules for direct examination. (A) is incorrect because, without more facts, it is not clear that this was error. In other words, it is not error per se to allow counsel to go beyond the scope of direct.

Leading questions are generally permitted on cross-examination, but the judge has discretion to limit them when the witness is friendly to the cross-examiner. (B) is incorrect because the judge's refusal to allow Defendant's attorney to cross-examine Defendant by leading questions would not be error.

(C) is incorrect because the credibility of the witness is a proper matter for cross-examination whether or not the issue is raised on direct.

The correct answer is (D). It is error for a witness who has not yet testified or been cross-examined to be allowed to remain in the courtroom to hear the testimony of other witnesses after a request for exclusion.

Answer to Question 154

(A) is the correct answer. It is always permissible to impeach a witness by showing his bias against or in favor of either party, and extrinsic evidence of bias is permitted. It can be shown by specific instances of conduct, so (D) is incorrect.

(B) is incorrect because Frank's character is not directly in issue in this case and character evidence cannot generally be admitted.

The majority of courts have ruled that the witness must be given an opportunity to explain or deny evidence that tends to show bias. But Frank is not the witness here, so Frank need not be given such opportunity, and (C) is thus incorrect.

Answer to Question 155

Although the language of the grant of the right-of-way in the deed of conveyance from Able to Baker did not specify the location of the easement, its location can be shown by the acts of the parties. Some time after the deed of conveyance 30 years ago and before Dorcas took title seven years ago, Baker built a driveway which was apparently used as the right-of-way granted in the deed. Evidence of such understanding and use by the original parties will fix the location of the right-of-way; a subsequent owner of the servient estate cannot select a different location. The right passes to subsequent owners of the dominant estate that is benefited. (A) is the correct answer, and (D) is incorrect.

The use of the driveway was not a prescriptive easement if the use was permissive, not hostile and adverse. The initial use of the driveway by Baker was apparently permissive under the terms of the deed of conveyance, and a use that was initially permissive remains so until permission is withdrawn or exceeded, so Dorcas' use was not hostile until Charlie requested him to cease using it. (B) is incorrect.

The fact that Charlie's proposal for a change in the location of the easement may have been reasonable does not affect Dorcas' right to the use of the easement once it had been established. (C) is incorrect.

Answer to Question 156

A seller of goods breaches its contract if it fails to make timely delivery unless the failure is excused. UCC §2-301. The buyer is entitled to treat this as a breach without showing material harm, so (A) is incorrect.

(B) is incorrect because this sort of *quid pro quo* should have been expressed in the agreement.

(C) is incorrect. Delay in delivery or non-delivery by a seller is not a breach of his duty if performance as agreed has been made impracticable by the occurrence of a contingency the non-occurrence of which was a basic assumption on which the contract was made. A transportation strike is a foreseeable contingency, however, which should usually be provided for in the written contract. In any event, the delay could perhaps have been avoided by Computer's undertaking some increased cost. Increased cost alone would not excuse Computer's performance, particularly because this contract is "F.O.B. Bank." When the term is F.O.B. the place of destination, the seller must at his own expense and risk transport the goods to that place and there tender delivery. UCC §2-319(1)(b). In other words, the risk of this contingency fell on Computer.

(D) is the correct answer. Under UCC §1-102, the parties' bargain includes implications from circumstances, including course of dealing, usage of trade or course of performance. A usage of trade may in effect modify the delivery term in this manner.

Answer to Question 157

(A) and (C) are troublesome choices. The applicable law is the UCC, so the common-law doctrine of impossibility is not really applicable. However, Article 2 contains the doctrine of "impracticability" which is similar to but not exactly the same as the doctrine of "impossibility" under the common law. The UCC concept is somewhat broader, containing also the doctrine of frustration of purpose. This statement is technically both true and false, but there is a better answer.

(B) is incorrect because there is no express or implied "best efforts" requirement in this contract.

(D) is the best answer. The doctrine of "impracticability" excuses the seller's non-performance when made impracticable by the occurrence of a contingency the non-occurrence of which was a basic assumption on which the contract was made. §2-615. However, the risk of Computer's inability to develop the technology was understood by both parties. This is not a contingency "the non-occurrence of which was a basic assumption" underlying the contract. The risk of Computer's inability to develop the technology remains on Computer. See *U.S. v. Wegematic Corp.,* 360 F.2d 674 (2nd Cir. 1966), where the court found no basis for the argument that "when an electronics system is promoted by its manufacturer as a revolutionary breakthrough, the risk of the revolution's occurrence falls on the purchaser."

Answer to Question 158

(A) is incorrect. A character witness may be cross-examined by asking about his or her knowledge of conduct by the person in question, but Defendant has not put on a character witness or brought his character into issue.

(B) is correct. Evidence of a person's character or a character trait is not admissible for the purpose of proving action in conformity therewith on a particular occasion. Thus, (C) is incorrect. Defendant's propensity for violence cannot be shown through other events or crimes as evidence that he was violent on this particular occasion.

(D) is incorrect because no issues have been raised for which it is relevant to show Defendant's identity, plan or motive as an exception to the general rule against attempting to prove the character of the accused.

Answer to Question 159

Although the factual statements in (A) and (B) are true, neither is sufficient to permit judgment for Bea.

A warranty deed contains not only a guarantee that the grantor's title is good, but also that he will assist in defending that title against claims by third parties. The covenant runs only to the grantee, however, so Celia did not have an option to sue Art. (D) is an incorrect statement of the law.

(C) is the correct answer. If Art's title was not defective, Bea cannot recover from him in a warranty action. There was no violation of the covenant of title because Bea was successful in defending the action.

Answer to Question 160

(A) involves the question of ripeness. Even though the issue might arise again upon a retrial, the court need not wait because the retrial would not serve to clarify the issues, which would probably be identical to those identified by Alex at the time of the first trial.

(B) is incorrect because mootness is not a matter of substantive state law under the *Erie Railroad* doctrine. Rather, it is a jurisdictional requirement for Article III courts under the Constitution and is a prerequisite for litigation in federal court, whether state or federal substantive law is to be applied. See, *e.g., Patriot Cinemas v. General Cinema Corp.,* 834 F.2d 208 (1987).

The correct answer is (C). If the passage of time or changes in the facts or law resolve the controversy, so that a party who had standing at the commencement of the litigation no longer has a stake in the outcome, then the case will be dismissed as moot. A moot case no longer satisfies the case or controversy requirement. *Liner v. Jafco, Inc.,* 375 U.S. 301 (1964).

(D) is incorrect because the case or controversy requirement must be satisfied regardless of the importance of the constitutional question involved. If the issue is moot as to the particular plaintiff, the courts should dismiss and wait until a plaintiff with a real interest in the outcome is prepared to litigate the issue.

Answer to Question 161

(A) is incorrect because an airplane crash is a proper case for the use of the doctrine of *res ipsa loquitur.* The plaintiff need not prove the cause of the crash but only that (1) the occurrence is of a type that does not occur in the absence of negligence, (2) the defendant had exclusive control over the instrumentality, and (3) there was no fault of the plaintiff involved. See *Newing v. Cheatham,* 15 Cal.3d 351, 124 Cal. Rptr. 193 (1975).

(B) is incorrect because the defendant is not entitled to a directed verdict where the plaintiff has made out a prima facie case based on the doctrine; the case must go to the jury, unless the defendant has positively ruled out the possibility of its own negligence.

(C) is the correct answer. The jury may infer negligence when the *res ipsa* rule is applied.

(D) is incorrect because common carriers are not held to a strict liability standard, although they are held to an enhanced duty, often called the highest duty of care. There must be a showing of negligence, if only slight.

Answer to Question 162

(A) is incorrect because the rational relationship test is not the applicable standard of review. In land-use cases raising Fifth Amendment taking issues, the Court has applied the higher "rough proportionality" test as described below.

(B) and (C) are both incorrect because the compelling government interest test is not applicable here. There is no fundamental interest such as free speech or the right to vote involved here, so the burden of proof issue is not determinative. The initial burden would be on Company in challenging the requirement to show that the case warranted strict scrutiny, at which time the burden would shift to City to prove that the requirement was necessary to vindicate its compelling interest, if applicable.

The correct answer is (D). The Supreme Court has held that a permit to develop property cannot be conditioned upon a requirement that the owner dedicate a portion of the property to public use unless the government can show that the impairment of the property owner's rights in being required to dedicate a portion of the land to public use is roughly proportional to the adverse impact that the property owner's proposed land development would have upon legitimate governmental or societal interests. *Dolan v. City of Tigard*, 512 U.S. 374 (1994).

Answer to Question 163

(A) is incorrect because a change of circumstances will operate as a defense to enforcement of an equitable servitude only if the benefit secured by the restriction is reduced as a result. The benefit of Ollie's five-acre lot restriction would continue to inure to property owners in the neighborhood if enforced.

The zoning code sets certain minimum requirements but does not prevent a grantor from imposing more restrictive covenants applicable to land he conveys. This is not a "conflict" with the zoning code. (B) is incorrect.

(C) is incorrect because the requirements for this restriction to run with the land are present. There was a binding covenant in writing, it touches and concerns the land, there was intent for the restriction to run with the land (shown by use of the words "heirs and assigns" in the deeds), notice, and privity.

(D) is correct. The provision imposed an enforceable equitable servitude.

Answer to Question 164

The correct answer is (A). Federal Rule 608(a) allows opinion evidence as to a witness's reputation for truthfulness. But Defendant has not taken the stand here, if Witness is his first witness, so Witness cannot testify to Defendant's reputation for veracity. Thus, (B) and (C) are incorrect.

Under Federal Rule 404, the defendant in a criminal case may introduce evidence of his good character to show that it is unlikely he committed the act in question. Thus, (D) is also incorrect.

Answer to Question 165

(A) is incorrect because it is not the ownership of the components alone but the message conveyed by the display that causes constitutional concern.

(C) is also incorrect because the lack of expenditure by the state is only one factor to consider as to whether there is excessive entanglement between the church and state in religious displays.

(D) is close to the correct answer because the fact that the nativity scene is displayed along with secular items would be important in appearing to give the display a secular purpose and message. However, (B) is the correct answer because it gives a more complete explication of the standard to be applied in assessing the constitutionality of such religious displays.

Answer to Question 166

(A) is incorrect because the police need not "know" what is in a container before they seize it; they merely need probable cause to believe it is contraband.

(B) is the correct answer. The seizure of the cocaine was the result of an unlawful search. Sandra abandoned it only after she had been stopped and detained, i.e., "seized." A stop is proper only if there is a reasonable suspicion of criminal activity based on the totality of circumstances in the particular case. *U.S. v. Sokolow,* 490 U.S. 1 (1989). Unprovoked flight when approached by police in a high-crime area may provide a reasonable suspicion of criminal activity. *Illinois v. Wardlaw,* 528 U.S. 119 (2000). However, Sandra merely walked away at the sight of the officers, which anyone might do, and she stopped immediately upon being ordered to do so.

(C) is incorrect because the police did not have probable cause to believe Sandra possessed cocaine merely from the facts that they had general information about the area and she walked away when she saw them.

Property that is abandoned by a fleeing suspect who has not yet been seized can be recovered by the police without implicating the Fourth Amendment. *California v. Hodari D.*, 499 U.S. 621 (1991). Once the suspect has been detained, however, the usual rules regarding warrantless searches apply. Here, Sandra had been stopped and effectively "seized" before she threw the item away. Although she had not been arrested, she had reason to believe that she was not free to leave. (D) is incorrect because her abandonment of the cocaine after that point does not remove it from Fourth Amendment protection.

Answer to Question 167

A certified copy of the judgment of conviction, as a self-authenticating document, is admissible under Federal Rule 902. Because this mode of proof is easily permissible, (A) is not the correct answer.

Defendant's conviction is a fact that can be testified to by a witness with first-hand knowledge. Thus, (B) is incorrect.

An admission by a party opponent is admissible under Federal Rule 801(d). Thus, (C) is incorrect.

The correct answer is (D). Federal Rule 201 forbids taking judicial notice of facts that are not common knowledge and are not shown by a source "whose accuracy cannot reasonably be questioned." Even if a personal call to the clerk would be deemed a sufficiently accurate form of verification, a judge may take judicial notice of proceedings only in the judge's own court, but not in other courts.

Answer to Question 168

(A) is the correct answer. The Rule Against Perpetuities applies to non-reversionary future interests, requiring that such interests vest within 21 years after a life in being at the creation of the interest. The interest Adam created is limited neither by any life in being nor a period of 21 years or less and thus would violate the rule unless construed as a reversionary interest in the grantor. Using the term "heirs and assigns" makes it possible that a third party other than Adam could exercise the right, so the interest violates the Rule.

(B) is incorrect because the Bank will be charged with knowledge of the language in the deed. Bank could have and should have demanded to see the deed before extending the loan.

(C) is incorrect because a purchase money lender takes priority over other creditors, but does not supersede a right preserved in the deed itself.

The consideration to be paid by Adam upon exercise of the right of reentry is not the issue here, so (D) is incorrect. If otherwise proper under the RAP, Adam could have stated that the right of reentry would be exercisable at his discretion without any payment to Betty.

Answer to Question 169

(A) is incorrect. The Board's offer of a pension was not conditioned on Loyal's immediate retirement. The Board was not bargaining for Loyal's early retirement.

(B) is the correct answer. Although not enforceable as a contractual obligation, the Board's promise reasonably induced reliance by Loyal. Thus, (C) and (D) are incorrect, although the Board's promise was a gift promise and Loyal did not provide consideration through his continued service as an employee-at-will. This was his preexisting duty and the company ordinarily did not have a retirement plan for such employees. Nevertheless, promissory estoppel causes the Board's promise to become enforceable.

Answer to Question 170

The correct answer is (B). The Congressional commerce power is probably broad enough to sustain this type of legislation. The Supreme Court has sustained under the commerce power some federal statutes which are designed to accomplish ends not closely related to interstate commerce. The current view of the Supreme Court is that, absent a countervailing, positive limitation in the Constitution, such as the Tenth Amendment, Congress has plenary power to regulate interstate commerce.

(A) is incorrect because the general welfare clause does not give Congress license to use its full legislative power for the general welfare of the United States; it only gives Congress the power to spend money for the general welfare.

(C) is incorrect. The Thirteenth Amendment prohibits racial discrimination as an incident of slavery. Congress could enact similar legislation to prohibit racial discrimination in housing under its power to enforce the Thirteenth Amendment, but that is not the case here.

(D) is incorrect because the Fourteenth Amendment, unlike the Thirteenth Amendment, is tied to the state action concept. It does not prohibit private actors from engaging in discrimination.

Answer to Question 171

The auctioneer was not a seller or supplier in the normal chain of distribution of this product, so he should not be held liable under a strict products liability theory. Liability for the sale of a defective product by one not in the chain of distribution would require negligence on the part of the seller. Thus, (A) is incorrect, and (C) is correct.

(B) is incorrect because the defendant auctioneer did not have a duty to inspect the tractor. One who buys items second-hand at auction is expected to know that such items are sold "as is" unless a warranty is expressly given. The seller is not a merchant in the business of selling goods of that kind, so no implied warranty of merchantability arises.

(D) is incorrect because in a comparative negligence jurisdiction Pratt's own negligence would not completely bar his recovery.

Answer to Question 172

(A) is incorrect because Minivanity Fair did not sell the van to Walker in reliance on Goodbar's promise to pay.

(B) is the correct answer. Minivanity Fair was an intended beneficiary because Goodbar intended to make payment to anyone who sold a car to Walker.

The suretyship provision of the statute of frauds is inapplicable because Goodbar's promise was not made to the creditor Minivanity Fair, and the creditor did not know of it.

(D) is incorrect because it is not necessary for an intended beneficiary to be named or aware of the promise. The *Restatement (Second) of Contracts* §308 provides that it is not essential to the creation of a right in an intended beneficiary that he be identified when a contract containing the promise is made. A creditor beneficiary need not know of or consent to the suretyship relation created by the promise to pay the debt of his debtor, but once he learns of it, he is required to proceed against the surety first.

Answer to Question 173

The issue here is the admissibility of the hospital record, not Doctor's competence as an expert witness since Doctor is not on the stand. Thus, (A) is incorrect.

(B) is incorrect because Doctor is not being asked his opinion on the stand, but if he were on the stand it would not be necessary for the facts underlying his expert opinion to be in evidence so long as they were of a type reasonably relied on by experts in the field.

(C) is incorrect because a statement of then-existing physical condition must be about the declarant's own condition, not another person's.

(D) is the correct answer. Hospital records are a form of business records, which are excepted from the hearsay rule if the custodian of the record is available to authenticate it and testifies that the record was made in the ordinary course of the hospital's regularly conducted business activities and that the entry was made by a person with personal knowledge or was transmitted to the maker of the entry by a person with personal knowledge. Doctor had personal knowledge of Plaintiff's condition through examination of Plaintiff's x-rays, and made a statement about this to Intern, who recorded it immediately on Plaintiff's hospital record in the ordinary course of the hospital's business.

Answer to Question 174

(A) is incorrect because the Fourteenth Amendment proscribes discriminatory state action, not action by private individuals or organizations.

(B) is incorrect because the organization's use of the public auditorium does not render the organization a state actor for purposes of the Fourteenth Amendment.

(C) is too broad a statement. While individuals do have a freedom of association that permits them to discriminate, the city could impose restrictions on the use of city facilities for gatherings that exclude women or other groups.

The correct answer is (D). The private organization is not a state actor and its activities are not subject to the Fourteenth Amendment.

Answer to Question 175

The tort of nuisance protects a number of personal interests of a property owner, from the right to be free of dangerous conditions to the right to be free of annoyances in the use of his property. Because forging a remedy for nuisance involves a balancing act, there are many factors that might be considered. Adam in effect is alleging a public rather than a private nuisance if any of these arguments is made because it is not just his own property that is affected in these ways. The strongest factor that Adam could point to, and the clearest ground for a declaration of public nuisance, would be a danger to the occupants of Townacres. Thus, (B) is the correct answer.

Answer to Question 176

Rescission for either mutual or unilateral mistake requires that the parties be mistaken about a basic assumption that has a material effect on their bargain. There was no mistake here because both parties knew that the boar's fertility could not be determined until it was one year old. Thus, (A) and (D) are incorrect.

(B) is incorrect because implied warranties are not made at auction sales, and no express warranty was made.

The correct answer is (C). Caveat emptor is the rule here. Breeder bought a two-month-old boar while aware that its fertility could not be determined until it was at least one year old. Thus, Breeder consciously assumed the risk of the boar's infertility.

Answer to Question 177

(A) is the best answer. An intentional intrusion on the plaintiff's land is a trespass, even if the intrusion is merely by light waves. Odors, smoke, gas and light intruding on another's property can also be nuisances if they interfere with the plaintiff's use or enjoyment of his property in some way. A nuisance action requires some degree of wrongdoing by the plaintiff, either intent or negligence. While intent to annoy the plaintiff is not a requirement for either trespass or nuisance, (A) is the correct answer because the others do not support the results given.

Economic interests such as property values are not the only interests protected by the law of nuisance, so (B) is incorrect. An action in nuisance would require a balancing of the utility of the spotlight to Homeowner against the adverse effects on Neighbor's use and enjoyment of his property. Neighbor's right to enjoy his view can be protected, but it would be relevant what hours the interference was in effect and the fact that the light would not impede Neighbor's view during the day. The utility of the spotlight to Homeowner's security would be a factor to be weighed in its favor. (C) and (D) are incorrect because while these are factors to be considered in a nuisance action, neither of them alone would be sufficient to result in recovery or denial of recovery for Neighbor.

Answer to Question 178

(A) is incorrect because all the elements that constituted the greater offense of manslaughter had not occurred at the time of the trial for the lesser offense. This is an exception to the prohibition against double jeopardy.

The statute of limitations does not apply to homicide charges, so (B) and (C) are incorrect.

(D) is the correct answer. Neither the statute of limitations nor double jeopardy should cause the indictment to be dismissed.

Answer to Question 179

(A) is a true statement. However, Seller need not have been authorized to speak for Defendant if the statement is an adoptive admission. Thus, (A) is not the best answer.

(B) is incorrect because an adoptive admission is admissible as non-hearsay.

(C) is incorrect because a statement against penal interest must be an assertion made by the declarant. Defendant made no statement that could be considered a statement against his penal interest.

(D) is the correct answer. If a statement is made to a party under circumstances in which an ordinary person would deny it if untrue, but the party remains silent, an inference arises that the party adopted the statement made to him. The statement and the fact of the party's silence are admissible as non-hearsay under the Federal Rules.

Answer to Question 180

The correct answer is (A). The Supreme Court has adopted an intermediate level of scrutiny for discrimination based on gender.

(B) is incorrect because the right to a jury trial by one's peers does not apply in civil cases that are contractually submitted to arbitration.

(C) is incorrect because the correct standard of review for gender classifications is intermediate, not strict scrutiny.

(D) is incorrect because the gender classification would be required to meet an intermediate level of scrutiny, not merely the rational basis test.

Answer to Question 181

A contingent remainder, unlike a vested remainder, means that the takers will be determined at a future time—here, at the end of Della's life. (C) is the correct answer.

Since T's descendants cannot be determined until the time of her death, their interests could not vest at the time of the writing of the will, so (A) is incorrect.

Because the remaindermen are to be Theresa's descendants, an alternative construction might hold that the remaindermen's interests vested at Theresa's death. However, the remainder has been found to be contingent, not vested, so (B) is not correct.

(D) is incorrect because Seth is among the contingent remaindermen who will take an interest in Blueacre after Della's death, if Seth is still alive at that time. The court could not and did not imply a life estate in Seth.

Answer to Question 182

Driver can be held liable for both Pedestrian's broken leg and her broken arm. Driver's negligence is a "but for" cause of her broken arm as well as the broken leg because she would not have slipped if she had not been on crutches as a result of the broken leg caused by Driver. Although Market was also negligent, its negligence alone would not have been sufficient to cause the injury. Driver's negligence was a substantial factor in the injury to Pedestrian's arm. Thus, (B) is correct and (A) and (D) are incorrect.

(C) is incorrect because Market has no liability for the broken leg. There is no causal relationship between the negligence of Market's produce manager and Pedestrian's broken leg.

Answer to Question 183

The correct answer is (D). The Fourth Amendment's arrest requirements apply within the territory of the United States. When an extradition treaty has not been invoked, a court may properly exercise jurisdiction even though the defendant's presence is procured by means of a forcible abduction from another country. *Ker v. Illinois*, 119 U.S. 436 (1886) ("in that transaction we do not see that the Constitution, or laws, or treaties, of the United States guarantee him any protection.") See also *U.S. v. Alvarez-Machain*, 504 U.S. 655 (1992).

If an officer is making an arrest in a home, even with an arrest warrant, most states and federal law require that he announce his purpose before entering; failure to do so renders the arrest invalid. States may permit an exception to this requirement, however, when the entry is made under exigent circumstances, such as a reasonable belief that there is a danger of harm to the officers or others or of destruction of evidence. Ker v. California, 374 U.S. 23 (1963). There is no blanket exception for felony drug investigations, but circumstances of the particular entry may justify dispensing with the requirement when the police have a reasonable suspicion that knocking and announcing would inhibit the effective investigation of the crime. Richards v. Wisconsin, 520 U.S. 385 (1997). The "no-knock" exception applies regardless of whether the entry would result in destruction of property. United States v. Ramirez, 523 U.S. 65 (1998).

Answer to Question 184

(A) and (B) are incorrect because Hope had a possible interest in the property which she gave up in executing the quitclaim deed. She did not know that the court would rule against her and thus her promise was valid consideration.

The correct answer is (C). Gourmet received what he bargained for, a quitclaim deed making no warranties. There was an enforceable contract.

(D) is incorrect because estoppel requires reliance by the plaintiff to her detriment on the words or acts of the defendant. Gourmet's payment of the first installment, although it was an act that affirmed Gourmet's belief in the validity of the contract, did not induce any further reliance by Hope than her execution of the quitclaim deed. This was merely the performance of her promise under the contract and constituted good consideration since the parties did not know at that time that it was worthless.

Answer to Question 185

(A) is the correct answer. A battery is a nonconsensual touching. Athlete's written consent was for Doctor to perform the operation, not Surgeon, so (B) is incorrect.

The facts that Surgeon was more skilled and that the operation was successful do not negate the commission of a battery. Even if Athlete has suffered no actual damages he may still recover nominal damages for the battery. Thus, (C) and (D) are incorrect.

Answer to Question 186

(A) is incorrect because the "Speech or Debate Clause," Article 1, § 6 of the Constitution provides protection of speech in Congress by making the conduct of U.S. Senators or Representatives engaged in legislative functions privileged against civil or criminal suit. There is also a judicially-recognized privilege as a defense by officers of government to civil damage suits for defamation and kindred torts, in addition to the absolute privilege granted by the Constitution to members of both Houses of Congress and their legislative aides in respect to any speech, debate, vote, report, or action done in session. *Barr v. Mateo,* 360 U.S. 564 (1959). The protection of free speech by legislators and their immunity from civil suit for exercising free speech stem from jurisprudence that long precedes and coincides with the U.S. Constitution. *Tenney v. Brandhove,* 341 U.S. 367 (1951). Senator cannot be sued for exercising her rights of free speech.

(C) is incorrect because the speech need not be germane to pending legislative business so long as it is delivered on the floor on one of the houses of Congress or in committee. *Hutchinson v. Proxmire,* 443 U.S. 111 (1979).

(D) is incorrect because the Speech or Debate Clause protection extends to legislative aides as well as to Congresspersons. *Gravel v. United States,* 408 U.S. 606 (1972).

Answer to Question 187

At common law, the language "to [A] and his heirs" was necessary to create a fee simple, but the conveyance would create a fee simple in A with no interest in the heirs. Under modern law, as reflected in the statute in this jurisdiction, such language is not required, but even if used, only a fee simple in the grantee is created.

(B) is the correct answer. Albert held title in fee simple and conveyed fee simple to Bea. There was no remainder, reversion or other interest created in favor of Donna by Oscar's deed and Bea's interest was not merely a life estate, so (A) is incorrect.

Albert had the power to disinherit Donna in this fashion, and she holds no interest jointly with Bea so (C) and (D) are incorrect.

Answer to Question 188

The crime of solicitation occurs when the defendant entices, orders or encourages another person to commit a crime, with the specific intent that that person commit the crime. The mere speaking of the words is the actus reus. Thus, the offense was completed at the time of Smart's original conversation with Johnson. (C) is the correct answer.

Solicitation should not be confused with conspiracy. The person who was solicited need not commit the act, take substantial steps toward committing the act, or even agree to do the act, so (A), (B), and (D) are incorrect.

Answer to Question 189

(A) is incorrect because this is a contract for the sale of goods involving more than $500, so the agreement must be in writing, and there is a writing that meets the UCC Article 2 statute of frauds specifying the quantity as 500 towels. The contract can be enforced only up to the quantity stated in the letter from Manufacturer, even though Retailer orally indicated a willingness to purchase up to 1,000 towels.

The correct answer is (B). A sufficient memorandum for purpose of meeting the statute of frauds under UCC Article 2 must specify the quantity term, but need not specify the price term. The price term may be supplied orally, so (D) is incorrect.

A contract for the sale of goods where the price is $500 or more must be in a writing signed by the party to be charged. Here Manufacturer is attempting to enforce the agreement against Retailer, so Retailer is the party to be charged, but only Manufacturer, not Retailer, signed the agreement. However, the Code also provides that where both parties are merchants and a memo that is sufficient against the sender is sent to the other party, the memo is also sufficient against the recipient unless the recipient gives written notice of objection within 10 days. The letter thus bound not only Manufacturer but also Retailer because he did not object, so (C) is incorrect.

Answer to Question 190

The states are forbidden to enact bills of attainder, but this is not a bill of attainder, so (A) is incorrect. A bill of attainder singles out individuals for punishment by attempting to make a law that is not universally applicable.

(B) is the correct answer. The Article IV privileges and immunities clause protects a nonresident from discrimination with respect to certain fundamental interests based upon the fact that he or she does not reside in a particular state. The right to employment or to practice one's profession is a fundamental right protected by this clause. The state of Red would have a heavy burden in justifying this restriction on Doctor's right to practice in the state. State discrimination against nonresidents with respect to fundamental interests such as employment can be justified only if the nonresidents are a peculiar source of the evil against which the statute is aimed, and the remedy must bear a substantial relationship to the problem caused by nonresidents. *Hicklin v. Orbeck*, 437 U.S. 518 (1978).

The due process clause would not be the most helpful to Doctor, so (C) is incorrect. The due process clause does not protect against discrimination unless the classification is totally arbitrary. The privileges and immunities clause, which aims to prevent precisely the sort of discrimination against nonresidents that the State of Red has adopted, would be a stronger basis for a challenge to the hospital rules.

This act does not violate the ex post facto clause and thus (D) is incorrect because it does not attempt to apply criminal penalties retroactively to Doctor's treatment of patients in Redville.

Answer to Question 191

The correct answer is (B). A mortgagee becomes liable for injuries to business invitees on the mortgaged property if the mortgagee in fact takes possession and control of the property, including collecting rents and profits and undertaking maintenance in an effort to protect its security interest. Marie is a mortgagee in possession on these facts.

A majority of states today in fact follow the lien theory of mortgages (under which the mortgagor retains the right to possession until foreclosure) and generally require language in the mortgage permitting the mortgagee to take possession after default but before foreclosure. Where the mortgagor abandons the real estate, however, the security interest is deemed sufficient to permit the mortgagee to take possession and protect the real estate until foreclosure. *Restatement (Third) of Property (Mortgages)* §4.1(c). Thus, (A) and (C) are incorrect.

Mortgagee in possession status does not arise where the mortgagee acquires possession as an agent of the mortgagor, but no agency agreement was expressly or impliedly reached on these facts, so (C) is incorrect.

Answer to Question 192

When Actor consented to being photographed by an amateur photographer, he may have reasonably assumed that the photograph was being taken for non-commercial use. Consent to being photographed did not constitute consent to its commercial use without Actor's knowledge, so (A) is incorrect.

(B) is incorrect because the fact that Actor is a public figure does not mean that his name and likeness is in the public domain for all purposes. Actor has a property right in his name and likeness and may sue for their unauthorized use for commercial advertising purposes. Some courts now call this a "right of publicity" where the plaintiff is a celebrity, to distinguish it from the tort of invasion of privacy by appropriation of the name and likeness of an ordinary, non-public plaintiff. The right of publicity includes the right of certain plaintiffs, such as entertainers and other public personalities, to control the commercial use of their names and likenesses. See *Carson v. Here's Johnny Portable Toilets, Inc.*, 698 F.2d 831 (6th Cir. 1983).

The correct answer is (C). Actor may recover for the tort of invasion of privacy by appropriation of his name and likeness (or the right of publicity) because Vineyard used these to advertise Vineyard's product without Actor's consent.

The fact that the statement made in the advertisement was true would not constitute a defense to the tort of invasion of privacy, so (D) is incorrect.

Answer to Question 193

Rule 801(d)(1)(A) provides that a statement is not hearsay if the declarant testifies at the trial or hearing and is subject to cross-examination concerning the statement, and the statement is inconsistent with the declarant's testimony, and was given under oath subject to the penalty of perjury at a trial, hearing or other proceeding. Witness's prior statement is not admissible under this rule because in effect he did not testify at Defendant's trial. Furthermore, a prior inconsistent statement of a witness is admissible substantively only if the prior statement was given under oath. Witness's prior statement regarding Defendant was not given under oath, so it is not admissible substantively. A prior inconsistent statement of a non-party witness may be used to impeach the witness if a foundation is laid; the witness must be afforded an opportunity to explain or deny the statement before extrinsic evidence can be used to place the statement before the jury. Witness's refusal to testify effectively made it impossible to cross-examine him about the statement, so not confronting him on the stand as in (D) is irrelevant. Because Witness's statement is not admissible substantively or for impeachment here due to his unavailability, (A) is incorrect.

(B) is also incorrect because the witness must be available to testify about a prior identification, and Witness has made himself unavailable.

(C) is the correct answer. Witness's prior out-of-court statement to Officer is hearsay, and it is not admissible as a prior inconsistent statement or prior eyewitness identification, as discussed above.

Answer to Question 194

At common law, contracts formed by offers that call for a return promise are bilateral contracts. Contracts formed by offers that call for an act are unilateral contracts. Unless the offer specifically states which is required, however, the offer can be accepted by either promise or performance. Under Article 2 of the UCC there is no distinction between unilateral and bilateral contacts; an order for goods may be accepted either by shipping the goods or by promising to ship them. §2-206. Seller accepted by return promise, so (A) is incorrect.

As between merchants in a contract for the sale of goods, an acceptance may state terms additional to or different from those offered and the additional or different terms become part of the contract unless the (1) offer expressly limits acceptance to the terms of the offer or the new terms materially alter the offer, or (2) the offeror notifies the offeree of his objection within a reasonable time. Buyer, the offeror here, effectively agreed to Seller's price term unless he objected to it within a reasonable time, so (B) is incorrect.

(C) is incorrect because Buyer made no assurance in the order that the offer to buy would not be revoked. Without such an assurance in a signed writing by a merchant, an offer can be revoked at any time.

(D) is the correct answer. Under Article 2, the order was an offer that could be accepted by Seller's letter of January 8. Traditionally, an acceptance had to be made by the same medium by which the offer was made, but Article 2 provides that an acceptance can be by any medium that is reasonable under the circumstances. Under either rule, Seller's letter on January 7 was a proper acceptance to Buyer's mailed order. Under the "mailbox rule," Seller's letter operated as an acceptance at the time it was posted, so Buyer could not revoke the offer on January 8.

Answer to Question 195

Hermit would have a defense of defense of property if he used only enough force to protect the property. The owner must first make a verbal demand that the intruder stop before using force, particularly where the intruder is merely a trespasser rather than a burglar. Potentially deadly force is not appropriate in defense of property alone; the property owner must believe that he or she is in imminent danger of death or serious bodily harm. (A) is the correct answer.

Proof of intent to harm intruders is not necessary since planting an explosive device was likely to cause serious bodily harm or death. See *Katko v. Briney,* 183 N.W.2d 657 (Iowa 1971) [loaded spring gun]. Thus, (B) is incorrect.

(C) is incorrect. The sign was not an effective warning since it referred only to prosecution, not physical harm. Furthermore, where the defensive device installed by the homeowner could inflict serious bodily harm or death, even a clear warning would likely not justify the use of such force unless the homeowner was in fact in apparent danger of the same.

(D) is incorrect because Hermit's fear of harm had to be a fear of imminent bodily harm before he would be justified in using potentially deadly force.

Answer to Question 196

The agreement with Charles is a sublease of a portion of Bertha's lease. The agreement is for a term of years, allowing him exclusive use of a portion of the leased property, and Bertha is charging rent. It is only a partial sublease, but that is prohibited by the clause in Bertha's lease from Adam.

Allowing Doris to use the fields to practice golf does not amount to a leasehold interest. Not only is Bertha not charging Doris rent, but Doris' use of the land would not be exclusive as to any space or time. Doris merely has been given a right to go on some portion of the land and do certain acts on the land. This right is in the nature of an easement or a license for the term of Bertha's lease, but it does not constitute an assignment or sublet.

Because only the agreement with Charles violates the provision against assignment or subletting, (A) is the correct answer.

Answer to Question 197

Even if Defendant had no intention of killing or causing serious bodily harm to Victim, Defendant could be liable if her act of pulling the trigger constituted a very high degree of risk to human life and if a reasonable person would have realized the risk, regardless of whether Defendant herself realized it. If the jury finds that Defendant's belief the gun was fake was reasonable, they should find her not guilty of either murder (the intentional killing of Victim) or manslaughter (the unintended but reckless killing). (D) is the correct answer, so the others are necessarily incorrect.

Answer to Question 198

Even though Del was negligent in failing to activate the motion detector on his security alarm, Del will not be liable to Paula if the inmate's criminal act is considered a superseding cause. Del's negligence constitutes a "but for" cause of Paula's injury, but it is also necessary to find that the inmate's act was not a superseding cause, so (A) is incorrect.

(B) is incorrect because Del's negligence alone, if not the proximate cause of Paula's injury, will not render him liable to Paula.

(C) is incorrect. The storage and sale of firearms is an activity that can be conducted reasonably safely and thus is not an abnormally dangerous activity as a matter of law.

(D) is the correct answer. The inmate's criminal act will not supersede Del's liability if theft and use of Del's firearms by criminals was foreseeable.

Answer to Question 199

The correct answer is (A). A statute will be found overbroad if it would criminalize a substantial amount of constitutionally protected speech. Prohibiting sales to adults of non-obscene materials that might be harmful to minors would violate their First Amendment rights, and yet such sales would be punishable under the language of this statute.

(B) is incorrect. In order for a conviction under a state statute punishing obscenity to stand, the statute must specifically define the conduct or expression which is proscribed as obscene. This statute does not meet that test, but states may have greater power to protect minors from material that is not defined as obscene. The standards in this area are somewhat unclear, but the First Amendment obscenity rules are not Corner Store's best defense since the statute is aimed at the protection of minors.

(C) and (D) are incorrect because the equal protection clause involves classifications among persons, not distinctions between pictures and printed words or material that might harm minors versus material that might harm adults as the subject of regulation.

Answer to Question 200

Fed. Rule 803(10) permits testimony that a diligent search failed to disclose a public record in order to prove the absence of such record. Thus, (A) is correct. This is an available hearsay exception, so (C) is incorrect.

Witness's testimony is not a summary. If applicable, the best evidence rule would permit a written summary of the contents of the documents surveyed, with the originals to be made available for examination or copying. It is not the contents of the prison records but the absence of a record of Defendant's incarceration that is at issue here, so the best evidence rule is inapplicable and (B) is incorrect. The records themselves need not be produced, so (D) is incorrect.

Made in the USA
Charleston, SC
17 June 2011